JOHN WESLEY
A Theological Biography

MARTIN SCHMIDT

JOHN WESLEY

A Theological Biography

VOLUME 1
From 17th June 1703 until 24th May 1738

Translated by
NORMAN P. GOLDHAWK

*Tutor in Church History and the History of Christian
Doctrine at Richmond College, Surrey*

ABINGDON PRESS
NEW YORK   NASHVILLE

© THE EPWORTH PRESS 1962

PRINTED IN ENGLAND BY
HAZELL WATSON AND VINEY LTD
AYLESBURY AND SLOUGH

Contents

Translator's Preface

DR MARTIN SCHMIDT, who is now Professor at the University of Mayence (Mainz), is a distinguished German church-historian who has included the study of Puritanism, John Wesley and Pietism among his special interests. The footnotes will indicate the wide use he has been able to make of such sources as the Halle and Herrnhut archives in the preparation of this book. At a time when something of a revival in Reformation studies is taking place in Britain and America, and when the particular emphases of the great Protestant traditions need to be clarified in view of ecumenical relations, it is valuable to have an informed critique of John Wesley by one who speaks from within Lutheranism.

For some months Professor Schmidt lived and worked in this college, and it is a pleasure to be able to acknowledge the value of his friendship by making this book available to English-speaking students of Methodism. In a few instances I have corrected slips or misprints in the text or the notes, and occasionally added to the latter. Such additions are always indicated. Over one matter I have ventured to introduce an alteration. This has been the substitution in the text of Sarah Kirkham for Betty Kirkham. My comment in note 4, page 73 explains, and I believe, warrants this liberty.

Quotations from John Wesley's *Journal*, *Diary* and *Letters* have always been reproduced according to the text of the Standard Edition.

Neither the Bibliography nor the Index was part of the original German edition.

Professor Schmidt's second volume is due to be published in Germany in the near future.

RICHMOND COLLEGE

ONE

The Task

JOHN WESLEY is well known as the founder of the Methodist movement in England in the eighteenth century, yet his significance is not confined to this fact. He was a man who thought of the whole world as his parish; he lived and acted as an ecumenical Christian; and he had the capacity of making this apparent even in the smallest matters. But from the historical angle also he belongs to the whole of Christendom, for the last of the great ecclesiastical organizations to have come into being in the development of Christianity originated from him. Although this ran contrary to his own wish it unites him with all those great figures before him who found themselves in similar situations. But his movement is one which took place in the modern era, against the background of the violent disruption of the Christian world-scene and the changing fortunes of the industrial masses. Again although John Wesley was greatly indebted to his Anglican inheritance, those traditional features and vestiges of the Middle Ages which played such a part in the Reformation had no place in this situation. He was an Englishman, and moreover a man of exceptional inner discipline and strongly realistic outlook. Age and nationality, historical circumstance, and mental equipment, all made him different from the great German, French and Swiss reformers, Martin Luther, John Calvin, and Huldreich Zwingli. He encountered the main stream in the Lutheran Protestantism of his time through German Pietism, but for all the affinity he had with its leaders, Spener, Francke, and Zinzendorf—an affinity due to the period and circumstances in which they lived—Wesley also differed from each.

Although his stature was on the whole less than that of the great Reformers, a biography must attempt to reveal it in its various aspects. In so far as Wesley himself undertook this task in his *Journal*, and performed it with extraordinary precision, he has made this enterprise both easier and more difficult. Unless a modern biography should aim at casting doubts upon the authenticity of this self-portrait by presenting a completely different evaluation of the material out of which it was constructed, it must draw principally upon this picture. On close examination such a reassessment would appear to be extremely hazardous, for the thing which strikes the reader is the integrity and devotion to—not to say fanaticism for— the truth in Wesley's autobiography. Our task accordingly is essentially a modest one. It consists in leaving out, in supplementing, and in drawing together connexions. It involves bringing the separate events into a whole, discovering the leading characteristics and the formative motives, appraising the importance of the influences from without and within, and so making intelligible the development and activity of the man—intelligible, that is, not by reducing his stature, but in relation to the distinctive thing about him, what Goethe meant by the significant, the 'fundamental truth'. Since in Wesley's case this was the central Christian message of salvation, his biography must be a theological one. In all the significant figures in the history of the Church it should be possible to see that the course of their lives, their personal piety, and their theological thinking, form in the end an essential unity. No unrelated event should be left protruding from the surface of their experience, for each one insists on being admitted into the subject's inner consciousness and becoming part of his thinking and acting. Contingency is turned into necessity. This scarcely ever happens all at once, but usually requires a lengthy process, to which inward conflicts, false solutions, hesitations and overhasty answers which nevertheless lead on to others, all belong. Could everything be arranged immediately in its final order, the development of the man would present no problems and would be incapable of seriously interesting anybody. He would simply be an ideologist or an organizer, whose essential nature could be described in a few sentences. Although John Wesley's life was firmly directed by a programme and by ordered thinking, to regard him merely as an ideologist would be hardly to understand him at all. On the contrary, the fascination of his life consists in the way in which his programme was gradually formulated and changed through encounters and controversies, new aspects of it arising out of the different crises.

Yet the theological structure and energy by which it was governed cannot be described only in theological terms. Fundamentally it was concerned with the basic realities of law, sin and grace, which characterize all theological thinking. Yet the attempt to understand the meaning of history in terms of abstract ideas only, so dear to the thinking of mankind, and through Hegel to the German mind in particular, is absolutely excluded from the first. This prohibition has special force in Wesley's case, for it was precisely the sharp impact of the isolated occurrence and the concrete situation which he experienced in their full strength. It has been truly said that he was a man more strongly influenced by events than by theories.[1] On the other hand the facts cannot just be left to speak for themselves, as if his life was built up in a positivist way from detached happenings. He was by nature a dominant personality, as far removed as possible from a plaything of events. Each isolated occurrence, in spite of its particularity, was drawn into his one life-purpose. A new, independent and unique unity arose from each encounter between purpose and event, theory and fact, programme and action, and this must be grasped.

The style of a biography must be suited to its subject. John Wesley loved clear-cut lines, and there was in him a strain of austerity which shunned compromise. It will be in line with this if the story of his life is told factually, precisely, and as succinctly as possible. A straightforward, essentially artless and sober style is demanded by the subject. The 'legend' or myth which Nietzsche's biographer, Ernst Bertram,[2] following Stefan George, rightly brought out in the account of his hero, has no place in the case of a personality like Wesley. The results of his activity are to be looked for in the field of pastoral work and organization, not in the realm of the legendary or mythical. On the other hand it is not possible to write a laudatory account of Wesley in the style used by Friedrich Gundolf, another pupil of George, in his biography of Caesar.[3] Wesley's type of preaching precludes his being conceived oratorically or his biography from being embroidered with rhetorical flourishes. Plainness is best suited to him. He is better represented by a drawing than by a painting, and the outlines must be bolder than the light and shade, the filling-in, or the colouring. A large-sized, impressive portrait would be essentially misleading, since it usually means that the surrounding figures and events, the formative forces of the period, are given less than their due. In such a picture they always appear less important than in reality they were. The central figure is too easily represented as the only inhabitant of his period, and his estimate of himself becomes too self-assured. Naturally his particular way of judging

[1] John S. Simon, *John Wesley and the Religious Societies*, p. 185: 'He was essentially a practical man, more deeply impressed by facts than theories.'
[2] *Nietzsche. Versuch einer Mythologie.*
[3] *Cäsar. Die Geschichte seines Ruhms.*

things and people cannot help but make a strong impression upon the biographer, and in this foreshortening of the perspective lies the temptation to isolate and over-emphasize. To a certain extent every biography does just this, since it has to portray great events which are common to all from the limited standpoint of one individual. This is doubly so in the case of a man who has already written his own life, and so cast it into one particular mould. In such circumstances the relationship between biography and autobiography cannot consist simply in the fact that the former should correct or improve the latter.[4] Although that may hold in particular cases, biography in general cannot treat autobiography as mere raw material. That could only happen when—as in the case of Carl Friedrich Bahrdt—obvious vanity and the need for self-justification has prompted the writing.[5] But whenever the autobiography has been written under the discipline of a desire to express the truth, it must be taken as the essential standard by anyone who subsequently recounts the life.

All autobiographies proffer the history of a self, but authors differ in the extent to which they reveal themselves. Throughout the whole of Europe John Wesley's time was an age of sentiment, but in England self-expression did not in general attain the lyrical character which it reached in the course of the century in Goethe's *Werther*, and which served to prepare the way for romanticism. England was disciplined to a far greater extent. It is not humours but genuine experiences, clear thinking, and firm resolutions which characterize the contents of the diaries. Actual situations come alive. This is understandable when earlier history is borne in mind, for in England the Puritan theology of conscience had taught the individual to look at himself as it were through the eyes of God, examining every detail, and directing his own purposes accordingly. Each step was reviewed to see whether it conformed to God's will. He was continually being warned against self-deception. The diary appeared expressly as the conscience fixed in writing, the 'witness between God and the soul'.[6]

---

[4] I regard it as an omission in the otherwise excellent work by Jan Romein, *Die Biographie* (1948), that the relationship between biography and autobiography is not discussed. On autobiography, cf. Georg Misch, *Geschichte der Autobiographie,* Vol. I (1909).

[5] *Geschichte seines Lebens, seiner Meinungen und Schicksale* (1790/1), newly published by Felix Hasselberg (1922; abbreviated).

[6] Cf. for example Henry Mason, *Tribunal of the Conscience*, p. 6: 'We read in the writings of the Ancients, that religious people have been accustomed to keep a day-book of their actions, and out of that to take an account for their life', ibid. pp. 36ff. *Regeln und Einte ilungsprinzipien für ein Tagebuch des Gewissens, An Account of the Life and Death of Mrs Elizabeth Bury (1644–1720)* (Bristol, 2nd

It was not written out of any necessity the writer may have felt of unburdening his heart or of enjoying his own feelings through objectifying them, nor even of making them of value to others. There was no question of such refined self-display: from beginning to end the whole undertaking had a strong ethical tone. The method was confessedly analytical and not primarily narrative. For this reason the older diaries in particular followed a stereotyped pattern, although they increasingly assumed an individual character because of the special experiences of their authors, the course of whose lives became for each a history of God's relationship with themselves. This was particularly true in the case of the two classic examples from the seventeenth century, the autobiographies of John Bunyan and George Fox, and then again of Jane Leade's also.[7]

When John Wesley is seen against this background the advance his *Journal* represents becomes evident. It sets out actual history, objectively related. Unlike the three instances mentioned above, the significance of each item is not stated in advance, but is left to follow the account and to grow out of the event. This is the reason why his *Journal* never gives the impression of having been deliberately composed or planned. The ordered and systematic impression it creates arises from the purposive character of Wesley's whole way of life. It is therefore a genuine expression of what he himself was. When one understands how to read it, what he has left us is suited in a particularly objective way to be the history of his own soul.

The same thing emerges from a consideration of his actual experience of life. The sensitive upbringing he received from his mother, the particular selection from the Romanic mystics with which he was familiar, the Puritan tradition as a whole, Henry Scougal, Jeremy Taylor and William Law, all introduced him to a particular type of spiritual culture. The stimulus to keep a journal he himself

edn, 1721), p. 9: 'Having set out for Heaven thus soon, and continuing her Resolutions for GOD, and Religion, and the Eternal Interests of her Soul: She often advised with herself and others, upon the properest and most effectual Means to promote and carry on her spiritual and pious Designs; and at last determined upon this as one, To keep a daily Memorial of what she did; which should be a Witness betwixt GOD and her own Soul (as she expresses it).'

[7] John Bunyan, *Grace Abounding to the Chief of Sinners*, George Fox, *Journal*, Jane Leade, *Ein Garten-Brunn gewässert durch die Ströhme der göttlichen Lustbarkeit* . . . (Amsterdam, Heinrich Wetstein, 1697). From the sixteenth century: *Two Elizabethan Diaries*, ed. M. M. Knappen (Chicago, 1933). On the whole question, Emma Danielowski, *Die Journale der frühen Quäker*, and my essay, *Biblizismus und natürliche Theologie in der Gewissenslehre des englischen Puritanismus*, Arch. f. Reformationsgesch (*ARG*) XLII(1951).198–220, XLIII. (1952).70–87, esp. 74–5.

traced back to the advice of Taylor,[8] and the urge became stronger when he read the spiritual biographies. It is no accident that these always meant a great deal to him and that he preferred above all to turn to them. Three stand out amongst them: the life of the French Count Gaston Jean-Baptiste de Renty,[9] the life of the Spanish-Mexican recluse Gregor Lopez, and the life of Thomas Haliburton, the Puritan. The first in particular he continued to recommend to the end of his days. When Wesley wrote the biography of his friend, fellow-worker, and designated successor, John William Fletcher (Jean Guillaume de la Fléchère), he put him alongside de Renty.[1] In his *Christian Library* and his periodical, *The Arminian Magazine*, he showed a preference for biographies, amongst them the life of Luther by the Halle Pietiest, Johann Daniel Herrnschmidt.[2]

The type of spiritual culture which was founded[3] during the modern era by the Romanic mystics of Spain and France, and mediated to the Pietism of the Netherlands and Germany through Pierre Poiret,[4] helped to mould John Wesley. The significance of the Romanic mystics for England in particular must be emphasized, and it could probably be shown how in that country their sensitive introspection hardens into a scrupulous, rationalistic and empirical analysis of the individual Ego.[5] The special characteristic of John Wesley's *Journal* consists in the fact that it hardly ever relates an event with-

[8] John Wesley, *Journal*, I.83–4 (Preface).
[9] Cf. my article '*John Wesley und die Biographie des französischen Grafen Gaston Jean-Baptiste de Renty* (1611–49)' in *Theologia Viatorum*, V.(1953) (*Jahrbuch der Kirchlichen Hochschule Berlin-Zehlendorf*).
[1] *Life and Death of Mr Fletcher*, pp. 223–4; *Works*, XI.364–5.
[2] E.g. *A Christian Library*, Vols. III–VI, include John Foxe's *Acts and Monuments*, i.e. biographies of the martyrs; Vols. XXVI and XXVII (1753) are given up entirely to biographies (*Lives* of Sundry Persons). Biographies of the authors always precede extracts from their writings, e.g. II.211–35, *The Life of John Foxe;* VII, *The Life of Robert Bolton;* cf. I.335–406, *The Life of Gregory Lopez.* In the *Arminian Magazine*, cf. I.(1778).9–17, *A Sketch of the Life of the Arminius;* I.68–77, 116–27, 165–75, 210–18, 264–72, *The Life of Martin Luther . . .* by John Daniel Herrnschmid; III.(1780).19–24, 81–91, 137–40, 194–9, *The Life of Armelle Nicolas* (1606–71).
[3] Max Frh v. Waldberg in his work, *Studien zur Geschichte des modernen Romans I': Zur Entwicklungsgeschichte der 'schönen Seele' bei den spanischen Mystikern*, has impressively worked this out, although with completely one-sided emphasis on the erotic factor.
[4] Because of this Max Weiser in his book on Peter Poiret is able to make his astonishing assertion, quite unjustified owing to its one-sidedness: 'The world which is the subject of this book has in my opinion little or nothing to do with religion—unfortunately today one must still use this expression from the eighteenth century! It is mainly the concern of psychology.' *Peter Poiret: Der Vater der romanischen Mystik in Deutschland. Zum Ursprung der Romantik in Deutschland*, p. viii.
[5] I hope sometime to demonstrate this.

out commenting on it, although in the fewest possible words. This unity of occurrence and comment reaches a high level of spontaneity, even if it is not entirely so, whereas in George Fox the narrative as a whole is still governed by the point of view which precedes it. For this reason it is much more difficult to see all that is implied in Wesley's compressed way of writing, and very careful attention is required to appreciate the various elements contained within it. Yet herein lies the peculiar fascination in recounting his life, and once the position is understood the introvert character of the biography becomes a necessity. But then even such a 'soul-history' which results from the inter-play between objective reality and subjective comprehension will not necessarily coincide without further modification with the theological way of thinking, even though they continually approximate to one another. One significant example of this may be given. On the day of his 'conversion' John Wesley wrote the review of his past life in terms of the Pauline distinction between law and grace, or works and faith, in order to show that justification, which at that time was the central article in his religious belief and theological thinking, had always been a reality in the depth of his own spiritual experience. Most biographers have followed him at this point because they have recognized that his theological understanding of himself was true for himself as he was at that particular time. Yet this is to short-circuit a process of growth which a subsequent critical review of the situation cannot repeat. Such a review must grant to every single moment, at least to every recognizable phrase in his inner development, its own right, and must deduce its meaning from the actual situation at the time.

The fact that the representation which follows, drawn from the spiritual and historical situation and from Wesley's own account, is the 'history of a soul', throws light upon one more theological circumstance. In the whole history of Christian thought Wesley scarcely has his equal as a practical counsellor in the experience of salvation. Thus everything moves in the end to a deep and final unity.

The Ecclesiastical and Historical Background

IT IS ONLY in a limited sense that modern English church history can be said to begin in the century which saw, as far as southern and northern Europe were concerned, the theological and ecclesiastical movement known as the 'Reformation'.[1] The questions which then agitated people and undermined the traditional order did indeed arouse resounding echoes in the British Isles, but they did not become historical forces of such weight or depth or extent. They did not set in motion any popular movement which might have led to the re-organization of Church or State, nor did they lead to any one compre-hensive and conclusive issue powerful enough to bring the succeeding period under the authority of its particular formulation of the questions. The controversy was rather contained within a cool atmosphere. Various features go to make up the over-all picture, such as the deliberations and decisions of rulers and church-leaders, who, driven by both opportunism and conviction, broke with or held to the connexion with the papacy; or again those ideas and writings of humanism, which by scholarly and critical study of the sources arrived at the ethical goal of a simple Christian life, combined at the same time with enthusiasm for antiquity. To an extent not found anywhere else the situation was governed both externally and from within by nationalistic, ecclesiastical-political considerations. In this way sixteenth-century England resembled the European Middle Ages of the fourteenth and fifteenth centuries, and might almost be thought

[1] Cf. James Gairdner, *Lollardy and the Reformation* and *The English Church in the Sixteenth Century from the Accession of Henry VIII to the Death of Mary*; Johannes Haller, *Papsttum und Kirchenreform*, I.375–465; A. F. Pollard, *Thomas Cranmer and the English Reformation*; Henry Eyster Jacobs, *A Study in Com-parative Symbolics: The Lutheran Movement in England during the Reigns of Henry VIII and Edward VI and its Literary Movements*; Frederick J. Smithen, *Continental Protestanism and the English Reformation*; Hans Leube, *Reforma-tion und Humanismus in England*, and '*Kirche und Glauben in England*' in *Die englischen Kulturideologie*, I.(1941).1–69; Herbert Schöffler, *Die Anfange des Puritanismus*; E. Gordon Rupp, *Studies in the Making of the Protestant Tradi-tion in the English Reformation*; Paul Meissner, *England im Zeitalter von Humanismus, Renaissance und Reformation*, esp. pp. 423ff.

of as a radical continuation of that period. The inherited national-ecclesiastical tendencies which determined events in France, especially from the time of Philip the Fair, in Bohemia from that of Hus, and in England itself from Wycliffe, reached their full strength under Henry VIII (1509–47). The term 'reformation', which for good reasons Luther avoided as a description of his work, is entirely appropriate to events in the British Isles, since it denotes the reorganization of the legal structure of the Church. Its political, nationalistic-ecclesiastical nature has imprinted itself on the whole of English church history as an enduring characteristic—to such an extent that one present-day writer would see in it an actual continuation of the Celtic priest-king conception.[2]

This is not to say that genuine conviction and passion were absent from the religious history of sixteenth-century England. On the contrary the England of that time was particularly rich in martyrs who were convinced of the truth of their Gospel, since each change in ecclesiastical direction led to the persecution of the adherents of the preceding one. Such a thinker as Herder regarded this violence as the most striking characteristic of the English Reformation.[3] It is consistent with this that the most significant and enduringly influential documents of the Reformation period should bear the mark of this ultimate witness to faith. Luther's own pupil, William Tyndale, the translator of the Bible, was executed in Amsterdam in 1536 and John Foxe wrote in 1564 the whole history of the Church in this period as a history of the martyrs.[4]

The primary effect of the stream of different religious proposals which flowed over the English people in rapid and often sudden succession was not, as might well have been expected, the formation of a large number of separate religious communities, each carrying on a more or less secret existence: instead the variety of influences and streams were once more successfully contained and forced into one mould, that of the Anglican Church. Under the leadership of the head of the State this entered the national life as a determinative

---

[2] Cf. Jürgen Wilhelm Winterhagen, *Die Ueberwindung des anglikanischen Kirchenbegriffs im ökumenischen Raum des 20 Jahrhunderts* in *Theologia Viatorum* II.(1950).80ff. (*Jahrbuch der Kirchlichen Hochschule Berlin-Zehlendorf.*)
[3] Johann Gottfried Herder, *Sämtliche Werke,* XXIII.123, 125.
[4] On Tyndale, cf. J. F. Mozley, *William Tyndale.* John Foxe's work is entitled *Acts and Monuments of the Christian Church;* there are two modern editions: ed. Cattley and Townsend, 8 vols (London, 1837–41); ed. Pratt, 8 vols (London, 1870). On Foxe, cf. esp. Rudolf Kapp, *Heilige und Heiligenlegenden in England,* Vol. I.

power, and in the succeeding centuries proved itself an important historical force. If Henry VIII could be said to have laid its foundation by England's break with Rome, his daughter Elizabeth (1558–1603) during her long reign gave to the new structure of the Church its legal status and determined the peculiar character of its life. The exceptional influence of Martin Bucer, the Strasbourg reformer, developed during his time as professor at Cambridge (1549–51), had served to prepare for this.[5] In particular his book, *De regno Christi* (*The Kingdom of Christ*), written while he was there, showed the way. Luther, in his teaching on the two authorities, had sharply stressed the difference which distinguishes the religious kingdom of love from the earthly kingdom of the secular power, and had sought their unity finally in the hidden rule of God.[6] Bucer on the other hand drew an impressive picture of the kingdom of Christ, characterized by the close relationship between Church and State so far as their standards, aims, undertakings and acts were concerned. The result was a religion whose institutions and personal outworkings were centred upon actual life, a strongly ethical and social type of Christianity particularly characteristic of England, and which time and again up to the era of Gladstone was to aim at the creation of a Christian State. Bucer founded no school, but his influence extended far. It affected both Anglicanism and Puritanism, and in this way created an enduring unity beneath those ecclesiastical and ecclesiastical-political tensions which were more immediately apparent.

Elizabeth's contribution to this era of the Counter-Reformation was to let her policy be determined wholly by anti-Roman considerations.[7] The chief motive behind her actions was the interest of the State rather than the wishes of the Church or even the promptings of her own personal faith. This remained her attitude. She was a politician of the Renaissance on northern soil, whom Schiller in his *Maria Stuart* quite correctly understood. In internal politics her anti-Roman point of view was given expression in her treatment of

[5] Cf. esp. Wilhelm Pauck, *Das Reich Gottes auf Erden. Utopie und Wirklichkeit. Eine Untersuchung zu Butzers 'De Regno Christi' und zur englischen Staatskirche des 16 Jahrhunderts;* August Lang, *Puritanismus und Pietismus. Studien zu ihrer Entwicklung von Martin Butzer bis zum Methodismus,* pp, 13ff; Wolfgang Mann, *Lateinische Dichtung in England vom Ausgang des Frühhumanismus bis zum Regierungsantritt Elisabeths* (1939), pp. 187ff.

[6] Cf. Franz Lau, *'Aeusserlich Ordnung' und 'weltlich Ding' in Luthers Theologie;* Gustaf Törnvall, *Geistliches und weltliches Regiment bei Luther,* esp. pp. 70ff, 159ff.

[7] Cf. esp. Arnold Oskar Meyer, *England und die katholische Kirche unter Elisabeth und den Stuarts,* Vol. I.

the Church. So far as personnel were concerned she began by removing from the life of the State all those Roman Catholic influences
which had been introduced during the reign of her predecessor,
'bloody' Mary. Urged on by the opposition she encountered, Elizabeth proceeded to the gruesome persecution of Catholics, and to the
present day Roman Catholic writers look upon that period of martyrdom as a glorious incident in the history of the Faith. In the realm
of law and organization it was the Parliament of 1559 which took the
decisive step towards the new form of the Church which suited best
the Queen's purpose, and Elizabeth assumed the title of 'Supreme
Governor of the Church', a cautious formula compared with the
earlier designation, 'Supreme Head of the Church'. It implied that
the teachers of doctrine, but not the doctrine itself, were to be subject
to the royal prerogative, and in this way Elizabeth hoped to retain
the Church's dogmatic characteristics for Catholics and so bring them
to break with the Pope. Although all the Catholic bishops refused the
oath to the Queen, nearly all the lower clergy submitted. The bishops
were accordingly deposed and a number imprisoned. Many went
abroad and at Douai in France founded a nursery of Catholic spirituality to flood the British Isles with its emissaries and printed matter.
Evangelically-minded clergymen, who had been forced to flee abroad
under Mary the Catholic, now accepted the bishoprics, and so the
episcopal system was retained. The Book of Common Prayer, which
had first been compiled under Edward VI (1547–53) from old-
English liturgies and the evangelical church-order of the former
Archbishop of Cologne, Hermann of Wied, was changed so as to
make it tolerable for Catholics. The Anglican Church henceforward
was to rest on the three pillars of the over-ruling authority of the
State, the episcopal office, and the uniform liturgy of the Book of
Common Prayer. Its authoritative theologians were John Jewel
1522–71) and Richard Hooker (1553–1600). The scholarly defence
of the peculiar ecclesiastical structure which they undertook in their
writings was intended first and foremost to avert the suspicion that
there had been any innovations. Jewel in particular sought by a
thorough-going exposition of the basic doctrines to demonstrate their
agreement with the Bible and the Fathers. In comprehensive fashion
Hooker traced the leading ideas of order and moderation, which he
took over from the ancient humanistic tradition, from the time of the
Divine creation to the building of the Church. In these writings the
fundamental character of the 'middle way' between the Roman

Catholic heritage and Reformation biblicism was established as the particular Anglican viewpoint, and it was claimed that in this way the true values of the early Church were better preserved and realized than in either the Roman Church or the Reformation Churches. Jewel made tradition, and Hooker reason, the great central principles of Anglican theology.

As a politician Elizabeth's concern was to unite the whole English nation in an anti-Roman direction. Accordingly she allowed a certain freedom in belief and practice within the Anglican Church, with the result that various tendencies could be contained alongside each other within it. This became the historical starting-point for Puritanism, which developed by prosecuting more strongly reformed energies and principles from the Continent. The reign of Mary the Catholic had brought many evangelically-minded refugees from England to Switzerland; also during these years the writings and the spirit of Heinrich Bullinger in Zürich and John Calvin in Geneva exerted an influence in the British Isles. Yet Puritanism knew how to combine with these influences the ethical and rationalist thinking of the Middle Ages, and the result was that characteristic type of Puritan preaching and devotional literature which might be called a rational empiricism in the tradition of the nominalism of the late Middle Ages. There came into being a reasoned and devout observation, analysis and penetration of the individual soul. In the time of Wycliffe William Langland had in fact already shown something of this in his poem 'Piers Ploughman', and it was carried farther by Edmund Spenser in the 'Fairie Queene'. It schematized, and yet continually broke through its own scheme, in order to hold to the reality of the soul's life and its concrete experience. The leading representative of this tendency was the Cambridge professor, William Perkins (1558–1602), who in the course of a short life achieved an astonishing amount. This served as a guide in the following century. The most influential devotional book at this time was *Practice of Piety* by Lewis Bayly (d. 1631), made out of sermons.

Ecclesiastical politics soon brought controversies into prominence. John Hooper (1495–1555),[8] from 1547 to 1549 an admiring disciple of Heinrich Bullinger in Zürich, was not prepared to wear the vestments of his office when about to become Bishop of Gloucester be-

---

[8] On him cf. principally M. M. Knappen, *Tudor Puritanism. A Chapter in the History of Idealism*, pp. 59ff, 70ff, 82ff, 89ff, 96ff, 483ff, August Lang, *Puritanismus and Pietismus . . .*, pp. 38ff.

cause they smacked too much of Catholicism. Behind his refusal lay Zwingli's cherished belief that God must be worshipped only in spirit and in truth. Hooper then launched a violent attack upon all accessories used in worship, such as pictures, altars, candles and crosses. With all the sharpness of Reformed polemics he condemned the Roman Catholic mass and also Luther's doctrine of the Bodily Presence of Jesus Christ in the sacrament, but Bucer's resistance to his radicalism was not without its influence upon him. He came to have a certain sympathy with the mediating position which Bucer took on the question of the sacrament, as represented in the Concord of Wittenberg of 1536, but the utmost concession he was prepared to make was to allow that the Spiritual Presence of Jesus Christ in the sacrament was a reality. Although Hooper's action was a prelude to what followed later, it can only with doubtful justification be called Puritanism, for Matthew Parker (1504–75) as Archbishop of Canterbury had pursued a harsh policy against those Puritans who were disposed to reform, and he had removed a number of the best preachers on account of their opposition to the Anglican ceremonies. Elizabeth let him alone, although severity was not her intention. The policy was not a success. In 1567 there came a split in the Church. The Puritans separated and so procured for themselves the possibility of holding services in small private groups in accordance with their principles.

Alongside the question of ceremonies, the organization of the Church was the other fundamental point of controversy. The leading protagonist in this instance was Thomas Cartwright (1535–1603) [9] As the youthful Lady Margaret Professor in Cambridge he pointed out in his sermons on the Acts of the Apostles, preached before a large audience, the contrast between the Anglican ministry and that of the early Church. He rejected entirely the episcopal hierarchy and demanded a Presbyterian system. According to his view the Church is not constituted from above, but from the congregation. His opponent John Whitgift was also a professor in the University, but soon became Vice-Chancellor and thereby gained the power to depose him, whereupon Cartwright went to Geneva to Calvin's successor,

[9] Cf. A. F. Scott Pearson, *Thomas Cartwright and Elizabethan Puritanism, Church and State*. On Puritanism as a whole, cf. my review of the literature in *Die Problematik des Puritanismus im Lichte seiner Erforschung Zeitschrift f. Kirchengesch.* (ZKG) LX.(1941).207–54, and William Haller, *The Rise of Puritanism*, together with M. M. Knappen, *Tudor Puritanism*, Geoffrey F. Nuttall, *The Holy Spirit in Puritan Faith and Experience* (in which the emphasis is upon the Quakers).

Beza. He soon returned to England and took up the struggle again, but once more he had to flee. This time he chose the Netherlands as an asylum and became minister of the English congregation which was still in existence among refugees of Mary's reign. He now began to formulate more sharply in violently controversial works the claims of the Presbyterian movement, and as soon as it seemed possible he returned to his homeland. Whitgift, who in the meantime had become Archbishop of Canterbury, had made up his mind to extirpate the Puritans. Cartwright spent the rest of his life pursuing the course to which he had set himself, in struggle and persecution. The harsh measures taken by the Anglican leaders resulted in a third of the total number of clergy being deprived of their office by the end of Elizabeth's reign.

As a Scottish Presbyterian, James I (1603–25), the son of Mary Stuart, was greeted with expectation by the Puritans, who hoped at last to obtain full legal status. At first it was also the new king's intention to unite the Calvinism of his Scottish homeland with English Anglicanism, and indeed he had far-reaching plans for bringing about the unity of Christendom. The French humanist Isaac Casaubon and the great Dutch scholar Hugo Grotius were his principal associates in these plans. But he soon gave precedence to the internal affairs of the English Church, because he saw in it the best foundation for the theocratic claim upon which he wished to establish his authority. The spiritual authority should sustain the temporal. The assertion 'No bishop, no king' became his favourite theme. James even introduced the episcopal system into Scotland, where however it remained a foreign growth in soil that was overwhelmingly Presbyterian. The most important theologian to strive for the close union of State and Church both in theory and in practice was William Laud (1573–1645), who was successively Dean of Gloucester, Bishop of London from 1628, and finally Archbishop of Canterbury from 1633. He regarded the sacrament as the focal point of worship, the altar as centre of the church, and the Christianity of the first centuries as the absolute norm. This made him the uncompromising antagonist of the whole outlook of the reforming Puritans. He expressed his Anglican-primitive church ideal in the celebrated formula, 'the beauty of the saints'. He became a fanatical champion of the liturgy. His real work was done under James's son, Charles I (1625–49), whose marriage to the French princess Henrietta Maria seemed to the people to bode ill, since she, as the daughter of Henry IV, was a Catholic. Everything that now happened, and especially Laud's activity, was interpreted as a further step towards Catholicism.

Under the two kings, James I and Charles I, the struggle against Puritanism and its conception of life became the official ecclesiastical policy. Charles's government intensified this attitude, because Laud's positive ideas in opposition to Puritanism became its driving force. The Puritans strongly stressed the hallowing of Sunday and they abominated the theatres. To strike at them, James I in 1618 issued the *Book of Sports*, which commended dancing, the theatre and archery. He required the clergy to read out its chief provisions from the pulpits. In Scotland, where great indignation had been aroused by the alteration of the constitution of the Church in the appointment of bishops, Laud in 1637 introduced an Anglican liturgy, embodying his principles, into the Cathedral Church of St Giles, Edinburgh. At this the storm broke out. Nobles and ministers drew up the form of a 'covenant', in which, after the manner of the Old Testament, the people bound themselves together before God to fight for His honour. This began the revolution which swept out the Anglican elements from the Church. In England Charles I had made himself unpopular by his autocratic rule, his dissolution of Parliament and particularly by his Navigation Tax. When at length he summoned the 'Long Parliament', it demanded the abolition of episcopacy and of Laud's liturgy. The nation, now aroused, detected Roman Catholic designs and influences everywhere, and the cry, 'No Popery', ran through the streets. In October 1641 there was a Catholic uprising in Ireland in which 12,000 men fell, for which the royal pair, especially the queen, were regarded as responsible. The king and queen were said to have planned to overthrow the troublesome English Parliament with the help of the Irish Catholics. Charles I fled from Puritan London, where he did not feel safe, and by so doing gave the signal for civil war. The 'Cavaliers' fought on the king's side against the parliamentary 'Roundheads'. Parliament, which regarded itself as too weak on its own, joined with the Scots, and the political alliance was strengthened theologically by the Westminster Assembly (1643–7). After lengthy deliberations this set forth in the Westminster Confession the common statement of belief for all Presbyterian churches. It was characteristic of Anglo-Saxon Christianity that it really turned on a point of practical piety, the Scottish conception of the Sabbath, rather than on theological doctrines like justification or predestination, and this became the distinctive mark of the Anglo-

American Christian tradition as a whole. The Great Rebellion, which held England in its grip for seven years (1642–9), produced such an outburst of spiritual energy and activity that it is tempting to call this the period of England's reformation.[1] A wealth of publicists and politicians appeared. Both individuals and groups were swayed by conviction and fixity of purpose, but also by propaganda and violence; by honourable motives and the desire to do great things, but also by fickleness and cowardice. Politics and religion, conceived for the most part apocalyptically, were mixed up together to a degree scarcely ever known before: secular history became church history under the sign of the End. Would it be possible to contain the cataract of propaganda and events? Would commanding figures appear out of ferment and create order? In the first phase John Pym (1584–1643), a real politician of inflexible determination, fulfilled this role, but then the mantle fell on the incomparably greater Oliver Cromwell (1599–1658), commander-in-chief and dictator, who in a unique way knew how to combine the spirit of the Old Testament and apocalyptic with political energy.[2] The common concern of all the various groups—baptists, mystic-spirituals, utopians, communists, simple pietists, and the upholders of natural rights—became freedom of conscience. This did not arise—as later in the Enlightenment—from weariness with religious quarrels: on the contrary its

[1] Hermann Weingarten, *Die Revolutionskirchen Englands*, cf. the latest brilliantly written account by Michael Freund, *Die grosse Revolution in England. Anatomie eines Umsturzes* (which goes up to 1642). From the point of view of Church history the thesis that Quakerism was the most noble product of the revolution still holds the field; cf. the researches of Theodor Sippell (*Werdendes Quäkertum*), in spite of his criticisms of Weingarten on points of detail. On the influence of Jakob Böhme: Wilhelm Struck, *Der Einfluss Jakob Böhmes auf die englische Literatur des 17 Jahrhunderts;* Nils Thune, *The Behemists and the Philadelphians*, also C. E. Whiting *Studies in English Puritanism from the Restoration to the Revolution, 1660–88*, pp. 295ff.

[2] Helmuth Kittel's attempt (*Oliver Cromwell: Seine Religion und seine Sendung*) to derive Cromwell's consciousness of his political mission from Luther's 'Freedom of a Christian Man' cannot be regarded as completely successful, in spite of his having noticed correctly a characteristic related to Luther in his opposition to the political Utopia of the Fifth Monarchy men. The difference lies in Cromwell being so strongly coloured by the Old Testament. Luther's way of thinking about the Old Testament, as Heinrich Bornkamm (*Luther und das Alte Testament*) has so clearly shown, rests quite differently upon the theocentric and Christocentric character of his thought, and upon salvation-history and general history seen in relation to God rather than upon the experience of the nation in God-given circumstances. Luther's 'political' exposition of the Old Testament (cf. Bornkamm, pp. 9ff) takes its forms and events as general examples of State action much more than as occurrences which can be actually identified with his own age. The German people do not become for him the People of God after the analogy of Israel, nor is the idea of election thought of as consummated or newly apprehended in them.

basis was a trembling awe before the power of the conscience through which God Himself spoke. Regard for the religious rights of individuals sprang from this awe. The characteristic outworking of this attitude was the North American colonies. Not without some truth has a recent writer described Oliver Cromwell as the first President of the United States.[3]

An abundance of lay preachers proclaimed their revelations. Since it was a time of war, they were mostly army chaplains. Political events pursued their own inexorable course. In 1649 Charles I was executed. Cromwell was now able to do that for which previously he had been too weak: as sole ruler he reorganized the State, dissolved Parliament, and in foreign and internal affairs went from one success to another. He united the three countries, England, Scotland and Ireland, made them the leading sea-power and the leading anti-Catholic power.

The freedom of conscience which helped to build up, if only in part, the North American colonies, made it possible for many religious denominations to live peacefully together in Cromwell's England also, and different types of leaders appeared simultaneously. Naturally the clergy who remained loyal to the king had to vacate their livings, but they retained, at least in theory, a fifth of their incomes. Thus the genuine Anglicans withdrew for a while from the life of the nation, and 'Puritanism' came to recognize more clearly the various shades of opinion of which it was composed. Continental influences appeared, among them that of the mystic Jakob Böhme, who through Jane Leade and William Law was powerful in seventeenth- and eighteenth-century England. Most important and influential among the leading figures were Richard Baxter (1615–91), John Bunyan (1628–88), and George Fox (1624–91). Baxter and Bunyan were representative of the average 'pietistic' Puritanism, which fostered a simple, dutiful life under God. Baxter laid emphasis upon the family and family worship, while Bunyan set the individual immediately before God. In his *Holy War* and *Pilgrim's Progress* his literary genius created for the whole of Christendom imperishable witnesses to English piety. In them he gave a unique dramatic description of the eternal theme of the human soul in its deep concerns with God, salvation and peace. The great Elizabethan tradition of dramatic poetry had also an influence upon the devotional literature

---

[3] Freund, *Die grosse Revolution in England* . . . , p. 16.

of Puritanism.[4] Different again was George Fox, the founder of the Society of Friends, or 'Quakers', an itinerant preacher similar to those in the early Church, who worked miracles of healing and by his emphasis upon the 'inner light' fought for the right of every individual to his own relationship with God and his own experience of God. During his lifetime he was instrumental in founding societies in England, Ireland, America, Germany, and Poland. A mission was started among the North American Indians. His successor, William Penn (1644–1718), the son of an officer, gave a stable form to the work begun in the Quaker State of Pennsylvania, where a silent type of worship, with neither hymn-singing nor liturgy, was cultivated. The congregation waited in silence and if anyone received a revelation in the manner of the charismatic gifts of the early Church, he communicated it to the others by prayer, exhortation, or instruction. Sometimes these illuminations were accompanied by nervous convulsions: hence the name 'Quaker'. If none was moved to speak, the company all sat in silence.

In addition to these peaceful elements in the land, there were others which more openly took the offensive. Amongst them was the greatest poet of the time, John Milton (1608–74), whose *Paradise Lost* gave expression to man's misery and his yearning for redemption. As a political publicist in the grand manner he demanded freedom for the Press as the basis of a true national life. William Prynne (1600–69) in his *Histriomastix* lashed out mercilessly against the theatre and court fashion, but entered the lists with equal violence against the revolutionaries when they dared to execute the king. Twice this undaunted fighter for his rights was punished by having his ears clipped, once under Laud, and again under Cromwell.

Cromwell's revolutionary political creation, the Protectorate, scarcely survived its founder. His son Richard, who tried to follow his steps, soon showed that he was incapable of doing so, and this suggested the idea of recalling the Stuart monarchy from France. How the abounding energies of the Great Revolution suddenly ebbed away to be replaced by the restoration of the monarchy defies explanation. At no point was this more clearly seen than in the affairs of the established Church. Charles II, the son of the Charles who had been beheaded, in 1660, two years after Oliver Cromwell's death,

---

[4] Cf. my article '*Eigenart und Bedeutung der Eschatologie im englischen Puritanismus*' (Arthur Dent, Lewis Bayly, John Bunyan); *Theologia Viatorum* IV (1952). 211–12 (*Jahrb. d. Kirchl. Hochschule Berlin-Zehlendorf*).

entered the London from which his father had fled in 1642. The rejoicing of the populace escorted him to his throne. In 1662 he renewed Queen Elizabeth's Act of Uniformity of 1559, the fundamental document of the Anglican Church. The supremacy of the king over the Church, episcopacy and the Book of Common Prayer, were once again constituted the standard order. Ordinations were examined. During the rebellion and the Protectorate many ministers had received presbyterian ordination, and now they had either to be episcopally reordained or vacate their livings. This was the dark year for Puritanism.[5] From a quarter to a third of the total number of clergymen lost their positions, and their economic situation became very uncertain. Lawful incomes generally were not open to them. In many cases they came to an agreement locally with the patron or their successor, by which they received a part of the revenue. In some instances the patrons endeavoured to persuade the ministers to submit to the regulations of the national Church. Frequently also the resolute found protectors amongst the nobility; a self-assistance fund was started; some had their own resources. But more serious than the economic need was the loss of their homes. The Act of Uniformity of 1662 was followed two years later by the Conventicle Act, which forbade more than five persons to meet in houses for worship. In this way congregations were to be broken up, although the result was that assemblies continued to meet in the greatest secrecy, often in forests and woods. Even this was not all. The last piece of legislation in this series was the so-called Five Mile Act of 1665, which was the harshest of all. It laid down that a minister who had been dismissed from his office should not come within five miles of his previous place of work. A very great many had to move their homes, which naturally they had made in the neighbourhood with friends or acquaintances. The children of Puritan ministers were excluded from the universities. When in 1768 John Wesley read an account of these times he was so shocked that he declared Charles II was worse than Bloody Queen Mary.[6]

On this basis Anglicans and Puritans, who were also called Nonconformists or Dissenters, pursued an unequal life in their districts, the one in possession of all rights, the other in a harsh struggle for existence. The literary battle over Church organization, liturgy and

[5] On this, cf. C. E. Whiting, *Studies in English Puritanism* . . . , pp. 1–42.
[6] Wesley's *Journal*, V.248 (11th February 1768).

ceremonies went resolutely on. Yet—and this was different from before—the consciousness of a common unity also grew. There were real points of contact between the opposed groups. Not only did the humanist and Puritan aim of a life pleasing to God unite earnest men in both parties, but Edward Stillingfleet (1635–99), Bishop of Worcester, advocated a conciliatory treatment of the controverted questions. Later he supported the actual admission of Dissenters into the Church of England. His spiritual successor, even if ecclesiastically and politically somewhat hesitant, was the great Bishop of Salisbury, Gilbert Burnet (1643–1715), author of an unsurpassed history of the Reformation in England and a history of his own times. Herbert Thorndyke, Prebendary of Westminster, was not prepared without qualification to call Quakers Christians, and thought that they were Mohammedans, or at best Gnostics or Manichaeans.[7] On the other hand he believed that the differences between Anglicans and Presbyterians could be overcome without too much difficulty. Jeremy Taylor (1613–67) held unequivocally to the divine right of the established Church and episcopacy, the rejection of which he could only account for as springing from a life opposed to God. He rejected all attempts to arrive at a theoretical unity in a common faith obtained through reduction or compromise. He regarded this as a 'fanciful peace'. Yet he stated that no one should be punished for his opinions, which were to be tolerated so long as they were not put forward violently or endangered national order. Finally, like the German Pietism of Philipp Jakob Spener and like Albrecht Ritschl, he appealed to the words of Jesus in John 7[17]: 'If any man will do His will, he shall know of the doctrine, whether it be of God.' He thus argued for the principle that ethics arbitrates about dogmatics and life about doctrine.[8] Even a man like William Prynne, the intrepid fighter in the time of Charles I and Cromwell, must have commended himself especially for his ideas on union, for he now strongly advocated the divine right of the king. On the other hand he found fault with the Book of Common Prayer, much of which contradicted the Bible. Richard Baxter wrote a *Nonconformist's Plea for Peace*. An anonymous writer issued a whole succession of fly-sheets with the title, *A Conformist's Plea for the Nonconformist:* he was Edward Pearse, a

---

[7] Herbert Thorndyke, *A Discourse of the Forebearance or the Penalties which a due Reformation requires* (1670), *Works*, V.381–488; cf. Whiting, *Studies in English Puritanism* . . . , p. 188.
[8] Cf. Whiting, *Studies in English Puritanism* . . . , p. 492–3.

Northamptonshire clergyman.[9] John Corbet tried to make the Established Church's royal oath tolerable for the Nonconformist ministers, who ought only to declare that they would abjure any attempt to oppose the king by force.[1] When Archbishop John Tillotson preached in Whitehall on 2nd April 1680, before Charles II, on Joshua 24[15] and deduced in an implacable way that the Established Church of England had the right to turn out the Dissenters, a nobleman jokingly asked the king if he did not hear from the pulpit the voice of the philosopher Thomas Hobbes, the spokesman for the sovereign rights of the State in religious affairs, so out of keeping with the spirit of the time was the desire to exclude, ignore or oppress the Dissenters felt to be.

Two factors favoured the idea of closer approximation. One was the growing Deism, often called 'atheism' by the representatives of the Church. It originated with Herbert of Cherbury in Cromwell's time. During the course of his frequent travels he had become familiar with other nations and religions, and so attacked the idea of Christianity as the criterion, and in its place set up 'natural religion' as the absolute standard. The second factor was the inclination of the Crown towards Roman Catholicism. This was already evident under Charles II (1660–85), and it led to the catastrophe under James II (1685–8). One event in particular was characteristic. In 1687 there appeared accounts of Christian charitable works under the title *Pietas Romana* (Roman Religion) and *Pietas Parisiensis* (Parisian Religion), which indirectly commended the charitable activities of Roman Catholic religious orders and congregations. In particular when James II, the Catholic, by his Declaration of Indulgence planned to gain the favour of Dissenters and Catholics by improving their legal status and then playing them against the Established Church, many Anglicans recognized the great danger. They perceived that in this matter they stood on the same side as the Puritans. A further factor contributed towards this end. The idea of a secular State was beginning to win its way. The State was no longer thought of as deriving from a transcendent order, but being looked at directly from the point of view of its tasks in this world, it appeared as a union for the accomplishment of certain ends. Questions of law and administration, the oversight of trade and commerce, and the re-

[9] Cf. Whiting, ibid. pp. 532ff. *The Conformist's Plea for the Nonconformist* (1681); *The Conformist's Second, Third, Fourth Plea* (1681–3).
[1] Whiting, *Studies in English Puritanism*, pp. 535ff. John Corbet, *An Enquiry into the Oath required of Noncomformists by an Act made at Oxford.*

duction of poverty, were seen to be the central concerns of domestic politics. Here was another factor which led to religious belief being regarded as a private concern, just as Cromwell's conception of the freedom of conscience on religious grounds had done. The separation of Church and State emerged as a serious possibility. William Penn was the most prominent champion of this idea.

The approximation between Anglicans and Puritans was possible in two ways. Either the Established Church could be made so broad and open that the greatest possible number could find entrance, or tolerance could be guaranteed to all kinds of belief on substantially the same terms, and each allowed to develop in its own way. The first idea was that of 'comprehension', the inclusion of all believers within the one Church. Because of the many different kinds of belief this would have meant the Church of England losing its identity and degenerating into a consulting room for all religious opinions. Its best representatives perceived just this. Accordingly the other way of toleration was necessarily the more attractive, since it allowed all forms of belief to subsist. Implied within it was the ultimate recognition of equal rights for all. Hence the idea of toleration prevailed over that of comprehension, and this soon became the case in political affairs also. The pro-Catholic policy of James II caused the two parliamentary parties, the Tories and the Whigs, in 1688 to summon to the country the nearest candidate to the title of the throne, James's son-in-law, William of Orange, the Stadtholder of the Netherlands. The anti-Roman spirit of Elizabeth's time was again aroused. In the 'Glorious Revolution' James II was expelled. He fled to France, the country to which the Stuarts had always turned for political support. In 1689 the new king, William III, issued the Toleration Act.

But his ascent of the throne created a fresh difficulty. Eight of the superior clergy and four hundred of the lower refused to take the oath to him because he was not considered to have succeeded legally to his office. They were churchmen imbued with the ideals of William Laud, and thus strongly committed to the Establishment. They held enthusiastically to the view which gave supreme importance to the early Church. On losing their positions they lived on as independent preachers or private persons as the Dissenters had previously done. They included in their number William Law, the author of religious works, and were known as 'Non-Jurors'. The differences which were aroused in this way extended into John Wesley's home. To his father's sorrow, his mother took this position. When Samuel Wesley

not reside in their parishes but led a life of ease in the town on incomes which accrued to them from rich benefices, of which they frequently possessed two or three. They left their ministrations and conduct of the regular services to curates, whom they paid, poorly enough, from their own means. Oliver Goldsmith's Vicar of Wakefield is an accurate representation of the frugal and uncertain existence of one of these curates. These conditions were typical of the late Middle Ages, but in Central Europe they had been challenged by the Reformation and, in the Catholic areas, by the Counter-Reformation which followed. A satirical picture, which admittedly comes from the year 1772, illustrates conditions in England and how they affected different men. It shows a fat collector of benefices sitting in a carriage with two churches under his arm, and holding pigs, geese and hens on his lap, while his hungry-looking curates, like drag-horses, are made to pull him along.

Social life also had its dark spots. England had become the great seafaring nation of Europe. The Peace of Utrecht, which ended the war of the Spanish Succession in 1713, gave her the monopoly of the slave trade. Wealthy planters returned from the North American colonies to spend their money in the more congenial homeland, bringing with them negroes and Indians whom they sold again. Even young Englishmen and women were sold to ships going overseas, after they had been lured into brothels. Alcohol and immorality also wreaked their excesses in the villages, and frequently went along with sport and entertainment. The brutal tormenting of animals was the order of the day. There were great economic and social inequalities, extremes of poverty and wealth existing side by side. A barbaric system of imprisonment of debtors put the law completely into the hands of the creditor and the holder of economic power. The helpless victims were frequently incarcerated in the same prisons with criminals.

Conditions were not of course everywhere the same. As always the towns were worse than the villages, which, as communities in which it was natural for people to grow up, formed a healthy barrier against the moral decay. The remarkable work of the Puritan preachers and writers in the field of moral training cannot have been without some effect. But the spirit of the age in the late seventeenth century and early eighteenth century was determind to a high degree by French influences at Court, political considerations, by complete indifference to Christian standards, by a general seeking after pleasure.

It is not therefore surprising that it was ment for the revival of the spiritual life o first place through the 'religious societies' leading figures were two clergymen, o Horneck (1640–97), and the other an Eng Horneck, a native of Bacharach, had co but before this he had been closely ass was influenced by Anna Maria von Sch ciple of Jean de la Badie. From 1678 the cultured classes had gathered arou by the desire for a change in view of society. Horneck, to whom they turn forthwith prescribed for them fixed r monastic rules of Benedict of Nursia also had affinities with those of m such as the Jesuits or the free societi Possibly he was also influenced by pupil of the Jesuits and a Roman (over to the Huguenot Church in F work in Geneva and Middleburg ideal church. Horneck's princi striking way with the prayers a was in conformity with the pract his pastoral method had the ef Anglican soil. It was a chur Christianity which was fostere merely with this concern for t undertake the care of the poo students. In the ancient univ made religion once more int women joined them, and th Associations came into bei and social evils, to found so

[3] The chief sources for the Re
of the Rise and Progress of the
their Endeavours for Reform
Simon, John Wesley and the
Anfänge der Laienmitarbeit
Missionsgedanke des jungen
Theologis viatorum, I.(1948–
year 1678 Spener's attention
in Amsterdam (Spener to F
City and University Library

prayed for King William, no 'Amen' came from her lips. When one day he noticed this, he stormed out of the house, and the couple lived apart for several months. The death of the king brought them together again, for both recognized Anne, the new queen.[2]

Anne (1702–14), the younger daughter of James II, once more took the High Church line which stressed the importance of the connexion between State and Church. They were bad days for the Dissenters, and their political representatives in Parliament, the Whigs, felt less than ever inclined to suffer slights. There was great unrest when Dr Henry Sacheverell in a sermon in St Paul's, London, in November 1709 violently attacked the Toleration Act of 1689 and so threw doubts upon the legality of the ecclesiastical set-up of the time. The ineptitude of the Whigs made him into a martyr in the controversies which followed, and in this way the Tories regained popularity and power.

Thus the Church history of Great Britain from the end of the Middle Ages presents a classic example of ecclesiastical politics. In scarcely any other country were the moving forces in Church affairs so strongly determined by events in the political sphere or by the action of the State authority. Tensions within the Church were constantly made more acute by external events, such as a change in government. A full measure of misery, suffering, injustice and oppression had given rise to much fidelity to conviction and readiness for sacrifice. In the tough struggle to maintain themselves the religious denominations and every one of their members had been forced to make decisions of far-reaching import and acute severity. This was a magnificent education in that independence and individuality wherein lay the true characteristic of the English ecclesiastical consciousness.

On the other hand there were serious weaknesses in the Church. The higher clergy frequently had an eye upon the Court, whose favour meant more to them than their own calling. Their sermons often praised in extravagant terms the prevailing system and the ruling persons, and were political speeches rather than messages of consolation or calls to repentance through the enlivening of conscience. But the greatest evil was the inadequate provision made for many congregations. Visitation and regular oversight and examination by ecclesiastical authorities were woefully inadequate. Many of the clergy did

[2] Maximin Piette, *John Wesley in the Evolution of Protestantism*, p. 219. His source, *Methodist Magazine* (1786), p. 606, is not available to me.

31

not reside in their parishes but led a life of ease in the town on incomes which accrued to them from rich benefices, of which they frequently possessed two or three. They left their ministrations and conduct of the regular services to curates, whom they paid, poorly enough, from their own means. Oliver Goldsmith's Vicar of Wakefield is an accurate representation of the frugal and uncertain existence of one of these curates. These conditions were typical of the late Middle Ages, but in Central Europe they had been challenged by the Reformation and, in the Catholic areas, by the Counter-Reformation which followed. A satirical picture, which admittedly comes from the year 1772, illustrates conditions in England and how they affected different men. It shows a fat collector of benefices sitting in a carriage with two churches under his arm, and holding pigs, geese and hens on his lap, while his hungry-looking curates, like draghorses, are made to pull him along.

Social life also had its dark spots. England had become the great seafaring nation of Europe. The Peace of Utrecht, which ended the war of the Spanish Succession in 1713, gave her the monopoly of the slave trade. Wealthy planters returned from the North American colonies to spend their money in the more congenial homeland, bringing with them negroes and Indians whom they sold again. Even young Englishmen and women were sold to ships going overseas, after they had been lured into brothels. Alcohol and immorality also wreaked their excesses in the villages, and frequently went along with sport and entertainment. The brutal tormenting of animals was the order of the day. There were great economic and social inequalities, extremes of poverty and wealth existing side by side. A barbaric system of imprisonment of debtors put the law completely into the hands of the creditor and the holder of economic power. The helpless victims were frequently incarcerated in the same prisons with criminals.

Conditions were not of course everywhere the same. As always the towns were worse than the villages, which, as communities in which it was natural for people to grow up, formed a healthy barrier against the moral decay. The remarkable work of the Puritan preachers and writers in the field of moral training cannot have been without some effect. But the spirit of the age in the late seventeenth century and early eighteenth century was determind to a high degree by French influences at Court, political considerations, by complete indifference to Christian standards, by a general seeking after pleasure.

It is not therefore surprising that it was in London that a movement for the revival of the spiritual life of the Church arose in the
first place through the 'religious societies', as they were called.[3] The
leading figures were two clergymen, one a German, Dr Anton
Horneck (1640–97), and the other an Englishman, Richard Smithies.
Horneck, a native of Bacharach, had come to England in early life,
but before this he had been closely associated with a group which
was influenced by Anna Maria von Schurman, the enthusiastic disciple of Jean de la Badie. From 1678 onwards young people from
the cultured classes had gathered around the two ministers, urged on
by the desire for a change in view of the empty life of the leaders of
society. Horneck, to whom they turned in their spiritual need, had
forthwith prescribed for them fixed rules, which resembled the great
monastic rules of Benedict of Nursia and Francis of Assisi, but which
also had affinities with those of more modern Roman Catholicism,
such as the Jesuits or the free societies of the French Count de Renty.
Possibly he was also influenced by Jean de la Badie, who had been a
pupil of the Jesuits and a Roman Catholic priest, but had then gone
over to the Huguenot Church in France, and who in the course of his
work in Geneva and Middleburg in Holland had sought to create an
ideal church. Horneck's principles were closely connected in a
striking way with the prayers and ordinances of the Church. This
was in conformity with the practice of the Roman Church. Moreover
his pastoral method had the effect of transplanting confession into
Anglican soil. It was a churchly rather than a private type of
Christianity which was fostered, but the young people were not left
merely with this concern for their own welfare. They had begun to
undertake the care of the poor, the sick, the imprisoned debtors and
students. In the ancient universities of Oxford and Cambridge they
made religion once more into an object of respect. Older men and
women joined them, and the movement grew to large proportions.
Associations came into being to take up the struggle against moral
and social evils, to found schools for the poor, and eventually even to

[3] The chief sources for the Religious Societies is Josiah Woodward, *An Account
of the Rise and Progress of the Religious Societies in the City of London and of
their Endeavours for Reformation of Manners.* On the Societies, cf. John S.
Simon, *John Wesley and the Religious Societies*, pp. 9–27; Theophil Funk, *Die
Anfänge der Laienmitarbeit im Methodismus*, pp. 15ff, and my article 'Der
Missionsgedanke des jungen Wesley auf dem Hintergrunde seines Zeitalters',
Theologis viatorum, I.(1948–9).82ff. It is worthy of note that as early as the
year 1678 Spener's attention had been drawn to them through Friedrich Breckling
in Amsterdam (Spener to Breckling, 5th April 1678, handwritten in Hamburg,
City and University Library Cod. Ms. *Supellex epistolica*, 4.VI.194.b.).

assume responsibility for religious work in the colonies. The most important of these foundations was the 'Society for Promoting Christian Knowledge', which is still in existence, and which welcomed support from those in any place who shared its outlook. In this way it became closely associated with August Hermann Francke in Halle.

These then were the conditions in the history of the Church in England which had been preparing the way for wellnigh 200 years for the coming of John Wesley and the rise of the Methodist movement. The nation had devoted an enormous output of energy to the solution of the problem of Christianity. Its relation to the political order had been taken as seriously as the nurture of individual Christians, and the same applied to the Church's sense of obligation both to the early Christian centuries and to the problem of a free community in an ordered society. The social task had been recognized and taken in hand at least on a small scale. Only in the sphere of dogma or the constructive aspect of theological problems or of doctrine had there been a retrogression. In its place English Christianity had developed a predominantly Old Testament biblicism which represented the people and events of Scripture in the first place as living, present realities, and indeed made them into its own possession.

THREE

Ancestors and Family Home

JOHN WESLEY came from an old family. Since the spelling of the name changed in an earlier age, there is plenty of scope for the imagination in constructing the family tree.[1] According to one possible tradition all the male members of the family over the age of sixteen must have lost their lives at the Battle of Hastings (1066). The widow of the head of the family found refuge with her little children on an estate in the County of Somerset, called Welswe or Welslegh.[2] This then would be the oldest form of the family name. Besides Welswe and Welslegh, Wellesleigh is found from the year 1420, later Wellesley and Welsly, and finally from 1539 Wesley. Only subsequently did the spelling Westley originate through mispronunciation. One branch of the family moved to Ireland, but kept in constant touch with England, principally by marriage—our John Wesley had Irish blood in his veins. The attempt has been made to trace to this source two characteristics he shared with his father, namely, the ease with which he wrote and his predilection for engaging in petty controversies.[3] The ancestors lived chiefly in the west and south of England, and in the hundred years at least before John Wesley's birth produced many clergymen. They experienced all the upsets of that critical period, which according to Hermann Weingarten's well-known dictum, ought to be called the age of England's Reformation.[4] We can follow the tracks of separate members of the family after his great-grandfather Bartholomew, who was born about 1600, although whether in Bridport, where he spent his youth, we do not know. Bartholomew's father, Sir Herbert Wesley, belonged to the lesser nobility, and his mother, Elizabeth de Wellesley, was Irish. Bartholomew studied medicine and theology concurrently, probably at

[1] George J. Stevenson, *Memorials of the Wesley Family*, pp. xi–xxiii, goes farthest in this respect; cf. Thomas F. Lockyer, *Genealogy of the Wesley Family, Proceedings of the Wesley Historical Society* I.(1898).67ff; John S. Simon, *John Wesley and the Religious Societies*, pp. 28–45.
[2] *Proc. of the W.H.S.*, IX.(1914).113–16.
[3] Eliza Clarke, *Susanna Wesley*, pp. 10–11.
[4] *Die Revolutionskirchen Englands*.

35

Oxford. In 1645 he became minister of the villages of Charmouth and Catherston in the southern English county of Dorset, near to the coast. He was brought into touch with public events in 1651 when, after the Battle of Worcester, he prevented the young King Charles II from escaping from the neighbourhood of Lyme Regis to France. This open intervention on Cromwell's behalf cost him his living after the Restoration, but he stayed on in the district, first in Bridport, then in Lyme Regis. He preached occasionally among private groups, but was mainly active in both places as a doctor, until his death at Lyme Regis in 1671. He was buried in the sea-washed cemetery, in distant view of the little valley where in the time of persecution he had held secret services with the few faithful members of his congregation. He was known for his candour of speech, with the result that his sermons were not always acceptable.

His son, who bore the same name as our John Wesley, although he spelt it Wesly, was in many respects prophetic of his famous grandson. A portrait of him which has survived shows him, in spite of his clerical dress, to have been of such an intrepid appearance that it might well be that of a soldier—yet not one who has been victor so much as one who is determined to hold to the right until the very last. He kept a journal which is unfortunately lost, but Edmund Calamy, the martyrologist of the Restoration, is at our disposal, and to him we are indebted for our principal information.[5] Even as a young schoolboy he had a distinct sense of his sins and a strong desire for deliverance and salvation. It was this which led him to keep a journal. It is probable that his grandson may have used an empty book of his grandfather's for the first notes of his own life in the year 1721.[6] Born at Bridport in 1636 John Wesley senior went to Oxford in 1651 and devoted himself to Oriental languages in addition to theology. He came to the notice of the Vice-Chancellor of the University, John Owen, a leading Puritan, who befriended him. After graduating Bachelor of Arts in 1655 and Master of Arts in 1657, he returned home again. In Melcombe Regis he joined John Janeway's Separatist congregation and, commissioned by them, went as a travelling preacher of the Gospel into the surrounding villages. In 1658 he was called to the charge of the quiet Dorsetshire village of Winterbourne Whitechurch, as was usual in this revolutionary age, without episco-

[5] *An Account of the Ministers, Lecturers, Masters and Fellowes of Colleges and Schoolmasters who were ejected or silenced after the Restoration of 1660;* cf. also M. Broadley, *The Dorset Wesleys in Proc.W.H.S.,* IV.(1904).1–4.
[6] Nehemiah Curnock, in Wesley's *Journal,* I.42.

pal ordination, but at the express wish of the congregation and in complete accord with local ecclesiastical order.[7] As might have been expected from his previous activity, he did not confine himself in his new appointment to the one congregation, but preached all around the neighbourhood. In fact he was only able to labour for two years, and then came the restoration of the Stuarts. Difficulties were created for him in his own congregation by partisans of the new order. These had long desired the change, and they now denounced their minister to the Bishop of Bristol. Presumably this indictment was made at the same time as John Wesley received the order to use the Book of Common Prayer. He was summoned before the Bishop, Dr Gilbert Ironside, and harshly examined.[8] This interview also can be looked upon as a prelude to the meeting between his grandson and Bishop Joseph Butler in the same place in the year 1739. The main point in the charge was that the preacher had not been ordained according to the regulations of the Anglican Church. The opposed points of view came out sharply and clearly in the conversation. John Wesley was conscious of himself as a servant of the Church of Jesus Christ, the bishop as a servant of the Church of England. Over against Anglican ordination the accused cited Romans 10[15] as his commission. It was a case of primitive Christianity standing over against history; the spirit in contrast to the law; service opposed to official position.[9]

[7] This follows clearly from the account (*Journal*, V.122; see following note): 'There was none presented to it these sixty years. Mr Walton lived there. At his departure, the people desired me to preach to them; and when there was a way of settlement appointed, I was by the Trustees appointed, and by the Triers approved.'

[8] John Wesley, the founder of the Methodist Church, published the account of this—presumably from family papers—in the *Journal*, V.120–4, under 25th May 1765, and it is also found in Adam Clarke, *Memoirs of the Wesley Family*, I.37–41. Further references to early printings in *Journal*, V.119, note 4. The date of the examination is not given. It must have been during 1661, since John Wesley gives his age as twenty-five (p. 122).

[9] *Journal*, V.120.
Bishop: By whom were you ordained? Or are you ordained?
Wesley: I am sent to preach the gospel.
B.: By whom were you sent?
W.: By a Church of Jesus Christ.
B.: What Church is that?
W.: The Church of Christ at Melcomb.
The early Christian expressions are noteworthy: 'sent to preach the gospel' is reminiscent of 1 Corinthians 1[17]; it is well known that ἐκκλησία (τοῦ) Χριστοῦ is not found in the New Testament, but the nearest to it is Galatians 1[22], ταῖς ἐκκλησίαις Ἰουδαίας ταῖς ἐν Χριστῷ; otherwise it is always ἐκκλησία τοῦ Θεοῦ. *Journal*, V.121: W.: I was called to the work of the ministry, though not the office. There is, as we believe, *vocatio ad opus, et ad munus* (A call to the work, and a call to the office). To understand 'work' as a translation of the early Christian word διακονία may seem hazardous, but John Wesley has two things in mind: on the one hand the

Wesley declared that the aim of his missionary and evangelistic preaching was to win men from ignorance and profaneness to obedience towards God.[1] The Puritan conception of godliness, the complete turning of life towards God, resounds in these words. It is possible that he caused the members of his congregation to enter into a formal covenant with God,[2] like that which he had come to know in Romanic mysticism from the example of Count de Renty.[3] He was proud of the fact that he could point to concrete results, and he very definitely offered to cease his activity immediately if the bishop could prove to him that his hearers did not conform to the Scripture requirements for godliness.[4] The proud consciousness of having been sent, which yet unreservedly subjects personal activity to the judgement of the Bible, the determination to conform to primitive Christianity, the stress on visible results as the fruit, and conversion as a definite aim—all this comes out again in his grandson.

John Wesley senior parted from the bishop with the promise that he would not be disturbed. But his opponents in the congregation, who held influential positions in the village, did not relax their efforts until they had him in prison and then removed from his office. Bartholomew's Day, 24th August 1662, was appointed as the day for his submission to the Book of Common Prayer, but John Wesley stood firm, and on 17th August preached his last sermon. The church after all met him so far as to provide him an income for the year following that which began at Michaelmas. The law provided that by a decree of the king part of the incumbent's living could be reserved for the discharged minister.[5] John Wesley stayed on for a few

essential nature of the 'work' which is more important than the validity of the appointment, and on the other the spontaneity of the service as opposed to the duty of the office. For further early Christian notes, cf. *Journal*, V.121, 122, where 'gifts and graces' corresponding to the Χαρίσματα are cited as criteria for the right to preach, and the basic principle. Ibid. p. 123: 'We have a plain, full, and sufficient rule for gospel worship, in the New Testament, recorded in the Acts of the Apostles, and in the Epistles.'

[1] *Journal*, V.123:
  W.: It pleased God to seal my labours with success, in the apparent conversion of many souls.
  B: Yea, that is, it may be to your way.
  W.: Yea, to the power of godliness, from ignorance and profaneness.
[2] Cf. Frederick Hunter, 'The Origin of Wesley's Covenant Service', *Proc. W.H.S.*, XXII.(1939–40).128. He makes it probable that this practice came to Richard Alleine from John Wesley senior, and from the life of Alleine by Thomas Haliburton to John Wesley junior.
[3] *Le Chrétien réel ou la vie du Marquis de Renty (1651)* (Cologne, 1701), pp. 318–20.
[4] *Journal*, V.123.
[5] John S. Simon, *John Wesley and the Religious Societies*, p. 39.

months in the village, then went to Melcombe Regis, but was turned out from there after a few weeks. He wandered about with his family until finally he found a private post in Poole, Dorsetshire, as minister to a little group of Nonconformists. But ecclesiastical legislation grew continuously more severe, and in particular the Conventicle Act of 1664 outlawed such a post as he occupied. He was repeatedly arrested and accordingly contemplated emigrating, probably to Dutch Surinam or to Maryland in America, where there was religious freedom. Nevertheless he remained in his native land as a persecuted private teacher and travelling evangelist. As a result of the hardship he endured he died in 1670 at the age of 34. His wife was the only surviving child of John White, the 'Patriarch of Dorchester', who, apart from a break of eight years due to the Civil War, laboured there as a clergyman from 1606 to 1648. He had also been a member of the Westminster Assembly. It was through him that the first move had come from Dorchester towards the founding of the strong Puritan State of Massachusetts in North America, since along with trades-people he had started a fishing-company for the sea-board there, intending at the same time to gather together the fishermen into a Christian congregation.[6]

Samuel Wesley was one of John's children.[7] He was born in the fateful year 1662, not long after the dismissal of his father, although his birth took place in the vicarage at Winterbourne Whitechurch. The baptismal entry, which is in his father's handwriting, is for 17th December. His childhood reflects the harsh circumstances of his parents' home during the period of persecution. At the death of his father he was barely eight years old; until his fifteenth year he went to the free school in Dorchester. His teacher there, Henry Dolling, had made a name for himself by translating into Latin a popular Puritan book of devotion, *The Whole Duty of Man*.[8] Friends among

[6] On this, cf. James D. Phillips, *Salem in the Seventeenth Century;* William Warren Sweet, *Religion in Colonial America*, p. 83; ibid. *Der Weg des Glaubens in den U.S.A. o. J.* (1950), pp. 53–4.

[7] On Samuel Wesley, cf. esp. Luke Tyerman, *The Life and Times of Samuel Wesley* (London, 1866); George Stampe, *The Rev. Samuel Wesley, M.A., Rector of Epworth, Proc.W.H.S.*, XL.(1918).1–7; John S. Simon, *John Wesley and the Religious Societies*, I.46ff.

[8] Simon, *John Wesley and the Religious Societies*, 46. The second edition (1667) of *The Whole Duty of Man, necessary for all Families* (1659) with an introduction by H. Hammond was available to me. This extremely widely circulated book belongs to the group of conduct-books which since Chilton Latham Powell (*English Domestic Relations, 1487–1653* [New York, 1917]) has been investigated principally by Levin L. Schüking (*die Familie im Puritanismus* [1929]). (On the Whole Duty, p. 33.) It is conjectured that Dorothy Pakington was the authoress (cf. Cata-

the Dissenters helped to make it possible for the gifted youth to be accepted in a Dissenting Academy in London. After a brief period there, he proceeded to another, the Academy at Stoke Newington. Its head was Charles Morton, a man of some consequence, who afterwards emigrated to America and became vice-president of Harvard College in Cambridge (Massachusetts), and whom Samuel Wesley always held in high esteem. Daniel Defoe, famous as the author of *Robinson Crusoe*, was one of his fellow-students.

Then the unexpected happened. Samuel Wesley was given the task of refuting an Anglican polemic against the Dissenters, but in the course of working on this came to the conclusion that its attacks were valid. Ever impetuous, the twenty-one-year-old young man broke with the whole rich tradition of his family. As wholeheartedly as this had been on the side of the Dissenters, so he now went over to the Anglican Church. Early one morning in August 1683 he set out for Oxford, in his pocket a carefully saved forty-five shillings, which was just sufficient for his entrance and caution money. He first became a sizar at Exeter College, earning money by private tuition and by preparing exercises for wealthy students who were too lazy to do so for themselves. By his indefatigable industry he acquired in this way a second solid education which, unlike the one he received from the Dissenters, was centred mainly upon classics and the historical and archaeological learning of the Enlightenment. The unusual course his life had taken explains the two features which subsequently characterized his outlook. On the one hand he always owed a great deal to the Puritan emphasis upon the importance of repentance, conversion and rebirth; on the other hand he had the historical interest of the Enlightenment. Although he severely pilloried conditions in the Dissenting Academies in an ungrateful satire which he wrote, he consciously retained the interest in the biblical instruction he had received in them. In London he visited such leading Puritan preachers as Stephen Charnock and John Bunyan. As a student he devoted his spare time to pastoral visitation in the prison, obviously under the influence of the social activity which characterized the movement for renewal within the Church of his time, that of the religious societies. Certainly he was a dedicated Anglican, a 'high church' man, as the term was then used. He desired the end of Dissent, but repudiated

logue of the *Oeffentlich Wissenschaftlichen Bibliothek*, Berlin D 3743). Together with the Bible John Wesley and his student-group at Oxford gave it to the prisoners! Cf. J. Wesley's Letters (Standard Edition by John Telford [1931]). I.129–30, Oxon, 18th October 1732, to Richard Morgan.

the use of all forceful means. He knew that he was truly at home in the Established Church of his country, but was conscious of being in the succession of Bishop Launcelot Andrewes and not that of William Laud. This is to say that he regarded as most important catholic continuity with the early Church and the whole Church on earth, rather than the system of the hierarchy and canon law. For these reasons he felt attracted to the free and broad spirit of the Established Church. In 1710 he came out strongly in support of the high church sermon preached by Dr Henry Sacheverell in 1709 in St Paul's Cathedral, which had demanded unconditional obedience to the king and made violent attacks on dissenters.[9] When Sacheverell was arraigned before Parliament Samuel Wesley drew up his defence.

He was ordained deacon on 7th August and priest on 24th February 1689. The first ceremony was performed by the Bishop of Rochester, Dr Thomas Sprat, in the episcopal palace at Bromley, Kent; the second by Compton, Bishop of London, in St Andrew's Church, Holborn. At first he did not find a living but had to support himself laboriously by his pen.[1] Through his political activity on the side of the Tories he won the goodwill of such noblemen as the future Duke of Buckingham and Normanby, who was able to obtain for him the small living of South Ormsby in Lincolnshire through his friendship with the patron.

While in London Samuel, at a friend's wedding in the year 1682, had become acquainted with the Annesley family. That same year he married the youngest daughter Susanna, then twenty years of age, and so once again entered a family with a great Puritan tradition. His father-in-law, Dr Samuel Annesley, was a leading dissenting minister and a close friend of Richard Baxter.[2] Like all the others he had been ejected from his office in 1662, but the fortune he had inherited enabled him to live without a stipend. Born in 1620 near Birmingham, at Kenilworth, made famous by Walter Scott, he was the only son of a wealthy land-owner and the grandson of a man who had been made a peer as a reward for his services to the British administration in Ireland under James I and Charles I. Francis Annesley became first Baron Mountnorris and then Viscount Valentia. Subsequently he suffered much at the hands of his rival, the well-known

[9] Luke Tyerman, *Samuel Wesley*, pp. 335–7, gives extracts.
[1] Simon, *John Wesley and the Religious Societies*, p. 56; Stampe, *Samuel Wesley*, Proc.W.H.S., XI.3, maintains that he had a curacy in London. I have not been able to clear up this point.
[2] Stampe, loc. cit.

Thomas Wentworth, Earl of Strafford, the ambitious favourite of Charles I. When Strafford met his end on the scaffold at the beginning of the Great Rebellion in 1641, his evidence had been of great importance at the trial. Viscount Valentia left two sons: Arthur, the elder, inherited the name and rank of his father in the Irish aristocracy; John, the younger, retained the name Annesley. In 1645 Arthur, commissioned by the Long Parliament, went to Ulster to conduct negotiations, but after Richard Cromwell's failure was active for the reinstatement of the Stuarts and the cause of Charles II. Under this ruler he soon rose to high office; he became a member of the Privy Council, and, as Earl of Anglesey, was a member of the English aristocracy. He used to the full his influence in favour of the Puritans. At the passing of the fateful Act of Uniformity in 1662 he fought to modify it so that the displaced minister might by the decision of the king retain a part of the stipend.

Samuel Annesley himself, the son of John, must also have been of strikingly distinguished appearance, tall and strongly built and with a sensitive dignity. He lost his father at the early age of four. At fifteen he entered Queen's College, Oxford, and was ordained in 1644. After a period of seven years at Cliffe near Gravesend he came to the capital in 1652, first to the Church of St John the Evangelist in Friday Street, and in 1658 to St. Giles', Cripplegate, on the nomination of the Lord Protector Richard Cromwell, whose father, the great Oliver Cromwell, had been married to Elizabeth Bourchier in this church in 1620. It was also a spot with other significant memories. John Foxe, the author of the Reformation martyr-history, was buried there beside Martin Frobisher, a colonial pioneer, who fought in the decisive battle against the Spanish Armada in 1588. Samuel Annesley was thus surrounded by some of the great history of his country, and he himself became unusually successful as a preacher. This may well have induced him to publish a volume of sermons which he and his colleagues preached in the church in the year 1661. They occupy an important place in the literature on the Puritan theology of conscience and the conscience-guided life.[3] Contrary to the modern advance in rational and psychological analysis, which has produced an extremely

---

[3] Samuel Annesley, *The Morning Exercise of Cripple Gate*, 1662 (1671). On this, cf. my article on *Die Gewissenslehre des englischen Puritanismus*, *ARG* XLIII (1952) (Ch. 1, note 6), pp. 80ff. John Wesley published many extracts from the sermons of his grandfather in his *Christian Library*, Vols. XXXVI (1754), 354ff, XXXVIII (1754), 297ff, 339ff, XLIV (1775). 273ff, 320ff, XLVI (1755), 331ff.

refined theory, his view of conscience is very much simplified. After losing his position at St Giles' he continued to preach among little groups of Dissenters in London, first in Spitalfields and later in Little St Helen's, where they were able to erect a meeting-house after the Declaration of Indulgence in 1672. The large income from his father's estate enabled him to support ministers who had fallen on evil days. It was in 1681 that he wrote his foreword to a book by the prominent Presbyterian Richard Alleine.[4] For more than thirty years after his ejection he ruled as a patriarch of Dissent in the capital until his death on 31st December 1696. It was also he who dared to undertake the first public ordination of dissenting ministers in Little St Helen's on 22nd June 1694. One of the seven young men then ordained was Edward Calamy, who wrote the history of the persecution of 1662.

This inflexible representative of Dissent, who, unlike such conciliatory spirits as John Howe, stood on the extreme right wing and would brook no compromise with the Established Church, must have found it hard to give his own daughter to an Anglican clergyman, and he a renegade from Dissent. But even that was not all, for Susanna herself went over to the Church of England. The wedding took place on 12 November 1688, in the old parish church in Marylebone.[5]

Susanna Annesley was the twenty-fifth child of her father, the youngest of the family, born on 20th January 1669. It is not unusual for the last child to possess the most resolute will and to be strongly independent. Almost nothing is known about her mother, the second Mrs Samuel Annesley, but her grandfather also happened to be called John White. He was a solicitor and sat in the Lower House as the representative of Southwark. As early as 1640 or 1641 he was a most vigorous supporter of presbyterian principles of government. As chairman of a parliamentary commission appointed to examine the personal conduct of the clergy of the land, he proceeded with great determination and, to conclude his activity, published a pamphlet entitled *The Century of Scandalous Priests*, which caused a great stir.[6] He took part in the opening of the Westminster Assembly, but died immediately afterwards on 29th January 1645. Learning came easily to Susanna, and she acquired a knowledge of French, probably

[4] Cf. Hunter, 'The Origin of Wesley's Covenant Service', *Proc.W.H.S.*, XXII.
[5] J. Telford in *Letters*, I.44. Nevertheless their first child, Samuel Wesley, was born in the house of their maternal grandfather in London in 1690; cf. Thomas E. Brigden, 'Samuel Wesley Junior, Schoolmaster, High Churchman, Minor Poet', *Proc.W.H.S.*, XI.(1918).25.   [6] Tyerman, *Samuel Wesley*, p. 123.

at an early age.[7] She was proficient in philosophy and literature, but her real interest lay in the questions raised by religion.

It was a strange fate which befell John Wesley's parents. Both came from a great and living succession, both had seen the personal sacrifice their fathers had made in the struggles over the Established Church, and indeed both had experienced something of the distress, which in particular overshadowed Samuel Wesley's childhood. Both knew the position they abandoned. What was the real cause of the break? Was it simply the rebellion of the younger generation against inherited tradition? Or, since Samuel Wesley said that as a Dissenter he had no prospects of success in his vocation, was ambition the motive? Such reasons are not sufficient. When Samuel himself spoke about his action he always claimed that the Anglican Church rested on the foundation of true doctrine, which Dissent did not secure for him.[8] Had he not been expected to take the part of John Biddle the Socinian from the age of Cromwell?[9] Added to this was the powerful early Christian and primitive Church motif in the Anglicanism of his day, of which perhaps the most impressive example in the field of scholarship was William Cave's influential book *Primitive Christianity* (1672),[1] while the programme of the 'religious societies' bore a similar witness in the practical sphere.

Samuel Wesley's subsequent development was altogether in line with this. His principal work, which occupied him for most of his lifetime and which was finally printed in his seventy-fourth year, was the studies in the Book of Job.[2] John Wesley had the honour of presenting in person the first bound copy to Queen Caroline on 12th October 1735, and at least heard a compliment paid to the binding.[3]

---

[7] Eliza Clarke, *Susanna Wesley*, p. 9.

[8] Tyerman, *Samuel Wesley*, pp. 77ff, brings his declarations together.

[9] Augustin Leger, *La Jeunesse de Wesley*, p. 7, speaks of a commission to translate the works of Biddle. This could only have been the making of a Latin version, since Biddle wrote in English. The purpose would have been to make the works known to continental scholars. According to Piette, *John Wesley in the Evolution of Protestantism*, p. 216, Susanna Wesley-Annesley inclined to Socinianism.

[1] On this, cf. esp. Erich Seeberg, *Gottfried Arnold*, pp. 240ff. Cave's book was the strongest impetus behind Gottfried Arnold's *Erste Liebe* (1696), simply because it provoked him to reply to it. The expressly primitive Christian character of the Anglican Church brought the French humanist Isaac Casaubon to England and prompted Hugo Grotius to fix upon it as the starting-point for a general Christian union.

[2] *Dissertationes in librum Jobi, autore Sam. Wesley, rector de Epworth in Diocesi Lincolniensi. Londini, Typis Gulielmi* [sic!] *Bowyer* (1736). I used the copy in the Main Library of Francke's Stiftungen in Halle, Signature 56.B.1.

[3] *Letters,* I.192, Gravesend, on board the Simmons, 15th, 17th October, to his brother Samuel. Adam Clarke, *Memoirs of the Wesley Family*, I.330.

The studies show an easy mastery of that English Old Testament scholarship which had been founded half a century earlier by John Spencer (1630–95) through investigation of the Hebrew ritual laws,[4] and which reached its climax in this period in the famous work by Robert Lowth on the sacred poetry of the Hebrews (1753).[5] Samuel Wesley combined dogmatic orthodoxy with careful regard for textual criticism and archaeology. He used all the available Hebrew editions but modestly disclaimed any pretension of having produced an exhaustive commentary.[6] He considers that Job is an historical figure who himself wrote the book,[7] and goes into all related questions with a thoroughness that could scarcely be surpassed. He discusses the style and compares it with Homer's; he goes into Job's knowledge of botany, mineralogy, military science, and jurisprudence; he deals with questions about Phoenician and Canaanite shepherds, magic, the Babylonian worship of serpents, Behemoth and Leviathan. In the discussion on the origin of evil he reveals his knowledge of ancient philosophy and non-Christian religions like those of Zoroaster and Mani.[8] This is all exactly in tune with the spirit of humanism and of the Enlightenment. On the other hand he argues emphatically that the meaning of the whole of Scripture, including the Old Testament, is to be found in Christ, and that accordingly this applies to the Book of Job also, and he protests against that rationalistic type of interpretation once practised by the Arians and now in his own day by the Socinians.[9] He stresses the fact that Job and Elihu believed in the

---

[4] Concerning John Spencer and his book *De Legibus Hebraeorum ritualibus aerumque rationibus* (1685), ed. Pfaff Tubingae (1732), cf. Ludwig Diestel, *Geschichte des Alten Testaments in der christlichen Kirche*, pp. 541–4. P. 543, n. 8, especially is correct in characterizing him as holding to the contemporary views of orthodoxy and at the same time giving expression in a clumsy way to very new perceptions which pointed in the direction of the Enlightenment.

[5] Robert Lowth (1710–87) wrote in 1753, *De sacra poesi Hebraeorum. Praelectiones Academicae Oxonii habitae.* This book was edited by Prof. Johann David Michaelis of Göttingen in 1758, furnished with notes, and stimulated Herder to produce his work *Vom Geist der ebräischen Poesie* (1782–3). On Lowth, cf. Diestel, *Geschichte des Alten Testaments . . .* , pp. 650–1.

[6] *Diss. in lib. Jobi . . .* , p. 1.

[7] Ibid, p. 16; p. 244, *Diss. XXX, De tempore Jobi;* p. 234, *Diss. XXIX, De patria Jobi.*

[8] Ibid, p. 43, *Diss. V, De Figuris;* p. 49, *Diss. VI, Parallela ex Homero;* pp. 255 ff, *Diss. XXXI. Scientia Jobi in arte militari;* pp. 258ff, *Jurisprudentia;* pp. 261 ff, *Metalla, Arbores;* p. 80 *Diss. X, De pastoribus Phoeniciis seu Chanaanaeis;* pp. 348ff, *Diss. XLVI, De Magia Veterum;* pp. 340ff, *Diss. XLIV, De Ophiolatria;* pp. 284ff, *Diss. XXXVIII. De Behemoth et Leviathan;* pp. 302ff, *Diss. XXXIX, De origine mali.*

[9] Ibid. pp. 388ff, *Diss. LI, De nupero modo interpretandi Scripturas.*

Trinity,[1] and that Job in the well-known reference to his Saviour who would awaken him from the dust (19[21]) was referring to Jesus and not to God, as Hugo Grotius maintained. He does not neglect to point out that this is in agreement with the position of the Church of England, which, in the seventh of the Thirty-nine Articles, strongly denies that the saints of the Old Testament looked only for earthly blessings.[2] It is true that in the discussion on the origin of evil the particular standpoint of the humanistic-rationalistic way of thinking comes out. Samuel Wesley traces evil back to God Himself—like Jakob Böhme, but significantly its origin lay not in God but it arose from the nature of the created world, and of man in particular. Only on the supposition that along with free-will God has conferred on man the propensity for sin and wrong is it possible to include it in the scheme of the creation. If this hypothesis is rejected, then incorruptibility has to be attributed to the creature. But this offends against both natural and revealed religion, which are characteristically placed alongside one another as if they were of equal dogmatic authority.[3]

Samuel Wesley did not write this vast work entirely by himself, but had an assistant for at least one chapter, that on Job's jurisprudence. He was Maurice Johnson, the founder and chairman of a small learned society in the little town of Spalding, to which such important men of the day as Isaac Newton the physicist, Alexander Pope the poet, and Joseph Addison the publicist, belonged.[4] Samuel Wesley and later also his son of the same name, John Wesley's eldest brother, were members of this distinguished circle, which was started in 1710. John Wesley himself recognized the vast amount of learning which lay behind the studies in Job, and yet not without disparagement of its kind and value.[5] As if in compensation for this barren

[1] Diss. in lib. Jobi, pp. 395ff, Diss. LII, De Fide Jobi et Elihi: The faith of Job and Elihu was in the Holy Trinity.
[2] Ibid. p. 387, Diss. L.: Ex supradictis judicet cordatus et candidus lector, an non satis probatum fuerit. Jobum fidem suam in Christum redemptorem et resurrectionem, non à morbo, sed à morte, ad vitam aeternam declarasse; unde sequitur, sicut ecclesia nostra in articulo septimo decrevit, 'Illos non audiendos esse qui fingunt, quod antiqui patres temporia tantam promissa expectabant'; p. 382, Refutatio sententiae Grotii: Article 7 of the Church of England states: 'The Old Testament is not contrary to the New: for both in the Old and New Testament everlasting life is offered to Mankind by Christ, who is the only Mediator between God and Man. Wherefore they are not to be heard, which feign that the old Fathers did look only for transitory promises.'   [3] Ibid. p. 302.
[4] Cf. W. B. Hoult, 'The Rev. Samuel Wesley and the Spalding Gentleman's Society', Proc.W.H.S., XXIII.(1941–2).145–53.
[5] The Arminian Magazine, VIII.(1785).151 ('Some Remarks on Article X of Mr Maty's New Review, December 1784): 'It [sc. the Book of Job] certainly contains immense Learning, but of a kind which I do not admire.'

exercise in scholarship Samuel Wesley also wrote a life of Christ in heroic verse. This was in direct opposition to John Dryden, the master of this style, who used his art in the cause of atheism, frivolity, and immorality.[6] Thus in the simple country parson there is seen the picture of a man of accomplished intellect, whose aims and enterprises extended far beyond his own limited circle, even if his results and achievements were not so impressive. In this way he shared in that great intellectual stirring which, consequent upon the earlier Enlightenment, went through the English parsonages and finally benefited all spheres of learning and poetry.[7]

Thus two factors, the Puritan heritage and the personal choice of the Anglican position, contributed to the faith of the parents and gave to it intensity and depth. The eldest son, Samuel, was quite correct in the verses he wrote about his father when he referred to the decision taken in his youth as the significant moment of his life.[8]

Although Samuel Wesley was of a domineering disposition, expecting his wife to be subordinate to him, Susanna was in no way merely

---

[6] Samuel Wesley, 'Upon my Father', *The Arminian Magazine*, I.(1778).142:

> Nor yet unmention'd shall in silence lie,
> His slighted and derided poetry.
> Whate'er his strains, still glorious was his end,
> Faith to assert, and virtue to defend
> He sung how God the Saviour deign'd t'expire,
> With Vida's piety, though not his fire.
> Deduc'd his maker's praise from age to age,
> Through the long annals of the sacred page.
> Not curs'd like syren Dryden to excel,
> Who strew'd with flow'rets fair, the way to hell;
> With Atheist doctrines loosest morals join'd,
> To rot the body and to damn the mind ...
> 'Nor would I write like him; like him to write,
> If there's hereafter, and a last great day,
> What fire's enough to purge his crimes away? ...'

[7] On this, cf. the comprehensive, statistical investigation by Herbert Schöffler, *Protestantismus und Literatur. Neue Wege zur englischen Literatur des 18 Jahrhunderts*, pp. 47ff.

[8] Samuel Wesley, 'Upon my Father', *The Arminian Magazine*, I.(1778).141–3:

> With op'ning life, his early worth began,
> The boy misleads not, but foreshows the man.
> Directed wrong, tho' first he miss'd the way,
> Train'd to mistake, and disciplin'd to stray;
> Not long, for Reason gilded error's night
> And doubts well-founded shot a dawn of light.
> Nor prejudice o'ersway'd his heart and head,
> Resolv'd to follow truth where'er she led,
> The radiant track audacious to pursue,
> From fame, from int'rest, and from friends he flew ... .
> No worldly views the real convert call;
> He sought God's altar when it seem'd to fall.

his shadow. The daughter of Samuel Annesley lived in the Romanic mysticism whose influence had been growing in England since the early days of Elizabeth.[9] One of her favourite books was the *Pugna Spiritualis* of the Italian writer Lorenzo Scupoli, which apparently did not come directly to England but was known through the Spanish version by the Benedictine Juan de Castaniza.[1] Only by handling such books in duodecimo or 16mo format is it possible to realize how much they meant to their owners. The *Spiritual Conflict* centred around the call to Christian perfection, which is derived solely from the idea of God. It is acquired chiefly through man apprehending the inexpressible goodness of God and at the same time his own nothingness. The greatness and beauty of the divine world appear in striking contrast to the misery and worthlessness of earthly life.[2] Man must therefore hate himself, renounce his own Ego, and turn with wholehearted love to God. It is not feeling but the understanding and the will which are addressed in the first place; hence this is primarily an intellectualist and voluntary mysticism, even if the

[9] This still requires elucidation through careful individual investigations after the model of Maria Hagedorn's study of the mystic Luis de Granada (*Reformation und spanische Andachtsliteratur* [1934]). See also Henry Thomas, *The English Translations of Guevara's Works*, Jose M. Galvez, *Guevara in England*, J. Fitzmaurice-Kelly, *The Relations between Spanish and English Literature.* The role of Romanic mysticism as the spiritual bond of unity in Europe in the seventeenth and eighteenth centuries is important and must be conceived in a new way. I have given a few indications in my contribution in *The History of the Ecumenical Movement*: 'The Ecumenical Movement in Continental Europe during the Seventeenth and Eighteenth Centuries' (London, 1954) otherwise cf. the very sketchy treatment, written from a political-pacifist point of view, by Paul Honigsheim in *Mystik als Faktor der Völkerannäherung in der Gerschichte*, 'Die Friedenswart' XL.(1949).1–30; on Susanna Wesley, see esp. John Kirk, *The Mother of the Wesleys.*

[1] Lorenzo Scupoli, *Il Combattimento spirituale.* No English edition was available to me. With the help of the catalogue of the British Museum I draw attention to the following: (1) Castaniza, *The Christian Pilgrim in His Spiritual Conflict and Conquest* (in two parts: [1] *The Spiritual Conflict* . . . First published in Spanish by . . . J. Castaniza . . . [2] *The Spiritual Conquest* in five treatises [Paris, 1752]). (2) *The Spiritual Combat* . . . translated . . . by R[obert] R[eade] (Paris, 1656). (3) *The Spiritual Conflict* . . . *put into the English tongue* (1658). (4) London, 1698. (5) London, 1710. (6) London, 1742 (and a whole series of editions during the nineteenth century). I used the Latin edition: *Pugna spiritualis sive de perfectione vitae christianae tractatus aureus Coloniae* (1666) from the City Library, Frankfort/Main, Myst. 504. c. (2).

[2] Ibid. p. 16: 'It [spiritual perfection] consists in nothing else but the knowledge of the Divine Goodness and Greatness, of our own nothingness, and proneness to all evil.' The basic scheme of the penitential and conversion preaching, which governs the classical book of devotion of early Puritanism, Lewis Bayly's *Practice of Piety*, recalls this very strongly. Cf. my article in *Theologia Viatorum*, IV.(1952).226ff, referred to on p. 26, note 4.

emotional element follows.[3] Through the whole book there runs an austere, masculine strain, more akin to the individual, warlike spirit, the *espiritu guerrero* of Spain, than to the military, organized soldiery which Ignatius Loyola fashioned from it.[4] God's will is set up as the one absolute after the manner of Kant's formalism. The human will is to be exercised by man doing nothing for his own advantage, but by looking only to God's command. The characteristic of such an attitude is necessarily renunciation—or as the ancient formula of Greek monachism expressed it—the mortification of the passions,[5] although it is not taken nearly as far. The demand for such an extreme state of impassibility is not raised.[6] In the place of *passio* (passion) is found *patientia* (a delicate play upon words!) or, still more clearly expressed, *virtus patientiae*, readiness to suffer.[7] To be prepared for suffering is everything, for God's purpose is a matter of suffering. Where is this more clearly expressed than in the suffering of His Son? Therefore in the words of Paul, the Christian can and should experience and know nothing but Jesus Christ crucified.[8] Without any effort on the part of the believer there comes into being a coincidence and conformity of his life with his Saviour. The believer does not first have painstakingly to create a situation similar to that in which Jesus found Himself, for the relationship rests much more beyond the earthly and the human, solely in the will of God. The Christian will indeed also set the Cross outwardly before his eyes and thankfully use all the means the Church provides, above all the

---

[3] This has been emphasized best by Erich Seeberg (*Zur Frage der Mystik*, pp. 18ff) when he speaks of the 'austerely ascetic spirituality'. In the *Pugna spiritualis* the sequence from cognition to willing is expressly brought out, when in the first place the *exercitatio intellectus* is required and a warning is given against previously mixing with this the will, because it befogs the understanding (*intellectum obnubilat*, pp. 34–5).

[4] On this, cf. Karl Vossler, *Die Bedeutung der spanischen Kultur für Europa* (1929) in '*Südliche Romania*' (1950), pp. 254–5, in conjunction with Angel Ganivet, *Idearium espanol* (Madrid, 1928), p. 47. The perception of this difference is more important than the way in which Erich Seeberg, ibid., relates Spanish mysticism in general (particularly *Teresa di Jesu*) to Ignatius of Loyola.

[5] Cf. Karl Holl, *Die schriftstellerische Form des griechischen Heiligenlebens Ges. Aufs. z. Kirchengesch II: Der Osten*, pp. 256ff. It would be a nice task to trace the connexion and parallel points running from the early Christian theory of mysticism in Clement of Alexandria and Origen to Romanic mysticism (cf. Walther Völker, *Das Vollkommenheitsideal des Origenes; Der wahre Gnostiker nach Clemens Alexandrinus. Pugna spiritualis* (see p. 48, note 1), pp. 16ff, 57–8 (Ch. 19). [Translator's note: The page references are to the Latin version used by Prof. Schmidt. This was not available to me, but where possible I have added chapter numbers so that references can be readily traced in English editions of *The Spiritual Combat*. I have not reproduced all the Latin references.]

[6] *Pugna spiritualis*, pp. 62–3 (Ch. 19).   [7] Ibid. p. 69 (Ch. 20).
[8] Ibid. p. 37 (Ch. 9).

Sacrament of the Eucharist, to make it contemporary. He will meditate upon every detail of the Passion. But the only thing which really
matters is the spiritual, inner fellowship. The goodness, love, and pain
of the Lord must cast their beams on all his ways.[9] The fundamental
law of the spiritual life and the instrument of true progress is therefore spiritual trial. As with Luther's Indulgence theses, Paul's saying
that through many tribulations we must enter the kingdom of heaven
is set in the centre. Jesus and all the saints have gone on before along
this road.[1] Education for perfection through trials—the pastoral purpose of the little book can be briefly formulated in these words.
Every temptation is overcome when man looks at God Himself, who
alone is victor in the spiritual conflict. Only in this way is a man
guarded against the greatest temptation, which is the presumption
of thinking that he has already attained the goal. The devil loves to
insinuate to those who have made some progress that they no longer
need to renounce their own wills. This pride of knowledge is more
dangerous than pride of will.[2] Once a man has withstood temptation
he will next time recall this victory and derive strength from it.[3] Not
only severe and gross enticements are to be resisted, but also the
smallest and apparently most trifling ones.[4] At all times the eyes must
be upon God. On the one hand man must consider how He rejoices
in the valiant fighter and not in any reward He holds in store for him.[5]
On the other hand in the midst of calamities which can scarcely be
endured he must think on God's goodness and love, which stand behind even this grievous circumstance and through it desire to enter
into even closer fellowship with him.[6] Scupoli's injunctions however
are not confined to instances which turn out successfully. It is their
particular virtue that they are also able to help the person who has
been beaten. On the one hand, in a true pastoral way, defeat is made
intelligible. Psychologically it is emphasized that a complete and
immediate dominion of that reason which is determined by God's
Word ought not throughout to be expected: oftentimes the intention
alone must suffice.[7] On the other hand Scupoli advises one who has
been overcome that he should first acknowledge his sin, but then completely forget it and think only of the divine love which purposes a

---

[9] *Pugna spiritualis*, pp. 142–3, 157–8, 173 (Ch. 56).
[1] Cf. Luther, Theses 94 and 95, *in Disputio pro declaratione virtutis indulgen-
tiarum, W.A.*, I.238.
[2] *Pugna spiritualis*, p. 53.   [3] Ibid. pp. 53, 56.   [4] Ibid. p. 59.
[5] Ibid. p. 67.   [6] Ibid. p. 73 (Ch. 20).   [7] Ibid. pp. 62–3.

complete union.[8] In every instance it is a question of not falling into despair but of manfully fighting on.[9] Temptations are sent for the honour and glory of God and at the same time for the sake of man's salvation.[1] The two are not to be separated.

It might appear as if this type of piety, centred in practice in the spiritual trial, were wholly individualistic, yet this is not the case. It was precisely this association of trial and temptation which issued in the urge to fellowship. It is part of the overcoming of the trials which come from the unpleasant things of life that one meets uncongenial folk. They are not to be looked upon as ordinary people but as saints, sent directly from heaven to expedite believers on the path to perfection. They are accordingly not adversaries but patron saints. This line of thought reaches its climax in the summons to love one's enemy.[2] To be sure the social aspect is secondary and is reached only indirectly, but for that very reason it is also organically joined on to the main content of the idea. In this connexion Scupoli utters a warning against the judgement which is made without love: it is not anger or contempt that has to be felt towards the person who irritates, but grief and compassion. At the same time one must pray to God that one does not fall in a way similar to this person.[3] In the school of the spiritual combat one is after all always a beginner, a recruit.[4] The greatest danger is to imagine that one can do a good work in one's own strength. A notorious sinner is more easily converted than a seemingly righteous man who covers his secret wickedness with the cloak of virtue.[5] Thus the book is directed against a limited ideal of perfection. It will not allow that pious acts and experiences such as fasting, mortification, frequent attendance at mass, or ecstatic experiences, are the marks of perfection. Its emphasis is upon the total attitude of the individual. It condemns the view which over-estimates the value of certain acts as if they had special advantages. It seeks to include the body as well as the soul in the area of spiritual discipline. In this way it transcended the traditional boundaries of the Roman Catholic Church and could become an effective instrument for the training in Christian piety throughout the whole Church.

A certain opposition is evident throughout between the aim of the

[8] Ibid. p. 101 (Ch. 26).
[9] Ibid. p. 62: *viriliter persiste, constanter pugnare necesse est.*
[1] Ibid. p. 94.   [2] Ibid. p. 75.   [3] Ibid. p. 79.
[4] Ibid. pp. 57, 117ff.   [5] Ibid. p. 16.

book and the particular setting in which it is expressed. The traditional concepts of Roman Catholic dogmatics are constantly met. The
superiority of the intellect over the will points back to Thomas of
Aquinas, and this applies even more to the anthropology which on
the one hand regards the rational faculties of man as a higher will,
and sensuality on the other hand as a lower will, and which conceives
the whole spiritual struggle as a conflict between these two forces.[6]
The injunction that man needs four kinds of spiritual weapons, mis-
trust of himself, trust in God, constant exercise, and devout prayer,
is still Catholic in its formal schematization, although its content
is biblical.[7] Naturally many pages are devoted to mystical piety,
particularly as it concerns prayer and meditation, and while the plan
of the little book is largely traditional, its contents everywhere transcend this limitation. The qualified acknowledgement and acceptance
of physical nature in the relationship with God is part of this. The
believer is to see to it therefore that this world of sense, which is
usually the gateway through which Satan attacks, becomes the door
through which God enters. Thus he must understand earthly beauty
as a foretaste of the divine.[8] God and His world, above all His mercy
and love, which is described in the vigorous language and picturesque
imagery of the Bible in terms of the shepherd and his sheep, governs
the whole method of thinking. Everything earthly has only a limited
value. Since understanding and will are summoned to tread the path
to God, the capacity for knowledge is poison to the soul if it gives way
to inquisitive inquiry and is directed towards useless things of earth.
This is the case even when such investigation is quite permissible.[9]

John Wesley's mother was well acquainted with this theocentric
mysticism and its emphasis upon the will.[1] She heard in it the mes-

---

[6] *Pugna spiritualis*, pp. 48–9. [7] Ibid. p. 10.
[8] Ibid. p. 90 (Ch. 23). [9] Ibid. p. 37 (Ch. 9).
[1] Augustin Leger, *La Jeunesse de Wesley*, stresses this somewhat one-sidedly.
A source for this is the important letter, written to John on 25th October 1732, by
(probably) his mother. It is printed in the following: (1) Adam Clarke, *Memoirs
of the Wesley Family*, I.336–9; (2) defectively (omitting the reference to Castaniza), in George J. Stevenson, *Memorials of the Wesley Family*, pp. 206–7; (3)
correctly: *Proc.W.H.S.*, XVIII.(1931/2).169–72, by E. H. Sugden. A distinction is made between the original letter and the transcript. F. F. Bretherton conjectures (ibid. p. 172) in a postscript to Sugden's reprint that the original came
from Samuel Wesley and the transcript from Susanna Wesley. If that were so it
would require a fundamental reassessment, for the attachment to Scupoli-
Castaniza would have to be ascribed to John Wesley's father. The question cannot
be decided now, since it would require a comparison of the handwriting. Nevertheless John Wesley would still be the heir to the Romanic mystical tradition,
even though its meditation through his father would mean somewhat less than if
it came through his mother.

sage of that love of God which alone is efficacious and all-powerful; and of that grace which takes up into itself human inability and worthlessness. But at the same time she heard the serious summons not to relax the struggle for perfection and to withdraw from the things of the world. When later she was awaiting her approaching death she could go so far as to reproach herself for having loved her son too much, and for having showed in this way how much she clung to earthly things.[2] She found fault with Scupoli-Castaniza for having directly glorified spiritual trials and for having thus contradicted the Lord Himself. Had not Jesus taught us to say in the Lord's Prayer, 'Lead us not into temptation'? Did He not warn His disciples, 'Watch and pray that ye enter not into temptation'? Thus she quoted the Bible itself against this mysticism of the theologian and in this was sufficiently independent to take advantage of the help even of a 'heretic' like the Deist Samuel Clark.[3] In general she refused to tie herself to any one devotional book. Rather in true feminine fashion she recognized the value of each one at different times, suited to the changing moods of the soul.[4] Thus she could place Baxter alongside or above Castaniza, and above them all a book which is met with everywhere in eighteenth-century England: Henry Scougal's *The Life of God in the Soul of Man*.[5]

In this book the conception of religion which is continually under discussion is expounded in terms of the idea of life. In a time which was disturbed by the great advance of theoretical and practical

[2] *Letters*, I.120–1. John Wesley to his mother, Lincoln College, Oxford, 28th February 1732.
[3] *Proc.W.H.S.*, XVIII.(1931/2).169–70.
[4] Ibid. p. 171.
[5] *The Life of God in the Soul of Man: or the Nature and Excellency of the Christian Religion. With the Methods of attaining the Happiness which it proposes. As an Account of the Beginnings and Advances of a spiritual Life.* With a Preface by Gilbert Burnet, late Lord Bishop of Sarum. I used the London Downing (1733) from the Main Library of Francke's Institution in Halle. Downing was the leading publisher for Puritan devotional literature. The name of the author, Henry Scougal, appears at the end of the book in the bookseller's advertisement. I hope to evaluate this most influential book on another occasion. It came to have particular importance for George Whitefield; cf. Luke Tyerman, *The Life of the Rev. George Whitefield*, I.16. The first edition appeared in 1677. Dugald Butler's *Henry Scougal and the Oxford Methodists* (Edinburgh and London, 1899) was not available to me. In 1770 John Wesley published a shortened version. It is probable also that Cambridge Platonism had something to do with Wesley's interest in Scougal. One of its representatives, John Norris, enthusiastically recommended those books which sought to explain Christianity as life rather than doctrine. John Wesley's father, Samuel, since his student days had been attached to Norris, and he drew John's attention to Norris's counsels; cf. Thomas E. Brigden, 'John Wesley', in Townsend, Workman, and Eayrs, *A New History of Methodism*, I.179–80.

atheism, many attempts at apologetic were made from the side of the Church. Scougal brushes them aside almost with a wave of the hand and summarily sets in their place the definition: 'True religion is a union of the soul with God, a real participation of the divine nature, the very image of God drawn upon the soul, or, in the Apostle's phrase, it is Christ formed within us.' [6] He calls religion life because it has the quality of permanence, but even more because it exhibits an inner, free, and spontaneous law of movement. It is the same with it as with love; greater than every command is the fact itself. Religion is a new nature, grounded in the love of God, whereas normal life is based upon love of self and the urge to self-assertion.[7] The religious man is therefore filled with an all-embracing will to love which knows no limits.[8] In the presence of God such a love is prepared to surrender everything. At this point the connexion with Romanic, quietist mysticism is immediately evident.[9] Love has an

[6] Henry Scougal, *The Life of God in the Soul of Man*, p. 4: 'They who are acquainted with it [sc. Religion] . . . know by experience that true Religion is an Union of the Soul with God, a real participation of the Divine Nature, the very Image of God drawn upon the Soul, or, in the Apostle's phrase, it is Christ formed within us.'

[7] Ibid. pp. 4–5. I choose to express it by the name of life, first because of its permanency and stability. . . . Religion is not a sudden start, or passion of the Mind. . . . It is true this Divine Life continueth not always in that same strength and vigour, but many times suffers sad decays.' Ibid. p. 6: 'The Love which a pious Man bears to God, and Goodness, is not so much by virtue of a Command enjoining him to do so, as by a new Nature instructing and prompting him to do it; nor doth he pay his Devotions as an unavoidable tribute only to appease the Divine Justice, or quiet his clamorous Conscience, but those religious exercises are the proper emanations of the Divine Life, the natural employments of the new born Soul.' Ibid. p. 13: 'Self-love . . . [is] . . . the effect of the animal life when it is neither over-powered by Religion, nor govern'd by natural reason.'

[8] Ibid. p. 15: 'As the Animal Life consisteth in that narrow and confined love which is terminated on a Man's self . . . so the Divine Life stands in an universal and unbounded affection . . . : The root of the Divine Life is Faith; the chief branches are Love to God, Charity to Man, Purity and Humility.' Ibid. pp.16–17: 'A Soul thus possessed with Divine Love, must needs be inlarged towards all Mankind in a sincere and unbounded affection, because of the relation they have to God being his Creature and having something of his Image stamped upon them.'

[9] Ibid. p. 16: 'The Love of God is a delightful and affectionate sense of the Divine Perfections, which make the Soul resign and sacrifice itself wholly unto him, desiring above all things to please him, and delighting in nothing so much as in fellowship and communion with him, and being ready to do or suffer any thing for his sake or at his Pleasure. Though this affection may have its first rise from the Favours and Mercies of God towards ourselves, yet doth it in its growth and progress transcend such particular considerations, and ground itself on his infinite goodness manifested in all the Works of Creation and Providence.' Ibid. p. 19: 'That sincere and devout affection wherewith his [sc. our blessed Saviour's] blessed Soul did constantly burn towards his heavenly Father, did express itself in an entire Resignation to his Will.' Ibid. p. 36: 'Perfect love is a kind of self-dereliction.'

irresistible power; it is a force which transforms everything. It be-
stows its own quality upon every attribute of the soul and gives to
them direction. The object of a man's love determines his worth: he
who loves vulgar things is himself vulgar; he who loves God partici-
pates gradually in the nobility of the divine world. As people in love
grow continually more like each other even in movement and voice,
so the image of God appears increasingly in His faithful ones.[1] But
love is more than a naturally abounding energy; it is something which
rests on clearly conceived objects. It embraces all men because God
created them and sent into the world for their salvation no less a one
than His own Son. God has imprinted His own image on them all,
and even if they have lost it, Jesus Christ came in order to restore
it.[2] God forces no one, but draws His own through love.[3] His Son
entered into the weakness of men, fully conscious of the humiliation,
in order to become the true minister of their souls. In this way He
awakened their dead hearts to the divine love,[4] and led them back to
their original state, to their true destiny. Should not this be regarded
as the most natural thing in the world?[5] Certainly a man who has received a strong impression of the greatness of the divine life of that
other world will realize with distress its difference from his ordinary
existence.[6] It was precisely for this reason that the Saviour appeared
in human form. Such a divine life at the same time affords the highest
happiness.[7] There is nothing which can make a man more blessed than
the presence of God in his heart. Scougal vigorously attacks those
theologians who would confine the Holy Spirit to Pentecost.[8] It is

[1] Ibid. p. 31.
[2] Ibid. p. 55: 'He created us at first in a happy condition, and now when we
are fallen from it, he hath laid help upon One that is Mighty to save, hath committed the Care of our Soul to no meaner Person than the eternal Son of his
Love....'
[3] Ibid. p. 116.   [4] Ibid. p. 56.
[5] Ibid. p. 57: 'Why should we think it impossible that true Goodness and
universal Love should ever come to sway and prevail in our Souls? Is not this
their primitive state and condition, their native and genuine constitution, as they
came first from the hands of their Maker? Sin and Corruption are but usurpers.'
[6] Ibid. p. 52.
[7] Ibid. pp. 30ff. Scougal uses Laud's favourite formula 'the beauty of holiness'
in connexion with a commendation of mystical mental prayer—ibid. p. 98.
[8] Ibid. p. 105: 'It is the formal Character of the new dispensation by which it
is distinguished from that of Moses, that in it we shall have a new heart and a
new spirit put within us, that God's Law shall not only be given us on Tables of
Stone, or any outward thing like those, but shall be inwardly engraven on our
hearts, that we shall be taught of God, and that his Spirit shall be poured out on
all flesh. This is most irreligiously restrained to the extraordinary effusion of the
Holy Ghost on the Day of Pentecost or to the other miraculous Gifts of the
Spirit in those beginnings of Christianity: This is clearly contrary both to the
promises of the Old Testament and the whole current of the New, and to nothing

rather a question of coming to know God here and now, since both for the person whose love is for earthly things and for the one who loves God the remoteness of the loved object is the greatest misery.[9]

In comparison with this strong affirmation of the love of God, which at times approximates to a transfiguration of the world amounting almost to pantheism, in the manner of Shaftesbury,[1] the practical outworkings of the faith are more feebly stressed. Scougal does indeed emphasize that the vital force of religion is more effectively expressed in deeds than in words, and he points to Jesus as the ideal of this.[2] There are four concrete qualities to which he refers as the most characteristic attitudes of the Christian: resignation, love, purity, and humility. These are the essential virtues which the Lord Himself practised in His own life.[3] But it is almost a religion without obligations, not far removed from intoxication with feeling. Scougal was apparently aware of this himself, and therefore he warns against putting too much emphasis upon experiences of joy and happiness.[4] He calls for an inexorable struggle against self-love, and takes up John Bunyan's expression of a holy war.[5] But on the whole the stress is upon the organic development of the new life. For this reason Scougal turns against religion as an external law. He calls attention to the dangers of education, and desires that it shall be suited to the stages in young people's growth to maturity. In this connexion also he claims that due understanding should be shown to those who temporarily turn away from the articles of the faith.[6] All schematization and fitting of the religious life into categories is to be rejected. The progress of the inner man requires that due consideration be shown to each individual case.[7]

When we consider the main positions of this impressive book, we can recognize both its strength and its weaknesses. The strongest point is the coherent way in which the idea of God is expressed. The greatness of God is the leading theme, and it consists in His love. This love is conveyed to man through the likeness which binds him to God, and it continues in that love for mankind which extends to

more than our Saviour's most Divine Prayer wherein he expresses that he was not interceding for his Disciples only, but for all that should believe on his Name through their word.'

[9] *The Life of God in the Soul of Man,* p. 38.
[1] Ibid. pp. 18, 135   [2] Ibid. p. 19.
[3] Ibid. pp. 17–18, 47, 49; pp. 21–8, it is centred on Jesus. Does this indicate a mystical tradition?   [4] Ibid. pp. 115–16.
[5] Ibid. p. 58. The connexion with Bunyan is certainly conscious. This is seen from the further application of this metaphor (esp. p. 62).
[6] Ibid. pp. 110–11.   [7] Ibid. pp. 122–3.

love for the enemy. The image of God in man is the foundation which supports the whole structure. Therefore those who forbear to know anything about this in themselves are to be pitied, not hated or treated with contempt.[8] In comparison with this the understanding of sin is weakly developed, and therefore also the conception of Jesus Christ. Indeed Scougal emphatically attacks the idea which limits Christianity to the mere forgiveness of sins. It is the possession of eternity, life in the divine world—very like Schleiermacher's definition later of immortality as becoming one with infinity in the midst of finiteness.[9]

The affinity with Scupoli-Castaniza is unmistakable. Both books are concerned with perfection, which consists in participation in God's own nature. But God's nature is love: hence the claim naturally follows that God's love enters man's sphere in order to make him again into the perfect image of his Creator. This happens through grace. Up to this point the two are on common ground, but then differences emerge. For Scupoli-Castaniza Jesus Christ the One who was tempted is central; for Scougal He signifies the ethico-religious Prototype. For Scougal man's likeness to God is arrived at from the original relationship in creation; for Scupoli it happens by becoming conformed to God. Scougal presents a Christianity of harmony, Scupoli-Castaniza a Christianity of dissonance. The curious result is that the Catholic book, in taking the Second Article in a redemptive sense, is nearer to the heart of the Bible than the Anglican, which understands the First Article and man's likeness to God in the sense of a natural analogy. Correspondingly the types of piety are different. That of *The Spiritual Conflict* is masculine, austere, disciplined, centred on the intellect and the will. Its main concern is with spiritual trial and its overcoming. That of *The Life of God in the Soul of Man*, on the contrary, is effeminate, tender, with a streak of fanaticism and abandon, and its chief characteristics are the aesthetic attitude and a devotion based rather on feeling. The divine life streams into the believer like an impersonal force and a higher nature. For this reason a special emphasis is laid upon Holy Communion.[1] It is not surprising that Scupoli's conception of a personal God, which implies

---

[8] Ibid. p. 137.
[9] Schleiermacher, *Ueber die Religion Reden an die Gebildeten unter ihren Verächtern* (Ed. Rudolf Otto), p. 133.
[1] Scougal, *The Life of God in the Soul of Man*, p. 140. For an appreciation of the place of Holy Communion in mysticism, cf. Heinrich Bornkamm, *Luther und Böhme*, pp. 203–4.

a strict I-Thou relationship, stands over against a mysticism which tends towards pantheism in Scougal.

Susanna Wesley was deeply affected by these influences, and through her they passed to her large family, especially John. It must not be overlooked that certain essential characteristics of John Wesley's own system are contained in them, and questions are apparent with which he was constantly concerned in his maturity.

In the year 1697 Samuel and Susanna moved to the village of Epworth in the county of Lincoln. Samuel Wesley was given the living at the express wish of the wife of William of Orange, Queen Mary, who had died three years earlier. This is evidence of a strong loyalty to the throne which was the only point of contention between an otherwise well-suited pair. Mrs Wesley was a Jacobite, although she did not make much of it. The rector and his wife came to a harsh spot.[2] Epworth was one of the principal places on the 'Isle of Axholme', a marshy moorland district formed by the rivers Trent, Don, and Idle. The inhabitants lived by agriculture, fishing, and the hunting of water-fowl. Their lot depended upon the water: the flooding of the rivers made their earth and land fertile but also threatened the safety of their dwellings, forcing them to seek refuge on the nearby hills. Their independence had been grievously reduced in 1626 when Charles I granted to one man, Cornelius Vermuyden, the right to drain the whole countryside. A third of what was thus reclaimed belonged to the Crown, a third to the contractor, and a third to the inhabitants, whose consent had not however been sought. It is probable that the king had been led to make this contract by his constant need of money, which at the sign of inflation considerably weakened the position of the ruler and contributed towards the outbreak of the rebellion. The result in Epworth was long-enduring resentment against the government; the inhabitants never forgave their king the seizure of their soil and land. They became a hostile community which defied all authority and went for each collector of taxes, rough-handling or by every conceivable device making life hard for him, even to the length of setting fire to his house. Not even Oliver Cromwell could subdue the people of Epworth. For various reasons Samuel Wesley had a difficult start there. Every stranger was unwelcome from the beginning as a matter of course, but this was especially the case with the new rector, since he assumed his office under the sign of the royal favour and was friendly with the tax-

[2] Cf. Piette, *John Wesley in the Evolution of Protestantism*, pp. 213ff.

collector most recently turned out. But Samuel Wesley was not
daunted. He carried out the duties of his position with a conscientiousness that was unusual: scarcely had he arrived before he began
to visit the members of his congregation in their homes and to show
his personal interest in them. He found out for himself the state of
their religious knowledge and kept a record about it. In this way he
won their respect by his attention, but made himself unpopular by his
strictness. In addition his political opinions were completely opposed
to theirs: he was conservative, and they were fundamentally liberal.
His militant temperament made it impossible for him to conceal his
views. On the contrary he openly canvassed for his party and its
ideas.

The parsonage, an old, thatched but comfortable building, was
able to accommodate the growing family in its seven rooms. Having
some land it provided opportunity for breeding cattle, and yet want
and privation were often experienced by the family, especially when
the father, in accordance with the harsh laws of the time, was in
prison because of his debts. In the year 1705 he was arrested in the
churchyard immediately after a baptism and put in Lincoln Castle.
He wrote from there a moving letter to Archbishop John Sharp of
York, who undertook the care of his wife and children.[3] In the rural
calm a typical picture of English family life developed, in a style
which grew out of a hundred years of deep and conscientious Puritan
thought and fashion, and which became the basis of a characteristic
middle-class way of life.[4] The marriage produced nineteen children,
of which eleven died young. The father undertook their instruction
in the ancient languages,[5] but otherwise devoted himself to the duties
of his office and to his learned studies. Consequently their education
was left entirely in the hands of their remarkable mother, who based
it upon the following principles.[6] The governing idea for outward
behaviour was regularity. From infancy the child was trained not
only to receive its food and have its clothes changed, but also to sleep,
at definite times, and for this purpose the cradle had to be rocked.
The mother prescribed at first three hours for sleep each morning
and each afternoon, until with the passing of time this was reduced

---

[3] Cf. Stampe, 'The Rev. Samuel Wesley', *Proc.W.H.S.*, XI.(1918).4–5.
[4] Cf. the comprehensive work by Levin L. Schücking, *Die Familie im Puritanismus*.
[5] Cf. Tyerman, *The Life and Times of Samuel Wesley*, pp. 320–1.
[6] Susanna Wesley to John Wesley, 24th July 1732; *Journal*, III.34–9, 1st August
1742 (in connexion with the death and funeral of his mother).

to two hours at each occasion. At one year the child was shown the rod as a means of correction, and in this way learned to 'cry softly', so that the loud crying of children was seldom heard in the parsonage at Epworth. Food was limited to three meals a day. At dinner the little children sat at their own table beside that of the bigger ones, watched over by a servant. Their wishes had to be whispered to the maid, who then came to their mother. Eating or drinking between meals was not allowed. Similarly the children were forbidden to go into the kitchen to ask anything of the servants when these were having their meals. As soon as they could handle a knife and fork they took their place at table with the grown-ups. Family prayers were held at 6 p.m., and afterwards the children were given their supper. At 7 p.m. the servant-girl began to wash them, so that all were in bed by 8 o'clock at the latest. Their mother did not allow anyone to sit by them until they had fallen asleep. This strict regularity in eating and drinking enabled them to swallow without difficulty even the most unpleasant medicine!

In the moulding of character Susanna Wesley regarded the mastery of the will as of decisive importance. She postponed until later the instruction of the mind, since it required time; but the subduing of the will must be done immediately. She expected no serious difficulties in the further education of those children who had the right respect for their parents and who had early been taught to obey. She was prepared to overlook many of their childish pranks and adolescent follies, or only mildly to punish them, but she strongly condemned obstinacy and the deliberate breaking of explicit rules.

Susanna Wesley's view of the subjection of the will as the essential presupposition for education in the things of God is an echo of Romanic mysticism.[7] Without it she expected nothing either from the direction or example of the parents. For her, self-will was the root of all sin and misery, and so she was well able to understand that the essence of Christianity lay precisely in the fact that man should do the will of God and not his own. Accordingly she regarded those parents who carried through a strict training of the will as fellow-labourers with God, while those who indulged their children were associates of the devil. She could sum it all up by saying that on the overcoming of self-will heaven or hell alone depends. Following Scougal she linked together piety and joy, holiness and happiness. The parent who promotes the salvation of his child also makes it

[7] *Journal*, III.36.

happy. Having placed so ultimate a responsibility upon the educational process, she undertook the direction of her own children's spiritual life with the greatest possible seriousness.

She taught them the usual things, such as the Lord's Prayer for morning and evening devotions, prayers for parents, collects, a short catechism and Bible passages. They had strictly to distinguish the Sunday from other days, and God's Name might never be spoken lightly or thoughtlessly. Even amongst themselves they could not address each other without prefixing 'Brother' or 'Sister' to their proper names.

She also ran a school for them in their house, carefully organized on austere lines. The lessons were from nine o'clock to twelve and from two to five. During these hours nobody was allowed to interrupt them, nor could a child leave the schoolroom except for a good reason and with special permission. On the first day all the letters of the alphabet were learned, and only John Wesley's two sisters, Molly and Nancy, required as long as one and a half days for this, while his eldest brother Samuel needed only a few hours. He then learned the first verse of the Book of Genesis, and after that the next, and he quickly recognized the words he had learned wherever he saw them again. By this method they all learned to read one after the other. No child was permitted to leave the schoolroom before it had completed its lesson. Susanna Wesley was particularly concerned for the education of the girls. She made it a matter of principle to teach none of her daughters sewing before she had completely mastered reading, and she was particularly happy that her daughters were able to read while still children far better than the average woman in England at that time. Later she began and ended their lessons with the singing of a psalm and a reading from the Bible.

A number of measures and rules were drawn up especially for the moulding of character, and among these education in truthfulness held the highest place. To prevent lying because of the fear of punishment, Susanna Wesley assured each child that it would never be beaten if it made open confession. Nor was a child to be punished twice for the same fault, and if it amended its ways it would never be reproved by being reminded of its earlier wrong. Every act of obedience should be recognized, even if the performance did not actually turn out well. Promises were to be kept unconditionally and rights of property to be honoured, even in possessions of the smallest kind or value.

Although this method of education was based upon fundamental principles, which Susanna Wesley consistently followed, it was in no sense mechanical. She regarded the soul of each child as a talent entrusted to her, for whose increase and improvement she was responsible before God,[8] and therefore each had to be given individual treatment. On each evening of the week she took one or two children on their own and talked with them about religious questions. John's turn came on Thursday.[9] While at Oxford he gratefully and fondly recalled this fellowship in God's Word which he had shared early in life with his mother.[1] We can form some idea of the subject of these personal conversations, since several of the mother's ideas for them are preserved.[2] Her chief concern was to make the greatness and perfection of God absolutely real to the children and to convince them of His continual presence.

It is significant that the impulse towards this care for the individual souls of her children came to Susanna Wesley from reading Ziegenbalg's and Plützschau's account of August Hermann Francke's Danish-Halle mission in Tranquebar in southern India.[3] In 1709 the letters of the two missionaries were translated into English by the German court-chaplain in London, Anton Wilhelm Böhme, a pupil of Francke, and they immediately attracted considerable attention. This little book again follows the familiar line, for the original motive for the missionary enterprise and task is ascribed principally to the love of God.[4] Both parents were one in their vital interest in missionary work. The father, Samuel Wesley, probably in the year 1706, had offered his services as a missionary in the East Indies, presumably only for a limited period, during which a curate would be at

---

[8] *Journal*, III.32. Susanna Wesley to her husband, Samuel Wesley, 6th February 1712: 'I cannot but look upon every soul you leave under my care as a talent committed to me under a trust by the great Lord of all the families both of heaven and earth. And if I am unfaithful to Him or you in neglecting to improve these talents, how shall I answer unto Him when He shall command me to render an account of my stewardship?'

[9] Ibid. p. 33.

[1] *Letters*, I.119, 28th February 1732, to his mother.

[2] Susanna Wesley's religious Conference, 1712 (*Publications of W.H.S.*, 3). Clarke, *Memoirs of the Wesley Family*, II.38–72; cf. Simon, *John Wesley and the Religious Societies*, pp. 59–60.

[3] *Journal*, III.33.

[4] *Propagation of the Gospel to the East, Being an Account of the Success of two Danish Missionaries, Lately Sent to the East-Indies, for the Conversion of the Heathens in Malabar.* I used the 3rd edition (London, 1718), see esp. pp. XVI, XVIII; cf. my article, '*Der Missionsgedanke des jungen Wesley*', *Theologia viatorum*, pp. 89ff.

Epworth.[5] It is not surprising that Susanna on her own account should assume responsibility for a special service for the congregation when from November 1710 until February 1712 her husband as a member of Convocation was away in London. On Sunday evenings she held a devotional meeting for her children and servants in the kitchen of the rectory. Some members of the congregation joined this of their own accord, from 30 to 40 in number, but shortly before her husband's return it reached 200, and this provided occasion for adverse criticism. Susanna put this on one side by remarking resolutely that she had long taken leave of the world, and that everything which conduces to the salvation of souls appears odd to others.[6]

John Wesley was born into this remarkable household on 17th June 1703.[7] It brought together the heritage of Puritanism, Anglican churchmanship, and that concern for the care of souls, social activity and missionary zeal, derived from the revival of the Religious Societies. At the same time it drew its sustenance from Puritan culture of family life and from the nurture of individual souls found in Romanic mysticism. To this was joined the influence of the Halle type of pietism. Finally a place was given to liberal scholarship, and the harmonious, mystical piety of a Henry Scougal was held in high esteem. To all this was added Susanna Wesley's personal gift as a teacher. Although this was charismatic in the deepest sense of the word, it was nevertheless most methodically cultivated and practised. Through this rich polyphony one leading theme resounds like a *cantus firmus*: it is that of the love of God which empowers man towards perfection. It might almost be said that here, in the cradle, the main content of John Wesley's thought was already being proclaimed.[8]

[5] Stampe, 'The Rev. Samuel Wesley', *Proc.W.H.S.*, XI.(1918).3.
[6] Journal, III.33. On the whole matter, cf. Eliza Clarke, *Susanna Wesley*, p. 101.
[7] John Wesley was well aware that he stood in a remarkable religious tradition. *Letters*, V.76, London, 15th January 1768, to Charles Wesley: 'Such a thing has scarce been for these thousand years before, as a son, father, grandfather, *atavus*, *tritavus*, preaching the gospel, nay, and the genuine gospel, in a line.' John L. Nuelsen (*Kurzgefasste Geschichte des Methodismus*, p. 14) rightly describes the Epworth rectory as the 'cradle of Methodism'.
[8] It is noteworthy that the old escutcheon of the Wesleys bore the inscription, 'God is Love'. Cf. Thomas F. Lockyer, *Paul: Luther: Wesley*, p. 138.

FOUR

Childhood and Youth

THE CALM of Epworth was suddenly interrupted by an event which for the time being broke up the family life and made a deep and lasting impression upon the child John Wesley. On Thursday night, 9th February 1709, between eleven and midnight, fire broke out in the rectory and completely destroyed the building.[1] The mother lay ill in her bedroom, and her husband was by himself in another room. The warning was given by one of the daughters, Hetty, when sparks fell on to her feet, and she rushed to her parents' bedroom. Meanwhile shouts of 'Fire' from the road had aroused Samuel Wesley. Quickly grasping the situation he aroused the whole family and gave his instructions. The children's maid took charge of the youngest children, while their mother painfully got herself up. The older children were able to look after themselves, some by jumping out of the windows. The father believed that he could hear one still crying from inside the house, and this was the little John.[2] A strong north-east wind drove the flames so furiously into the building that every attempt to enter it was frustrated. In this moment of extreme danger the father knelt down and commended to God the soul of his little son. Meanwhile John himself was surprised because he saw his room brightly lit up. He ran to the door, but the smoke made it impossible for him to get any farther, so he climbed on to a chest of drawers and looked out. Somebody outside saw him and wanted to rush for a ladder, but someone else said there was no time, and suggested standing by the wall of the house so that a lighter man might get on to his shoulders and take the child from the window. This was done. Scarcely had the little boy come out when the roof fell in. When they brought the rescued child into a neighbouring house his father was overwhelmed and cried out: 'Come neighbours, let us kneel down: let us give thanks to God! He has given me all my

[1] Mrs Wesley's account, written in a letter to a neighbouring clergyman, Joseph Hoole of Haxey, is printed in the *Arminian Magazine*, I.(1778).31–2, with a postscript by John Wesley—ibid. pp. 32–3.
[2] John Wesley himself denied that he had cried out—ibid. p. 32.

eight children; let the house go: I am rich enough!' The next day he went into his garden and picked up a page from his polyglot Bible upon which the Latin words were still legible, which read: 'Go, sell all thou hast, and take up thy cross and follow me.' So this extreme challenge from primitive Christianity was used to interpret to this scholar and writer the loss of his home, his books and manuscripts. His son however always regarded his preservation from death as a sign of God's direct call, and until his twenty-third or twenty-fourth year nothing affected him so deeply.[3] He liked to refer to himself in the words of the prophet[4] as a brand plucked from the burning.[5]

In addition to the material loss this misfortune meant that the process of educating him, which his mother had so carefully undertaken, was jeopardized. The children had to be separated. After they had returned to their newly-built house, she recorded what bad habits they had acquired in the meantime. Association with serving folk had been all too close; they had given up strict observance of Sunday; they brought home with them bad language and songs, and altogether their behaviour had taken on a clownish and coarse quality which could only be removed with difficulty.[6] The relationship between the brothers and sisters was a normal one, and on the whole they were held together by true affection, which occasional provocations did not break. In particular John grew close to Samuel, the eldest of the family.

John left his parents' house when he was ten and a half. On 28th January 1714 he entered the famous school of Charterhouse in London.[7] Founded as a monastery in the time of Wycliffe in 1371 by Sir Walter de Manny, in 1535 it became a victim in the general

---

[3] *Arminian Magazine*, VIII.(1785).152: 'The strongest impression I had till I was 23 or 24 years old.'

[4] Amos 4^{11}, Zechariah 3^2.

[5] *Journal*, I.328, 17th March 1737, and IV.90, 26th November 1753, where the words appear in the inscription he wrote for his tombstone, consequent upon his illness. It is noteworthy that Luther quoted this text in the letter he wrote to Archbishop Albrecht of Mainz to accompany the 95 Theses on 31st October 1517. He uses it as an example of the difficulty in attaining salvation (*WA*, Br.I. (1930).110): 'For the way which leads to life (Matthew 7^{14}) is so narrow that the Lord addresses those who are saved through the prophets Amos (4^{11}) and Zechariah (3^2) as brands plucked from the burning.'

[6] *Journal*, III.37–8, Susanna Wesley to John Wesley, 24th July 1732.

[7] Cf. Edward Weaver, 'Wesley and Charterhouse School', *Wesleyan Methodist Magazine* (1912), pp. 936ff; H. A. Butz, 'John Wesley and Charterhouse', *Methodist Review*, XCV.(1913).449–50; T. B. Shepherd, 'John Wesley and the Charterhouse', *Proc.W.H.S.*, XXI.(1937/8).25–30. The biographies which deal with this period most fully are those of Robert Southey, *The Life of John Wesley*, I.25, and John Telford, *The Life of John Wesley*, pp. 25–6.

dissolution which, particularly in England, was carried through with such ruthlessness.[8] It fell into private hands and, after more than one change of owner, was acquired in 1611 by Thomas Sutton, upon whose estate at Newcastle upon Tyne the first collieries were just being opened up. In this way he became a wealthy man. At his death he directed that an infirmary for eighty old men, a school for forty boys, and a chapel should be founded in the beautiful and stately grounds. He laid down that the school should be for the sons of those parents whose means were not sufficient for an education in keeping with their position. John Wesley was admitted to it in its centenary year [9] expressly as a 'poor scholar'. He was on the foundation, one of the small number who occupied free places, and he had been nominated by the Duke of Buckingham. As a mark of his new status he received a uniform type of clothing, consisting of a narrowly-cut jacket made of black linen, which was worn open in summer and buttoned up in winter, knee-breeches and a kind of hat, as well as a white collar similar to those worn at the more aristocratic institution at Eton.

Life in his new surroundings was hard and frugal. The scholars got up at five in the morning, and not until eight were they given breakfast, which consisted of bread, cheese, and beer, tea or coffee being much too costly. John had promised his father that he would run three times round the garden before breakfast, and thus it is clear that from early days he strove to harden his body. Dinner was at twelve or three. Shortly before bedtime came supper, at which once again only bread, cheese, and beer were provided. Between midday and evening the boys could ask for a slice of bread from the storeroom. The fare was certainly not luxurious and was even further diminished through the evil system of fagging, by which the older boys took away the younger ones' meat. For a long time John Wesley's staple diet was just bread. The boys had always to sleep two in a bed.

It was a fact of special significance that both school and infirmary were part of one institution, since it meant that a note of seriousness was added to the life of the boys through the constant sight of age and decrepitude.[1] One master was head of both sections; when

[8] Cf. S. B. Liljegren, *The Fall of the Monasteries and the Social Changes leading up to the Great Revolution* (1924) (Lund Universitets Arsskrift, N.F., I.19). He shows that it was the rising middle class which became the usufructuary of the secularization, not the State, as in Germany.

[9] This is noted by John Telford, *The Life of John Wesley* (5th edn, 1929), p. 23. The school was founded on 3rd October 1614.

[1] Telford, ibid. p. 26, draws attention correctly to this; see also *Letters*, I.xiii.

Wesley went there it was Dr Thomas Burnet, a grand old man of the theological enlightenment, who died twelve months later in his eightieth year. He had acquired a European reputation through a series of books, particularly by a learned and pious work on earthquakes, which Addison had celebrated in a Latin ode.[2] He had successfully resisted the Roman Catholic tendencies of James II, who had attempted to introduce a catholic into the school. Through the recommendation of Archbishop Tillotson he was made secretary and chaplain to William III. His successor at Charterhouse, Dr John King, had already been Preacher of the institution for two decades. Of King it was said that he always carried about with him a copy of the *Imitation of Christ* by Thomas à Kempis.[3] Under his care John Wesley passed his schooldays, although the direction of the school itself was in the hands of the 'Schoolmaster', Dr Thomas Walker. At the time of Wesley's arrival he too was past his prime, being sixty-seven years old, and having occupied the post since 1679. Previous to that he had been assistant master for four years, and so he had spent the whole of his working life in the one sphere. It may well be that this definite but unobtrusive emphasis upon the school tradition which he saw in these men made an abiding impression on the boy. Walker left behind him the reputation of a man with an excellent knowledge of the ancient languages, Latin, Greek, and Hebrew. Some of the leading figures in the cultural life in the England of that day had received their grounding from him—men like Richard Steele, Joseph Addison, Bishop Law of Carlisle, Martin Benson of Gloucester, and Dr Davies, President of Queens' College, Cambridge, who was considered to be the best Latin scholar in the country. Walker had a high regard for Wesley on account of his diligence, conscientiousness, and regularity, and the boy acquired great facility in the composition of Latin verse, while he learned Hebrew with unusual rapidity. An apocryphal story is told about the usher, Andrew Tooker, who was a mathematician. He was struck by the fact that John Wesley was usually found standing among the smaller boys, addressing them. On being asked why he did not keep with the others of his own age, he replied: 'Better rule in hell than serve in heaven.' It is of course highly improbable that there is any truth in this.[4]

John usually spent his Sundays and his holidays with his brother

[2] Telford, ibid. Was it in this way that the example of the French Count Gaston-Jean Baptiste came to exercise its influence? [3] Ibid.
[4] T. B. Shepherd, 'John Wesley and the Charterhouse', *Proc.W.H.S.*, XXI.25–30, comments justifiably: 'It savours too much of Southey's ambitious theme.'

Samuel, who was fifteen years his senior, and who was usher at Westminster School, where he lived in Dean's Yard. Epworth was too far away, and the journey too expensive. He also got on well with his young sister-in-law, although later he found fault with her for a certain tendency to resentment.[5] He gratefully recognized the help his brother was to him.[6] When he left in 1720 to go to Christ Church, Oxford, he received a prize of twenty pounds in addition to an exhibition for the same amount. In his last week at school he had an amusing experience when he happened to meet Dr Henry Sacheverell, the opponent of the Dissenters and the man whom Wesley's father had assisted in the controversy over obedience to authority. He greeted Wesley with the words: 'You are too young to go to the University; you cannot know Greek and Latin yet. Go back to school!'

Like anyone who has spent the formative years of his life in such a place, John Wesley retained an abiding love for his school, which in return regards him as one of the greatest of its sons.[7] As often as he could Wesley returned there. On 12th December 1727, under the direction of Dr King, he and two other former scholars acted as stewards at the annual dinner, which was part of the celebrations in honour of the founder, Thomas Sutton. At that time, apart from a break from 1720 to 1726 and from 1728 to 1739, this was held in the school itself.[8] Later Wesley visited the old rooms at least once a year and spent hours of solitary meditation in them. He lodged in the institution for an extended period immediately after his return from Germany in the late summer of 1738. Prior to this he had become friendly with an invalid tradesman, Jonathan Agutter, who was forty-nine years of age and had lived in the infirmary as a 'poor brother' since 1733.[9] He seems to have provided Wesley with a quiet room in which he was able to stay for months at a time, and it is likely that one of the first little Methodist fellowship-meetings met there. It was

[5] *Letters*, I.17, 18th June 1725, to his mother.
[6] Ibid. pp. 26–7, 21st March 1726, to his brother Samuel.
[7] Ibid. p. 3:

    Wesley, John Wesley, was one of our company,
    Prophet untiring and fearless of tongue,
    Down the long years he went
    Spending yet never spent,
    Serving his God with a heart ever young.

[8] Cf. Robert Birley, 'Charterhouse Notes, III: John Wesley as a Steward at Founders' Day Dinner', *Proc.W.H.S.*, XXVII.(1949).56–7.
[9] Cf. ibid. IV: 'Petition of Jonathan Agutter to be Nominated a Poor Brother at Charterhouse, 1733', XXVII.(1949).83.

here that Wesley prepared either the first Methodist hymn-book of
1739 or the edition of 1740, and here he wrote letters to his friends.[1]
In this way the old monastery became once again the centre of a
spiritual movement. When in September 1757, at the age of fifty-
four, John Wesley once more walked through the buildings he made
the observation which is usual when a grown man looks again on the
scenes of his childhood: what was then so big now seems so small!
This changed impression, a common experience of life, prompted
in him the sombre reflection that since the Deluge men have grown
neither in stature nor understanding.[2] Charterhouse meant for him a
second home. Two things he had learned in his parents' home he
found being continued and emphasized there—the strict regulation
of his life and a modest style of living. The application to scholarly
work which he had seen in his father now became his own, particularly in the study of the ancient classics.[3] But these were really only
formal matters. These years produced no recognizable gain so far as
his religion was concerned: it was the new sphere which was to bring
a decisive change.

[1] *Journal*, II.77.D [Diary], 25th September 1738, pp. 130–55.D (17th January
to 27th March 1739).
[2] Ibid. IV.232, Monday, 8th September 1757.
[3] H. A. Butz, 'John Wesley and Charterhouse', *Methodist Review*, XCV.449–
50, correctly brings out these two points, regularity and scholarly work. While
Luke Tyerman, *The Life and Times of John Wesley* (6th edn, London, 1890)
I.22, following an uncritical acceptance of Wesley's comment about himself made
on the day of his conversion (24th May 1738), says, 'John Wesley entered the
Charterhouse a saint, and left it a sinner', Butz goes too far in the other direction
when he asserts: 'He was nearer a saint when he left Charterhouse School than
when he came.' In the review Wesley made of his life, to which reference has
been made above, he said: 'However, I still read the Scriptures, and said my
prayers morning and evening' (*Journal*, I.466). Of his sins, which he views with
the uncompromising eye of the newly-converted, he says merely: 'Outward re-
straints being removed, I was much more negligent than before, even of outward
duties, and almost continually guilty of outward sins, which I knew to be such,
though they were not scandalous in the eye of the world' (ibid). This implies no
more than a half-conscious loosening of the basic principles he had learned from
his home.
During his time at Charterhouse School ghostly effects occurred at his parents'
home between 2nd December 1716 and the end of January 1717. Later John
Wesley himself wrote an account of these—*Works*, XIII.459–64 (Hilton Park,
26th March 1784). The point which stands out in this report of the eighty-one-
year-old Wesley is the intrepidity of his father. When some friends advised him
to vacate the house, he replied: 'No, let the devil flee from me: I will never flee
from the devil'—p. 464. John Wesley not only regarded the phenomena with
youthful curiosity but took them as confirming the reality of a supernatural world,
especially of the existence of the devil. He repeatedly mentioned similar phenomena in such letters as the following: *Letters*, I.6, 23rd September 1732, to
his mother; pp. 10–11, 1st November 1724, to his mother; pp. 13–14, 18th December 1724, to his mother; on this question, cf. Tyerman, op. cit. I.22ff.

The University of Oxford, to which he went on 24th June 1720, on becoming a member of Christ Church, was situated in a pleasant city which was still rural and medieval. The approaching traveller could see towers, with meadows and fields stretching up to the city walls, within which were the college buildings and dwelling-houses. The Bocardo prison, in which, under Mary the Catholic, the Protestant martyrs, Cranmer, Ridley, and Latimer, had lodged before they were burned, and the Castle, which dated from early Norman times, spoke eloquently of an earlier age. Among the colleges Christ Church and Lincoln were pre-eminent: the former was founded by Henry VIII's Catholic chancellor, Thomas Wolsey, and the latter had been started a hundred years earlier as a theological counterblast to the false teaching of Wycliffe. Political changes had strongly affected the city itself; under James I and again under James II it was for a time a royal residence. Hence it had been particularly suspect by Cromwell and William of Orange. Political discussions and party organizations were prominent features there. The effects of the high life of Court, with its loose morals, were not quickly eradicated amongst the students. On the other hand the official attitude of the University emphasized most strongly adherence to the king and the Church of England, and proscribed everything which smacked of dissent or enthusiasm. It was a world full of tensions into which John Wesley entered, as if destined to be the centre and starting-point of a great movement. At first to be sure it produced in him no unusual reactions. He allowed himself to be captivated by the spirit of the place, and with all the normal enthusiasm of youth entered into the students' recreations. He sat in the coffee-houses and read the newspapers, he tried his hand at topical romantic verse in the manner of Horace and Tibullus, and at times got into debt. He was able to ride, swim, row, and play tennis, even though his constitution was not robust. He walked a great deal and also hunted. At home in the holidays he kept up the friendships he had made and was often a guest in neighbouring parsonages, where he danced with young people of his own age. Hence it is not surprising that at Oxford he was rarely alone either at meal-times or when studying. Yet for all this he did not neglect his academic work, and in this at least he differed from his contemporaries. Nevertheless he constantly reproached himself for idleness; it seems as if during the first years he lacked constancy and concentration in his course of study. Like most gifted students he covered a remarkably wide field and read whatever came to hand.[4]

Nevertheless by his nineteenth year, towards the end of 1721, all this had completely changed. He now began to draw up a regular plan for all his activities and to adhere to it. After the first brief reaction against the strict discipline of his home and the Charterhouse, he reverted to that basic pattern which Puritanism had impressed upon English life. It is evident that he did not feel at home for long in the easy atmosphere of the average undergraduate. The change was expressed in his decision to keep a daily note-book, and this was quite in line with the tradition.[5] At first the book was only concerned with details of his work, and it enumerated under each day the things he intended to do. There are entries about Hebrew and Greek, and alongside them the Latin poets Ovid, Terence, Juvenal, Horace, Virgil, as well as French writers, are mentioned. Wesley toyed with the idea of preparing a new edition of Horace.[6] His studies were interspersed with personal correspondence, and the few examples which have been preserved show his complete candour. They are straightforward accounts of events, and include occasionally a remodelled Horatian ode, especially when writing to his brother Samuel, the poet.[7] Only a few refer to religious questions. Once he relates a ghost story in which the chief character bears the Messianic name from Isaiah 9[6] of פליא אלת, Wonderful God, and remarks that it must have been the devil, since the title belongs only to God.[8] Another time he says that the book by the physician George Cheyne, *Essay of Health and Long Life*, with its recommendations for moderation and the hardening of the body, has made a great impression upon him. The book did indeed make quite a stir, as had been foreseen by its author, who felt that in his main concern he was so much on God's side that he attributed the opposition he would meet to the world, the flesh, and the devil.[9] John Wesley himself soon adopted the moderate, restricted diet which he recommended.

We should like to know more about his teachers at Christ Church

---

[4] On Wesley at Oxford, cf. Tyerman *The Life and Times of John Wesley*, I. 24ff; Curnock in *Journal*, I.4ff; Simon, *John Wesley and the Religious Societies*, pp. 64ff. [Translator's note: see also especially V. H. H. Green, *The Young Mr Wesley*, for a much fuller account, based upon material not hitherto used.]
[5] *Journal*, I.43, facsimile.   [6] Curnock, ibid. p. 47.
[7] Cf. Thomas E. Brigden, 'Samuel Wesley Junior, Schoolmaster, High Churchman, Minor Poet, and his circle, 1690–1739', *Proc.W.H.S.*, XI.(1918).25–31, 74–81, 97–102, 121–9, 145–53; *Letters*, I.8–9, Oxford, 17th June 1724; pp. 27–9, 21st March 1726; p. 30, 4th April 1726.
[8] *Letters*, I.6, Oxford, 23rd September 1723, to his mother.
[9] Ibid. p. 11, 1st November 1724, to his mother.

and Wesley's opinion of them. Academic study in England is to this day fundamentally different from that in Germany because of the close association of the student with his tutor, an association which amounts almost to dependence. The first of these men in Wesley's experience was George Wigan, a biblical linguist after the style of the Enlightenment, who carried a stage farther the research into the Septuagint undertaken by the notable German scholar, Johann Ernst Grabe (1666–1711), who had himself gone to Oxford.[1] In the autumn of 1723 Wigan retired to a country living in order to devote himself completely to his studies. Did John Wesley learn from him that care in the treatment of biblical texts which later distinguished his *Notes on the New Testament*? His second tutor, Henry Sherman, has not left any particular reputation, but Wesley always remembered him with great gratitude.[2] He gave Wesley Tasso's *Jerusalem Delivered* in an English translation.[3]

Thus the first years at Oxford were similar in character to the schooldays at Charterhouse: the emphasis was upon formal instruction and education in principles and fundamentals. His tutors evidently confirmed him in the course which he had naturally taken, even to his partiality for poetry.

But the year 1725 was radically to change this. Suddenly statements about religious matters are found in various places from the months of April and May. All at once long-repressed energies were released. On 5th April he began to fill his note-book with entries about his spiritual life, and from this time he subjects himself to incessant self-examination and spiritual discipline. On 28th May he propounds to his mother a theological subject for the first time. So far as we can trace the reasons, two external circumstances were responsible for the new situation, his approaching ordination and his acquaintance with the clergyman's daughter, Sarah Kirkham, at Stanton. It is understandable that both facts should affect him deeply, for one led to his life's vocation and the other to the possibility of a wife. However normal this may have been, it nevertheless went beyond the usual experience of the young man. Both impulses tended towards the same direction. The association with Sarah Kirkham, in which each used assumed names, he Cyrus and she Varanese, presumably following a literary model which is how-

---

[1] On Johann Ernst Grabe, cf. esp. Hans Leube, *Kalvinismus und Luthertum im Zeitalter der Orthodoxie*, I.351ff.
[2] Cf. John Telford, in *Letters*, I.5, notes 2 and 3.
[3] *Letters*, I.12, Christ Church, 18th December 1724.

ever no longer known, was his first serious and yet timid approach
to the other sex. The romantic element is restrained, perhaps actually
replaced, by the religious. Probably Wesley destroyed the correspondence, so that the further possibilities can only be a matter of
conjecture.[4] When on 26th January 1725 his father referred to his
intention of being ordained deacon, he strongly emphasized that the
chief motive for the ministry must be God's honour and the edifica-
tion of one's neighbour. All other ideas had to be relegated to the
second place. But alongside them he allowed that certain personal
considerations, such as the securing of the means of living, should be
considered within their proper limits, while concern for one's own
spiritual welfare, of which inner discipline was an extreme expression,
was quite fitting. Above all however he warned him against entering
this office unprepared. The fundamental requirement is a personal
familiarity with the Bible, based upon a knowledge of the text in the
original languages. To the question as to which was the best commentary, he, the scholar, replied: the Bible itself. Then far behind this
he placed Hugo Grotius.[5] In such a way John Wesley was directed
with commendable clarity to the central thing. His father's counsel
combined the methodology of the Enlightenment with orthodox
belief. His mother on the other hand suggested that he should read
practical divinity.[6] It is also likely that Sarah Kirkham encouraged
him, and she appears to have introduced him to Jeremy Taylor's
books on *The Rule and Exercises of Holy Living* and *The Rule and
Exercises of Holy Dying,* and to the *Imitation of Christ* by Thomas à
Kempis, although not without certain reservations.[7]

Jeremy Taylor (1613–67) is one of the classic writers of the Anglican Church. He is the Shakespeare of English prose. The two aforementioned books, which are only a part of his literary legacy, occupy

[4] Nehemiah Curnock's careful investigations, given in the Introduction to
the *Journal* (I.13ff), are authoritative. Leger, *La Jeunesse de Wesley*, p. 99, and
James Harrison Rigg, *The Living Wesley* (2nd edn., 1891), pp. 47–8, stress too
one-sidedly the romantic element. Leger would conclude from the entry in the
Diary for 20th September 1725 ('talked of marriage with Griffiths, walked round
the meadow'—*Journal*, 1.59) that his disappointed love for Varanese prompted
him to seek true happiness in God, and this is often held. Yet against this must
be set the fact that Wesley's decisive turning to God had begun six months earlier.
[Translator's note: Dr Green (*The Young Mr Wesley*) considers that Mrs Harrison in *Son to Susanna* (Penguin edn, pp. 40ff) has established that Varanese
was Betty Kirkham's elder sister, and says (p. 207, note 3): 'It can now be
stated categorically that Varanese was Sarah Kirkham.' Accordingly I have sub-
stituted 'Sarah' for 'Betty' in Prof. Schmidt's text.]
[5] *Arminian Magazine*, I.(1778).29–30.
[6] Tyerman, *Life and Times of Samuel Wesley*, pp. 391–2.
[7] Curnock, *Journal*, I.15–16. The criticism appears in *Letters*, I.19.

a permanent place in English religious writing.[8] In the first, *The Rule and Exercises of Holy Living*, he expounds on the basis of Titus 2^{12} Christian sobriety, Christian justice, and the Christian religion. Under the first heading he presents a type of Christian individual ethics, under the second a social ethic, and under the third a doctrine of divine worship and the personal relationship with God. It is difficult to say what the basic conception is, since there runs through all the thoughts and injunctions an harmonious trait. The first impression made upon the reader is of a peculiar medley,[9] but on closer examination the fundamental position becomes clear. The real background of every assertion is the fact of God the Creator and man the creature, and this relationship governs Taylor's thinking. For this reason he can use Old Testament Psalms as prayers[1] and quite naturally places the petition for bodily health with equal emphasis alongside the desire for salvation.[2] As a remedy for gossip among people he proposes as subjects for conversation the greatness of the cosmos and the course of the stars.[3] The sanctification of marriage, although not based on its sacramental character, rests upon the fact that the New Testament used it as a simile of Jesus' relationship with the Church.[4] He finds the greatness of God in Nature, especially storms, and he understands earthquakes as an exhortation to humility.[5] In general he is remarkable for his keen observation of Nature.[6] His confession of faith begins with thanksgiving for all the gifts of natural life like sun and moon and the beauties of the countryside, it goes on to thanksgiving for a cheerful spirit and a good conscience, and it ends with thanks for God's providence and the promise of eternity.[7] Is not all the world God's family? he asks.[8] The function of man consists in being God's Temple,[9] and his end is to enjoy everlasting felicity.[1] The whole of life becomes a walk blazing with light in the constant presence of God.[2] Sacrament and prayer are the external aids; contentment, humility, a quiet and modest life which

---

[8] On Taylor and his significance, cf. the complete edition with biography by Reginald Heber, *The Whole Works of Jeremy Taylor* (London, 1847–54); Gosse, *Jeremy Taylor* (1904); Herbert Schöffler, *Protestantismus und Literatur*, p. 136; Taylor's two books: *The Rule and Exercises of Holy Living* and *The Rule and Exercises of Holy Dying*, in Heber's edn, Vol. IV. August Lang, *Puritanismus und Pietismus*, pp. 276–81, gives an account of their contents.
[9] Lang, *Puritanismus und Pietismus*, p. 278.
[1] Heber, *The Whole Works of Jeremy Taylor*, IV.46–7.
[2] Ibid. pp. 49ff.   [3] Ibid. pp. 100–1.   [4] Ibid. p. 73.   [5] Ibid. p. 102.
[6] Cf. Schöffler, *Protestantismus und Literatur*, p. 69.
[7] Heber, *The Whole Works of Jeremy Taylor*, IV.114–15.   [8] Ibid. p. 108.
[9] Ibid. pp. 33, 73, 140.   [1] Ibid. p. 12.   [2] Ibid. p. 37.

offends nobody, its results. Man calmly sees death approaching, since each night has been the grave of the departing day.[3] All things take place of themselves without trouble, therefore the Christian religion, in so far as it makes moral statements, can be nothing but the Law of Nature.[4] Temperance, which was both a humanist and Puritan ideal, an inward balance, follows logically as the practical ethical task. The example of the characters and words of the ancients as of the Old Testament also, make this evident.[5] Biblical commandments and rational rules of prudence come to the support of each other: since earthly pleasures and desires bring only disappointment in their train, man must give the priority to heavenly ones.[6] But over all there hangs a veil of mysticism which makes the Augustinian tradition in the early Church come alive again. Chastity appears as a duty which God mystically intended by the law of circumcision, virginity ranks as the angelic life which frees the soul from cares and fills it with prayers.[7] Imperceptibly the author passes from the first article of the creed to the second and third. Thanksgiving for the blessings of creation turns into praise for redemption, since God's providence is also efficacious in this. The end of life is the perfect man in Christ, created for all good works.[8] A holy way of life is demanded and striven after. For this reason sin and individual sins must be heeded with the greatest watchfulness, and the passions mortified.[9] The emphasis upon humility or lowliness, which was characteristic of the early Church and the Middle Ages, receives a new splendour. Man must be content to be undervalued and esteemed as of little worth.[1] Yet this is established again in a completely rational manner: the human body is weaker than those of many animals and human beauty cannot be compared with that of flowers.[2] Afflictions which come to man often prove themselves great temporal benefits.[3] On the other hand God meets man most closely and deeply in troubles, and demonstrates in them the greatness of His promise.[4] The majesty of God consists in the fact that He brings good out of evil.[5] At this point Taylor was able to break through the bounds of natural religion

[3] Ibid. pp. 49, 134.   [4] Ibid. p. 56.
[5] Ibid. pp. 56ff Cf. Levin L. Schücking, *Die Familie im Puritanismus*, pp. 1ff (in conjunction with earlier studies); Helmuth Exner, *Der Einfluss des Erasmus auf die englische Bildungsidee*, and my review of this book in *Zeitschr. f. Kirchengesch.*, LIX.(1940).491.
[6] Heber, *The Whole Works of Jeremy Taylor*, IV.59.
[7] Ibid. pp. 70ff.   [8] Ibid. p. 49.   [9] Ibid. pp. 94, 50–1, 45, 72, 76, 140–1.
[1] Ibid. p. 91.   [2] Ibid. p. 86.   [3] Ibid. p. 124.   [4] Ibid. p. 37.
[5] Ibid. p. 125: 'For God esteems it one of his glories that he brings good out of evil.'

and theology, and with the daring of the Reformers put his trust in the promise of God. 'If all natural means fail, it is certain that God will rather work a miracle than break His word.' [6] To believe means to take God's promises seriously, to receive God's word humbly without calculating its possibilities, to obey the conditions of His promises which He has laid down in His commandments. Repentance and growth in holiness cannot be dissociated from belief in the forgiveness of sins. To have faith means to know oneself as a child of God, to trust Him unconditionally as Father, and at the same time to feel oneself a stranger in this world and to have before one's eyes the heavenly reality. Such a faith holds within itself the whole world, life, vocation, and possessions. In a way similar to that with which Luther, in his celebated preface to the Epistle to the Romans, asserted that good works followed from faith,[7] Jeremy Taylor writes: 'Faith, if it be true, living, and justifying, cannot be separated from a good life.' [8] It works miracles, it makes a drunkard sober, a lascivious person chaste, a covetous man liberal. It overcomes the world and works righteousness. It makes us diligently to do and cheerfully to suffer whatsoever God hath placed in our way to heaven.[9] Such faith finds external aids in the festivals of the Church year, Trinity Sunday, Ascension Day, Easter and Christmas. They are particularly useful for simple folk who are not able to grasp the contents of the faith by their own spiritual ability. It is also said that hope and fasting are the two wings of prayer and so of faith, although Taylor qualifies this when he calls fasting the wing of a bird, while hope is the wing of an angel. He continually comes back to the Word of God and definitely confines it to the Bible, although not to any one part of it. All commandments and revelations, promises and threatenings, stories and sermons in the Bible belong to the Word of God, but this applies only to the Bible. Even the best books of devotion or sermons cannot be compared with it. 'The Holy Ghost is certainly the best preacher in the world, and the words of the Scripture the best sermons.' [1]

It was certainly of significance for John Wesley's development that

[6] Heber, *The Whole Works of Jeremy Taylor,* IV.132.
[7] W.A., *Deutsche Bibel,* 7.9–10.
[8] Heber, *The Whole Works of Jeremy Taylor,* IV.183: 'Faith, if it be true, living, and justifying, cannot be separated from a good life. It works miracles, makes a drunkard become sober, a lascivious person become chaste, a covetous man become liberal, "it overcomes the world – it works righteousness" (2 Corinthians 13⁵, Romans 8¹⁰), and makes us diligently to do, and cheerfully to suffer, whatsoever God hath placed in our way to heaven.'
[9] Ibid. pp. 180–3, *passim.*   [1] Ibid. pp. 203–4.

in this book he was so strongly directed to the Bible. As was many times demonstrated, the Church in its cultus and sacraments conforms to the Bible. In this connexion to be sure Taylor makes some fairly considerable modifications, as for instance in his estimate of fasting. Not only does he require that considerations of health should be intelligently borne in mind, but he looks at it completely in relation to prayer. It is to free man from all earthly desires and direct his thoughts exclusively to God. If it is to help towards repentance it must be short, sharp, and afflictive. On the other hand if it is to subdue inordinate appetite for food, drink, or sexual desire, it must be undertaken gradually. Similarly with Sunday observance, he represents throughout the cause of Christian freedom and allows harmless recreation. He finds the meaning of Sunday by relating it to the fact that God created the world, and so the person who visits the sick, reconciles differences and performs acts of charity, will best fulfil the divine purpose. Sunday is the day appointed for the exercise of Christian love.[2] Holy Communion [3] is given the greatest emphasis; Taylor seeks to understand it as the continuation of the pre-Christian sacrificial cult and as the present representation of Jesus' sacrifice on Golgotha. In spite of this the psychological effects are emphasized as much as the dogmatic import. The communicant must enter completely into the life of Jesus Christ and allow His image to be realized in and through himself. By disputing the secret of the mystery its efficacy is lost; a man must be satisfied with the real presence of the Lord. In a phrase which has a typically mystical sound, this is a presence to the soul.[4] At the same time the participants are joined with each other and to their Head, Jesus Christ. Thus the effects far exceed the individual's experience. The Holy Sacrament also affects our bodies, which receive the seed of an immortal nature. From all this it follows naturally that Taylor should recommend frequent reception of the sacrament.

The whole book is like a symphony based on the theme of the relationship between man the creature and God the Creator. By harmonious transition the Christian faith arises out of natural religion, and Taylor expressly professes four fundamental truths: that there is one God, that God is invisible, that God cares for all things,

[2] Ibid. pp. 207ff.
[3] Ibid. pp. 265ff.
[4] Ibid. p. 271: 'Dispute not concerning the secret of the mystery, and the nicety of the manner of Christ's presence: it is sufficient to thee, that Christ shall be present to thy soul.'

and that He rules over all the world. God is the Creator of all things outside Himself. He finds these perceptions of natural religion repeated and set forth in the first four precepts (according to Reformed reckoning) of the decalogue.[5] Thus with the word 'calling' he can pass imperceptibly from activity in this world to the heavenly call, and in one breath he can include under the word 'promise' both earthly and heavenly blessings.[6] In the very nature of the case synergism is introduced in the assertion that God and man must work together in salvation. Greatly as Taylor endeavours to hold to the Word of God and to justifying faith on the one hand, time and again the human factor is emphasized. This is clearest of all when it appears in its most refined form, when he speaks about love. Love is the greatest thing that God can give us, for He Himself is love; but love is the greatest thing we can give to Him, for in so doing we give Him ourselves. For this reason the apostle calls it the band of perfection. It is the old and the new, the greatest commandment which includes all the commandments in itself. It is the fulfilling of the law. In love God and man meet; it is the point of identity between them. The human factor becomes still more evident when Taylor tries to describe the incentives which create love and indicates that they are perfection and usefulness. On man's side these two qualities call forth admiration and desire.[7] The first of these qualities arises from the contrast between our small and lowly nature and the greatness and dignity of the Creator; the second between man's well-being and his misery. In both instances the point of view is determined by the creation-relationship; hence the ideas with which John Wesley had been familiar since the days in his parents' home were once again set before him. The leading concepts of Scupoli-Castaniza and Scougal were also the love of God and perfection.

In several respects Taylor points in the direction of Roman Catholicism. Piety based upon the cultus, the mortification of the self, and individual sins receive an unusually strong emphasis. This

[5] Heber, *The Whole Works of Jeremy Taylor*, IV.212.

[6] Ibid. p. 177 ('calling'), pp. 115, 129, 187 ('promise'); note especially p. 129: 'Christ . . . made express promises that we should have sufficient for this life.'

[7] Ibid. p. 193: 'Love is the greatest thing that God can give us, for himself is love; and it is the greatest thing we can give to God, for it will also give ourselves, and carry with it all that is ours. The apostle calls it the band of perfection; it is the old, and it is the new, and it is the great commandment, and it is all the commandments; for it is the fulfilling of the law. . . . There can be but two things create love, perfection and usefulness: to which answer on our part 1. Admiration and 2. Desire; and both these are centred in love.' Page 256 is another significant reference and is a discussion of baptism.

however is the point where the final balance in the harmony of the book fails. If on the one hand there is found the profound primitive Christian truth that the conversion of every individual sinner to God redounds to the glorification of Jesus Christ,[8] it is surprising on the other hand to find an uncertainty about salvation which imprisons the individual in his own efforts.[9]

The practical ethics which are derived from all this must also be said to lack consistency. On the one hand, where the reference is to God, the utmost seriousness in deep repentance and complete sanctification is required—in one word, perfection.[1] But on the other hand the service of God is made to suit the capacities of each individual.[2] Contradictions are even found in the wording of the text: in principle purity of intention may be demanded,[3] yet it is stated—perhaps in opposition to the Roman Catholic view—that even the noblest intention is not able to sanctify an unlawful action.[4] Seen in relation to God the practical guidance given seems in more than one place to be an epitome of civil behaviour, even in the way it is expressed.[5] What is lacking is the sense of the tragic, the courage to be different or daring.

The second of the two devotional works, *The Rule and Exercises of Holy Dying,* is much the weaker. It is a continuation of the tradition of the Middle Ages on the *ars moriendi,* but in an unusually broad and general way it elaborates the everyday theme of the transitoriness of all earthly things. The understanding of death as the wages of sin is only incidental; it is much more the law of nature. The emphasis lies upon practical, almost commonplace counsels. The pages are full of such things as the individual's attitude during illness, starting with a general exhortation to patience, and moving on to the special summons to confession of sins; the visitation of the sick by the Christian minister and the warning against carrying ecclesiastical

---

[8] Ibid. p. 264: 'The conversion and repentance of every sinner is part of Christ's glorification.'   [9] Ibid. pp. 261-2, 382.
[1] Ibid. p. 179: 'Faith believes the revelation of God, hope expects his promises, and charity loves his excellencies and mercies. Faith gives us understanding of God, hope gives up all the passions and affections to heaven and heavenly things, and charity gives the will to the service of God. Faith is opposed to infidelity, hope to despair, charity to enmity and hostility, and these three sanctify the whole man, and make our duty to God and obedience to his commandments to be chosen, reasonable, and delightful, and therefore to be entire, persevering and universal'; cf. also p. 45.   [2] Ibid. p. 39.
[3] Ibid. pp. 25ff.   [4] Ibid. p. 30.
[5] Ibid. pp. 103-4: 'Abstain from wanton and dissolute laughter, petulant and uncomely jests, loud talking, jeering, and all such actions, which in civil account are called indecencies and incivilities.'

discipline too far at the immediate approach of death. In comparison the comfort which is derived from the resurrection of Jesus Christ receives only slight emphasis.

Taylor's books had a definite effect upon John Wesley, but this was due, not to their general viewpoint, but to the directions they contained for the practical exercises of religion. Various points in the arrangement and practice of prayer come back to him later, and this applies especially to the advice about wandering thoughts and the recommendation to utter short ejaculations to God rather than lengthy petitions.[6] There was also the challenge to examine every day his relationship to God, as well as the method for so doing, which was in line with the Puritan way of life. There were also exhortations to frequent communion, and the book provided a large number of printed prayers. It is probable that Varanese made use of it herself in this way and urged John Wesley to do likewise, but his scheme of general rules for governing his life [7] shows a completely independent working out of Taylor's directions. At the head there stands as the governing idea the beginning of every action by considering how God would have it done, and direct imitation of God is introduced without further consideration as the ethical standard. In the rules for the employment of time which follow, the resolution to begin and end every day with God has pride of place. Moderation in sleep, diligent work in one's calling, not surrendering to the passions, avoiding drunkards and busybodies, renouncing curiosity and gossip, nightly self-examination—these are the fundamentals of a judicious life which ensures the greatest possible spiritual gain. It is a rationalized mode of life which is conscious of being directed by the will of God, similar to that set forth by August Hermann Francke,[8] only less rigorous. When Wesley insists upon consecrating every free hour, or at least one in the day, to personal devotion, it is merely a logical expression of this. Particularly searching is the way in which he examines himself about wandering thoughts in prayer, thoughts which draw him away from God. He reproaches himself for idle talk, unprofitable reading and slothfulness, and proposes to himself an earnest and moderate course of conduct. He will shun light company, and above all guard against too free and familiar acquaintance with young women. He will avoid too highly-seasoned meals. He will resist the first beginnings of lust, not entering into an argument with

---

[6] Heber, *The Whole Works of Jeremy Taylor*, IV.226–7.   [7] *Journal*, 1.48.
[8] Cf. *Kurtzer und einfältiger Unterricht,* esp. chapter XII.37ff.

it, but immediately thinking of something else or going into company. In conclusion, frequent and fervent prayer is to help.

He also submits his intentions to an inexorable examination. In every act he is to think on its end. He may not leave off any duty because temptation assaults him in the doing of it; such cowardice is not to be tolerated. Every action must begin in the name of the Trinity and with prayer.

When this is compared with Jeremy Taylor the points common to both are unmistakable, but Wesley has cast them all into a permanent form and strictly systematized them. The result is something temperate and disciplined, with the emphasis no longer upon feeling or the striking of a pious attitude. The character of the whole is completely changed. The song of praise to God and the creation has become a command to sally forth, and John Wesley kept to the course. Thus on 1st December 1725 he reproaches himself with having broken the promises which he had made. He has been careless in fixing days for the mortification of the flesh, by which he evidently refers to fasting. He has been proud because of his special endowment for holiness, eager for praise, but also peevish and idle. He has slept intemperately, sinned in thought, and then been uselessly angry. He has not had a strict enough concern for truth, he has rashly censured others and despised them; he has not shown due respect to governors, and has desired to seem better than he really was. As a result he resolves to fast once a month on a Wednesday.[9] On 29th January 1726 he draws up a new scheme for his monthly review. Large Roman letters indicate the compartments into which his life was divided: the religious exercises, the different languages, dealings with his pupils, his travels, and the unexpected happenings of the day. Each question which he puts to himself is answered in characteristic fashion, not with a general 'Yes' or 'No', but quite concretely with a resolution. Thus to the question, 'Intemperate sleep?' he answers, (Get up) 'At five'. To the query, 'Unclean thoughts?' he replies, (Think on) 'God's omnipresence'. He asks, 'Irreverent behaviour at Church?' and answers, 'Never to laugh or talk idly there'. To the question, 'Pride?' there follows the resolve, 'Consider death, the Scriptures'.[1] This disciplining of the inner life, in its form reminiscent of Ignatius Loyola, although in its details essentially different from his theory of method, is sustained by a genuine prayer-life, which finds expression in the two ejaculations, 'Lord, help me!' and, 'The Lord have mercy on

[9] *Journal*, I.51.   [1] Ibid. p. 52.

thee!' which Wesley always transcribes in Greek—an indication of his familiarity with the liturgy and the New Testament.

What John Wesley was doing in these instances serves as his own personal introduction to the practice he later introduced into his societies. Every Saturday he reviewed his spiritual life, as the Puritan theology of conscience had prescribed a century earlier, and which was based on God's contemplation of His creative work on the seventh day.[2] As Nehemiah Curnock has finely said, it was a band-meeting with God and himself as the only members.[3] Yet for all its severity there is no sign of a limitation of his outlook or of a narrow-minded viewpoint. Wesley continues to read Juvenal as usual.[4] Only on the one point of his association with young women was he obviously over-scrupulous: he asks himself whether he has valued being with them during the Christmas holiday with the Kirkhams at Stanton more highly than fellowship with God in worship.[5] To be sure it may well be doubted whether he continued to visit the coffee-houses so frequently to pass the time in care-free conversation, or whether he gave as much time as previously to sport.[6] Yet it is unlikely that a formal break resulted.

How fundamentally his development was affected is evident from the first theological controversy in which we know him to have been engaged. It concerned the *Imitation of Christ* by Thomas à Kempis, that classic example of the monastic piety of the late Middle Ages, the 'most beautiful rose in the garden of the Brethren of the Common Life', as Karl Hase has described it. It is one of the books which have gradually won for themselves a place of honour throughout Christendom. Sarah Kirkham had introduced him to the work, which was translated into English as early as 1502, but which only received its proper recognition fifty years before John Wesley's ordination.[7] Once

---

[2] Cf. chapter 1, note 6.   [3] *Journal*, I.51.
[4] Ibid. p. 52.   [5] Ibid.
[6] His daily diary for 18th September 1725 shows that he visited a coffee-house and that he played tennis on 20th and 21st September (*Journal*, I.58–9). The great Dr Samuel Johnson (1709–84), who was at Oxford the same time as the Wesley brothers, said: 'John Wesley's conversation is good, but he is never at leisure. He is always obliged to go at a certain hour. This is very disagreeable to a man who loves to fold his legs and have out his talk, as I do' (quoted by T. F. Lockyer, *Paul: Luther: Wesley*, p. 238).
[7] Cf. Augustin de Backer, S.J., *Essai bibliographique sur le livre De Imitatione Christi* (Liège, 1864), 149ff; Jacobus Rosenthal, *De Imitatione Christi, Catalogus XXXVIII Monachii* (Bavariae, n.d.), pp. 103–15, completes and corrects him. There were six English editions between 1677 and 1726. Wesley used that of 1726 by George Stanhope. The earliest English translation was by William Atkynson and Princess Margarete (London, 1502; new edn, London, 1893). Peter Böhler said of the book: 'The art which we have to learn to believe in the Saviour is

again the subject of the book is the perfection of the Christian, but it differs from Scupoli, Scougal, and Taylor in that the goal of religion lies wholly beyond this world and in the mystical subjectivity of the individual. For the sake of eternal life man must despise the things of earth.[8] The world is viewed in a completely negative fashion. Once again love to God is reckoned as the highest human affection.[9] It is however at the same time one-sidedly conceived as longing for the heavenly Fatherland.[1] This spiritual enlistment requires the fiercest struggle with oneself. The renunciation of one's own will must be daily renewed, and as an exercise in this, unconditional obedience to a superior is to be given.[2] All spiritual aids, beginning with submitting oneself to the life of poverty and bitter suffering of Jesus [3] to the severe ecclesiastical discipline of Roman Catholicism, in particular to the sacramental mysticism to which the whole of Book IV is devoted, and to the highest exercises of monastic asceticism,[4] are pressed into the service of this one aim. The social aspect is completely absent, and this is due to serious defects in the great one-sided development of two themes in the Church of the first centuries and the Middle Ages—humility and renunciation.

John Wesley reacted against this whole point of view with all the impetuosity of a young man.[5] He could indeed grant that Thomas's personal piety was to a high degree genuine, he could also admit him to the ranks of the great, God-given men, but he knew that his own position was essentially different. His objection was that Thomas makes belief in God's creative will incredible. Wesley argues: Did God place men in the world only to keep them perpetually miserable? If so, then every endeavour after happiness in this life is at once sin. Why are there innocent little pleasures if men may not taste them? It is true that we are to take up the cross. But is that to mean that all joy and all satisfaction must disappear from life? How then can Solomon call the ways of religion the ways of pleasantness and the paths of peace? Has Adam left his sons this patrimony, that they are

much too easy for the Englishmen, so that they are not able to adjust themselves to it, though if it were a little more ingenious they would accommodate themselves to it. The best people in England, especially the scholars, talk only of imitating Jesus.' Peter Böhler's Diary, London, 18th February 1738 to the end of May, Manuscript in Archives of the United Brethren at Herrnhut, R.13.A.Nr.4.

[8] *De Imitatione Christi Opera omnia Thomae à Kempis*, ed. Michael Josephus Pohl, Vol. III.(1904).2.1, 3.48, 1.17, 3.41, 3.38.

[9] Ibid 1.1.; cf. 2.12, 3.5; also 3.21.   [1] Ibid. 1.23, 3.48–9, 3.6, 3.21, 4.4.

[2] Ibid. 3.13, 3.37, 2.11.   [3] Ibid. 1.1, 1.25, 2.1.

[4] Ibid. 2.9, 2.12, 3.6, 3.58, 4.3, 4.10, 4.14; also 3.10, 3.56.

[5] *Letters*, I.16, Oxford, 28th May 1725, to his mother.

destined to continual wretchedness? Undoubtedly heaven is a sufficient recompense for all the afflictions which men suffer here, but this
comfort by itself would convert few to Christianity, were not the yoke
of Jesus easy even in this world, and one which gives rest here.
Wesley rebels even more against the prohibition of all joyful feeling.
So his words, questions, and accusations tumble over each other,
although this is not the really significant thing.

It is the position from which Wesley makes his protest which is
noteworthy. In his words there speaks not simply the healthy feeling
of youth, with its acceptance of life and the world, nor Wesley's
concern for those writers of antiquity who taught him to delight in
life. Better to regard it as an echo of Jeremy Taylor's pantheistic
type of belief about the creation, in which all earthly things are seen
as proceeding from God and returning to Him. But none of this
touches the real point. Wesley is thinking biblically. His chief
references are to the Old Testament, the Psalms, and Wisdom literature.[6] But he also takes the word of Jesus about the easy yolk and
light burden (Matthew 11^{30}) so literally and seriously that it is used
to support his argument. On the other hand he repudiates the simple
view of Thomas, which refuses to recognize that to the Christian
anything is really suffering or misfortune. Instead, Thomas in God's
name would make him so insensitive to every affliction that he thanks
God for them. In Wesley's opinion this is completely contrary to
God's real purpose. God wills to humble men through affliction,
which must accordingly retain its sting, and may not be so radically
softened down that it loses its severe character. The example of Job
teaches how affliction is to be experienced and overcome—and of him
the Scriptures expressly say that in all this he did not sin.

In this early period therefore John Wesley's thinking included an
acceptance of the natural as the good creation of God. He is aware
that this coincides in the deepest sense with the Bible itself. This
creation-belief is so living, so elemental and unconditional, that he
even maintains it against the man from whom he learned it, or from
whom he could have done so—Jeremy Taylor. His mother substantially agreed with his criticism of Thomas à Kempis,[7] and even his
father, who treasured the book as an old friend and guide, conceded

[6] He refers particularly to Psalm 68^3: 'Let the righteous rejoice and be glad in
the Lord. Let them also be merry and joyful.'
[7] Her letter of 8th June 1725 to John, in Tyerman, *The Life and Times of John
Wesley*, I.34. She ends with the following opinion: 'I take Kempis to have been
an honest weak man, that had more zeal than knowledge.'

that it was one-sided, and granted that this was due as much to the peculiarity of the monastic life as to the obscurity of mystical theology. From that position the complete rejection of the world becomes understandable. Nevertheless, he wrote, mortification remains an unconditional Christian duty, for the world is a siren, whose enticements conceal dangers. Thomas at least merits admiration and emulation for the heroic efforts he made to attain humility.[8] What John Wesley is attacking is the standard of values, fostered and hallowed by a way of life which runs from Augustine, through Gregory the Great, and the whole phenomenon of monasticism and its influence upon the Middle Ages.[9] Taylor demands that a man should not desire any esteem, but be satisfied with being underrated or not noticed at all, that he should show no gratification at being praised, and should not flatter himself by thinking of himself as one of the misunderstood, if he is misjudged. He expects that a man should consider himself the worst among those present in any company, and thank God for every weakness, every deformity, every imperfection, since He helps in this way to resist pride. He goes even farther. He takes Christian humility so far that he requires repentance for the whole of his life, and leaves the believer uncertain whether God has forgiven him.

If repentance consists in all this it becomes impossible and intrinsically incredible. Wesley allows that there is an absolute humility measured by our relationship to God, but in relation to our fellow men it can only be a question of a comparative humility. An atheist is in any event worse than a believer. A man who endeavours to please God is undoubtedly to be preferred to one who defies Him. If absolute humility presupposes a corresponding knowledge of God, comparative humility presumes a corresponding knowledge of our

---

[8] His letter, Wroot, 14th July 1725, *Arminian Magazine*, I.(1778).30.

[9] Wesley expressed his criticism of Jeremy Taylor in two letters to his mother (*Letters*, I.19–20, Oxon, 18th June 1725; I.21–2, Oxon, 29th July 1725). The investigation of the concept of *humilitas* from the early Church through the Middle Ages and the Reformation to the end of the confessional period would show the essential motives in the history of piety. For the western world the leading characteristics already appear in Augustine, principally in *De civitate Dei*. *Humilitas* is there opposed to *superbia* and is quite central. Later it plays on important role in Gregory the Great, and even stronger monastic qualities than appear in Augustine are ascribed to it. Since Alfred the Great translated Gregory's *Cura pastoralis* into Anglo-Saxon the particularly powerful influence of this work in England must be recognized. From the English Middle Ages reference need only be made to John Wycliffe. His theology can be understood as a commentary upon the Augustine theme of *Christus humilis,* as I hope to show more particularly in studies on 'Luther in England'.

neighbour. In these forceful, decisive sentences a second feature, which characterized Wesley all through his life, appears alongside his creation-belief, namely, the unconditional claim of truth. This was part of his very nature, and for that reason it comes out inexorably in every dispute. It is not confined to this, however, but is seen very powerfully in logical argument, by which it is made more acute. Practical truth and theoretical truth go hand in hand, and the result is something of unconditional validity.[1] John Wesley unconsciously carried on the heritage of the rationalist empiricism, by which Puritanism had ruthlessly and conclusively analysed reality, especially the spiritual reality of man. So it was in this case. He has already said enough to demolish Taylor's treatment of humility, but he embarks upon a further line of argument, centring around a discussion of faith. According to the biblical declaration it is impossible to please God without faith. But faith means assent to a proposition upon rational grounds, and therefore faith is never the acceptance of what is contrary to reason. In this there is seen the unbroken continuation of that rationalistic tradition in English thought, which was not interrupted by the convulsion brought by the Reformation, while at the same time the new value put upon reason by the Enlightenment also comes out. Wesley pursues the matter farther. His objections against humility cannot be refuted from the point of view of reason, but since there is a close connexion between faith and reason, the attempt to impugn reason contradicts faith also. The important thing about these statements is not the actual argument, which can be easily shaken, but the strength of purpose behind the will which cannot rest until it has subjected everything to the authority of God. The Bible word that without faith it is impossible to please God is the position by which everything is in the end decided.

This is another instance in which biblicism is authenticated. On the question of the certainty of salvation, however,[2] Wesley attacks Taylor with his own weapons and vindicates the power of sacramental grace in the Lord's Supper. If Taylor is correct when he

---

[1] As indicative of this, cf. the following passage from *Letters*, I.21 : 'We have so invincible an attachment to truth already perceived, that it is impossible for us to disbelieve it. A distinct perception commands our assent, and the will is under a moral necessity of yielding to it. It is not, therefore, in every case a matter of choice whether we will believe ourselves worse than our neighbour or no; since we may distinctly perceive the truth of this proposition, He is worse than me; and then the judgement is not free.'

[2] *Letters*, I.20.

states that in the sacrament Jesus Christ takes up His abode in believers, that He becomes their own and they His, that the seed of the resurrection body is implanted in them, then a *sensibility* must arise in them from all these remarkable facts, and they must *experience* something of regeneration. Further this implies that they become certain of their final salvation. Moreover previous sins are not allowed to rise up against them, unless they commit them again. The sacramental grace is so strong that it confers complete forgiveness of sins, and such forgiveness extends to the Judgement. In this polemic it is not difficult to recognize characteristics of John Wesley's later theology, which is actuated by an 'experience fanaticism', the desire for a demonstrable experience of salvation.

It was chiefly the question of humility, lowliness, which had aroused Wesley and called forth his opposition against those who were the authorities for his religious life. Without the connexion being recognizable in each instance, his uneasiness extended to further problems. First and foremost there was the question of predestination. It is characteristic of the seriousness of John Wesley's conception of God that he met this problem so early and that he was preoccupied with it for at least three months.[3] Fundamentally everything revolved around the understanding of God's nature. Again he carried on a correspondence, longer than the previous one, with his mother on the subject. Her main contention was that all idle speculation about the secrets of God's saving methods should be avoided,[4] but she did not put a stop to the discussion. When John raised the subject he unerringly hit upon the main point, the tension

---

[3] On 23rd September 1725, five days after his ordination as deacon, he spoke about predestination with Mr Rigby, presumably an undergraduate (*Journal*, 1.59, Introductory [Diary]). [Translator's note: Dr Green (*The Young Mr Wesley*, p. 70) points out that John Rigby was Wesley's contemporary at Christ Church.]

[4] Letter from Wroot on 18th August 1725, in Tyerman, *The Life and Times of John Wesley*, I.39–40. 'I have wondered that men should be so vain as to amuse themselves with searching into the decrees of God which no human wit can fathom, and do not rather employ their time and powers in working out their salvation. Such studies tend more to confound than to inform the understanding, and young people had better let them alone. But since I find you have some scruples concerning our article, Of Predestination, I will tell you my thoughts of the matter. If they satisfy not, you may desire your father's direction, who is surely better qualified for a casuist than I.

'The doctrine of predestination, as maintained by the rigid Calvinists, is very shocking, and ought to be abhorred, because it directly charges the most high God with being the author of sin. I think you reason well and justly against it, for it is certainly inconsistent with the justice and goodness of God to lay any man under either a physical or moral necessity of committing sin, and then to punish him for doing it.

between God's justice and His mercy. The question which he formulated recalls, even to the form of words, the one which had arisen from his reading of the *Imitation of Christ*. Is it merciful to ordain a creature to everlasting misery? What he had said about God the Creator is now applied to God the Saviour. Does not God become the author of sin and injustice, Wesley further asked, and how is this consistent with His perfection? To be sure he also brings the freedom of man into the discussion. He feels that it contradicts human dignity to lie under a physical or moral necessity. But this is not his main point. In the end it was a question for him of respect for God's Word. There is something very impressive about the straightforward sentences in which he takes his stand directly on logical deductions: 'God is true; therefore what He says is true. He hath said this; therefore this is true.'[5] Perhaps he would even have accepted predestination if he had found a certain foundation for it in the Bible. So in this instance also a characteristic feature of his later thought shows itself: the rejection of the Calvinist doctrine of election, and the extension of salvation to all mankind—the point which led him to declare his emphatic agreement (which people today find too emphatic!) with the Dutchman Jakob Arminius against the Cal-

---

'I firmly believe that God, from eternity, has elected some to eternal life; but then I humbly conceive that this election is founded on His foreknowledge, according to Romans 8 [29-30]. Whom, in His eternal prescience, God saw would make a right use of their powers, and accept of offered mercy, He did predestinate and adopt for His children. And that they may be conformed to the image of His only Son, He calls them to Himself, through the preaching of the gospel, and internally, by His Holy Spirit; which call they obeying, repenting of their sins and believing in the Lord Jesus, He justifies them, absolves them from the guilt of all their sins, and acknowledges them as just and righteous persons, through the merits and mediation of Jesus Christ. And having thus justified, He receives them to glory – to heaven.

'This is the sum of what I believe concerning predestination, which I think is agreeable to the analogy of faith; since it does in no wise derogate from the glory of God's free grace, nor impair the liberty of man. Nor can it with more reason be supposed that the prescience of God is the cause that so many finally perish, than that one knowing the sun will rise tomorrow is the cause of its rising.'

In this letter of Mrs Wesley the main points in Wesley's case against double predestination appear with remarkable clarity. The first sentence could have been repeated exactly by John Wesley: the task of the Christian is not to pry into the secrets of God but to be engaged in the real concern of his own salvation. But in so far as the theoretical question comes up, it is in the first place to be decided from the conception of God, and the idea of God cannot be considered apart from God's activity on and for men. God is an active, creative God, whose deeds and creativity are determined by certain clear purposes. The historical acts of salvation in their inception and execution constitute the point of view from which predestination is rejected.

[5] *Letters*, I.23, Oxon, 29th July 1725, to his mother.

vinism of Dutch orthodoxy,[6] and which brought about his temporary break with George Whitefield. His mother, like all theorists about predestination, sought for a verbal compromise: God has elected certain people to salvation, but this choice rests upon His omniscience. He chose those whose subsequent acceptance He foresaw. Although in this way she was still close to Augustine, her son wanted to go substantially farther in the co-operation of God and man; God has chosen a definite number from eternity, yet it is in the power of every man to belong to that number. Since, however, this conception could not be made to conform with Article 17 of the Church of England on predestination, he saw no other alternative than to allow exceptions: he thinks that those who do not belong to the number of the elected can also be saved.[7] In the end God is not bound by His own decree.

Eighteen months later he was occupied with the question of original sin,[8] although apparently only cursorily. He stated it first of all as a personal existential question in relation to the matter of his own imperfection, which, in the style of Paul, he looked upon as a thorn in his flesh, but he went on to relate it to the conception of God. The answer he gave was to the effect that God must have been concerned with him in the beginning of sin in order at least to allow him to attain a certain degree of virtue: God alone had the power to bring so much good out of evil. He ended in wondering and thankful praise for the omnipotence which he had come to know working providentially in his own life.

This then is the picture of John Wesley at the age of twenty-two. He is shown as an unusually serious and decided young man of independent judgement, who in his thinking penetrates to the ultimate and the highest in the rational understanding of God, and yet at the same time imposes upon himself the most rigorous demands, and pursues them further by scrupulous self-examination. Has the happy undergraduate become an austere, prematurely developed,

[6] John Wesley himself qualified this and dissociated himself from polemics (*Arminian Magazine*, I.(1778). VII–VIII, esp.VIII): '. . . we have no reason to believe that there is so general a reception of those Decrees (*sc.* absolute predestination) in Protestant countries. Whatsoever was the case in times past, very few now receive them even in Holland. And in Geneva they are universally rejected with the utmost horror. The case is nearly the same in England. Not one in ten, not one in an hundred, if we look through the nation, have the least esteem for Absolute Predestination: so that nine in ten, yea, ninety nine in an hundred, will take no offence at an open, avowed opposition to it.'
[7] *Letters*, I.23.
[8] Ibid. pp. 41–2, Lincoln College, 19th March 1727, to his mother.

world-denying Pharisee?[9] In no sense is this true. The change to a stricter way of life was certainly decisive, and yet at the same time a natural development of his energies. An important indication of this is the friendly intercourse and the large correspondence which he still kept up. He does not retire into solitude or become a monk.

On 19th September 1725 John Wesley was ordained deacon by John Potter, the Bishop of Oxford.[1] Shortly before, his father had been given the living of the village of Wroot as an addition to that of Epworth, and he had gone to live there. The rural calm, the beautiful garden, the large number of domestic animals, continued to form an idyllic atmosphere, which his eldest son Samuel with affection described in some happy verses.[2] As far as money went the rectory was indeed poor, but at least the scarcity of bread, which had often distressed Susanna Wesley, came to an end. This then was the world into which John Wesley now entered, with its peaceful seclusion and its rich personal associations. After his ordination he went there during the summer months from April to September 1726 to assist his ailing father in his pastoral duties and also with his work on Job. On two further occasions he did this for periods of a year, from August 1727 to September 1728 and from October 1728 to the end of November 1729, and in this way made himself thoroughly familiar with the life of a country parson. He was entirely at liberty to spend his time between work and recreation. In his free hours he worked in the garden. He took a delight in the flowers and looked after them for his sisters;[3] he went swimming in the nearby river; he walked into the neighbouring villages, and in particular often visited Joseph Hoole, the clergyman at Haxey, who was his mother's special friend. He read Spenser's *Fairie Queene*, partly to his sisters and partly on his own; he studied *The Spectator*, the leading weekly newspaper, and he took a special interest in the child of his young married sister Anne Lambert (Nancy). In this way the days passed easily and equably, although he never neglected his times of strict self-examination.

---

[9] It seems to me that Curnock (in *Journal*, I.35) somewhat exaggerates the negative aspect of Wesley's self-examination.
[1] *Journal*, I.59.
[2] Printed in Eliza Clarke, *Susanna Wesley*, 150–1.
[3] Cf. Curnock, 'John Wesley's Early Life in the Light of Unpublished Diaries', *Journal*, I.21–2.

FIVE

The Student Circle at Oxford

THE YEAR 1725 had so decisive a meaning for John Wesley that it can be readily understood why some modern biographers should regard it as the time of his real 'conversion'.[1] In many respects the basic course of his life was then determined. He was never to give up the practice of strict self-examination, and he had started on the path of 'holiness'.

His material circumstances were suddenly changed for the better when on 17th March 1726 he was elected to a fellowship at Lincoln College, a position which he might hold for the rest of his life. He wrote a letter of thanks to his brother Samuel, in which he said that he attributed his success chiefly to him and his interest.[2] It was not only himself but his father also who rejoiced at what had happened. He addressed his son jocularly as 'Dear Mr Fellow Elect of Lincoln'! Life might have brought him many disappointments and denied him the final realization of his hopes, yet the main thing was, his son was Fellow of Lincoln! So he wrote in a letter which was full both of pride and self-pity.[3] The period of debts was now at an end, and John could make do for himself and also help his family for the rest of his life. At first there was not overmuch to do in the University city. Many of his colleagues gave themselves up to a comfortable life, and Wesley obtained permission to assist his father in his work at Wroot and Epworth. After a pleasant summer at his country home he returned to Oxford, and in November 1726 became a tutor at Lincoln College, his duties being to give instruction in Greek. At the same time he was preparing for his master's degree, which he obtained on 14th February 1727. The subjects on which he gave his three statutory lectures in Latin are significant: one in natural philosophy was on the soul of animals, one in philosophy was about Julius Caesar,

---

[1] Principally Augustin Leger, *La Jeunesse de Wesley*, p. 366; Maximin Piette, *John Wesley in the Evolution of Protestantism*, pp. 244, 305ff.
[2] *Letters*, I.27, 21st March 1726, to his brother Samuel.
[3] Tyerman, *The Life and Times of Samuel Wesley* (1866), p. 399; Telford, *The Life of John Wesley* (London, 1929), p. 43.

and the third, a theological one, was on the love of God.[4] He felt very much at home in his college; it was distinguished from others by its friendly atmosphere.[5] He was concerned about suitable lodgings and good companions for his younger brother Charles, who was at the time leaving Samuel's care at Westminster School and going to the University.[6] On Sundays he frequently rode out to the surrounding villages to preach, often in two churches, one after the other.[7] During the week he gave himself to his studies with admirable diligence. In his plan of work for the year 1727, Monday and Tuesday are given to Greek and Roman classics, Wednesday to logic and ethics, Thursday to Hebrew and Arabic, Friday to metaphysics and natural philosophy, Saturday to rhetoric and poetry, including his own efforts, and Sunday to theology.[8] Of course these particular subjects did not take up the whole day; it was probably the ordeal of the master's examination which determined the selection and arrangement, so that afterwards Wesley was able to let them drop. Part of the time he worked alone, at other times with a number of students. Like a polyhistor he devoted himself to theology, which unquestionably occupied pride of place, and to mathematical, medical, physical, zoological and historical books of the day.[9] He read every book twice on principle, at first cursorily, then with pen in hand in order to make extracts. He learned French and made himself familiar with the literature of France.

His work with his father at Wroot and Epworth, for all their mutual affection, had its darker side. His father was irritable, asserting his authority in the family, and most of all in parish duties. Hetty, the young married daughter, had aroused his displeasure and nobody dared stand up for her against him. Knowing this John preached on the unconditional duty of love, which knows no limits. He had previously discussed with his mother the text of his sermon, even the individual phrases. His father took it in bad part, and even appealed to a canon of the Anglican Church which forbade a doctrine that had previously been preached to be attacked in the same or an adjoining church. He came near to handling the incident at an official level. This shows more clearly than anything the lengths to which he could take his high-church point of view. John was com-

[4] *Letters*, I.39, note 1.
[5] Ibid. p. 30, Lincoln College, 4th April 1726, to his brother Samuel.
[6] Ibid. p. 33, 5th December 1726, to the same.   [7] *Journal*, I.60–1.
[8] Telford, *The Life of John Wesley*, p. 49.
[9] A list is in the *Journal* (I.65–6).

pletely ignorant of all this until his brother Charles told him, where-upon he went to his father and reconciliation followed. John put his seal to this by working several days running solely for his father.[1]

Further problems presented themselves to him as a result of his pastoral activity, and from his preaching in particular. They arose quite naturally. One of his sermons on the rule of God and His righteousness from Matthew 6[33], possibly the first he preached after his ordination, had been criticized by his brother Samuel.[2] In his reply John tried to say more clearly what he had meant. In the first point, he used the words of 2 Kings 17[41], 'These nations feared the Lord and served their graven images', to attack a divided service of God, thus heightening the moral implication of the words. The biblical reference is to the Samaritans in contrast with the Jews, but Wesley speaks of the Jews, whose standard must be transcended by Christians. At the Old Testament stage God did not expect that His own should show love towards the wicked. But are not the people of the new covenant called to tasks not laid on those of old? Is not revenge, which in the case of the others was occasionally overlooked, entirely forbidden to them? In such a way, Wesley thinks, the gospel is superior to the law. Further he does not allow the force of the unconditional command of love to be weakened even by reference to Jesus, who certainly showed sharp anger against His opposers. In such doubtful cases Wesley prefers to follow the precepts of the Lord rather than His example, since the Master was superior to His own directions, while His disciples are subject to them. This carefully considered interpretation of an organic relationship between Jesus and believers, which takes into account the difference between Him and His followers, is far better than an unthinking, mechanical view which imagines that a direct imitation of Christ is possible, and which inevitably leads to a legalistic attitude.

[1] *Letters*, I.35–9, Lincoln College, 6th December 1726, to his brother Samuel.
[2] Ibid. I.32, Lincoln College, 5th December 1726, to his brother Samuel. The conjecture that this refers to his first sermon after ordination preached on 26th September 1725 in the Church of South Lye (Leigh) cannot be established with certainty. I regard the allusion to 2 Kings 17[41] at the beginning of the sermon as decisive. It appears in *Standard Sermons* (ed. Sugden [1921],I.496ff) in a later form. Should the assumption be correct it would be a remarkable repetition of the fact that Philipp Jakob Spener adduced the beginning of his definite activity for Pietism to a sermon on the subject of the greater righteousness of Matthew 5[20], preached on the 6th Sunday after Trinity, 1669 (Spener, *Wahrhaftige Erzehlung dessen, was wegen des sog. Pietismi in Deutschland vor einiger Zeit vorgegangen* [1697], pp. 42–3. The sermon itself appears in *Erste geistliche Schiften* [1690], pp. 109–36). On Wesley's sermon, cf. Curnock, *Journal*, I.59–60. He leaves it an open question whether we still possess it.

While it was ordination which aroused John Wesley into action, another factor can be discerned which links him with Luther. This is the idea of calling, which influenced the reformer so characteristically when he was engaged on his doctorate.[3] In Wesley's case this remained with him throughout the whole of his life: his type of religion was determined in the strongest possible way by the events which befell him and by the tasks with which he was faced. The very course of his life was in itself a way to God. In this he was a man of the modern world. He was aroused and urged by practical considerations, not theory; by tasks rather than problems; by human beings, not books.[4] This was shown immediately by a second characteristic occurrence. At the very moment when theological questions became important for him he knew that he was called to pastoral and missionary work.[5]

In the summer of 1725 he put a question to his young associate, John Griffith, which recalled Jesus' conversation with Peter.[6] He wanted to know if Griffith really was his friend, and if so, why he would not do everything in his power out of affection for him. It was an unusually solemn moment, for they were going to the funeral of a young woman whom they had both known well. Griffith vigorously repudiated this doubt cast on his friendship with Wesley. The latter then came directly to the point. He begged Griffith to give him the pleasure of making him a whole Christian. The young man could do Wesley no greater kindness, as both would be fully convinced when they came to follow the young woman. At this Griffith became very serious and kept his grave disposition in the days which followed. Eighteen months later he died suddenly in his parents' home. In accordance with his wish John Wesley preached at his funeral service in the church of his home-village. The text was 2 Samuel 12[23] : 'Now he is dead, wherefore should I fast? can I bring him back again? I shall go to him, but he shall not return to me.' Wesley began without any sign of personal sentiment. Almost harshly he emphasized

---

[3] Cf. Hermann Steinlein, *Luthers Doktorat*, pp. 25ff.

[4] Cf. his own statement *Letters*, I.39–40: I am perfectly come over to your opinion that there are many truths it is not worth while to know. Curiosity, indeed, might be a sufficient plea for our laying out some time upon them, if we had half a dozen centuries of life to come; but methinks it is a great ill-husbandry to spend a considerable part of the small pittance now allowed us in what makes us neither a quick nor a sure return.

[5] Unfortunately Johannes Schempp in his comprehensive investigation *Seelsorge und Seelenführung bei John Wesley* 1949 has not brought out this basic principle. He has in general given too little attention to the actual pastoral care.

[6] John 21[15ff].

the uselessness of mourning. He repressed all personal feeling in concise, unpretentious sentences which were nevertheless full of meaning, but then he went on to bring consolation, based on Thessalonians 4[13, 14, 18]: 'I would not have you to be ignorant, brethren, concerning them which are asleep, that ye sorrow not, even as others which have no hope. For if we believe that Jesus died and rose again, even so them also which sleep in Jesus will God bring with him. . . . Wherefore comfort one another with these words.' He brought it to a close with the great words from 1 Corinthians 15[55]: 'O death, where is thy sting? O grave, where is thy victory?' Wesley was at the same time preaching the sermon to himself, for he knew only too well that his own condition did not correspond to what he had said.[7]

John Griffith came from the vicarage in Broadway, Worcestershire, and this was one of three which John Wesley often frequented during his Oxford years, 1725–9. The other two were Buckland and Stanton. Stanton was the family-home of a clergyman, Lionel Kirkham, while the Tookers lived at Buckland. Wesley liked staying at Stanton best of all, for he was particularly friendly with Sarah, the young woman who had introduced him to Thomas à Kempis and Jeremy Taylor. He frequently preached there. The rector of Buckland, Tretheway Tooker, must have been a very original character, full of native wit and entertaining to all visitors.[8] The Granville family also lived there, the two daughters Mary and Anne being friends of Miss Kirkham. Mary was one of the most eminent women of the day. Highly accomplished and devoted to music and painting, she moved in the highest circles in society and was eventually at Court as the friend of George III and Charlotte. With equal self-possession she knew how to be at home in a plain country parsonage. When she was nineteen years old, Händel came to her parents' house and kept up a life-long connexion with her.[9] Later Edmund Burke paid her an extravagant compliment when he described her as the highest bred and most fashionable woman in the

[7] Works (1860), VII.63–8, on 2 Samuel 12 [23]. The decisive pastoral correspondence of the summer, 1725: Letters, I.40, to his mother, Lincoln College, 25th January 1727; ibid. p. 43, to his mother, Lincoln College, 19th March 1737. Curnock, Introductory, in Journal, I.62, proves that the designation of Epworth as the place where the sermon of 15th February 1727 was preached, as stated in the Works, is incorrect. It was given at Broadway, the residence of Griffith's parents. Thus it becomes understandable why Wesley should send his mother a copy of the text.
[8] Mrs Delany's 'Account of Parson Tooker' in Life and Correspondence of Mrs Delany, I.13–14; Journal, VIII.324.
[9] Edward Dent, Händel in England (Hallische Universitätsreden 68), 5–6.

world.[1] Her first marriage was with the land-owner Charles Pendarves, who was years older than herself, but she was early left a widow. Shortly after this she came to know Wesley, who was three years younger. She heard him preach at Stanton and asked for a written copy of the sermon. From this a correspondence developed, in which, as in the case of Sarah Kirkham, nicknames were used. John Wesley was again 'Cyrus', Charles Wesley 'Araspes', Sarah Kirkham 'Varanese', Mary Pendarves 'Aspasia', her sister Anne Granville 'Selima', while it was probably in connexion with this that the name 'Robin' was associated with John Griffith.[2] Various sermons which John Wesley preached in the years 1726 and 1727 on such subjects as Holy Communion, Election and Reprobation, led to the first serious conversations between him and Mary Pendarves. In 1743 she married a clergyman, Dr Henry Delany.

It was among this group of friends, made up of young men and women, that John Wesley's gifts for conversation and dealing with people were awakened and developed. It happened quite naturally and imperceptibly. As in German Pietism the female element was of considerable significance and played almost a leading part.

The concern for the pastoral care of souls, which was evident in the disturbing experience with John Griffith, determined the future course of John Wesley's life in a way that was of great consequence. It is true that an inclination for solitude also came over him, for he could see in this the necessary preliminary to equipping himself for a true Christian life and for implanting in his mind those habits which go along with it. But it was only to be for a limited period.[3] In reality his nature was drawing him into society, in which he wanted to grow, to mature, to make an impression and cut a figure, and indeed to rule. On 21st October 1729 an urgent letter from John Morley, Rector of Lincoln College, summoned him immediately to Oxford. All the junior fellows were to undertake the instruction and supervision of undergraduates in order at last to promote the reform of morals in the university. So on 22nd November he returned to the academic world and threw himself zealously into his studies and the oversight of undergraduates. He discovered that three students from different colleges met in a group on four evenings of the week to read ancient authors and the New Testament in the original language—a procedure completely in accord with the Anglican ideal of culture—

[1] See *Letters*, I.166. [2] Cf. Curnock, *Journal*, I.59.
[3] *Letters*, I.42, 19th March 1727, to his mother.

while on Sunday evening they discussed religious books. Its members were Robert Kirkham (the brother of Sarah), William Morgan and Charles Wesley. Perhaps it was the latter who had been the prime mover in the project. The procedure of the group would not yet have become too stereotyped nor its life very highly organized. It was simply a free kind of fellowship for study, but behind it there was a serious ecclesiastical and academic responsibility.[4] This rules out any resemblance to the highly-organized society, built up by Count Zinzendorf among the Wittenberg students, who, as 'slaves of virtue' and 'confessors of Christ', bound themselves from the first to work for Jesus Christ.[5]

John Wesley soon became the effective leader. He was so dominant a character that a student who joined the group said that were he to describe one of the two Wesleys he would describe both, for Charles was a complete copy of John.[6] During the next year several men of decided character were added to their number: of these John Gambold was outstanding. Other members were James Hervey, Benjamin Ingham, William Morgan, John Clayton, John Whitelamb, who later become the incumbent of Wroot, and Westley Hall, afterwards brother-in-law to the Wesleys. In the course of the year seventeen people belonged to the meeting, and then a steady if moderate increase took place naturally. Some of the young undergraduates whom John, and soon Charles also, supervised joined of their own accord. John Wesley felt himself personally responsible before God for each of them; he watched over the way they spent their days, their attendance at worship and their reading. When on one occasion he was failing to make any progress with one of the students, he applied directly to William Law, the religious writer, because his books were read by all the group together, and were used by each individual in his private devotions.[7] A scheme on which the young people based the examination of themselves has

[4] On this, cf. Tyerman, *The Oxford Methodists;* David Brook in Townsend, Workman and Eayrs, *A New History of Methodism*, pp. 135–58; Curnock in *Journal*, I.6ff. [Translator's note: V. H. H. Green, *The Young Mr Wesley*, pp. 145ff]. John Wesley himself related the history of the circle in the letter to the father of his friend, Richard Morgan, 18th October 1732, *Letters*, I.123ff. John Gambold's account is in Tyerman, *The Oxford Methodists*, pp. 175ff., and in John Wesley's *Journal*, VIII.265–8. I have not been able to find in the sources the nickname 'Bible-Moths' which one often meets in secondary accounts: probably it is taken from one of the polemical writings which are only available in England.
[5] Cf. Heinz Renkewitz, *Zinzendorf* (2nd edn), pp. 13ff.
[6] Gambold, in *Journal*, VIII.265.
[7] *Letters*, I.161ff, Lincoln College, 26th June 1734.

been preserved, and is an eloquent witness to the thoroughness with which they conducted their lives.[8] On Sunday the main topic in their conversations and exercises was the love of God and simplicity. The means by which they sought to attain their goal were prayer and meditation. They asked themselves: 'Have I been *simple* in everything, i.e. looked upon God, my Good, my Pattern, my One Desire, my Disposer, Parent of Good; acted wholly for Him; bounded my Views with the present action or hour? . . . Has this simple view been distinct and uninterrupted? . . . Have I done any thing without a previous perception of its being the Will of God? . . . Have I prayed with fervor? At going in and out of Church? In the Church? Morning and evening in private? . . . Have I in private prayer frequently stopt short and observed what fervor? Have I repeated it over and over, till I adverted to every word? Have I at the beginning of every prayer or paragraph owned I cannot pray? . . . Have I duly used Ejaculations? i.e. Have I every hour prayed for Humility, Faith, Hope, Love, and the particular Virtue of the day? Considered with *whom* I was the last hour, *what* I did, and *how*? . . . Considered the next hour in the same respects, offered up all I do to my Redeemer, begged his assistance in every particular, and commended my soul to his keeping? . . . Have I used a Collect at nine, twelve, and three? . . . Have I duly meditated? . . . From six, etc., to prayers? From four to five, (What was particular in the Providence of this day?) How ought the Virtue of the day to have been exerted upon it? How did it fall short? (Here faults.) On Sunday from six to seven, with Kempis? From three to four on Redemption, on God's Attributes? Wednesday and Friday from twelve to one on the Passion?'

Monday was given over to the love of man. Each asked himself: 'Have I embraced every probable opportunity of doing good, and preventing, removing, or lessening evil? Have I pursued it with my might? Have I thought any thing too dear to part with, to serve my neighbour? Have I spent an hour at least every day in speaking to some one or other? . . . Have I, before I spoke to any, learned as far as I could, his temper, way of thinking, past life, and peculiar hinderances, internal and external? . . . Have I, in speaking to a stranger, explained what Religion is not, (not negative, not external) and what it is, (a recovery of the image of God) . . . ? . . . Have I persuaded

---

[8] 'A Scheme of Self-Examination used by the first Methodists in Oxford', *Arminian Magazine*, IV.(1781).319–22.

all I could to attend public Prayers, Sermons and Sacraments? And in general, to obey the laws of the Church Catholic, the Church of *England*, the State, the University, and their respective Colleges? . . . Have I, when any one asked Advice, directed and exhorted him with all my power? Have I rejoiced with and for my neighbour in Virtue or Pleasure? Grieved with him in pain, for him in sin? Have I received his infirmities with pity, not anger? . . . Have I duly used intercession? 1. Before, 2. after speaking to any? 3. For my Friends on Sunday? 4. For my Pupils on Monday? 5. For those who have particularly desired it, on Wednesday and Friday? 6. For the Family in which I am, every day?'

This is an example of the way in which the Puritan practices of self-control and self-criticism have been intensified and formulated into an extraordinarily exacting oversight of the individual's affairs. John Wesley and his associates were here building on the great Anglo-Saxon tradition of a religion of conscience.[9]

It was a young Irishman, William Morgan from Dublin, who first stimulated them to reach out beyond the confines of the University. In the summer of 1730, partly out of curiosity and partly from compassion, he had paid a visit to the Oxford prison and spoken with a man who had murdered his wife. He had been surprised at the way in which criminals and debtors were herded together, a feature of the penal system of the time which offends against every healthy instinct and which provoked the attack of contemporaries. Deeply moved by his experience he returned home and would not rest until on 24th August John and Charles Wesley went with him. This became a regular custom once or twice a week. Again prompted by Morgan, visits were soon made to the sick as well as the prisoners, and later a few poor families were assisted. At his wish John Wesley obtained permission from the bishop to preach once a month to the prisoners, and since they came to an understanding with the parish clergy about visits to the sick, everything was done properly and in order. The practice itself was no innovation in the England of the time, since the care of prisoners and the sick was part of the activities of those groups within the Church, the so-called 'Religious Societies', which had spread from London since the year 1678–9. Even the further step, the founding of a school, came well within their scope. John Wesley installed a woman teacher, and saw to it that the girls

[9] On this, cf. Levin L. Schücking, *Die Familie im Puritanismus*, pp. 1ff, and my essay on the Puritan theology of conscience in *ARG*. XLII.198–220, XLIII.70–87.

99

learned to knit and spin. Nevertheless all this aroused violent opposition against the young men. At first they were ridiculed, but soon
actual hostility showed itself. Their strict churchmanship and regular
attendance at Communion every Sunday would have been more
easily excused than this social activity, and the reason is not difficult
to find. It is likely that the leading groups among the student-body
were justifiably afraid that this revival from within the Church
would soon encroach upon the rights of their autonomous associations within the University. Possibly they saw in the activities of the
club the beginnings of a general attack, planned by the Religious
Societies. A whole range of nicknames was given to the students
associated with Wesley. They were called the Sacramentarians, the
Holy Club, but most frequently the Godly Club, a title which is
reminiscent of the Puritan emphasis upon 'godliness'; and finally the
Reforming Club, which recalls one of the Religious Societies. They
were also condemned as enthusiasts and 'supererogation men'. John
Wesley acted with deliberation. When they had embarked upon
social activities he sought his father's advice and received a *'Valde
probo'* (I strongly approve) in reply.[1] Samuel Wesley, who in his
youth had also undertaken social work, saw in the activity of the
young people a struggle against the world and the devil, and recommended them to use equal energy to combat the flesh. They were on
the right path. He, 'a warrior now on the retired list', proud of his
three doughty champions, would have liked to adopt William Morgan
as his own son. In praising their work in this way he was applying to
it the strongest expressions which Christian language provides.[2] He
did so once again when he used Paul's joyful exclamation from 2
Corinthians 7[4], which he wrote out in the original Greek.[3] It was also
he who said it was necessary to obtain the bishop's consent. At the
same time he warned them against becoming spiritually proud. John
Wesley then sought confirmation about the regularity of their efforts
from another clergyman, probably Joseph Hoole, his family's friend,
at Haxey. He also laid before his companions a series of questions in

[1] Samuel Wesley (father) to John, 28th September 1730, from the extract in
Letters, I.125ff.
[2] The threefold powers which tempt men, the combination of which is found in
the west from the time of Augustine, have not yet been investigated, and the same
applies to their antecedents in the Greek of the early Church, but see the preliminary treatment by Johannes Meyer, *Historischer Kommentar zu Luthers
Kleinem Katechismus*, pp. 100ff. Fritz Blanke, *Der verborgene Gott bei Luther*,
p. 22, note 22, announced his intention of investigating the development of the
conception.
[3] *Letters*, I.27.

which he quite openly set the activity of the group under the early Christian conception of 'doing good'[4] according to the word and example of Jesus. The works of mercy, concerning which Jesus would ask in the day of judgement, were given a prominent position; Matthew 25[35-40] was referred to in detail. Behind it all is evidence of that concern which accompanied Wesley throughout his life and which so impressed itself upon the Methodist revival: the desire 'to save souls from death'. In Wesley's opinion this entailed a rigorous discipline both in a man's spiritual life and in his vocation, loyalty to the Church and its regulations as well as application to study. It required inner discipline and outward zeal. He held that individual work, that which is done in a man's own sphere, is in no way opposed to social action. Both are required and each enhances the other. It is a well-thought-out programme which is outlined in these questions to the students. It only requires application on a large scale, and the Methodist movement as a whole can be seen. Even the essential points in Methodism's theological basis are present: a characteristic combination of a strong desire for sanctification with a rejoicing in salvation, and of holiness with happiness. The view that happiness follows inevitably from doing good runs right through the whole position.[5]

A movement of considerable proportions developed. The hostility became increasingly violent, but at the same time support for the charitable work increased through voluntary gifts. The fortunes of the enterprise varied. In the summer of 1731 the group came near to extinction because its leading members left Oxford to take up duties, often as curates, elsewhere. Then it once again went forward. In the year 1732 John Clayton, the son of a Manchester bookseller, joined, and he was instrumental in their deciding to observe the regulations of the Church on fasting which nobody heeded at the time. It was

---

[4] 'To do good', 'doing good', are the actual words. In addition to this reference it is found in *Lettters*, I.183, 30th September 1735, to John Robson; *Journal*, VIII.285, John Burton to John Wesley, 8th September 1735; *Letters*, I.191, John Wesley to John Burton, 10th October 1735.

[5] *Letters*, I.128–9. The formula 'holiness is happiness' belongs to the fundamental data of Wesley's theological thinking and constitutes the root of his later 'perfectionism'. So far as I know this fact has not been recognized hitherto in Wesley research, although the nearest approach to it is in the great work of C. N. Impeta, *De Leer der Heiligung en Volmaking bij Wesley en Fletcher*, esp. pp. 60, 226–7. The formula is anticipated not only by Laud's favourite expression, 'the beauty of holiness', but by the whole of Puritanism and goes back eventually to Augustine. I hope to demonstrate this sometime in a separate study; cf. the previous reference in my article, *'Eigenart und Bedeutung puritanischer Eschatologie'*, *Theologia Viatorum*, IV.(1952), *Beiträge zur Eschatologie*, pp. 261–2.

probably at about this period that the name 'Methodists' became current, and this is the one which alone has remained. It was by no means a new title. At the time of the Great Rebellion under Cromwell it was being used as a sect-name, although it does not indicate to whom the term was applied, and leads rather to the conjecture why anyone should have earned such a term of reproach. Presumably it referred to a particularly strict, puritanical conception of worship, type of preaching, or way of living; later it was applied to a particular interpretation of justification before God.[6] It was also used of a school of doctors who practised a certain method of healing.[7] Outside England it was known in France as early as 1634, although once again its exact meaning is not apparent.[8] It appears in Germany in 1691 in connexion with orthodox polemic against the Pietists, and was used by Philipp Ludwig Hanneken, a professor at Giessen.[9] Thus before its application to the group of Oxford students it was a familiar title; as so often in the history of the Church, a name of opprobrium was to become a title of respect.

Besides Clayton, Thomas Broughton, a later secretary of the Society for Promoting Christian Knowledge, and Benjamin Ingham joined the group in the year 1731. Clayton had the effect of strengthening the tendency to observe the practices of the early Church, as might be expected from one who had been influenced by the Nonjurors in Manchester.[1] These men, while holding to the establishment of the Church, considered that William of Orange's occupancy of the throne was invalid, and at the same time they clung tenaciously to the traditions of the early Church. There were several schools of thought among them. One confined itself to a formal protest, and

---

[6] Thomas Jackson, *The Life of the Rev. Charles Wesley, M.A.,* I.17–18.

[7] J. Telford, *The Life of John Wesley,* p. 59.

[8] Jean Daillé, *La foy fondée sur les Saintes Ecritures contre les nouveaux Methodistes* (Charenton, 1634).

[9] Hanneken to the *Gymnasialrektor Hoschius* in Erfurt, 18th February 1691, Ms.Cod, *Supellex epistolica,* fol. XC.260–1, in the City Library, Hamburg: 'The very new Professor of Theology in this place, D. Majus, is also a Collegiatus of Spener and devoted to Quakerish Methodisterey.' This would appear to suggest that the word 'Methodisterey' was originally aimed at the Quakers. The connexion between Pietism and Quakerism has been familiar since the *Historia Quakeriana* by the Dutchman, Gerhard Croese (3 vols, Amsterdam, 1696); the statement of Hanneken quoted above is probably the oldest (written) evidence for this so far known. To be sure, the word 'Methodisterey' could be taken to mean merely 'theory of method'. Spener definitely rejected any connexion with Quakerism. *Praefatio zu Joh.Henrici Vindiciae exegeticae dicti Luc.,* 18.8.1696, *Wahrhaftige Erzehlung dessen, was wegen des sog. Pietismi in Deutschland von einiger Zeit vorgegangen* (1697), *Consilia theologica latina,* III.(1709).770ff (referring to the year 1698); cf. also Paul Grünberg, *Philipp Jakob Spener,* I.(1893).277, note 1.

[1] Cf. J. S. Simon, *John Wesley and the Religious Societies,* pp. 99ff.

merely omitted the name of the king in the prayers from the Prayer Book. A second stricter group had founded its own Church and took as its basis an earlier, in part rejected, version of the Prayer Book, which originated in the reign of Edward VI. A third group sprang from the second. Its leader, Dr Thomas Deacon, acted as bishop in Manchester, although doubts were cast upon his consecration. He built up his ecclesiastical and liturgical practice entirely upon the 'Apostolic Constitutions', a Church Order of the third century. Since he considered it genuine it served as his irrevocable standard, but the other Non-jurors accused him of having a passion for innovations. It was from him that John Clayton inherited his principles. Moreover Clayton was attracted by Romanic mysticism, and said that it meant a great deal to him that he was beginning to understand what was meant by the union of souls, so much talked of by Malebranche and Antoinette Bourignon.[2] He evidently made such a good impression from the beginning that he became the deputy-leader of the student group and brought to it further members from Brasenose, where he was a tutor. Two years later the little band once again sunk to four members, with apparently three visitors.[3] In 1733 there had been something of a palace revolution. Some of the undergraduates had appealed to John Locke's philosophical uprooting of authority.[4] The strictly regulated day, which for John Wesley and a few, though not all others, began at five in the morning, contrasted sharply with the way in which the majority idled away the time. On the five evenings in the week the 'Methodists' spent two hours together in prayer with the Greek New Testament and devotional books, while others sported and drank. They saved every penny for their poor fund, while others squandered their money on the amusements of the day. John and Charles Wesley walked the whole way to Epworth in order to save the cost of the journey. Every day one of them went to visit the prison.

All these characteristics were strengthened and intensified, and the self-assurance of the young men grew. They resolutely declined to admit to their 'important hours' others whose experience in piety they judged to be insufficient.[5] John Wesley had no doubts that their

---

[2] John Clayton to John Wesley, Oxon, 1st August 1732, in Tyerman, *The Life and Times of John Wesley*, I.83–4; cf. also his accounts in letters written to John Wesley in London and Epworth on 1st August and 4th September 1732, *Journal*, VIII.275–81.

[3] *Letters*, I.151, Oxon, 15th January 1734, John Wesley to Richard Morgan.

[4] Ibid. p. 136, 13th June 1733, to his father.

[5] Ibid. p. 144, 17th December 1733, to Richard Morgan.

course was right, but he expressly submitted it to the judgement of God, and was willing to listen to all genuine correction.[6] It was the purpose of the whole enterprise which mattered to him. He was not interested so much in the externals to which many objected, nor in a display of churchmanship which might exist alongside a worldly life, but in following Jesus completely. His concern was therefore to do those things by which the soul might recover the true image of God, as he expressed it in words which recall the language of Henry Scougal. He could ask, How will a man pass through the hour of death unless he has served God with all his powers? Will a man be able to answer God in the judgement that he has obeyed Him according to the custom of the place he was in? Can there be excess when the highest possible is required?[7] One of his pupils truly observed that in Wesley's eyes lukewarm Christianity was the worst thing of all, worse than open sin.[8] It was essentially this devout radicalism which sustained him and drove him on, and which at the same time commended him and his cause to others.

This is seen most clearly in the extended correspondence with Richard Morgan in Dublin, the father of his friend. A painful experience had seriously affected the group. William Morgan, who had been responsible for guiding them towards social works, died on 26th August 1732 after a long illness, apparently in spiritual darkness. Samuel Wesley, John's elder brother, wrote a moving poem in memory of him.[9] As early as February his condition had been so hopeless that Wesley wrote: 'He can neither sleep, read, stand, nor sit . . . he is a burthen to himself and almost useless in the world; his discharge cannot be far off.' But his natural will to live sustained him for a further six months. John Wesley marvelled because, unlike a year before, he was no longer ready to die.[1] In June he left Oxford and went to his parents' house in Dublin, where he died. Student gossip in Oxford said the group of 'Methodists' were responsible; excessive fasting had undermined the health of the young man. This had not actually been said by his father, but doubtless the rumour had reached his ears, especially as six months later it found its way into the newspaper.[2] John Wesley took up the challenge immediately

[6] *Letters*, p. 132, 18th October 1732, to Richard Morgan.
[7] Ibid. pp. 152–3, 15th January 1734, to Richard Morgan.
[8] Ibid. p. 149, Richard Morgan to his father, Oxon, 14th January 1734.
[9] *Journal*, I.103–5.
[1] *Letters*, I.120, Lincoln College, 28th February 1732, to his mother.
[2] *Fog's Journal*, 9th December 1732; cf. Simon, *John Wesley and the Religious Societies*, p. 97.

and wrote to Richard Morgan what was not merely an apology on behalf of the group but also a most urgent pastoral appeal. It was easy to rebut the charge about his son's health: John Wesley himself had begun to fast only six months before. William Morgan was by that time seriously ill and had not fasted at all for eighteen months. Wesley was certainly concerned to assert and defend his own honour. He contests most decisively any suspicion that he is over-zealously pious or too exacting with his pupils.[3] The real point at issue depends upon something quite different. William Morgan now stands before the eternal Judge who sees the truth. *He* will decide whether it was blind zeal and complete misunderstanding of religion which led him, or whether he finished his work in haste as a true servant of his Lord, having a just sense that the time was short. Yet even this is not enough. One day Richard Morgan himself will stand there and have to answer for his own life, for his comfortable conception of 'religion'. Will he then still be disposed to suspect that seriousness in the Christian way of life is too extreme, or to find fault with an over-zealous love of the Master?[4] Will it not then be overwhelmingly clear that the question about God is not a technical affair of the theologians, but one which determines eternal salvation? Will he not then regret too late that he has rejected it? Will it not then become apparent to him that it is not the gross sins we have committed, but the delicate sins of omission which are the most dangerous, since it is on account of them that condemnation follows in the Judgement (Matthew 25[41])? Will he not then abandon that easy-going attitude which imagines that God has issued only prohibitions, and not meant His commandments to be taken seriously? How will he come to terms with the requirement of Jesus that the righteousness of His disciples should exceed that of the Scribes and Pharisees?[5]

It is possible to find much deserving of censure in this letter. It is not free from impertinence, and the reference to the hour of death is reminiscent of the rhetorical flourishes found in literary models.[6] But looked at with reference to John Wesley himself, the significant

[3] *Letters*, I.146-7, 17th December 1733, to Richard Morgan: 'I acknowledge your goodness in having a far better opinion of me than I deserve, or, I trust in God, shall ever desire. I have many things to add when time permits, but one I dare not defer a moment. 'Tis absolutely necessary to guard your surviving son against the least suspicion of my over-great zeal or strictness. You are fully sensible he is in no danger of either. But if he once fancies I am, that fancy will cut me off from all possibility of doing him any substantial service.'
[4] Ibid. p. 153, 15th January 1734, to Richard Morgan.
[5] Ibid. p. 159, 15th March 1734, to Richard Morgan.
[6] Cf. my essay in *Theologia Viatorum*, IV.232f, 265, note 172.

fact is that he assumes the part of both theologian and pastor, while his thinking only reaches its conclusion when he has brought everything under the judgement of God.

Richard Morgan was not won over by the pastoral and missionary efforts of this correspondence, but he allowed his suspicions of the Oxford Methodists to drop, and entrusted his younger son Richard to Wesley's care. This was a moral victory. In the disputes caused by the death there intervened one of the leading religious writers of the day, William Law, a former Anglican clergyman, who was at the time without an appointment because of his opposition to William's succession to the throne. In July 1732 John Wesley visited him and obviously impressed him favourably. Law defended the Oxford society in a pamphlet which went through three editions.[7] He emphasized that their law of life was the gospel, their rule the scriptures, and their orders those of the (Anglican and primitive) Church. For this reason they were particularly devoted to the observance of Christian usages, prayer, fasting, and reception of the sacrament. The money saved through fasting they devoted, in accordance with the precepts of the early Church, to the poor, the sick, and prisoners. Their early rising and their ordering of the day was to ensure that the greatest possible time should be dedicated to the glory of God. John Wesley and his friends could not have wished for a better apologist.

It is principally through two works, *A Practical Treatise upon Christian Perfection* (1726) and *A Serious Call to a Devout and Holy Life* (1728),[8] that William Law influenced his own and subsequent generations, right up to the present time. The subject of the first of the two books shows that Christian perfection was a common expression of that time. It was Law's intention to free it of the associations it had for many people. It was felt to be a special, almost monastic type of sanctity, which was neither attainable nor worth striving after by normal folk. Over against this Law recognizes only *one* holiness which applies to all and only *one* Christianity which saves all. He takes the early Christian emphasis upon unity as it is used in the Epistle to the Ephesians and applies it to his argument: *one*

[7] *The Oxford Methodists, Being some Account of a Society of Young Gentlemen in that City so denominated* (1733 and 1737, with great alterations and improvements 1738). Extracts from the 1st edn in Simon, *John Wesley and the Religious Societies*, pp. 97ff.

[8] I used the following editions: William Law, *A Practical Treatise upon Christian Perfection* (1726) in the *Works of the Rev. William Law*, in 9 volumes, Vol. III (New Forest, 1893), and *A Serious Call to a Devout and Holy Life* (1728), ed. J. H. Overton (London, 1898). August Lang (*Puritanismus and Pietismus*, pp. 281–96) used the old editions in the library of Francke's Institution in Halle.

faith, *one* baptism, therefore *one* religion and *one* perfection. He asks further whether it is possible to fulfil the requirements of Christian perfection under different outward circumstances of life, and replies with a definite affirmative. The decisive requirement which is always demanded is the inner disposition.[9] In this way he establishes a point of view which transcends all external actions. Perfection as the condition of happiness means perfection of purpose. The primary thing is not the end attained but the earnest effort towards it, not the actual performance but the disposition to do it, not the result which is produced but the genuine resolution to effect it. The difference is between falling short of our perfection after our best endeavours, or stopping short of it, by not endeavouring to arrive at it.[1] He was thus quite justified in prefacing his treatise with the words of Paul: 'Not as though I had already attained, either were already perfect' (Philippians 3[12]). So there is found here the statement of what afterwards became the theme of the *Serious Call*: in the Christian life everything depends upon purity of intention. Yet for Law Christianity is much more than a demand; it is at the same time, in the words of the Second Epistle of Peter (1[4]), participation in the Divine nature. He does not hesitate to apply to this the Augustinian word 'enjoyment'.[2] This requires a complete transformation of nature, as is aptly expressed by the word about the new life. This new life appertains entirely to God, and only on the basis of this principle does the requirement that Christians should renounce the world become intelligible. The new life comprises both a new birth and a state of death at the same time. Humanly speaking it is a dying.[3] In the detailed working out of his theme, renunciation of the world is Law's favourite topic. He works with the sharp contrast between the kingdom of Christ and the kingdom of this world.[4] In the long run mankind has only one enemy, the devil. He examines

[9] Behind this there is probably the scholastic distinction between *habitus* and *actus* as the unrecognized tradition; cf. esp. Law, *Christian Perfection* (1893), p. 6. It must always be borne in mind that the Reformation in England failed to make a complete theological and historical breach.

[1] Law, *A Practical Treatise upon Christian Perfection* . . . (1893), pp. 6ff. The sentence with a play on words is on p. 9: 'For surely it is a very different Case, to fall short of our Perfection after our best Endeavours, and to stop short of it, by not endeavouring to arrive at it.' [Translator's note: In the text I have not translated Dr Schmidt's whole sentence, since he points out that Law makes a play on words which cannot be reproduced in German.]

[2] Ibid. Chapter 1: 'The Nature and Design of Christianity that its Sole End is to deliver us from the Misery and Disorder of this present State and raise us to a blissful Enjoyment of the Divine Nature.'

[3] Ibid. pp. 31, 85.   [4] Ibid. pp. 36ff.

every actual life-situation with puritanical austerity from this point of view, and as a consequence enjoins acts of mortification and self-denial with all the passion of a catholic mystic.[5] They are as important to him as acts of charity to the poor.[6] Like Tolstoy he raises again the unconditional demands of the Sermon on the Mount for the renunciation of all claims to property, rights, and honour.[7] So he oscillates between biblical radicalism and the methodics of Catholicism, which systematized these demands into the institutional pattern of monasticism, but it is the biblical reference and attitude which ultimately prevails. Following Jesus, to which he devotes the last chapter but one,[8] is to be sure conceived largely in the customary reduced and mechanical way as direct imitation, and from this John Wesley detached himself. But when he calls the daily taking up of the cross the essence of self-denial and mortification, he is again at the biblical centre. Like a Puritan of a century before, he condemns popular literature,[9] and in particular the stage.[1] 'Vain and impertinent books'[2] is how he describes this whole field of writing. The aesthetic value of poetry, in the sense in which it had been fundamentally esteemed in England in an unbroken succession since the Middle Ages, and such as can be gathered perhaps most clearly from Edmund Spenser's *Fairie Queene*, he denies altogether. Only its educational value for morality and religion is recognized. Because of this extended emphasis it is easy to get the impression that Law put all his stress upon the renunciatory aspect of Christianity, and undoubtedly he has often been understood in this way. The concluding sentence of the book, the exhortation based on I Corinthians 15^{58} to labour tirelessly and faithfully in the work of the Lord, confirms this.[3]

Although the basic conception is similar in many respects to those

---

[5] In my opinion Lang (*Puritanismus und Pietismus*, pp. 291ff) has over-emphasized the catholicizing tendency.

[6] Law, *Christian Perfection*, p. 83.

[7] Ibid. p. 92.

[8] Ibid. Chapter 13: 'All Christians are required to imitate the Life and Example of Jesus Christ.'

[9] Ibid. pp. 150ff.   [1] Ibid. pp. 170ff.

[2] Ibid. p. 150. 'So must we look upon all those Books as corrupt, which do not improve and confirm our Hearts in Virtue, or, in the Apostle's Words, such as do not *edify and minister Grace* to the readers' (p. 151). On this subject, cf. the important first chapter in Herbert Schöffler's *Protestantismus und Literatur*, pp. 1ff.

[3] Ibid. p. 250: 'Do you but sincerely labour in the Lord, and then neither Height nor Depth, neither Life nor Death, neither Men nor Devils, can make your Labour in vain.'

works of Henry Scougal and Jeremy Taylor which we have discussed
—perfection and the regaining of the Divine likeness are always to the
fore—yet in comparison with these books the *will* is much more
strongly stressed. There is a greater awareness of the reality of the
ordinary situation in which man finds himself in the battle of faith.
The opposition between God and Satan, the kingdom of Jesus Christ
and the kingdom of this world, is much more sharply worked out.
So Law could say that Christianity was a 'calling'—in the double
sense of vocation (*Beruf*) and summons (*Berufung*)—which puts an
end to all other callings. This is a question of the one thing which
is needful.[4] By the necessity of continual decision for and against
God earthly life receives an importance which is quite foreign to
mysticism, and this too is in line with the fundamental Puritan aim
which used eschatology to drive home the call to repentance.[5] In
spite of this the large setting in which this appeal to the will is placed
must not be forgotten or neglected. It is all too easy to conclude
that Law preached a religion of works by his emphasis upon the
striving after perfection.[6] He begins with the revelation of Jesus
Christ which made known to man God's great secrets, His design
to save the world. This redemptive purpose is directed to the new
man, and so to the perfecting of man in general. In this there lies
everlasting rest and happiness.[7] As has already been stated, its final
purpose is likeness to God. The divine birth of the new men is made
manifest in three ways: they have overcome the world, they commit
no sin, and they love as God Himself loves. Their love knows no
limits and embraces all mankind. At its highest it proves itself by
love for the enemy.[8] Their perfection establishes hatred of sin as the
basic disposition of their natures. They may indeed fall again into

[4] Ibid. p. 37.
[5] Ibid. p. 14: 'This Knowledge of ourselves makes human Life a State of infinite Importance, placed upon so dreadful a point betwixt two such Eternities.'
On the place of eschatology in the summons to repentance in Puritanism, cf.
esp. pp. 221ff and 263ff in my article in *Theologia Viatorum*, Vol. IV.
[6] This tendency can be seen especially in Law's statement (*Christian Perfection,*
p. 9): 'Though it may be true, that People will be admitted to Happiness, and
different Degrees of Happiness, though they have not attained to all that Perfection to which they were called, yet it does not follow that any People will be
saved who did not endeavour after that Perfection.'
[7] Ibid. p. 11: 'It has pleased the infinite Goodness of God to satisfy all our
Wants and Inquiries by a Revelation made to the World by his Son Jesus Christ.
This Revelation has laid open the great Secrets of Providence from the Creation
of the World, explained the present State of Things, and given Man all the
Information that is necessary to quiet his Anxieties, content him with his condition, and lead him safely to everlasting Rest and Happiness.'
[8] Ibid. p. 28.

sin at any time, but their fundamental dispositions are not thereby changed.[9]

The perfectionism which Law sets forth, although limited in practice, is clear in principle. The new life is covered, not by a torturing uncertainty which causes a man to watch and secretly suspect every step, but by an assurance of standing on firm ground which he has not struggled after or won for himself. Fasting is a characteristic example of something which is seen under the conditions of everyday life. Law is able to set it free in its different methods and degrees, since each man is to determine its form as it concerns his own personal situation in the sight of God. This counsel is combined with the fullest insistence upon repentance. This too consists not in fixed degrees of sorrow and pain for sin, but is suited to each person in the same way.[1] Equality before God does not exclude differences among people but includes them, and the true expression of the religious life is not mechanical uniformity but organic individualization.

The other work, the *Serious Call*, was in many respects the practical outworking of the teaching on perfection. In this Law also begins by changing the common meaning of his basic concept. He rejects the popular idea which restricts devotion to religious exercises and prayers, and insists upon the unity between divine worship and morality in daily life.[2] Indeed he expressly calls attention to the fact that in the whole Gospel there is not a single command which regulates the observance of the public worship of God.[3] All life must be surrendered to God, and the intention of pleasing Him in every action must determine its whole course.[4] By means of concrete illustrations and the introduction of sharply-drawn types of characters, a favourite device of the eighteenth century,[5] he makes this claim a living thing. He describes the rich man of the world, Flatus, whose wife decks herself with pearls and adds to her natural beauty by the use of cosmetics, in his constant restlessness. He flits from one amusement and from one project to another. Social diversions, invitations, balls, hunting, visits to the opera, fill his days. He spares no effort to get more out of these things. He learns Italian in order to understand the opera. He is then captivated by serious things

---

[9] Law, *Christian Perfection*, p. 27   [1] Ibid, p. 111.
[2] William Law, *A Serious Call to a Devout and Holy Life* . . . (1898), pp. 1ff.
[3] Ibid. p. 5.   [4] Ibid. pp. 13, 16.
[5] Cf. Addison and Steele in England, La Bruyère in France, Rabener in Germany.

like a passion for building. Then one day he grows weary of his luxurious life and becomes a vegetarian, which is the first result of his so reflecting with himself.[6] In contrast to him there is Miranda, the example of Christian character. In everything she does she thinks of God and what He requires of her, of Jesus and His example. She concerns herself with the spiritual welfare of her neighbours and her servants, and denies herself every comfort and pleasure to help the poor. She takes in three children from their depraved home and brings them up in such a manner that afterwards they convert their parents.[7] Every sentence and illustration is expressed in an extremely practical way. The Bible is made into a book of law, and God's readiness to forgive is said to apply only to those sins which are unavoidable in a man's life: it is not for those sins in which he lives without the intention of avoiding them.[8] The question whether Gospel-perfection can be fully attained is not under discussion; the important thing is whether a person comes as near to it as a sincere intention and careful intelligence can carry him.[9] A true Christian will not ask whether God will forget his failings and follies, his spurious pleasures, his vain outgoings, the luxury of his household, the dissipation of his time, but rather whether God is pleased with these things and whether they are the appointed ways of gaining His favour.[1] Although wellnigh every occupation falls under condemnation on account of its worldliness—as in the tract on idolatry by the early Church writer Tertullian—yet Law emphasizes that earthly occupations can be made holy, and ought so to be, by being done as a service to God and in conformity with His will.[2] The book is not without its contradictions. Although at the outset the public worship of God is given such a limited connotation, the second part of the book gives precise directions and suggestions, even to the times for prayer.[3] The historic facts of salvation in general are not at all prominent. The emphasis lies upon the moral austerity in which the Christian must train himself. But on the whole the close relationship with the teaching of perfection is preserved. The negative statement that worldliness is not happiness,[4] and its positive counterpart that

[6] Law, *A Serious Call*, pp. 53ff.
[7] Ibid. pp. 66–7.   [8] Ibid. p. 18.
[9] Ibid. p. 19.   [1] Ibid. p. 14.
[2] Ibid. p. 29: 'Worldly business is to be made holy unto the Lord, by being done as a service to Him and in Conformity to His Divine will. (This should be set against Lang (*Puritanismus und Pietismus*), who exaggerates Law's monastic catholic withdrawal from the world.)
[3] Ibid. Chapters 14–16.   [4] Ibid. pp. 117ff: 'Worldliness is not happiness.'

holiness and happiness go together,[5] are both found. It was the latter, found both in the Puritan tradition and in contemporary theology, which expressly lay behind John Wesley's bringing together of joy in salvation and the pursuit of holiness.

The difference between Law's viewpoint and that of Scougal and Taylor, in spite of all their affinity, lay in the summons to the will. As a result of this John Wesley was in some respects directed once again to the Romanic mysticism which he had known in his childhood. It is not surprising that this conception of Christianity, expounded in so practical a way, exerted an irresistible attraction upon the group of Oxford students. It is already understandable why John Wesley found it so difficult later to break, both personally and theologically, with such a man.

If John Wesley at this stage appears to us as vigorous and disciplined to the point of harshness, there is another picture from the same period which shows him in a much more tender light. This is seen in the correspondence with Mary Pendarves, the young widow from Buckland, who had lived in Gloucester since 1727 when not at Court in London. This interchange of thoughts and sentiments seems to act as a counter-balance to the purely male group of students in Oxford. In a letter to her sister she jokingly called Wesley 'Primitive Christianity', which indicates that by that time the return to the practice of the early Church had been noticed as the mark of the Oxford Methodists.[6] The letters which John Wesley exchanged with her are a peculiar mixture of pastoral pronouncements and repressed eroticism. His words are prompted by sentiment in a way quite unusual for him, yet the result is not an unconstrained artlessness but a style which is affected and fanciful. Exaggerated declarations of gratitude and protestations of his devotion are repeatedly found.[7] John Wesley admired the young lady as a paragon of holiness and virtue—although not her alone, since he felt the same about her sister Anne Granville and her friend Sarah Kirkham. Regarding the disparity between himself and his models of virtue, Wesley could not

[5] *Law, A Serious Call*, p. 116: 'If we desire real happiness, we have no other possible way to it but by improving our talents, by so holily and piously using the powers and faculties of men in this present state, that we may be happy and glorious in the powers and faculties of angels in the world to come.'

[6] *Letters*, I.50, Introduction by the editor, John Telford.

[7] James Harrison Rigg (*The Living Wesley*, p. 50) has rightly drawn attention to this characteristic, not found in any other of John Wesley's writings, so far as their style is concerned.

sufficiently extol the condescension of these noble ladies.[8] He believed he could shelter himself under their protection from the lowering contact with the bulk of mankind.[9] Their help was indispensable to him for his strivings after holiness. Above all he esteemed Mary Pendarves as the epitome of true humility; on account of his religious pride she was so necessary to him. He could regard her as innocent compared with himself, the penitent sinner.[1] She of course vigorously repudiated the character which Wesley attributed to her, and stressed her own weakness: for her part she admired *his* degree of holiness.[2] On the other hand he was gratified that he was allowed to assist her as spiritual adviser, and yet again he suspected that it was ambitious on his part to pretend to be of any use to her.[3] The conversations with her, the prospect of seeing her, give wings to his feelings and thinking. To this group the highest aim in life appears to be a devout and enjoyable love for God, containing within itself belief in a providence to which man must be resigned, but leading also to resolute activity. All pain and every act of renunciation would be gladly borne. Zeal in prayer and the partaking of the Sacrament were the outward manifestations.

Over all this relationship, in which each really feels superior to the others, there hangs an over-refined, delicate, decadent atmosphere. In this correspondence John Wesley certainly paid his tribute to the age of sentiment in which he lived. The inheritance of Henry Scougal, and in part of Jeremy Taylor, representing a late and

---

[8] *Letters*, I.52–3, 12th September 1730; p. 57, 3rd October 1730; pp. 72–3, 11th January 1731; pp. 75–6, 11th February 1731; p. 79, 5th April 1731; p. 81, 14th April 1731; p. 103, 12th August 1731; p. 109, 28th September 1731; p. 165, July 1734. As evidence against interpreting the relationship in a romantic way, which even the otherwise cautious and delicate Rigg (*The Living Wesley*, p. 47) presupposes, is to be set above Wesley's letter of 28th December 1730 (*Letters*, I.67–8), in which he submits his attitude to critical judgement. With unbiased honesty he places his attitude to her alongside his earlier and still continuing relationship with Sara Kirkham (Varanese). Sarah Kirkham was his 'religious friend'. He characterizes the significance of Mary Pendarves as one who recommends virtue to him. When he accuses himself of the suspicion of mixing self-love with the friendship, it might be concluded that he was referring to a secret romantic feeling. Yet the chief consideration is that immediately another factor obtrudes itself, his liking for being considered, his desire of being admired by her as a pastor, and his longing for esteem and honour. This tallies with his reproach of himself that he lacks humility. Moreover it fits in with his praise of her, whose humility was the very thing he felt to be her most outstanding characteristic.

[9] *Letters*, I.79, 5th April 1731.

[1] Ibid. pp. 75–6, 11th February 1731; p. 80, 5th April 1731; p. 81, 14th April 1731; pp. 96–7, 24th July 1731; p. 97: 'You have kept yourself unspotted from the world: I am sullied with many stains.' Cf. finally, p. 165, July 1734.

[2] Ibid. p. 95, 21st July 1731.

[3] Ibid. p. 68, 28th December 1730; p. 90, 19th June 1731.

weakened version of the spirit of Augustine, can also be discerned. It is not surprising that Pascal was quoted with approval.[4] The enjoyment of God—this was the leading idea. It was at this point that Wesley's characteristic formula that holiness also means happiness originated[5]—at this point it was bound to do so.

Yet all this was, as it were, by the way, and not in any sense his central course. The strict, not to say inexorable, earnestness which sustained and fashioned John Wesley's efforts after personal holiness did not cease during this period; indeed through all the effusiveness of feeling it is found in these letters. Time and again Wesley struggled against his unhappy tendency towards pride in his religion, and as a Christian minister counselled Mary Pendarves not to stand still but to resist and to attack the devil, instead of remaining on the defensive. For him sanctification was not a passive affair but something active, and he applied this to the intellectual field also. To that end he called for an assault against the deism and atheism of the day, the half-belief and the unbelief, by doubly strong representation of Christian truths. The more the leading thought of the day degrades the Son of God to the human level, the more zealously let them emphasize His divine nature; the more the credibility of the Bible is doubted, the more resolutely let them testify to its unconditional authority![6] He felt that Matthew Tindal's book, *Christianity as Old as the Creation*, the Deists' bible, was an assault on the honour of

[4] *Letters*, I.76, 11th February 1731: 'Who can be a fitter person than one who knows it by experience to tell me the full force of that glorious rule, "Set your affections on things above, and not on things of the earth"? Is it equivalent to "Thou shalt love the Lord thy God with all thy heart, soul and strength"? But what is it to love God? Is not to love anything the same as habitually to delight in it? Is not then the purport of both these injunctions this—that we delight in the Creator more than His creatures; that we take more pleasure in Him than in anything He has made, and rejoice in nothing so much as serving Him; that, to take Mr Pascal's expression, while the generality of men use God and enjoy the world, we, on the contrary, only use the world while we enjoy God?'

[5] Ibid. pp. 92–3, 19th July 1731: 'My present sense is this—I was made to be happy: to be happy I must love God; in proportion to my love of whom my happiness must increase. To love God I must be like Him, holy as He is holy; which implies both the being pure from vicious and foolish passions and the being confirmed in those virtuous and rational affections which God comprises in the word charity.' Cf. also p. 114, 17th November 1731, to his brother Samuel.

[6] Ibid. p. 101, 12th August 1731, to Mrs Pendarves. It should be noted that in England these expressions implied generally not a radical denial of God but more a conscious deviation from ecclesiastical orthodoxy, which from the time of Elizabeth found its normal form of political and religious practice in the life of the Anglican Church. Paul Meissner (*England im Zeitalter von Humanismus, Renaissance und Reformation*, p. 511) has correctly drawn attention to this. On the other side Puritan polemics were directed sharply against a Renaissance attitude which was combined with genuine atheism. Cf., above all, Henry Smith, *God's Arrow against Atheists* (1639).

Christ, taking away His meaning as Saviour for salvation.[7] He considered Deism much more dangerous than Catholicism, and strenuously attacked the way in which, especially in London, people were advised against popery rather than summoned to attack the common enemy of Christianity.[8]

In fact, Wesley was as truly the spiritual counsellor in this group as amongst his students. Fundamentally all his conversations and letters, like the resolutions and acts in his personal life, were included in his pastoral purpose. This demanded an appreciative accommodation to each situation and each individual. If in the correspondence with Richard Morgan, in which he had to set himself against indifference, he displayed a devout radicalism with a distinct and at times cutting severity, yet in the interchange with the women he could be surprisingly tender. He was resolutely committed to one thing, the task of promoting by all possible means his own and other people's sanctification. Mary Pendarves inquired on one occasion whether it was legitimate for her to go to a concert on a Sunday evening. John Wesley answered her with a detailed exposition of the meaning of Sunday and the things which were allowable on it. He classifies them principally into two groups, works of mercy and works of natural necessity, like cooking and washing. All others are to be judged by whether they promote holiness. Should that not be the case they must be rejected. It is not sufficient to be sure that they do not actually obstruct holiness; they must rather result in a definite advance in it.[9] But when Mary Pendarves told him of a young girl who was reproached for her lack of attention in prayer and uneasiness in receiving Communion, he replied that really he envied the young woman her tender conscience. Her reactions were obviously involuntary, and so she ought to console herself with the thought that God's goodness punishes nobody for offences they could not avoid. She ought not to imagine that while on earth she can attain to the perfection which belongs to the angels. As to her own case, he recommended her to pray more often and more frequently to receive the Sacrament.[1] Similarly, after the manner of Jeremy Taylor, he wrote to Anne Granville, when in a pessimistic mood she was bemoaning her shortcomings, that she must learn that on earth we have to attain

---

[7] *Letters*, I.91, 19th June 1731, to Mrs Pendarves.
[8] *Journal*, I.357–8, 25th May 1737.
[9] *Letters*, I.78, 4th April 1731, Mary Pendarves to John Wesley; and pp. 81–2, 14th April 1731, John Wesley to Mrs Pendarves.
[1] Ibid. p. 102, 12th August 1731, to Mrs Pendarves.

to purity of heart and not perfection of the deed. She must cling on to the fact that Jesus speaks of a forgiveness which reaches to seventy times seven. He might just as well have said a thousand times a thousand. The sin against the Holy Ghost, which causes her uneasiness, comes into consideration, according to Mark $3^{22, 29\text{-}30}$, only when we revile Jesus against our better knowledge. But Satan loves to use this word in order to disturb those whom he cannot otherwise get into his power. She must, she ought to believe that forgiveness avails for her as for everyone. All things are possible to one who believes. She must not of course expect to be freed immediately from her distress, for God educates His own through temptations. Inconstancy in those things which pertain to our relationship with God belongs to our human lot, and we ought not to let our feelings influence too much our judgements about ourselves, which should be soberly based upon what we do.[2] In this instance greater stress is laid upon faith than hitherto, and this was to be further enhanced at the time of Wesley's conversion, yet at this time the statement is an isolated case, from which nothing can be deduced with certainty.

On one occasion John Wesley gave expression to his opinion about the principles which governed his work of spiritual instruction. In this case also he puts gentleness and forbearance in the first place, for the wrath and severity of man do not work the righteousness of God. Ten years is the shortest period which ought to be given to the case of one individual. How long, he exclaims, hath God had pity on thee? By reading and conversation he desires to show the young student of theology, for whom as tutor he is responsible, what the 'law of Christ' is, so that he shall understand it and make it his own, in order that he can practise it, and in the end teach it to others. The law of Christ means however being freed from love of the world in order to become free to love God. It is noteworthy that he limits it in this way: all love which is not subordinated to the highest and true end must be given up. Already love to God, the love which gladly obeys Him, is seen as the essence of Christianity. He who assents to this and puts it into practice will make use of the external aids which the Church provides in prayer and sacrament, entirely of his own accord. To what extent and in what order they are to be used, Wesley decides afresh with each individual according to his character and

---

[2] *Letters*, I.110–12, 3rd October 1731, to Anne Granville. For the origin of this in Jeremy Taylor, see his *Holy Dying*, Ch. 5, sect. V (quoted by Wesley, *Letters*, I.47–8).

spiritual condition, and for this he depends upon the direction of the Holy Spirit. Further he draws upon his own experience and his own reflection and in emergencies follows the advice of his friends. But his supreme rule of action is always longsuffering.

John Wesley's own spiritual evolution is embedded in this pastoral activity, and from it his own sanctification naturally developed. He was indebted to Jeremy Taylor for the basic perception that forgiveness of sins is at the same time sanctification. Taylor stressed the fact that forgiveness is not a hidden word but one which can be read in a visible change for us. Accordingly the believer, in the words of Johannes Hofmann, the founder of the Erlangen theology, required only to turn to himself, the Christian, in order to confirm his being in a state of salvation. The biblical basis for this is Acts 3^{26}, which Taylor translates: 'Christ came to take away our sins, by turning every one of us from our iniquities.' This also was to bear fruit in the future. Forgiveness in the sense of actual dominion over sin became Wesley's continuing concern.[3] For this reason he directed his efforts so strenuously to himself, and with a searching of self which was both torturing and exacting, gave a continuous account of himself. His favourite way of expressing it was as follows: his aim in life was of necessity to become as happy as possible, and this required being as holy as possible, for happiness consists in loving God, and to love Him one must be as He is, holy. Thoughts, words, and deeds must be directly aimed at the high prize of victory which the divine call holds out to us. As often as he is able he must use all the regular means of help which the Church offers in its ordinances, such as prayer, sacrament, and Bible-reading. But in addition there were other aids which must be taken into account and chosen without constraint. In connexion with them he made it his rule that nothing is indifferent: the particular means in question either promotes or hinders his spiritual progress.[4] Once again with the radicalism of faith he sharply repulses every sign of lukewarmness. When in despair he could say that he was still completely entangled in earthly

[3] Ibid. pp. 47–8, Lincoln College, 28th February 1730, to his mother. So far as I know this early statement of Wesley's doctrine of sanctification has not been noted even in the detailed researches of C. N. Impeta, *De Leer der Heiligung*, David Lerch, *Heil und Heilıgung bei John Wesley*, Harald Lindström, *Wesley and Sanctification*. It is not possible to determine what John Wesley meant by the Perfectionists, which he referred to in a letter to his mother on 14th February 1734 (*Letters*, VIII.269).

[4] Ibid. pp. 92–3, 19th July 1731, to Mrs Pendarves, similar in part even in the form of expression to his brother Samuel (*Letters*, I. p. 114, 17th November 1731). My account collates the two statements.

things, and beg his mother to help in his struggle for the renunciation of the world, since she herself has made definite progress. As once at home she had devoted Thursday evening to him for forming his judgement, she might do it now for correcting his heart. In a state of alarm he confessed how swiftly life was flying away and how slowly he advanced in holiness. He feared to die before he had learned to live.[5] The thought of death and the judgement awaiting him beyond it drove him when writing to his mother to the utmost clarity and resoluteness in matters of faith. She had endeavoured to restrain somewhat his too great preoccupation with the problems of salvation, and urged him to talk less about them. He denied the reason she gave, that he would think as she did when he was her age, by stating that it was questionable whether God would grant him so long to live. A right faith is as worth striving for at thirty as at sixty, and the actions which result from it merit the same reward now as then. Now is the time to throw off the affections of the earthly Adam and to put on the image of the heavenly, so that he may not be found wanting in the divine balance.[6]

Wesley knew that this seriousness and the striving consequent upon it marked him out as a singular character.[7] He was continually hearing reproaches against the enthusiasm of his ways,[8] and that he was too strict, that he set his demands too high and took his life too seriously—objections similar to those brought against the Puritans a hundred years before. He could only reply that if this was so then the law of God itself was not strict enough.[9] The experience which he gained as spiritual leader of the Methodist circle at Oxford led him to a veritable 'martyr theology', which became ever more rigorous. It belongs to the true Christian life to be misunderstood, despised, persecuted, and this actually ought to be a matter of pride. A whole series of biblical references (such as Matthew 10^{25}, John 15^{19}, 1 Corinthians 1^{20}, Matthew $5^{11, 12}$) prove that these things must happen to the disciples of Jesus, and have happened to them from the beginning. The Christian has to bear his cross like his Lord, and

---

[5] *Letters*, I.119–20, 28th February 1732, to his mother.
[6] Ibid. p. 134, 15th February 1733, to his mother.
[7] Ibid. p. 114, 17th November 1731, to his brother Samuel: 'But it will be said I am whimsical.' Page 136, 13th June 1733, to his father: 'My singularity.' Page 137, 17th August 1733, to his mother: 'The thing that gives offence here is the being singular with regard to time, expense, and company.'
[8] Ibid. p. 86, 11th June 1731, to his mother.
[9] Ibid. p. 92, 19th July 1731, to Mrs Pendarves.

further, God uses persecution in order to mortify in His own their love of the world.[1]

Yet this rigorism also is still contained within the sphere which is determined by the unconditional supremacy of the love of God and of the formula, 'holiness is happiness'. In all this John Wesley never actually became a fanatic for the law. He holds to the basic position of his thinking, which makes everything lead to God Himself, His will, His judgement. A deep and passionate concern for God runs through his declarations, informs his choice of words, and directs his resolutions and acts. This is shown in a decision to which he ultimately came. In spite of all the hostility John Wesley nevertheless felt that Oxford was the right place for him. To be sure he had constantly to reckon with variations in the state of his health, particularly in the year 1734, and this caused his mother to write anxiously that he ought to look after himself: but by the strict regularity of his life he succeeded in overcoming his disorders.[2] Meanwhile his father was increasingly feeling his advancing years and reckoned on dying soon. He wanted to keep the two livings of Epworth and Wroot in the family, particularly in order that his wife might remain in receipt of the stipends. He first proposed that his eldest son, Samuel, should succeed him, but Samuel declined on the ground that he wished to remain in the teaching profession. His thoughts then turned to John, and in January 1733 the project was for the first time discussed in the parents' home. For all that he wanted to help his mother, John showed no particular inclination for the proposal: he thought the two villages were too easy-going for him. He was constrained by the expectation that the assault of the hostile world would soon come upon him in full force at Oxford. There he could and must prove himself a faithful minister of Christ, by honour and dishonour, through evil report and good report (2 Corinthians 6[8]).[3] Earlier indeed he had considered certain small posts,

[1] Ibid. p. 86, 11th June 1731, to his mother; p. 90, 19th June 1731, to Mrs Pendarves; pp. 96–7, 24th July 1731, to Mrs Pendarves; p. 113, 17th November 1731, to his brother Samuel; p. 132, 18th October 1732, to Richard Morgan; p. 134, 15th February 1733, to his mother; p. 136, 13th June 1733, to his father; p. 137, 17th August 1733, to his mother; and most comprehensively: pp. 175ff, 10th December 1734, to his father.
[2] J. S. Simon, *John Wesley and the Religious Societies*, p. 105. Cf. on this subject, Ralph Butterworth, 'John Wesley's Health', *Proc.W.H.S.*, XIV.(1924).162–5.
[3] *Letters*, I.134–5, 15th February 1733, to his mother. The basing of his refusal on this point has been overlooked so far by all biographers. It invalidates the usual charge of religious egotism.

such as a school in Yorkshire and a small living near Oxford.[4] But by now the student circle had grown into a strong group, the importance of which was shown by the opposition it aroused. To leave Oxford would seem to him like desertion. The fact that he asked his bishop whether his ordination obliged him to undertake parish work was an indication of his scrupulous conscientiousness and his unconditional adherence to the regular orders of the Church. He did this because the meaning of the oath was decided, according to canon law, not by the one who takes it but by him who requires it. When the bishop replied in the negative to his question, Wesley was completely convinced.[5] Barely two years after his first request his father repeated the invitation, but John flatly refused it, nor was his elder brother, Samuel, able to make him change his opinion. Under twenty-five points he gave so well-considered and comprehensive a reason for his refusal that four years later he published it in precisely its original form.[6]

In the primary place he set God's glory, and emphasized that this was not his highest consideration, but his only one. The course of life however which tends most to it is that in which we can best promote holiness in ourselves and in our neighbours. These two belong inseparably together, otherwise God would be making a strange schism in His Body, the Church. The physician's first concern is always to heal himself before trying his skill on others, but he himself is not yet healed or ready in this sense fully to work on others. He must still grow and mature, and there is nowhere better fitted to this than in college at Oxford. He has there a band of like-minded young men around him, while he can at any time seek out retirement. He is not over-troubled by annoying, superficial visitors who merely rob him of time and endanger his true Christian life because they are only lukewarm Christians. He is free from cares, and when he hears in the Gospel about 'the cares of this world', it sounds to him like something from another world. He is thus unusually free for the Lord's work and the service of God. This is what Paul meant when he wrote to the Corinthians (1 Corinthians 7^{32}): 'I would have you be without carefulness.' Further, Oxford provides him with ample opportunities for regular worship. Were he to give up

---

[4] *Letters*, I.42, 19th March 1727, to his mother; p. 48, 28th February 1730, to his mother.

[5] Ibid. p. 182, Oxon, 4th March 1735, to his brother Samuel (quote).

[6] *Journal*, II.159–66, 28th March 1739. (An abbreviated version of the long letter to his father written on 10th December 1734, *Letters*, I.166–78.)

all this he would be throwing away these provisions for the support of a true soldier of Jesus Christ, and he would lose immediately his disciplined life and become an easy prey for the adversary. While he preached to others he might himself be cast away.

It is evident that he is held by the ideal of monasticism. It is not freedom but restraint which he values; not spontaneity, but discipline; so much so that he can disdainfully and expressly reject a life without rules as a type of Christian freedom which is too high for him.[7] What is being described in every one of his sentences is none other than the monastic state with its advantages and its weaknesses. Its aim has rarely been so sympathetically appraised from outside Roman and Byzantine Christianity.

The consideration which in his first refusal he had advanced in this case now comes last, but to compensate for this it is stated more comprehensively and fundamentally than ever before. It concerns the meaning of persecution for the Christian. Wesley holds that the opposition which the disciple of Jesus meets is a perfectly normal thing. It denotes being in the state of salvation, and is the unconditional presupposition for fruitful work in the service of God. Through being contemned a man becomes a better Christian. To be sure he could and would find the same opposition in Epworth as in Oxford, but in Oxford he has it already. He repeated the same argument to his brother Samuel, only more briefly and abruptly, adding as a further drawback his poor health. He obstinately argued against abandoning in any way the opportunity he had of working with students. He could more easily be replaced at Epworth than in college, while to sweeten the fountain is more important than to purify the particular streams.[8] So the idea of leaving Oxford was set aside, and John Wesley remained a pastor to students. At the same time he shows that he retains his attachment and devotion to scholarship. Just as earlier he had expressed surprise at people who considered the text of the Septuagint faultless,[9] now in the manner of the Enlightenment he can extend the analysis of an idea into an article of encyclopedic proportions.[1]

[7] *Letters*, I.179, 13th January 1735, to his mother.
[8] Ibid. p. 180, 15th January 1735. Page 181, 13th February 1735, John Wesley appealed to the same principle for showing the importance of the minister's work as the German Pietists Philipp Jakob Spener (particularly in *Pia Desideria* [ed. Aland, 1940], pp. 67, 18) and August Hermann Francke (especially *Idea Studiosi theologiae* [1723], pp. 4ff, *Paränesis*).
[9] Ibid, p. 65, 11th December 1730, to his father.
[1] Ibid. pp. 178–9, 13th January 1735, to his mother.

For all its exclusiveness the Oxford environment was capable of containing and producing a rich variety of people, associations, and problems. John Wesley was alone and yet not a solitary; he had quiet and yet ministered to others; he was constantly engaged in conversations. His parents, so different in disposition from each other, his friends, his critics, the circle of women, his books, and the father of his friend Morgan, both demanded from him and presented him with opportunities for very different attitudes. He was able to watch over his little world without too much trouble, but for this reason the two thousand souls in Epworth and Wroot seemed too many for him.[2] He also possessed the ability to benefit from the varied characteristics of his situation, so that in spite of the limited environment in which his life was spent and the restricted extent of his work, he did not himself become confined in outlook. He never exaggerated the importance of the experiences which came to him or his associates. He was always concerned about the whole situation, the underlying principle, and that which was significant.

At Oxford John Wesley thought of himself primarily as a spiritual overseer, but in his personal practice, counsels, exhortation, decisions, and methods he was at the same time a theological thinker who traced everything back to the idea of God. Accordingly he could never be indifferent to questions which seemed to be merely theoretical. He examined them in the light of their importance for sanctification, or how they appeared in relation to the biblical and early Christian conception of God, and attained in this way to a type of 'existential thinking' which possessed complete inner coherence. Theory as such never played an entirely independent role, and it was for this reason that the atmosphere of Oxford, soaked as it was in the principles of the Enlightenment, was unable to make any strong impression upon him. Gratefully and frankly he took over its formal methods, but just as decisively rejected its attack on such fundamental dogmas as salvation through Jesus Christ, the God-man. He sharply repudiated Matthew Tindal, the leading figure of Deism, in whom he found this assault, yet this was not done theoretically, but by the reproach that such a view encouraged the denial of Jesus Christ in the present. At the same time he was aware of the place of such a standpoint in the history of dogma, and put Tindal alongside Faustus Socinus.[3] From

---

[2] *Letters,* I.174, 10th December 1734, to his father.
[3] Ibid. pp. 90–1, 19th June 1731, to Mrs Pendarves. Tindal's main work, *Christianity as Old as the Creation*, had appeared in the previous year (1730).

an early age his independence of judgement was evident, even if it was completely contained within the limits marked out by the thinkers of his own time, Scougal, Taylor, and Law. Superior to every type of literary evidence he found theological authority in Holy Scripture itself, and there primarily in the Person of Jesus and in His disciples. It was Christ he desired to obey, the disciples he wished to emulate. The group of Oxford students was to become in fact another early Christian congregation, a persecuted Church, continually growing more resolute, true, and pure, on behalf of its Lord. Accordingly Wesley repudiated every authority which was opposed to him in favour of the one original authority. When Richard Morgan put forward the judgement of the bishops against his radical religious practices, Wesley replied that the question of eternal salvation is not to depend upon the decision of ecclesiastical dignitaries, but on God's Word. Even though they are 'angels' there is the word of Galatians 1^8: 'Though an angel from heaven come and preach any other gospel, let him be accursed!'[4]

A number of influences had directed him expressly to the Bible, in particular those of his father and William Law. But in what sense did he understand it? The Word of God spoke to him of the summons to conscience and the utmost gravity of the problem of existence, i.e. the question of sin. He understood this as the challenge to holiness, as the way to happiness. But this means that he understood it basically as law. The complex of gospel, grace, and faith was missing, and the limited nature of such a conception of holiness implied that the reference to the Holy Spirit was also lacking. This concept does of course emerge,[5] but only as an incidental criterion in cases when decision is difficult, and not as the principle which determines the whole process of sanctification. The limits of natural theology are not transcended, since the ethical correlative to this is the law. The question of salvation has not yet been seriously faced, but is considered only as an appendix to the belief in God as Creator. This result is finally verified by his understanding of love as the deepest possibility of the law. He always speaks about love for God, never of the love which is God's.

[4] *Letters*, I.158, 15th March 1734, to Richard Morgan.
[5] Ibid. p. 138, 17th August 1733, to his mother.

SIX

Georgia

JOHN WESLEY never imagined that his work among the students in Oxford could come to a sudden end. His declining the Epworth living meant that he had given himself to it afresh, and apparently he counted on years which he still wished to spend there. Then came a very different call. Dr John Burton, tutor at Corpus Christi College, who was seven years Wesley's senior, asked him if he were willing to go to America as minister to the newly founded colony of Georgia.

This most recent of settlements owed its beginnings to humanitarian, military, political, and strategical considerations. Its founder was James Edward Oglethorpe, an officer and still a young man, who later became a general.[1] Himself the son of an officer, he was born in London in 1696, and had fought in the War of the Spanish Succession under Marlborough and Prince Eugene in Flanders, Germany and Hungary, been present at the siege of Belgrade, and had taken part in the battle of Schellenberg. When he returned home he went to Corpus Christi College at Oxford. On inheriting his father's property he devoted himself wholly to social work after the manner of philanthropy characteristic of the Enlightenment. He took part in the assault against smugglers and the gangs which disguised themselves as policemen in order to rob the Mint. Above all he gave himself to prison-reform. The condition of the prisons shocked every visitor, and they have been eloquently described by that shrewd Swiss traveller, Beat Ludwig von Muralt. By his extensive journeys in the 1720's he came to know France, Holland, and England, and was one of the first to draw the attention of the Continent to the distinctive importance of Anglo-Saxon culture. His letters, written in French, on the English and the French penetrate behind external appearances to the people themselves, and in this way combine

[1] On Georgia, cf. principally Leslie F. Church, *Oglethorpe: A Study of Philanthropy in England and Georgia*, a detailed biography; Ralph Butterworth, 'A Voyage to Georgia begun in the year 1735,' *Proc.W.H.S.*, XI.(1918).108ff.

pietistic questionings about the new man with concern for the natural man, typical of the Enlightenment.[2] Englishmen for their part had long since noticed the evils in their own land. At the beginning of the century, in the years 1699 and 1700, the most important of the religious societies, the Society for Promoting Christian Knowledge, had undertaken an energetic campaign for the improvement of conditions in London's chief prison at Newgate. The main troubles were the negligence of the warders, who joined with the prisoners in perpetrating crimes, the uncontrolled drunkenness, the dice-playing, and the absence of any kind of religious services. Old prisoners corrupted the new arrivals. The greatest harm to the prisoners themselves, as has been already noted, came from the herding-together of criminals and debtors. One of the victims of this deplorable system was the architect Robert Castell, who in the year 1728 ran into debt through the cost of printing an important archaeological work on the estates of late antiquity. He died in the Fleet Prison in London as a result of catching smallpox. Oglethorpe, a subscriber to the book, had visited him while there and was deeply affected by his death. This case set going a great inquiry into the prisons. Newspapers were full of descriptions of the conditions, but owing to opposed interests which were also at work the two prison-warders, who were chiefly responsible, received only mild punishment. Feeling among the people ran high. William Hogarth, the painter of contemporary manners and the great popular educator of eighteenth-century England, portrayed one of the governors, Thomas Bambridge, as a mixture of cruelty, scoundrelism, anguish, and remorse. Samuel Wesley, John's eldest brother, far in advance of the time, wrote an enthusiastic poem on the opened prisons. The public conscience was aroused by Oglethorpe's energetic lead, although, in accordance with English practice and tradition, the evil conditions were only very slowly removed, and not until 1869 did imprisonment for debt disappear.

Oglethorpe's charitable interests were directed to wider spheres and areas. He applied himself to the sailors in the King's Navy who received insufficient pay and who were the victims of disciplinary oppression from the junior officers. In the British Parliament, that incomparable home of fearless public criticism and free expression of

[2] On Beat Ludwig von Muralt, who as a Pietist opponent of the Berne national church was banished, and his *Lettres sur les Anglais et sur les Français*, cf. Paul Wernle, *Der Schweizerische Protestantismus im 18 Jahrhundert*, I.126ff, 159ff, 162ff, etc.

ideas, he attacked alcoholism and pleaded on behalf of the poor, especially the unemployed. The increase of poverty meant that commerce was denied the necessary flexibility. A law of 1601 tied the poor to the parish so that no settlement was possible. In 1723 a step forward was taken. Every two or three small parishes joined together to build a workhouse, but the majority of these institutions were breeding-places for idleness and drunkenness. Probably the only solution of the problem of unemployment was emigration, and this was one of the chief considerations in the founding of the Georgia colony. But there were other reasons also.

Thomas Bray, one of the founders of the Society for Promoting Christian Knowledge, had long contemplated as one of his dearest projects the conversion of the Negro slaves of America. For this he first found an isolated benefactor, then he collected further private donations, and finally obtained a body of trustees for the fund. These were known as Dalone's Trustees, after the first one, d'Alone. From 1730 Oglethorpe became one of the patrons of the various undertakings which Bray had initiated. He was in the happy position of having received still further private bequests, and he proposed to combine them all in one fund. The intention was to acquire land in the West Indies for a settlement of a hundred debtors discharged from prison. His chief associate in this was Viscount Perceval, afterwards the Earl of Egmont. In order to commend the project to such a man, who obviously looked at it more from the political angle, Oglethorpe emphasized in particular the fact that the new colony could quickly become a bulwark against the Indians and the French. An acute danger strengthened these considerations. The settlers in South Carolina were threatened by run-away negroes who had gone over to the Spaniards in Florida. By 1717 Sir Robert Montgomery had planned to establish a new colony there in no-man's-land, but only after the decisive conversation between Oglethorpe and Perceval in April 1730 did the idea really take shape. On 27th January 1732 the project was laid before the king, after it had gone through the various initial legal stages, and on 30th April 1732 it was approved, almost two years after the petition had been submitted. The reason for the delay must be sought in the fact that the project gave little promise of much economic gain and the members of Parliament who had committed themselves to its support must have been afraid of losing their seats. It was the great statesman, Robert Walpole, the Prime Minister, who allayed their fears. With the approval of the king, the trustees agreed to a constitution which guaranteed them full authority over the new colony which was to be set up. The legal administration was entrusted entirely to them; they alone were to appoint or dismiss the leading persons and the setting-up of a colonial force was to be in their hands. Constitutionally the new community was to be completely separate from South Carolina and only from the military point of view was there to be any connexion: the Governor of South Carolina was to be commander-in-chief of the forces. After twenty-one years, supreme authority was to pass to the king, but until then the trustees were to act in his place. From a constitutional point of view the whole thing was an experiment which imposed the highest responsibility upon those who initiated it. No such legal basis had been granted to the other English colonies in North America.

An important helper in the New World was the Welsh-Swiss Jean-Pierre Purry (1675–1736) from Neuchâtel, who founded a Swiss colony in South Carolina in 1730 and gave it its name, Purrysbourg.[3]

Only one hundred debtors had originally been contemplated as settlers for Georgia, although the further development of the Colonial plan showed larger dimensions. Nevertheless the first transportation was to be confined to 114 people, consisting of those who were in difficult circumstances in England. But on 12th October 1732 there was brought to the notice of the trustees a very different group— that of the Salzburg Protestants. The first ship left England on 17th November 1932 with Oglethorpe in personal charge. The Governor of South Carolina mustered all available help and provided twenty negroes and eight men, who used four saws to fell trees and prepare the ground for the new settlement. He also won the friendship of the Indians in the neighbourhood. Amid many troubles Oglethorpe himself, with Colonel Bull from South Carolina, searched for a spot suitable for the colony. The starting-point was the settlement at Beaufort on the Savannah River, near to which a trader named Musgrove lived. His wife, a half-caste Indian, became the interpreter for the colony, and it was she who negotiated the interchanges with the Indian chief Tomo-Chichi and the Indians in general. The first conversation laid the foundation of an abiding friendship.

Since the colony had been brought into being principally from philanthropic motives it aroused a lively interest among the British

[3] On Purry, cf. Türler-Attinger-Godet, *Historisch-biographisches Lexikon der Schweiz*, V.(1929).300.

public. John Wesley's own father welcomed the undertaking, for he had himself had personal experience of the rigours of imprisonment for debt. In 1732 John's eldest brother Samuel volunteered to collect money for it, and became the custodian of a silver chalice and paten, presented by an unknown donor, for use in the first church in Savannah. He could hardly have suspected that in so doing he was keeping the Communion vessels in readiness for his own brother.[4]

In view of all that lay behind the project the provision of churches was bound to occupy a principal place in the building up of the colony. On the first voyage Oglethorpe was accompanied by a clergyman who gave his services, Henry Herbert, who afterwards died in Carolina. In addition, Arthur Johnson, the son of the Governor of South Carolina, placed his services at their disposal. Finally Samuel Quincy, who was born in Massachusetts, was installed as minister in Savannah and worked there from 1732 until 1735, the first Anglican clergyman in Georgia. From the beginning Oglethorpe had in mind the conversion of the Indians. He did his best to understand their mode of thought, their morals, and their ways of life, and came to have a high regard for a great deal about them the more he came to know of them. They abhorred adultery and polygamy, and in one tribe, the Creeks, robbery was forbidden, although among the Uchees it was common and was even regarded as honourable. Murder was considered a crime, except when done to an enemy, when it was rather regarded as a vendetta. This, together with drunkenness, which was so often copied from Europeans, Oglethorpe considered to be the chief hindrance in the way of making them Christians.[5]

The colony grew slowly. During the first months the new arrivals slept in tents, but by 7th July 1733 the first forty wooden houses were built and by February 1736 there were more than a hundred larger

[4] *Journal*, VIII.283. Extracts from the *Journal of the Georgia Trustees*.
[5] Letter from Oglethorpe to the Hon.———, 9th June, 1733, in the *Gentleman's Magazine*, III.(1733).413–15 (*The Weekly Miscellany*, No. 35, 11th August 1733), in Church, *Oglethorpe*, p. 245: 'There seems a Door open to our Colony towards the Conversion of the Indians. I have had many conversations with their chief Men, the whole Tenour of which shows there is nothing wanting in the conversion, but one, who understands their Language well, to explain to them the Mysteries of Religion; for as to the moral Part of Christianity they understand it and assent to it. They abhor Adultery, and do not approve of Plurality of Wives. Theft is a thing not known among the Creek Nation, thou' frequent and even honourable among the Uchees. Murder they look upon as a most abominable Crime, but do not esteem the killing of an enemy, nor one that has injur'd them, Murder. The Passion of Revenge which they call Honour, and drunkenness which they learned from the Traders, seem to be the two greatest obstacles to their being truly Christians: But upon both these Points they hear Reason; and with respect to drinking of Rum, I have warned those near me a good deal from it.'

ones, many three stories high. In the middle of the year 1734 the population of Savannah was 259, and in February 1737 there were 386 males from all countries. In addition to the British administrative element, made up of English and Scots, there were Vaudois, Piedmontese, Salzburgers, Jews, Swiss, Germans and Moravians. It was the intention of the trustees that the British character of the colony should be strictly preserved. The Piedmontese were responsible for introducing the silk industry, and in addition potash was produced, medicinal plants were grown, indigo, rice, cotton, and vines planted, the ground cultivated, timber felled and bricks made. Finally there were the household personnel. For the first year the food to a large extent came from England and was stored in warehouses and distributed in fixed rations. A working man received 312 pounds of pork or beef a year, 104 pounds of rice and the same amount of Indian corn or peas and flour, 12 pounds of butter, while a woman or a child had 260 pounds of meat. A few settlers were allowed to farm and still fewer to hunt, so that gradually they were able to provide food for themselves. A series of five larger settlements were formed to be designated as towns: in addition to Savannah there were Augusta, Ebenezer, Darien and Frederica, the latter being originally a small fortress. As the cultivation of no-man's-land progressed the Spaniards also advanced from the south. A long period of skirmishing developed in 1739 into a proper little war, and in this Oglethorpe was able to make good use of his experience as a young soldier in Europe. As neither side secured a decisive result the disputed territory remained in the hands of the English.

The Europeans and the Indians lived side by side in patriarchal friendship, although in separate areas. There was very little intermarriage between the two races. The drinking of alcohol was subject to rigid restrictions. When the trustees allowed rum in 1742 Oglethorpe made an unsuccessful protest. By the Indians he was revered as a father. In 1734 he brought to England the chief of the Creeks, the aged Tomo-Chichi, with whom he had concluded a territorial and commercial agreement on 10th June 1733. With the chief was his wife, his nephew and heir-apparent, his chief of war and six dignitaries. They were presented to the King and Queen and to the Archbishop of Canterbury, Dr William Wake, at Lambeth Palace. When questioned about becoming Christians they maintained a reserve, since dismal memories of the methods of evangelism used by Spanish Catholics made it impossible for them to entertain the prospect with any enthusiasm. The father of the old chief had been burned because he would not become a Christian. On the return voyage they were accompanied by the first batch of Salzburgers.[6]

This was the spot to which John Wesley was to go: a greater contrast to his previous life could hardly be imagined. To be sure both places were in reality quite small, enabling him to keep in touch with the people with whom he had to do. But at Oxford he was taken up with the limited world of a great academic tradition, a rich intellectual life and the education of the students, while in North America a completely new country awaited him, the possibilities of which were quite open, and accordingly problematic. The folk with whom he would be concerned were a very mixed assortment. It might have been expected that he would have refused to go, as in the case of Epworth, since he must have been well aware of the lack of comforts, the primitive conditions, and the uncertainty of the new life. There was no guarantee at all that his work would bear fruit, and it might just as easily come to grief. The whole undertaking was in the nature of an experiment.

Surprisingly enough when John Burton's enquiry reached him he consented forthwith. Burton knew Oglethorpe well and the latter had at least a passing acquaintance with John Wesley's father. It was therefore natural that they should think of him. At first John Burton had thought not only of John but also of one or other of his companions in the group at Oxford, since he looked to their fellowship to produce something in the field of education. Here then was a project completely in line with the purpose of the fellowship of the Methodists. This decided the matter: the question whether they intended to remain a self-contained group or set about a task which urgently needed doing was posed in all its sharpness. Burton had shrewdly pointed out that not everyone could be accepted for the service which was being offered, but only those persons were required who were ready to forgo the comforts of normal life. They must be men capable of putting up with the austerities of a hard life, which was expected to be a genuine example of the Christian pilgrimage. In pointing out that this was a special opportunity 'of doing good' he was also taking up a phrase that these young men had made peculiarly their own.[7]

John Wesley presented himself in person to Oglethorpe. He con-

[6] Von Reck to Zinzendorf, Windhausen, 4th December 1734, handwritten in the archives of the United Brethren in Herrnhut, R.14.A.3.11.
[7] John Burton to John Wesley, 8th September 1735, *Journal*, VIII.285.

sulted his brother Samuel, his friend Clayton, and finally his mother. She replied: 'Had I twenty sons, I should rejoice that they were all so employed, though I should never see them more.'[8] Burton was overjoyed with his acceptance and in a later letter described in detail the problems and possibilities. Pastoral work among the colonists in Savannah and missionary service among the nearby Indians were to be the main parts of his new activity, but also there was the further missionary commission to preach the Gospel to the negro slaves belonging to the settlers in Purrysbourg. Moreover, Burton did not forget to mention in particular the great opportunities for evangelism amongst the passengers on the ship during the outward voyage. In almost every sentence he makes reference to the work in language reminiscent of primitive Christianity. As the apostles preached from house to house, so also will he do amongst his people. Those to whom he will speak are babes in the faith and like Paul he must not give them strong meat but milk, becoming all things to all men in order to gain some. In particular he drew attention to the importance of Old Testament history, such as the journeys and sojournings of the patriarchs, the 107th Psalm, the Books of Ezra and Nehemiah, since all of this is something actually experienced by the settlers. Not for nothing did Jesus value preaching in parables.[9]

All this John Wesley laid to heart, although he was of far too independent a nature to rest there. He went on to develop his own reasons for coming to a decision, and these sharpened Burton's view of the situation and put forward some quite new ideas.[1] Only with reluctance did he express himself on his own motives, about which he had been silent until then, because few would know how to judge them, and favourably disposed critics might find them presumptuous. He knew very well that he was speaking about things of the greatest importance. His first sentence is the celebrated statement which has so often been misinterpreted: 'My chief motive, to which all the rest are subordinate, is the hope of saving my own soul.' This is not re-

[8] Henry Moore, *The Life of John Wesley*, I.(1824).234; cf. J. S. Simon, *John Wesley and the Religious Societies*, p. 111; Maximum Piette, *John Wesley in the Evolution of Protestantism*, p. 293.
[9] Burton to John Wesley, 28th September 1735, *Journal*, VIII.287. The Old Testament consciousness of the Dispersion in its New Testament form of the Christian as a stranger on earth was aroused amongst the Salzburgers also on the voyage to Georgia; cf. my study, *Die Anfänge der Kirchenbildung bei den Salzburgen in Georgia 'Lutherische Kirche in Bewegung'* (*Festschrift* of the Martin Luther-Bund for Friedrich Ulmer) (1937), p. 31.
[1] On this see my essay on the missionary ideas of the young Wesley referred to in Chap. 2, note 21. The source is John Wesley's letter to John Burton 10th October 1735, *Letters*, I.188ff.

ligious egotism.[2] In the letter written to his father in the previous December, in 1734, he had stated that he could only view his own holiness and that of others in the closest connexion with each other. That observation carried with it a very strong conception of the Church, one which took seriously the indissoluble nature of the Body of Christ. In the present instance the emphasis on the salvation of his own soul is only the subjective side of a similar strong conviction. John Wesley is here concerned with the original understanding of the Gospel, and this is only revealed in a situation akin to the original one, that is, in a heathen environment. It was a question of the true meaning of God's Word, and that could only be discovered in an actual repetition of the first Christian preaching to the heathen. The Word of God cannot be received and communicated from books, after the manner of the Enlightenment, as abstract teaching or the learning of the principles of religion. Only in a living encounter does it disclose its content, its extent and its challenge.

In this way Wesley was giving even stronger expression to the contemporary urge to make the primitive Christian early-Church tradition vital in the present. He now saw that the best way for him to do this was to go to the heathen world, whereupon a wealth of early Christian associations and possibilities suggested themselves almost involuntarily to his thinking. The heathen, whom to be sure like Defoe and Rousseau he thought of in idyllic and idealistic terms, are not only particularly open to the Gospel as a result of their being untouched by civilization, which means that they are in an unspoiled state, but they are also like children in their humility, their willingness to receive and eagerness to learn, their obedience, their moderation in food and clothing, and their freedom from care, which shows itself in their renouncing the laying up of supplies on earth where moth and rust only consume them.[3] Is not the call of Jesus to His disciples to be as children realized in their manner of life? On the other hand John Wesley expects to lose his own pride and reliance upon self through his intercourse with them, and by his faltering speech in a strange tongue to avoid that vain speaking to which his natural eloquence leads him. He recalls in this connexion Paul, the missionary to the heathen, both in his readiness to accommodate himself and in

[2] E.g. Nehemiah Curnock, *Journal*, I.159; Leslie F. Church, *Oglethorpe*, p. 195, corrects Piette, *John Wesley in the Evolution of Protestanism*, p. 290.

[3] *Standard Sermons*, ed. Sugden (1921), I.478–9. (Sermon XXIII, Sermon VIII on the Sermon on the Mount, begun on 29th January 1736, on the voyage to Georgia.)

his renouncing eloquence of speech. Further he hopes in a manner reminiscent of early Christianity to become free from all ties with the female sex, since there will be no women of his own kind. He counts on living like the first Christians in a spirit of sacrifice, sharing his goods in common with others. The promise of Jesus that what is lost shall be restored a hundredfold makes it easy to leave home and relations. Persecution is the only factor in the primitive Christian situation which is missing. At Oxford Wesley had laid very strong emphasis upon this, and the fact that he now omits it is due to the idyllic notion he has of the heathen. But that he expected to meet lack of understanding, even hatred, when he got to America is quite definitely shown by a remark he made later on.[4] Hence a situation which entirely corresponds with that of the early Church rises before his imagination. That typical urge in his thinking, which will not rest until he has brought everything into relation with the idea of God, is evident in this case also. He thinks that the very monotony of his surroundings will prevent his eye, ever susceptible to the allurements of sense, from being diverted, whereas the cedar-trees will raise his attention to God, who alone is exalted. In this way he pays tribute to a sentimental age which inclined to nature symbolism, yet more significant is the fact that in doing so his thought mounts up to God Himself. He desires to serve his neighbour, and how better can he do this than by the Gospel? He does not anticipate any immediate success, for he is still an unworthy, unconverted instrument in God's hand. But then, if God will give him insight into His Word and the power to proclaim it, he will be making some contribution to the glorifying of His Name to the ends of the earth. Even failure has a deep meaning: it shows that men can do nothing, but God alone all things. Everything of value which he has renounced belongs to this world and is comprised under the text: 'The grass withereth, the flower fadeth, but the Word of our God shall stand for ever.' These are the reasons why the mission to the heathen seems to him a better way to salvation than remaining at home. In America he hopes not only to do good but more good than in England. But also he decided upon his new life for the further reason that in religion the man who chooses the more comfortable but less trustworthy way, when faced with two alternatives, cannot ever hope to please God. Here is the same religious radicalism as that which characterized the Oxford Methodists, a radicalism which recognizes only an Either-Or.

[4] *Journal*, I.371, 23rd July 1737.

Obviously it was the idea of the mission to the heathen which completely laid hold of John Wesley.[5] John Burton had put before him two tasks, but one, the pastoral work amongst the settlers, Wesley pushes aside, and concentrates entirely upon the other. To be sure he considers the question—the very wording of which in this connexion is significant—whether there were not enough heathens at home to whom the Gospel ought to be brought, but he replies summarily: 'They have Moses and the prophets.' Indeed it is most likely that he saw the missionary urge and missionary successes of his time as a judgement upon the deism and atheism of Europe.

The concept of mission here expressed by Wesley is fundamentally different from that represented by two other movements, the religious societies in England and the Danish-Halle Mission, whose missionary ideas naturally affected him, since they were part of his environment. For the former everything centred upon the missionary; he was the important person, especially in his love and his wisdom as a pastor and educationist. In the latter case the missionary was the servant of the Church who knew himself entirely dependent upon the work of the Holy Spirit. Wesley was more like the second, although of his own accord he went much farther. He saw in missionary activity the key to the original meaning of the Gospel, the rebirth of primitive Christianity, the existential way towards his own salvation. These principles were concentrated for him into a living awareness of history, bounded by eschatological horizons. He saw the majesty of the Word of God standing so absolutely alone that all human activity lost its value. Since both the missionary and the pagan are the same in the presence of the Word, Wesley came to see that there is in consequence a mysterious solidarity between the one who brings the message and the one who receives it.[6]

It is impossible not to recognize the intrinsic greatness of this concept of mission. In its reverence for the Word of God, derived from a daily study of the Greek New Testament, it is already a step in the direction of Luther. Obviously the external impulse was required clearly to bring out its full strength. How much greater is this letter accepting the Georgia offer than the one which refused

[5] This goes to the extent of regarding his brother Samuel's responsibility for the education of his pupils as a particular instance of the mission to the heathen, seen in his letter to his brother written on 15th October 1735. He cautions him against basing his school lessons upon immoral classical authors and concludes the paragraph with these words: 'For assure yourself, dear brother, you are even now called to the converting of heathens as well as I' (*Letters*, I.192).

[5] *Journal*, I.239, 1st July 1736.

Epworth! In the latter he looked for holiness basically in a catholic and ascetic way from the undisturbed practice of spiritual exercises, from guarding against the world, from intercourse with his fellows in the 'cloister', from persecution. And yet it depended essentially upon his own deliberate action. But now Wesley entrusts everything to the Word of God itself, and this reveals its dynamic power in the actual situation. It is this which the one new factor, that of the mission to the heathen, has accomplished.

The significant spiritual change which the removal to Georgia produced in Wesley's life is seen directly in the result it had on his writing. He now began to keep an exact and fully-transcribed journal, setting his own reflections alongside the account of events. His careful puritan watching over himself lost its schematic and uniform character. It was set free and it became autobiography.[7]

The departure to the New World followed very soon. On 10th October 1735 the trustees approved John Wesley as minister for Georgia, and he had then to receive his ecclesiastical commission from the Society for the Propagation of the Gospel in Foreign Parts. This was not completed until 16th January 1736, by which time he was well on his way to his destination.[8] The terms were that he was to receive no salary, but that he would have free food, house and clothes.[9] Nothing is known about his actual departure from Oxford. The student group continued in existence, but John Clayton had left the university some time before and become a clergyman in his home-town of Manchester, where Wesley had visited him to discuss the American project. The leader of the group in Oxford was now John Gambold, who afterwards went over to the Herrnhuters and who for a long time was one of Wesley's most valued friends.[1]

Only four days passed between Wesley's acceptance by the trustees and his departure. He was accompanied by three companions: his brother Charles, his friend Benjamin Ingham, and the son of a London merchant, Charles Delamotte, who had only just been persuaded

---

[7] It cannot of course be maintained with certainty that the finished form of the *Journal* originated at this time. It is possible that Wesley only made notes, which he later put into literary form. As the separate parts of the *Journal* are lost there is room for various conjectures. But even if—which seems unlikely to me—the formal account was written later, it is still significant that he made the transcription of the notes into a detailed journal begin at the voyage. He was conscious of a change. Concerning sources see Curnock, *Journal*, I.106.

[8] Cf. R. Butterworth, 'Wesley as Agent of S.P.G.', *Proc.W.H.S.*, VII.(1910). 99–102.

[9] *Letters*, I.211, Savannah, 16th February 1737, to John Hutchings.

[1] *Journal*, V.40, 5th November 1763.

to go to America, despite the displeasure of his father. It was during these days that John Wesley had an audience with the Queen, who accepted from him his father's book on Job, although with only a non-committal comment about the binding! Charles Wesley was ordained priest on 12th October in London by the bishop, Edmund Gibson. This was only eight days after his ordination as deacon, and he himself was not happy about this. Apparently John Burton and his brother pressed him because of the task which awaited him in the sparsely populated place to which he was going. The two brothers stayed in Westminster with a clergyman, John Hutton, a non-Juror who was closely associated with the Religious Societies, one of which met in his house. John Wesley was invited to preach to it, and the son, James Hutton, was so deeply impressed that he would gladly have gone to America with the young men.

The four went on board on Thursday 14th October in London, probably at Westminster steps. The trustees had chartered two ships for the voyage, the *Simmonds* and the *London Merchant*. A company of two hundred refugee Salzburgers were travelling in the second, led by the Hanoverian nobleman, Friedrich von Reck from Windhausen, who as English commissioner for the Georgia colony was particularly concerned with transport. On the *Simmonds* was a private party of twenty-six Moravian Brethren from Herrnhut, led by the sixty-year-old Bishop, David Nitschmann, a simple straightforward character.[2] There were about eighty English passengers on board, including General Oglethorpe himself. The whole convoy consisted of six large vessels.[3] The four Methodists had their quarters on the *Simmonds*. The voyage from London to Gravesend took seven hours.

John Wesley wrote in his *Journal*: 'Our end in leaving our native country was not to avoid want, God having given us plenty of temporal blessings, nor to gain riches and honour, which we trust

[2] This is derived from the travel-diary of David Nitschmann and his companions, which has not hitherto been fully used. It exists in a handwritten version in the archives of the United Brethren at Herrnhut, R.14.A.6, Nr.6c.1. Extracts in an English translation in Adelaide L. Fries, *The Moravians in Georgia*. In the handwritten journal for 3rd October 1735 it says: 'When we went on the ship H. v. Reck unexpectedly came to us with great joy . . . on the 4th November I [sc. Nitschmann] visited the other ship where the so-called Salzburgers are. . . .' This settles the question raised by P. A. Strobel, *The Saltzburghers and their Descendants*, pp. 75ff, as to whether the Salzburgers played any material part in Wesley's meeting with the 'Germans' on the voyage. The 'Germans' were only the Herrnhuters; cf. also *Journal*, I.117, Diary, Monday, 10th November 1735.

[3] *Journal*, I.109, note 8.

He will ever enable us to look on as no other than dung and dross; but singly this—to save our souls, to live wholly to the glory of God.'[4] In these words Wesley indicates that his motives were different from those who emigrate, that is to say, from normal worldly concerns. He thought of his departure at this particular moment wholly in terms of early Christianity. How strong this influence was is indicated by a remark which follows. The ship's cabin which he occupied with his brother had been originally allocated to another member of the Oxford club, Westley Hall, but shortly before he had married Martha, a sister of the Wesleys. John Wesley makes no direct reference to his own close relationship to this event, but dismisses it with the word from Luke 4[20]: 'He had married a wife, and could not come.' This sounds as if he had nothing to do with his brother-in-law, and indeed this can be accounted for by some doubtful experiences. His new relation had a bad reputation for instability, especially in connexion with women.[5] Yet the significant point is that John Wesley should account for his absence in these words taken from the primitive Christian tradition. All other ties had to be sacrificed. Here is the impulse towards ascetic renunciation of a man's homeland similar to that which drove the Iro-Scottish and Anglo-Saxon monks to the Continent a thousand years before.

The way of life followed by the four young friends was a continuation of their practice at Oxford. After a few days John and Charles Wesley gave up taking meat and wine in order to extend self-denial to the smallest things. They contented themselves with biscuits and vegetables, and in particular rice. John Wesley was in the happy position of being entirely free from seasickness. Delamotte was affected the most, Charles Wesley had severe headaches, and Ingham was not at all well. Accordingly John Wesley was able to get through a full day's work from four in the morning until nine at night. This was devoted not only to his own religious reading, but also to reading

---

[4] Ibid. p. 109.
[5] Westley Hall, a typical deceiver of women, first became engaged to Wesley's youngest sister Katharina (Kezia), and advanced so far in her confidence that it became generally recognized by the Epworth congregation. On becoming acquainted with her older sister Martha (Patty) he showed his preference for her. He broke off his engagement with Kezia, married Patty, but took Kezia with him into his home. In 1738 he became closely associated with the group around Peter Böhler, belonged to the early Methodists, but broke with them after several romantic misdemeanours had occurred. He made all preparation to go to Georgia and was ready up to the last moment. He had been ordained expressly with this in view, but then maintained that his wife and all his relations had opposed the plan. Cf. *Journal*, VIII.147–52.

to the passengers and to pastoral work among them, such as was prescribed in the directions of the Society for the Propagation of the
Gospel. John Wesley was brought into contact with all sorts of
people. One he brought back from unbelief, another from Quakerism. In conformity with his Anglican principles he rebaptized all
who were members of other Churches, with the exception of the
Roman Catholics, since like the Anglicans—and as he was soon to discover, the Moravians from Herrnhut also—they had preserved the
apostolic succession.[6]

The friends met in the Wesleys' cabin for reading and prayer. The
daily round was regulated with precision, and in particular all external diversions were avoided. Right from the beginning of the
voyage John Wesley instituted regular services with communion. On
the first Sunday there was a large attendance at the sermon, but at
the celebration of the communion only three passengers besides his
friends were present. Nothing daunted he was convinced that God
would increase the little flock in His own time. Every weekday at
8 a.m. Morning Prayer was said, at which thirty or forty of the
English passengers would be present. At this John Wesley expounded
the Book of Common Prayer in sections and earned the thanks of
many for so doing. In addition Charles Wesley instructed the children. Between six and seven in the evenings two of the four friends
read in their cabins with the passengers passages from religious books.
From the start John Wesley was fascinated by the people from

[6] On this, cf. Spangenberg's account in the handwritten diary, 30th June to
28th October 1736, in the archives of the United Brethren in Herrnhut, R.14.A.
6.d.12.d: 'He has moreover several quite special principles, which he still holds
strongly, since he drank them in with his mother's milk. He thinks that an
ordination not performed by a bishop in the apostolic succession is invalid.
Therefore he believes that neither Calvinists nor Lutherans have *legitimos doctores*
and *pastores*. From this it follows that the sacraments administered by such
teachers are not valid: this also he maintains. Therefore he thinks that anybody
who has been baptized by a Calvinist or Lutheran pastor is not truly baptized.
Further, nobody can partake of the holy meal without being first baptized: accordingly he baptizes all persons who come from other sects, although not those who
have been baptized in Roman Catholicism. He considers Nitschmann's and
Anton's baptism valid. Reason: they have an episcopal order from the apostolic
church. But he thinks it a great wrong in the Herrnhut community that they
allow their children to be baptized by H. Rothe (the Lutheran pastor of the
neighbouring congregation at Berthelsdorf, in whose jurisdiction Herrnhut came).
He will therefore not share the Lord's Supper with anyone who is not baptized
by a minister who has been ordained by a true bishop. All these doctrines derive
from the view of the episcopacy which is held in the Papist and English churches
and which rests upon the authority of the Fathers. Above all he believes that all
references in Scripture of doubtful interpretation must be decided not by reason
but from the writings of the first three centuries, e.g. infant baptism, footwashing,
fast days, celibacy and many others.'

Herrnhut. He was struck by their primitive Christian resoluteness of character. He concluded that they had left everything for their Lord, that they were dead to the world, and that they were filled with faith and the Holy Spirit. By 17th October he had begun to learn German, while at the same time the bishop, David Nitschmann from Hemsdorf and Andreas Dober, applied themselves to English. John Wesley was soon joining in their singing meetings at seven o'clock and he came to love their hymns. At eight the young friends met again for conversation and retired to bed between nine and ten. Charles Delamotte was learning Greek, presumably in order to be able to share with the three Oxford men in their study of early Christianity. John Wesley visited the sick and spoke with them on spiritual matters: he hoped, often vainly, that illness would have a sobering effect. During the day between one and four o'clock religious passages were read or discussed with individual passengers or their questions were answered. Benjamin Ingham instructed the children, but John Wesley also interested himself in them and compiled a catechism for them. In this way the sea-voyage became a time of intensive application to Church affairs.

John Wesley experienced both joy and disappointment. Even under the most uncongenial conditions the people thronged to hear the Word of God. On the other hand he found that many who at first responded to his work became increasingly hostile. This was particularly the case with several women; attacks and backbiting produced some unpleasant results, but this quite naturally confirmed him in his ideas about cross-bearing and made him see in the hatred of the world the essential mark of the true Christian. John Wesley took his pastoral work extremely seriously and did not exclude even General Oglethorpe from his ministrations. When Oglethorpe read in a devotional book a passage about the forgiveness of sins he was reminded by the 'Methodists' that shortly before he had insulted one of his subordinates, possibly the second mate, who had been insolent to his face and then to the general relief transferred to the accompanying warship. Oglethorpe immediately pardoned the insult, and was in fact a model of behaviour during the whole voyage. He went to great pains on behalf of everybody, he insisted upon order being kept without being excessively strict, he gave up his bed to a woman who was sea-sick and himself slept in a hammock. At first only Charles Wesley shared his meals with him, since he was his secretary. From Christmas onwards John joined them, no doubt by invitation, and took the opportunity of talking with him about religious questions. At the same time John Wesley devoted himself with the same energy to his three friends. Naturally young Charles Delamotte stood most in need of guidance, since he had only just joined them. Evidently the events of the day were scrupulously examined and set in the light of God's Word. No one was permitted anything without consulting the others. Doubtful points were decided by a majority vote, and when they were equally divided they prayed for God's guidance and then decided by lot—a method they probably learned from the Herrnhuters. Such then was the stern discipline with which the young men prepared themselves for their tasks.[7]

In the little library of religious books which Wesley had brought with him, there were two books that, in addition to the *Imitation of Christ* by Thomas à Kempis and Law's *Christian Perfection*, occupied an important place: August Hermann Franke's *Nicodemus* and *The Life of Gregory Lopez*.[8] He had come to know the first of these two books only shortly before; immediately prior to embarking he expressly recommended it to one of his pupils at Oxford and probably read it himself.[9] August Hermann Francke for a considerable time had personally borne the cost of this book which, though small, was rich in content. It was finished in 1701 after several years of continually interrupted work.[1] It faithfully represented his own character and his opinions. John Wesley was attracted to it to a remarkable degree. He read it in an English translation made in 1706 by Franke's pupil, Anton Wilhelm Böhme, from Oesdorf, near Pyrmont in Waldeck. Boehme had worked in London from 1701 until his death in 1722, at first in wretched circumstances as a teacher of German children, and later as court chaplain to the Prince Consort George of Denmark.[2] As a true pupil of the Halle Orphanhouse he

[7] *Journal*, I.127, Diary, 9th December 1735; I.131, Diary, 15th December 1735.
[8] Ibid. I.124, Diary, 24th November 1735.
[9] *Letters*, I.183, 30th September 1735, to John Robson.
[1] August Hermann Francke, *Segensvolle Fussstapfen des noch lebenden und waltenden liebreichen und getrewen Gottes zur Beschämung des Unglauben und Stärkung des Glaubens entdecket durch eine wahrhaffte und umständliche Nachricht von dem Wäysen-Hause und übrigen Anstalten vor Halle* (1701) 1709, pp. 71–2. John Wesley at this time read this book in the English version under the title *Pietas Hallensis* (*Journal*, I.116, Diary, 6th November 1735).
[2] On Böhme, cf. Johann Jakob Rambach, *Anton Wilhelm Boehmens erbauliche Schriften Altona* (1731) (with biography and index of writings and translations); Gustav Kramer, *August Hermann Francke, Ein Lebensbild*, II.58ff; Wilhelm Irmer, *Geschichte des Pietismus in der Grafschaft Waldeck*, pp. 26–41; and my article. *Das hallische Waisenhaus und England im 18 Jahrhundert'*, *Theol.*

made good use of his position abroad and his influence at court to spread the spirit of the Pietism of Halle. He became the English translator of the literature from Franke's Institution. In *Nicodemus* Francke with an inquisitor's acute sense and ruthless severity attacks the 'fear of man'. With a shrewd sense of reality he reveals its extent, its external causes and its subjective motives, its characteristics and manifestations, and the excuses it brings forward. Like Spener's outline of his objectives in *Pia Desideria*, written in 1675, the book is intended for ministers of religion. Like Spener's book it works with the basic idea of the Body of Christ, of which the author feels himself to be but the meanest member, but into which there flows the life, strength, and spirit of the Head.[3] This work must have commended itself to such a man as Wesley, who would recognize in it a conception of the Church similar to his own.[4] But above all, a similar primitive Christian motif determined Francke's thinking, and he too demanded the resolute renunciation of the things of the world. To be sure the Gospel permits marriage and property, but at the same time Paul requires a man to have a wife as if he had her not, and to sell as if he had no possessions. The pattern of the poor, lonely, despised, and suffering Jesus should be reproduced in His messengers and servants, but Francke fails to find this in his fellow-ministers. The clearest indication of this is the fear of men, which was unknown to the servants of God in the Old and New Testaments. So he comes to his main theme. As the object and requirement for preaching and the exercise of the office of a minister he sets up the simple truth as it is in Jesus Christ and the power of the Holy Ghost.[5] The reason for these being lacking lies entirely in the fear of man, which is apparent

Zeitschr. (Basel, 1951), pp. 40–1. His devotional works found a particularly ready welcome in Sweden, cf. Ove Nordstrandh, *Den äldre svenska pietismens litteratur* (1951), pp. 100ff.

[3] August Hermann Francke, *Nicodemus oder Tractätlein von der Menschen-Furcht Halle* (1707), a.3a: 'Dearly beloved brethren, For the sake of the love which God has towards us in His Son it is granted to me, the least and meanest of the servants of Jesus Christ, to dedicate and adapt for you this work. Though I am the meanest member of the spiritual body of our LORD Jesus Christ (thus will man reckon me) yet I share in the life, spirit and strength of our highly exalted Head; and what flows from Him is not mine but His and imparts itself in the strength of the Head not only to the weak and abject members but also to the strong and honourable, who cannot do without the weakest member, so that the whole body performs its work of improving itself.' It is noteworthy in this instance that in the example of the body an essential function is given to the weaker members acting on behalf of the stronger, whereas normally the opposite view prevails.

[4] See above, p. 132.

[5] Francke, *Nicodemus* (1707), a.5a ff.

in two ways: on the one hand as the dominance of sin among those who have not been born again, and on the other, as Francke says with characteristic discernment, as defects which still cling to the regenerate. He does indeed allow that it is a necessary feature of the fight of faith, but in Schleiermacher's words it is the inferior degree of self-consciousness which has to be overcome by the God-consciousness.[6] This psychological formulation of the problem determines the whole direction of the thought. Francke seeks out the fear of man in all its manifestations. He pertinently observes that it is more prevalent among those in high positions than those in lower ones, since they have more to lose.[7] But it is most dangerous of all in ministers of religion, since pride of office prevents their knowing themselves. They imagine from their vocation that they are converted Christians, and they cling on to their faults, the greatest of which is quite naturally the fear of men, which they instil into others. Indeed frequently enough they themselves become the object of such fear. In every case the fear of man, whoever has it, is 'a vicious thing and an idolatrous sin, which arises from unbelief, since man disregards the fear of God, and takes in hand, speaks or does an evil thing, or forbears from undertaking, speaking or doing a good thing, by only looking towards men when he ought simply to follow the Word of God and set it in his doing and not-doing as his own rule and standard'.[8] Thus the fear of man is made the opposite of real Christianity as well as the expression of attachment to the world and of indifference. Accordingly among its principal causes there appear those enticements which

[6] *Nicodemus*, pp. 3–4. 'It is here treated of the fear of man, both as a ruling sin among the unregenerate and as a failing which clings to the regenerate; even the sins of weakness must ever more and more be laid aside and overcome, while believers must through the power of Christ continually enter into the strength of the heart and the joy of faith in greater measure.' This distinction had been already indicated in the spiritual mysticism of, e.g., Joachim Betke, *Excidium Germaniae* (1666), pp. 123, 254, 266; Christian Hoburg, *Arndus redivivus* (1677), esp. pp. 43ff, 62ff, 67ff, 88ff; the whole book of Balthasar Köpke, *Dialogus de templo Salomonis* (*cum praefatione Dn. D. Speneri de Perfectione Christiana*) (Lipsiae, 1689), German edition (Neuruppin, 1695), Latin again (without Spener's preface) (Amsterdam, 1698). Köpke bases the attainability of a certain perfection on the superiority of the New Testament and its sanctity to the Old (Latin ed. [Amsterdam, 1698], pp. 15ff; German ed. [1695], pp. 8ff). The opposition of Lutheran orthodoxy to Spener was directed in particular against his perfectionism, although its limited extent was recognized; cf. Jacob Wächtler, *Drey christliche Beicht-Kinder wolten bey Herrn D. Philipp Jacob Spener zur Beichte gehen* (Wittenberg, 1697), esp. pp. 145ff.

On Spener, cf. in addition my article '*Speners Wiedergeburtslehre*', *Theol. Litz.* (1951), p. 22; and on English Puritanism, in Arthur Dent, *The Plaine Mans Pathway to Heaven* (1625), p. 21, Lewis Bayly, *Practice of Piety*, pp. 72ff, Richard Bernard, *Christian see to thy Conscience* (1631), pp. 290–1.

[7] Francke, *Nicodemus*, p. 5.   [8] Ibid. p. 6.

proceed from the world—in a word: 'The love of the world and of
the things in the world, that is, the lust of the eye and of the flesh
together with an arrogant demeanour.'[9] In particular these things
consist of false prudence, which judges divine things by human
considerations; false humility, which submits to human authority
rather than to God; worldly ambition, which desires to reach a higher
position; the false opinion that a man can please God and the world
at the same time; the self-deception of the human heart, which knows
how to conceal the true nature of all the vices. Finally—and this is
the most profound aspect—the fear of man consists in a lack of
experience of God. There is no disposition on the part of man in his
conflicts seriously to venture upon God or to abandon himself to Him
alone.

Corresponding to these, yet sharply differentiated in thought, are
outward things, of which the chief are wife and children, the esteem
gained in the world, the too great intimacy with the children of this
world, the promises and also the threats of the world. By reckoning
in a casuistical way Francke enumerates in all seventy-two of these
characteristics,[1] which include wrongfully keeping silent too long in
the presence of injustice and having a false fear of going too far when
in reality a man does not go far enough; the wrong kind of respect
for authority, which makes a person afraid of displeasing it; a false
fear of making use of St Peter's keys in confession, that is, by denying
forgiveness to all; giving heed to common rumour, which prevents
true friendships being made with genuine Christians; and the fear of
being thought singular and the like. The tenor of all this might be
expressed in one sentence: 'The divided character is not acceptable
to God.'[2] Although this sounds like legalism, that is by no means
the final impression. The heart of the book is reached when it sets the
fear of man over against faith. The great positive message of the book
is that in faith the fear of man can be and actually is overcome. The
command of Jesus, 'Fear not, only believe!', although not expressly
stated, is the note which resounds through the whole work. Faith is
the result of the power of God in the human heart. The holy Spirit
is first the Spirit of power and only then the Spirit of love and
discipline.[3] For this reason Francke refers expressly to the 'joyful

[9] Ibid. p. 7.
[1] By a different arrangement these appear in the 5th edn of 1729 as 73, in the
English edn of Anton Wilhelm Böhme (1706) as 74, in John Wesley's edn (Newcastle, 1744) as 21. In the third German edn of 1707 they are on pp. 13–34.
[2] Francke, *Nicodemus*, p. 149.   [3] Ibid. p. 125.

heroes of faith' who are described in Hebrews 11,[4] and directly
applies to faith the great statements from Romans 8: 'Who shall
separate us from the love of God? Shall tribulation, or distress, or
persecution, or famine, or nakedness, or peril, or sword? As it is
written, For thy sake we are killed all the day long; we are accounted
as sheep for the slaughter, but in all these things we are more than
conquerors through him who loved us. For I am persuaded, that
neither death, nor life, neither angels, nor principalities, nor powers,
nor things present, nor things to come, nor height, nor depth, nor any
other creature, can separate us from the love of God, which is in
Christ Jesus our Lord.'[5] The person who recognizes and esteems
this fact about the children of God is lifted right above all fear of
men, for faith saves not only from all dangers to body and soul but
also establishes a man in all happiness and in all the fullness of God.[6]
When the Bible is read aright we know that every good thing that
ever happened in the world was done through faith, because by faith
God is united with man so that all things become possible to him.[7]
This derives from the pattern of faith seen in Abraham. Faith is not
Luther's simple unconditional trust in the word of promise, but a
force which enables man to do great things. The important point is
that man should taste and experience the fruits of faith.[8] Faith is in
essence union with God, participation in His fullness. Accordingly
Francke is able to quote a favourite text in Pietism, the promise
from 2 Peter 1[4] that the children of God are to share in the divine
nature.[9] Similarly he viewed the history of the Church as the history
of the heroes of faith, and he cited the martyrs and Martin Luther
in support of this.[1] Faith is freedom from fear. 'For the man who
trusts in God is joined by faith with the strength of the living God
and the Creator of heaven and earth in such wise that he is stronger
than the whole world, be it visible or invisible.'[2]

This little book was John Wesley's companion not only on his
voyage to Georgia but throughout his whole life. In later years he
made an abridged version of it.[3] He found that it confirmed that

[4] *Nicodemus,* p. 123: 'It is no small quickening of faith when there is frequently
placed before us the joyful heroes of faith of both holy scripture and history. In
this way Paul sought to arouse the Hebrews in Chapter 11 of the epistle he wrote
to them, when they were becoming weak. And this chapter, because it is a glorious
epitome of the whole Old Testament, is worthy of greater consideration and
ought to be used for strengthening faith in every outward and inward struggle.'
[5] Ibid. pp. 122–3.   [6] Ibid. p. 181.   [7] Ibid. p. 179.
[8] Ibid. p. 178.   [9] Ibid. p. 150.   [1] Ibid. pp. 124–5.   [2] Ibid. p. 147.
[3] *Nicodemus, or a Treatise on the Fear of Man.* Written in German by August
Hermann Francke, abridged by John Wesley (Newcastle, 3rd edn, 1744).

devout radicalism of the primitive Christian attitude which he demanded of his student circle at Oxford, yet at the same time, in its characteristic conception of faith as union with God's almighty power, the dimension of religion as mere demand was transcended.

The other book which John Wesley eagerly read at this time was the *Life of Gregory Lopez*.[4] This was part of that deep enrichment which came to Wesley through Romanic mysticism, a characteristically intense type of spiritual culture. Lopez, a Spaniard from Madrid who lived from 1542 to 1596, spent the greater part of his life as a recluse in Mexico. At the age of twenty he renounced the world to devote himself entirely to the pursuit of salvation.[5] His aim was to perfect himself in love to God and neighbour. In order to attain to complete conformity with God's will he repeated continuously the third petition of the Lord's Prayer: 'Thy will be done on earth as it is in heaven.' These words expressed for him his whole life as a Christian.[6] His room contained only a Bible, a globe, and a pair of compasses.[7] Naturally, he read the Bible every day; indeed he had set himself the task of learning the whole of it by heart. He was especially attached to the Pauline epistles.[8] Occasionally he read other books as well, principally Church history and general history. He read through the works of Teresa di Jesu in twenty hours, and yet nobody could have given a better account of them.[9] His diet was remarkably frugal; for a long time he lived only on corn and herbs, sometimes on milk and cheese only.[1] He slept for not more than two to three hours and spent the rest of the night in prayer and contemplation.[2] His life as a hermit attracted attention, but at the same time aroused suspicion because it was not directly regulated by the Church. He caused offence because he did not belong to any Order and even more because he did not attend mass. That he could plead his great distance from the nearest church was of no account. The Archbishop of Mexico instituted an inquiry after he had received a number of protests, although the priest who was appointed to see Lopez actually became his advocate, friend, and eventually his biographer. The thing which particularly impressed him was that the

---

[4] The only copy available to me was that in John Wesley's *Christian Library*, L.(1755).335–406. John Wesley published the biography a second time: *Arminian Magazine*, III.(1780).249–55, 305–7, 362–7, 417–19, 474–7, 529–38, 580–92, 637–50.
[5] *Christian Library*, L.(1755).343.   [6] Ibid. pp. 347–8.   [7] Ibid. pp. 354–5.
[8] Ibid. pp. 351–2.   [9] Ibid. p. 353.   [1] Ibid. pp. 351, 349.
[2] Ibid. p. 369.

hermit could answer all his questions with biblical texts.[3] The words
he spoke to people by way of spiritual counsel, based always on the
Bible, were sought after and prized by men and women of all ages,
and he had a special gift for comforting those who were in distress.
They felt as though a heavenly light shone down on them from his
eyes and through his words.[4] When he had to go into hospital he
remained for the most part silent, especially at meal-times, which
were enlivened by the noisy conversation of others, yet when it was
a question of testifying to, or discussing, spiritual truths he spoke
with such authority and conviction that those most impressed were
the monks connected with the hospital who were trained in theology.[5]
His power in prayer was so great that it completely transformed
himself and his visitors also. His biographer, Francisco Losa, received such an enduring impression of the presence of God that it
remained with him in all he did.[6] Even great personages like Don
Luis de Velasquo, Marquis de Salinas, the viceroy of New Spain and
later of Peru, visited him several times and spent two or three hours
with him, since the hermit knew how to help him not only in spiritual
matters but also how to give him advice about political decisions.[7]
Lifted above the ordinary affairs of the world with its cares so much
to the fore, and utterly dedicated to God's eternal world, he seemed,
in his completely self-renouncing love and his humility, to be a true
portrait of Jesus. He was able to say of himself that it was not he but
Christ who lived in him.[8] Yet he was entirely without the visionary
trait of Teresa di Jesu. In his case everything depended upon the
individual will being subordinated to God's, and being directed
continually to Him in pure love.[9]

This recluse naturally calls to mind the great representatives of
eastern monasticism, from Antony the Egyptian to the Russian *startzi*
of recent times. It was his singleness of purpose towards God and
his continual living in God's presence which attracted Wesley to
him.[1] Here was Wesley's yearning after perfection in the love of
God. Once again he was reminded of the theme he had been taught
in his home, especially by his mother from the *Pugna Spiritualis* of

[3] Christian Library, L.349ff, esp. 357.   [4] Ibid. pp. 258, 364, 367, 374ff.
[5] Ibid. p. 360.   [6] Ibid. p. 377.   [7] Ibid. p. 368.   [8] Ibid p. 399.   [9] Ibid p. 393.
[1] Statements in John Wesley's later letters show this clearly. *Letters*, V.283, 6th
October 1771, to Philothea Briggs: 'A continual desire is a continual prayer—
that is, in a low sense of the word; for there is a far higher sense, such an open
intercourse with God, such a close, uninterrupted communion with Him, as
Gregory Lopez experienced, and not a few of our brethren and sisters now
alive.' Similarly *Letters*, V.338, 31st August 1772, to the same; VI.293, 10th
December 1777, to Miss March.

Scupoli-Castaniza, and which had been repeated and strengthened by William Law. It was to dominate his whole life. He discovered again that early Christian renunciation of the world which he had made into an inner principle and which he now expected to realize in the heathen wilderness of Georgia.[2] It sounds like an echo from his reading of this particular biography when he cried at the end of the voyage: 'How hard it is to serve God without distraction in the midst of secular business.' To be sure he immediately added, as if correcting himself: 'Happy are they who are delivered from this heavy cross, and so are they who bear it in the spirit of their Master.'[3] Yet the positive attractions in Gregory Lopez, including in the first place his strong Bible piety and constant use of Scripture, greatly outweighed those features which he found unsatisfactory and strange.

The talks with the Herrnhuters were naturally about religion and the Church, especially as they followed the singing-meetings in which John Wesley took part. From the beginning the hymns of the Moravian Brethren made a very stronge impression upon him, and he was not content until he had translated them and so made them available for the use of his own church people.[4] On 25th October he and Oglethorpe, true to the Anglican tradition, asked for information about the consecration of bishops, the Church order and the confession of faith of the Brethren. On 2nd November the subject at the singing-meeting, raised on this occasion apparently by the Herrnhuters themselves, was the falling away from the state of salvation and the loss of power by many Christian ministers. John Wesley was surprised that the Brethren did not say the Lord's Prayer, but David Nitschmann told him that its contents formed the basis of every prayer. Oglethorpe found it hard to believe that the Moravian bishops were plain, simple men; he imagined they must be 'grand personages . . . as was the case with the Catholics'. On another occasion they discussed the Holy Communion, and one of the three asked about its meaning and the frequency with which they celebrated it. The questioner stressed the fact that it was a sacrifice which promoted

[2] In the *Christian Library* (L.[1755].342) he comments frankly in a note: 'It is absolutely certain that this Resolution is not to be justified on Scripture-Principles: And consequently Lopez is not to be imitated in this; however GOD might wink at the Times of Ignorance.' Wesley is referring here to Acts 17[30]. Later (*Letters*, VII.198, 21st November 1783, to Ann Loxdale) he even says: 'Yet I do not wonder at the horrid temptations of Gregory Lopez; because he was in a desert—that is, (so far) out of God's way.'

[3] *Journal*, I.150, Saturday 7th February 1736.

[4] Cf. John L. Nuelsen, *John Wesley und das deutsche Kirchenlied*.

holiness and amendment of life, and moreover declared his intention of going to Herrnhut. This was on 19th January 1736, and it is impossible to say who this unnamed English clergyman was, although there is much to be said for thinking it was John Wesley, who was personally, theologically, and ecclesiastically the outstanding man. If this is so it means that already at this early stage he had formed the idea of seeing the home of the Brethren for himself, which he did under very different circumstances two years later. In other respects the subjects at the singing-meetings were those normally associated with Pietism, such as rebirth by the living Word of God according to 1 Peter 1^{23}, the sprinkling with the Blood of Christ which purifies the soul—in connexion with which the details of the sufferings of Jesus were in particular emphasized—sanctification, election, and importunate prayer and its being heard.[5] From the first meeting, when he began to learn German, John Wesley uttered the fervent cry: 'Oh may we be not only of one tongue, but of one mind and of one heart!'[6]

But all his previous impressions counted for little in comparison with his experience in a severe storm towards the end of the voyage. For some time the sea had been getting rougher, especially at night. John Wesley discovered to his shame how little he was prepared to die. He could not get away from the judgement which lay behind the thought of death. He reflected: 'Oh how pure in heart must he be who would rejoice to appear before God at a moment's warning!'[7] He did not feel that he was at all prepared for such a judgement. Yet when next morning the sea was calm again, life went on as usual once more, and everything seemed normal to the majority of the passengers and the sailors, who had only been moved to think of God and eternity in the danger. From this experience Wesley was made aware of the deep truth, which accorded well with his general line of thinking, that a person who is not drawn to God through love will not obey Him through fear.[8] He recognized that his own personal faith was in question. The climax came on 25th January 1736. The ship was driven by the sea, the waves washed over the deck, and the

[5] This is all from the handwritten Travel-Diary of David Nitschmann in the archives of the United Brethren at Herrnhut, R.14.A.6, No. 6.c.1.
[6] *Journal*, I.112, Monday 20th October 1735. [7] Ibid. p. 138.
[8] Ibid. p. 139: 'I will never believe them to obey from fear who are dead to the motives of love.' How central *love* had become for his understanding of the Christian position is shown by his comment after the storm at sea, in *Journal*, I. 143, Monday 26th January 1736: 'We now enjoyed the calmer weather. I can conceive no difference comparable to that between a smooth and a rough sea, except that which is between a mind calmed by the love of God and one torn up by the storms of earthly passions.'

mainsail split because the wind was blowing in all directions. The passengers were all transfixed with fear. Shortly before an English child had been baptized, and this put Wesley in mind of Jeremiah, who bought a field when the Babylonians were approaching Jerusalem (Jeremiah 32). It gave him the same confident expectation of life in the face of the destruction which threatened. He records in his *Journal* the changes in the weather, the ebb and flow of the storm from hour to hour. Even on such a day he joined in the singing-meeting of the Germans. He had already been surprised by their unassuming behaviour. They performed the most menial tasks on the ship, the things which none of the English were prepared to do, and for which they took no money. They never complained about improper treatment, although they often had to put up with it in various forms. But it was now that their real test came. David Nitschmann had just struck up the opening hymn from Psalm 115[14, 15]: 'The Lord increase you more and more, you and your children. Ye are blessed of the Lord, which made heaven and earth.' It was at this moment that the sail split and the English passengers were seized by panic. John Wesley moved quickly from one to the other, calling upon them earnestly to repent. The difference between the believers and unbelievers, the God-fearers and the ungodly, was manifest for all to see. The Herrnhuters remained completely calm: neither men, women, nor children showed the slightest fear of death. Wesley was deeply impressed and wrote in his *Journal*: 'This was the most glorious day which I have hitherto seen.'[9] It was the real turning-point of the voyage.

It is a striking fact that Christmas receives no special mention or consideration, but New Year's Day led Wesley to write: 'Oh may the New Year bring a new heart and a new life to all those who seek the Lord God of their fathers!'[1] At the end of the voyage he saw a depressing sight, when many of the passengers, presumably following the example of the crew, got drunk. Wesley's first act on landing was to make a personal vow to abstain from flesh and wine; his second was to stave in the rum-casks.[2]

John Wesley's experiences on the voyage were in many respects an anticipation of his life in his new sphere. On 4th February the ship

[9] Ibid. pp. 141ff, 25th January 1736, and the Travel-Diary of David Nitschmann, 5th February 1736 (unlike England, Nitschmann reckons according to the Gregorian calendar): 'I felt quite well, for our life is in God's Hands, He does what He will with us, no fear at all during the whole night until morning.'

[1] Ibid. p. 134, 1st January 1736.

[2] Ibid. pp. 149–50, Diary, 6th–7th February 1736.

cast anchor. David Nitschmann climbed up the mast to pour out his heart to God. He prayed that He would scatter and plant the Brethren like grains of seed. The evening text was: 'He regardeth the prayer of the destitute, and despiseth not their supplication.' First of all they ran alongside Tybee Island. When Oglethorpe, Nitschmann and the four Methodists set foot on American soil on 6th February they knelt down to give thanks to God from full hearts.[3] Then John Wesley held a service, based on the lesson for the day from Mark 6. He found the sufferings of John the Baptist and Jesus's walking on the sea both particularly suited to the occasion, and the central message was: 'Be of good cheer: it is I; be not afraid.'[4]

Before he entered upon his ministerial duties in this new sphere a significant event took place which must have strengthened the impression he had gained of Herrnhut. The ship was lying off the coast of Tybee Island. Oglethorpe took a boat up the Savannah River to the town of Savannah and brought back with him the leader of the Herrnhut settlement, August Gottlieb Spangenberg, the close colleague and later the successor of Zinzendorf at Herrnhut itself. He was an unusually practical and far-seeing person, and the preceding year he had brought a company of the Moravian Brethren to Georgia. He had been responsible for technical preparations and organization and had conducted the negotiations and sought out with considerable foresight the right spot for the settlement near Savannah. His care of his people had gone to the lengths of himself preparing the meals in the kitchen whilst they got the land outside ready for cultivation.[5] He now came to greet the new additions to his community. The fact that Oglethorpe brought him back is an indication of the cordial relations which existed between Oglethorpe and the Brethren. Oglethorpe immediately noticed how happy they were, particularly over David Nitschmann's arrival, and he fully shared their joy. He had already told Spangenberg about John Wesley.[6] Now the two men stood side by side, the Anglican minister and his counterpart from Herrnhut, of almost the same age. They immediately took to each other.[7] Since the boat which was to take Spangenberg back waited for a day there was time for them to have three conversations, from

[3] *Journal*, I.146ff, Friday 6th February 1736; David Nitschmann's Travel-Diary.
[4] Ibid. p. 149.
[5] Gerhard Reichel, *August Gottlieb Spangenberg, Bischof der Brüderkirche*, pp. 99ff.
[6] Spangenberg's handwritten Diary in Georgia (1734–6) in the archives of the United Brethren at Herrnhut, R.14.A.6.No. 6.
[7] The hitherto unused diary confirms this from Spangenberg's side.

which John Wesley learned more about the Brethren and their way of life, and Herrnhut, and the events which had led to Spangenberg's breach with the Orphan-house at Halle. In this way he heard about the difference which existed between the two groups in Pietism,[8] and this was soon to be confirmed for him from the other side by the Salzburgers' minister. When he asked Spangenberg about his plans for the future the answer he received made a particular impression upon him. Spangenberg mentioned the possibility of visiting a settlement of some people from Herrnhut in Pennsylvania and then said simply: 'I am blind. I am a child. My Father knows; and I am ready to go wherever He calls.' Spangenberg told him of Count Zinzendorf's testimony that he had been so full of the love of God since childhood that he had never felt the love of the world for so much as a quarter of an hour. He must have seemed to Wesley like a second Gregory Lopez, and it is against this background that Wesley's statement, made later after his conversations with the Salzburgers, becomes intelligible: 'He likewise is but a man.'[9] The result of Spangenberg's account was that a month later Wesley sent a short letter in Latin to the Count himself, written on the same day on which Wesley took possession of his parsonage in Savannah. He begged the favour of Zinzendorf and his people to include him in their prayers, and yet not merely in general terms such as would impose no binding obligation. Instead he expresses his desire for their prayer in the words of a verse by Freylinghausen which he had got to know from the singing-meetings of the Brethren:

> *Then the dauntless mind*
> *Which, to Jesus joined,*
> *Neither life nor treasure prizes,*
> *And all fleshly lusts despises,*
> *Grant him, Highest Good,*
> *Through Thy precious blood.*

[8] Cf. Gerhard Reichel, *Die Entstehung einer Zinzendorf feindlichen Partei in Halle und Wernigerode Zeitschr.f.Kirchengesch.*, XXIII.(1902).549–92.

[9] *Journal*, I.375, 1st August 1737; cf. also Spangenberg's opinion of the Count and Herrnhut in his writing: '*Declaration über die zeither gegen uns ausgegangene Beschuldigungen, sonderlich die Person unsers Ordinarii betreffend* . . . (1751), pp. 15ff, paragraphs IX, X, XIII, esp. 6. 18: 'I cannot deny that to me his speech has often seemed paradoxical and his behaviour extraordinary. I must also confess that I have often had scruples about it. . . . Yet . . . he is a servant of Jesus Christ. . . . If he has a failing . . . so has the sun its spots, yet we thank God for it.'

He felt that he himself was the smoking flax and the bruised reed of the Gospel, but because he saw in Zinzendorf a disciple of Him who would not break either, he sought fellowship with him.[1]

This absolute trust in Providence, which gave to Spangenberg's account of himself its peculiar character, had its origin in the conversion-experience of his student days at Jena. He had been gripped by the preaching of several ministers 'who proclaimed God's Word with power', and had accordingly resolved wholeheartedly to serve God. He had given up jurisprudence and become a theological student. His revolutionary spiritual experiences drove him into solitude and paralysed his normal bodily functions. When he could endure it no longer he went to an experienced Christian, but found that he was unable to speak. During the following days he could not even say yes or no, nor could he understand anything or follow any conversation. The one to whom he had gone recognized his condition and advised him to do what God's Providence was obviously calling him to—to take up theology and devote his life to the work of a minister.[2]

The impression which this account made upon Wesley is seen, not in statements about feelings, but in the precise way in which he relates it, which is in line with his disciplined attitude to objective fact. He was for the first time powerfully directed to sudden conversion as the beginning of faith.

The main subject of the first conversation was Herrnhut and that of the third, Spangenberg's life, but the second was about John Wesley himself and his task. He had stressed his plan for evangelizing the Indians and the fact that he desired to carry this through in the manner of the early Church. He thought that one of the brethren from Herrnhut might go with him, but there ought to be also ordained deaconesses in order to be able to conform to the early Christian practice of baptism by immersion for women. His standard for primitive Christianity was in general the concensus of opinion from the Fathers of the first three centuries. So runs Spangenberg's account of the meeting.[3] The effect of the conversation on John

---

[1] *Letters*, I.195, Savannah, 15th March 1736. The verse comes from Freylinghausen's hymn: *'Wer ist wohl wie du, Jesu, süsse Ruh.'*

[2] I must follow Wesley's account of Spangenberg's narrative of his conversion-experience in Jena, since here it is a question of its effect upon him. Gerhard Reichel, *August Spangenberg*, pp. 24ff, relies entirely upon Spangenberg's own sources, especially upon his letters to Leonhard Dober in the year 1735. He has not drawn upon Spangenberg's account in relation to Wesley.

[3] Spangenberg's Diary (see note 6, p. 150).

Wesley was quite different. From the first the question of his own Christian faith was intimately bound up with his task. To be sure he was going to the heathen in order to comprehend the original meaning of the Gospel and so to save his soul. But whilst he himself had proceeded from his personal concern to the practical one, and hoped to find the answer to his personal need from the practical task, Spangenberg now showed him the reverse way. Before replying Spangenberg requested that he might put a few questions to him. They followed the typical Herrnhut pattern. 'Do you know yourself? Have you the witness within you? Does the Spirit of God bear witness with your spirit that you are a child of God?' (Romans 8[16]). So surprised was John Wesley that he remained silent. Spangenberg noted this and went on: 'Do you know Jesus Christ?' Wesley replied: 'I know He is the Saviour of the world.' 'True,' said Spangenberg, 'but do you know He has saved you?'; to which Wesley answered: 'I hope He has died to save me.' When Spangenberg went on, 'Do you know yourself?', Wesley replied, 'I do'; but in his account he adds: 'But I fear they were vain words.'[4] In this way the question as to his own faith was posed with the most radical urgency, and it became a goad, throwing him into a state of unrest which was ultimately to bear fruit. It urged him on his way until it received effective answer in the conversion-experience of 24th May, 1738. Spangenberg seems to have failed to note the effect which he had produced, since he gives a much more favourable judgement about Wesley's condition: 'I observe that grace really dwells and reigns in him.'[5] With regard to the pastoral work he gave Wesley the sound advice not to meddle too much with women, but only to speak with them about the most essential matters and to ask God to do the rest[6]—a problem which already had exercised Wesley on the ship.

A second important meeting took place on Tybee Island with the Indian chief Tomo-Chichi (Tomochachi), who two years previously had been in England with Oglethorpe. He was accompanied by several grandees, including his wife Sinauky and his nephew Theenouhee, the 'Crown-prince'. Some of them were in picturesque Indian costumes, but the chief and his wife showed their friendly attitude to England by wearing English dress. The meeting, which John Wesley describes in terms appropriate to a State-reception, took place in a cabin on the boat. The Indians waited there until John Wesley and his companions came in, wearing their surplices and

[4] *Journal*, I.151.   [5] Spangenberg's Diary.   [6] *Journal*, I.155.

Oxford hoods, after they had prepared themselves by praying together. At their entrance the Indians stood up, which so far as the
women were concerned was contrary to their usual custom. They all
shook hands, and Sinauky, the chief's wife, presented a jar of milk
and another of honey, for she hoped that the English ministers would
feed them, the children, with milk and speak with words as sweet as
honey. Then Tomo-Chichi the chief, with lively movements of his
hands and head, delivered a speech, which Mrs Musgrove, the Indian
woman who had married an English trader, interpreted. With the
plain man's predilection for repeating the same turns of expression
he said, 'I am glad you are come. When I was in England, I desired
that some would speak the Great Word to me; and my nation then
desired to hear it. But since that time we have been all put into confusion. The French have built a fort with one hundred men in it in
one place, and a fort with one hundred men in it in another. And the
Spaniards are preparing for war. The English traders, too, put us
into confusion, and have set our people against hearing the Great
Word. For they speak with a double tongue; some say one thing of
it and some another. Yet I am glad you are come. I will go up and
speak to the wise men of our nation; and I hope they will hear. But
we would not be made Christians as the Spaniards make Christians:
we would be taught before we are baptized.' To this John Wesley
replied: 'There is but One, He that sitteth in heaven, who is able to
teach men wisdom. Though we are come so far, we know not whether
He will please to teach you by us or no. If He teaches you, you will
learn wisdom; but we can do nothing.' The four young Methodists
then withdrew. When John Wesley had opened his Greek New
Testament before going in to the Indians he had chanced upon the
words in I Thessalonians 2^{14-16}, which speak of the opposition of the
powers hostile to God against the proclamation of the message of
salvation.[7] It now seemed like an echo of Tomo-Chichi's disappointment over the conduct of the Europeans which had contradicted the
Gospel.

The two meetings at the beginning of the work in Georgia were
both providential and symbolic, for it was from the contact with the
Herrnhut Moravians and concern over the mission to the heathen
that the two decisive spiritual impulses and motives in Wesley's

[7] *Journal,* I.159–61. Benjamin Ingham gives a briefer account of this meeting
in his Journal in Luke Tyerman, *The Oxford Methodists*, pp. 75–6. His note
runs: 'We put on our gowns and cassocks, spent some time in prayer' (p. 75).

thought and action proceeded. Both pointed in the same direction and supplemented each other. Together with the daily reading of the Greek New Testament they helped to make primitive Christianity a vital and contemporary experience, and thus to clarify the original meaning of God's message.

The Indians stayed on Tybee Island for a day and representatives of other tribes presented themselves also. Wesley was impressed with their fine physique and attractive bearing. It was then that the work in connexion with the settlement began, and the four friends were at first separated. Oglethorpe sailed with Benjamin Ingham and about fifty Englishmen approximately 150 kilometres farther south along the coast to the new settlement at Frederica, while the Wesley brothers and Charles Delamotte went inland to Savannah. In accordance with their main purpose the first visit made by the three was to Tomo-Chichi's Indian village,[8] and only after this did they seek out Thomas Causton, the Chief Magistrate. There they met Spangenberg and were taken by him to the Herrnhut settlement, and in this way the two meetings they had had on the island were repeated, this time in reverse order. Prior to this they had all conversed in the Chief Magistrate's garden with Samuel Quincy, up to this time the clergyman at Savannah. With the Herrnhuters they took part in the evening singing-meeting, thus continuing the practice which John Wesley had come to love during the voyage. After a short sleep of three hours in the Chief Magistrate's house they returned during the night to their ship. In his Diary John Wesley put down beside this first day a significant word of caution: 'Beware America, be not as England!' He was thinking of the indifference towards the Church, the growing Deism, and the opposition which his group of students had experienced in Oxford. Finally on 24th February he left the ship for good and took the opportunity of speaking seriously to the passengers who still remained by reading to them from William Law.

Oglethorpe returned shortly after and took Charles Wesley with him to Frederica as his secretary. Hence only John Wesley and his young protégé Delamotte went to Savannah. There were no proper lodgings for their use as yet: Oglethorpe had promised the English missionaries that he would build a log-house for them, and during the first few days they looked out a place for it on their own account. The parsonage was still occupied by Wesley's predecessor, conse-

---

[8] Ibid. I.166, 19th February 1736: 'My brother and I took boat, and, passing by Savannah, went to pay our first visit in America to the poor Heathens.'

quently the two new arrivals had at first to live under the same roof with the Herrnhuters. Presumably they shared a room with them. The daily round brought them ever closer to one another, and this took place through the usual prayer and singing. But there were also talks, especially during walks. Wesley discussed at length apostolic succession and mysticism with Spangenberg, who, as the only trained theologian amongst the Brethren, was naturally cast for the main part. It was through his friend John Gambold in Oxford that Wesley had been brought into close contact with mysticism, and Spangenberg definitely professed his agreement with it, which accorded well with his previous experience with the separatist Pietists in Jena and Halle. It was natural that Wesley should also once again devote himself to the study of German and make use of Spangenberg's assistance. On 1st January 1736 Ingham and he had begun to compile a dictionary for learning the Indian's language under the guidance of Oglethorpe, but now their preoccupation with this grew less. Once again Wesley admired much that he saw among the Brethren; he noted their industry, which prevented them from sitting idle. He experienced their cheerfulness and good humour. He never heard them use violent language nor did he notice any signs of acrimony. When he had seen one of their number who was seriously ill he mentioned it to Nitschmann, who smiled and said: 'He will soon be well; he is ready for the Bridegroom.'[9] In all, Wesley discovered that the Moravians gave evidence of their high calling of being living witnesses of the Gospel, and already he reckoned that God had richly compensated him for what he had given up in England. He had left there many faithful friends and must have feared that their love was now growing cold. He had been separated from ten of his fellow-travellers, but God had opened to him the door into a whole Church.[1] At a consecration of a bishop he felt himself transported right back into the early Church, and it seemed to him that he was present at a meeting before the time the Church had either form or state, when Peter the fisherman and Paul the tent-maker presided, yet with demonstration of the Spirit and of power.[2]

The congregation which awaited John Wesley presented a motley appearance. It included Anglicans and Dissenters, although its direction was definitely in the hands of the Anglicans, a position

[9] *Journal*, I.180, 7th March 1736. John Wesley used the same expression for the death of a Methodist (*Letters*, V.51, 18th June 1767).
[1] Ibid. p. 169, 24th February 1736; p. 171, 29th February 1736.
[2] Ibid. pp. 170–1, 28th February 1736.

which was strengthened by their appointing a clergyman. As to its personnel, groups and individuals of very varied types belonged to it. In the first place there were debtors, mostly poor, but on the whole steady characters, although some were easy-going spendthrifts and swindlers. Then there were avowed adventurers and work-shy types who could not settle to any order, as well as folk who had made shipwreck of their lives and who were now intent upon making a fresh start. Then there were also the highland Scots, who lived in a group apart, industrious and disciplined. In addition to the English folk there were also French, French-Swiss and Spanish Jews.[3] This variety was naturally reflected amongst the leading personalities: it had not been possible to inquire into their background or standing, and they had to be accepted as they were. It was a world full of contrasts and hidden tensions which might break out at any moment. In sharp contrast to this diverse and motley crowd were the two quite distinct groups from Salzburg and Herrnhut.[4]

The same lack of precise definition and determination applied to the tasks with which John Wesley and his friends had been entrusted. He himself originally considered that he was appointed to missionary work, but now, at least at the beginning, he was to be a parish minister. Charles Wesley was reckoned as 'Secretary for Indian Affairs' and soon became General Oglethorpe's right-hand man. Ingham was to work solely as a missionary and did begin in this way, but he was soon claimed as minister for Savannah and Frederica, so that he had to be able to divide his attention between the two tasks. Delamotte had to instruct the children. The congregations were small and for that reason decidedly difficult. They had to be built up in very harsh circumstances. The proximity of Indians and Spaniards, with the French on the other side, the uncivilized life, always on the verge of war, and the great measure of freedom which was the occasion of dangers from within and without, all contributed towards these. The inadequate methods and means of communication made the Church work considerably more difficult. In all this John Wesley had to manage as best he could. There was no fund of experience accumulated by the Church's tradition upon which he could draw. There

---

[3] Ibid. p. 389: '. . . The Colony of Georgia is composed of a mixed number of Christian members of the Church of England and Dissenters, who all or most part would willingly attend Divine Ordinances and communicate with a faithful pastor of the Established Church.'
[4] Ibid. pp. 345-6, 4th April 1737; and earlier, p. 299, Diary, 26th November 1736.

was no bishop whose advice could be sought or to whose authority he could appeal: the responsibility for every decision rested alone upon him and his friends. It was indeed a pioneer existence, a great contrast to the sheltered life he had known in Oxford.

There was no church building. To be sure the trustees had provided a site for one, but the building had not yet started. Services, and probably the children's instruction, were held in the court-house.[5]

It was significant again that Wesley preached his first sermon on Quinquagesima Sunday, 7th March 1736, on 1 Corinthians 13, the hymn to Christian love. He impressed upon his congregation the truth he had learned from his own life and reading, that to love means to set God above all things, to live always in His presence and to act in accordance with His will. Once again this implied the characteristic equation of holiness with happiness.[6] In the Second Lesson too the words in Luke 18^{28-30} took on special significance for him. He saw himself and his friends as disciples who, in the words of Francis of Assisi, followed 'naked their naked Lord'.[7] A very large congregation crowded into the room, and their attention was so exemplary that Wesley experienced great joy in conducting the service. He afterwards added in his *Journal* that he was once again deceived about the real condition of the Christian in the world, which is loneliness and persecution. From the congregation he became friendly in particular with the doctor, John Reinier, a Frenchman by birth, whose parents, being Huguenots, had emigrated to Vevey by the Lake of Geneva. Even as a young man he wanted to seek a quiet place far away. He had acquired sufficient for his profession from his father, who was also a doctor, and apparently never studied anywhere else. He had been imposed upon by the captain of the ship in which he travelled from England to Pennsylvania and so lost his money. He found himself in the New World with nothing to his name and he struggled along laboriously as a domestic servant, cobbler, and button-maker. In the end he found what he was seeking with the Herrnhuters in Georgia. John Wesley was always interested in medicine. While at Oxford he was attracted to Dr Cheyne's famous *Book of Health and Long Life*.[8] In later years he himself

[5] *Journal*, I.174.
[6] The sermon, naturally in a more developed form, appears as Sermon CXXXIX, 'On love' (Works [5th edn, 1860], VII. 494–9); cf. esp. p. 495: 'Now, what is it to love God, but to delight in Him, to rejoice in His will?'
[7] *Journal*, I.179.
[8] *Letters*, I.11, 1st November 1724, to his mother.

wrote a little book of simple prescriptions which to his surprise was much read.[9] With John Reinier he read a book on anatomy.[1]

On the second Sunday, 14th March, Quincy preached and Wesley administered the sacrament, thus beginning a practice which he repeated every Sunday. Eighteen people took communion, and he anxiously asked: 'Which of these will endure to the end?'[2] The next day he was able to move into the parsonage, since Quincy had gone away to South Carolina. With his extraordinary love of order Wesley gave the rooms a thorough cleaning and carefully arranged his books. This occupied the whole of Monday, but his attachment to the Herrnhuters was so strong that he was only away from them during the daytime. He and Delamotte still spent the night with them. He grew especially fond of the parsonage garden, not only for recreation but also for the opportunity it provided for manual work, which reminded him of his childhood and his habits when he was his father's curate. His eye for flowers, plants, and trees made him sad when he saw the way they were neglected in America in comparison with England. It was a real joy to him when he came across a properly tended garden, as in Ashley Ferry near Charlestown.[3]

His day was very fully occupied. As a rule he got up at five, sometimes at four. Then he took part in morning prayers with the Herrnhut Brethren and afterwards himself read the Anglican Office of Morning Prayer in the court-house. Then he had religious talks,

[9] Cf. G. Gisler, 'John Wesley's *Tätigkeit und Bedeutung als Arzt*' in the '*Schweizer Evangelist*', 35.(1928).221ff; William Kirkby, 'Wesley's *Primitive Physic or an Essay and Natural Method of Curing Most Diseases*', Proc.W.H.S., XVIII. (1931–2).149–53; Frederic Jeffery, 'John Wesley's *Primitive Physik*', ibid. XXI. (1937–8).60–7. The book appeared first in 1747 and reached its twenty-fourth edition in 1792. The first edition contained 725 prescriptions, the second 808, and the sixteenth (1774) 1,012. John Wesley based it upon his reading and personal experience. He knew the medical writers of the time, particularly Dr Tissot, Dr Mead, and Dr Dover, but he depended most on Dr George Cheyne, because he advocated a natural way of living and method of healing. Accordingly he recommends simple lightly seasoned food, fresh air and moderate amounts of sleep and early to bed. This is his recipe for health. For curatives he wanted to see only household medicines used, which could be easily prepared and applied. The medical work of John Wesley is also briefly treated by Frank Collier, *John Wesley among the Scientists* (New York), pp. 30ff. John Wesley expressed his surprise at the friendly reception given to his book (*Works* [3rd edn, 1831], XIV.330). [Translator's note: See also A. Wesley Hill, *John Wesley Among the Physicians* (London, 1959).]
[1] *Journal*, I.176, Diary, 6th March 1736; p. 180, Diary, 8th March 1736.
[2] Ibid. p. 182.
[3] Ibid. p. 348, 15th April 1737: 'I walked over to Ashly Ferry, twelve miles from Charlestown, and thence in the afternoon, went to Mr Guy, the Minister of Ashly, and to colonel Bull's seat, two miles farther. This is the pleasantest place I have yet seen in America, the orchard and garden being full of most of those sorts of trees and plants and flowers which are esteemed in England, but which the laziness of the Americans seldom suffers them to raise.'

which he sometimes held during walks. After that he breakfasted with the Herrnhuters, wrote letters, read religious books, and wrote up his *Journal*. In between he kept free some periods for prayer. After dinner he read the Bible with the Herrnhuters, had further pastoral talks, and read the book on anatomy with Reinier, the doctor. Then once again he gave himself to devotional reading, worked in the garden, and prayed with Delamotte. After supper he read again and took evening prayers, with an exposition of Scripture for the congregation. Then he went to the Herrnhuters and, if he was in time, took part in their singing-meeting: otherwise he meditated on his own. After evening prayer he went to bed at ten. On many days he kept a strict fast and took only such nourishment as was absolutely necessary for himself. He and his young protégé Delamotte tried living for several days on only *one* kind of food, such as bread, and found this excellent, just as he had found from his Oxford experience that abstinence from wine was best for him.[4] Later too when all four were together again they continued an ascetic life. They slept in the parsonage upon the bare boards rather than in beds and ate the simplest dishes, although they could have had the best food from the store-house. When the Herrnhuters wanted to give them something better they declined it.[5]

In his reading Wesley kept in the main to the books which had previously appealed to him. His method was to absorb the contents for himself and then to pass on to his associates and hearers as much as possible. Contact with people always meant more to him than books; hence among books his preference was for biographies and accounts of personal religion from the early Church, such as the First Epistle of Clement, Clement of Alexandria and Ephraim the Syrian. He liked to summarize or make tables of the contents of the books he had just read: in this way he had already begun to lay the foundation of his great collection in the *Christian Library*, which began to appear in 1749.

His relationship with the Herrnhuters could hardly have been closer, and yet it seems to have grown stronger. On 30th March Spangenberg had gone to Pennsylvania, which meant that next to Bishop David Nitschmann—who soon left Savannah also—Johann Töltschig was the leading man. For the theologically accomplished

---

[4] *Journal,* I.188–9, 30th March 1736.
[5] Töltschig's handwritten Diary, 7th May 1736, in the archives of the United Brethren at Herrnhut, R.14.A.6.D.5.

Wesley, who had found in the select circle of the University at Oxford a second home, the meeting with these sons of peasants, working men, and characteristically lay-Christians, must have been a new experience. As Töltschig was walking on 1st April 1736 with one of Wesley's three companions in the little Herrnhut plantation, they began to consider how they might influence the Englishmen more and how the truth of the crucified Saviour could be made more real. On 20th May (German reckoning) Ingham asked Töltschig for the second time whether the Herrnhuters were prepared to receive him completely into their community. Töltschig put him off with the argument that they must get to know each other better. The next day John Wesley came with the same request. Töltschig replied that through the constant daily intercourse they had indeed come to love him very much, and they were also assured of his love. Yet they were not prepared to receive anyone so hastily fully into their fellowship. Wesley then asked what their conditions were. In his reply Töltschig referred to Paul's doctrine of justification and grace, which he set out with a wealth of biblical references: God has concluded all under sin and unbelief in order that he might have mercy on all and that no flesh should glory before Him. All men lay under sin and were its slaves, all did their own will and lived thus without God in the world. Therefore they were the most wretched and unhappy creatures under the sun. All the seeds they sowed brought forth nothing but corruption. So long as they remained the slaves of sin they had no part in God's promises. But Jesus Christ, the eternal Son of God, appeared as the seed long promised of God in order to destroy the works of Satan and sin. In the days of His flesh He did all things well and brought healing, shed His blood for us and bought us with a price. He has purchased us for eternal salvation, so that we should no longer be the slaves of men and of sin, serving its lusts, but of Him who died and rose again for us and is exalted to the Father's power.

In this plain, 'simple' way, said Töltschig, the Herrnhuters regard men's souls. Accordingly they try first 'to lead people out of themselves' so that they themselves ask how it is with themselves. When the word of power—a typical expression of Pietism—breaks in on them and pierces them through, when they are apprehended by grace, then their souls are tended in the way which best ensures that they grow in grace from one step to the next. But they are not admitted into the true fellowship to glorify the body and blood of Christ until they have genuine forgiveness of sins and are reconciled to God through Christ and have peace with God. This is the meaning of confirmation, after which a considerable time often elapses before they are admitted to the Lord's Supper. At confirmation questions concerning the whole plan of salvation and Jesus's way of saving man have to be answered. They must promise to dedicate soul and body to the Lord, to cleave to Him, to give themselves to the service of the Church, and to submit themselves gladly and willingly to its discipline.[6]

In further conversations, which Töltschig recorded under 31st May and 1st June, they discussed the historical validity of the consecration of bishops among the Moravian Brethren, a question which naturally suggested itself to the Anglicans. When Töltschig related how the first three elders whom the old Unitas had elected had been consecrated by the Waldensian bishop Stephanus,[7] and that subsequently an unbroken succession had been maintained, Charles Wesley and Ingham were very gratified. They recognized the Brethren as the oldest true, i.e. non-Roman, Church. On the other hand John Wesley criticized the Herrnhut community for allowing their children to be baptized by the Lutheran minister at Berthelsdorf, Johann Andreas Rothe, because he was not episcopally ordained.[8] As previously John Wesley and Ingham still desired to become full members of the Herrnhut congregation, but Töltschig continued to bring forward the objections already referred to, and mentioned obligations which they would probably find difficult to keep. These included a strict rule of ecclesiastical discipline that they should not baptize anyone not converted, whereupon they became very quiet and sighed over the degeneracy of their own Church. Töltschig invited them to share as visitors in their sacrament, but they did not avail themselves of the opportunity.[9]

In this way John Wesley's request was decisively refused. He could not submit to this long process of admission, and yet it is significant that he had sought so soon the most intimate fellowship with the Herrnhuters. It was natural in view of this that he should discuss with them till the last all his questions, pastoral problems, and personal difficulties. On the other hand Töltschig came to the Anglican

---

[6] All this from the same source.

[7] This tradition is now recognized to be a legend; cf. Joseph Theodor Müller, *Geschichte der böhmischen Brüder*, I.124ff, esp. pp. 135ff.

[8] Spangenberg's (?) handwritten Diary, 30th June to 28th October 1736, in the archives of the United Brethren at Herrnhut, R.14.A.6.d.12.d.

[9] Töltschig's Diary, loc. cit., R.14.A.6.D.5.

Morning Prayer.[1] Then a long letter from Count Zinzendorf himself arrived in reply to the one Wesley had sent on 15th March. The Count had written in Latin on 23rd October 1736, probably from Stolp in Pomerania, where he stayed for a few days on his journey from Königsberg to Berlin.[2] He enclosed a missionary appeal to the Indian King Tomo-Chichi,[3] in which he referred to the king's desire for wisdom, stressing the fact that true wisdom consists in the recognition of one own's ignorance and pointing him expressly to Jesus Christ, who is the saviour from all folly. In few words, written as if to a child, he tries to explain the meaning of Jesus for man's salvation. In the letter to John Wesley he takes up Wesley's quotation from Freylinghausen's hymn, 'Who is blessed as Thou', and altered it into:

> *Now may Westley own,*
> *Through Thy blood alone,*
> *A dauntless mind.*

He assured Wesley that he would remember his request in prayer before Jesus Christ, his God, and at the same time pointed out that as true Man Jesus was familiar with all the needs of miserable men from His own experience. In this way he expressed in a few words the basic principles of his own religious system, but in addition he proposed to Wesley a series of theological questions in order that their new friendship might be based upon agreement about fundamentals and not just personal qualities.

These doctrinal statements are typical of Zinzendorf's whole theology. On the one hand they carry farther the basic idea that the Person of the incarnate and crucified Saviour should be the focal point in every Christian affirmation, including speculations about the nature of God. On the other hand the Count strongly emphasized that the work of salvation is a fact which must be simply accepted. He will not allow any attempt at penetrating the mystery of the divine nature or its mysterious origin. One is to think of the blood

---

[1] *Journal*, I.209, 2nd May 1736.

[2] A handwritten copy of this letter is in the archives of the United Brethren at Herrnhut, R.13.A.17.2a–c. It is curious that it was not included in the Standard Edition of John Wesley's *Letters* published in 1931 by John Telford, although before 1914 it had been photographed with all the Wesley correspondence for Nehemiah Curnock, the editor of the *Journal*. Accordingly it has not been previously used.

[3] Handwritten without date in the archives of the United Brethren at Herrnhut, R.14.A.6.d.8.

of Christ as literally and really a ransom, like a sum of 1,000 thalers which might purchase the freedom of slaves condemned to death in Algiers. The first two questions concern the Person of Jesus, the third His blood as the ransom for sinful humanity, the fourth the sacrament of the altar, the fifth baptism, and the sixth the Church. Zinzendorf wanted to know if Wesley allowed that God the Son was in every conceivable way one with God the Father, so that baptism in the name of the Triune God was one and the same thing as baptism in the name of Jesus. He asked further if the word of the Triune God, 'Let us make man in our own image', was also a reference to the incarnation of the Son, so that Jesus was as much the Triune God as the first 'divine' Man.[4] He went on: 'Do you also believe that the Messiah, who was really born of the Virgin, was true Man from His childhood to His resurrection?' This implies according to 1 Corinthians 15 that He will at the last give back His rule to the Father. Zinzendorf saw here—and this was his own independent contribution—that same renunciation of His own works as that with which He began to obey God from the time when in His mother's womb. He does not confine the basic christological idea of the humiliation to the earthly appearance of Jesus, but makes it universal, cosmic, and eschatological. It characterizes the whole salvation-event both in heaven and on earth, the beginning and the end of God's method. Further he stresses the fact that Jesus was delivered up to every temptation, affliction, feeling, and passion associated with human existence. By the steadfastness with which He withstood them He attained the highest point of the 'divine humanity' which was possible and which He desired to reach. In His lowliness and obedience He surpassed all His brethren. Yet He does not cease with the loss of His humanity, for the 'eternal Word' will endure, even if destitute of the flesh. He is now inseparably joined to the Father and the Spirit. The eternal divinity of Jesus, the majesty of which He cannot be deprived, has the same status as the divinity of the Father and the Son. It is noticeable that Zinzendorf strenuously resisted the view that Jesus was humbled merely to accomplish the work of salvation: at the same time he was concerned to maintain strictly the scriptural statements about Him with something approaching anxiety.

In connexion with the Lord's Supper Zinzendorf affirmed that the

[4] Cf. the modern exposition of this idea in Karl Barth, *Die Kirchliche Dogmatik*, III.2, esp. pp. 47ff, and his disciple Heinrich Vogel, *Gott in Christo* (1951), pp. 440ff.

body and blood of Jesus Christ are realities which belong to the form of the Cross and do not reflect His glory. This form of the Cross is eaten in a manner which is real and which yet cannot be comprehended, and it is mingled with the bodily, mental, and spiritual substance of the one who partakes. Up to this point his view corresponds to a large extent with the Lutheran doctrine of the sacrament, but he then begins to deviate from it, since he asserts that the unregenerate receive no benefit. God's judgement actually falls only upon those who, in full awareness of what is involved, despise the gift, and it is to them that Paul's word of caution in 1 Corinthians 11 is directed. Accordingly Zinzendorf is against the wholesale admission of the regenerate to the celebration: they should be examined by the pastor to see whether they are really taking seriously the battle of faith. If this is not so they are in danger of taking hold of holy things with unclean hands. Yet people who are depressed or of little faith ought not to be regarded as among the unworthy. As to baptism Zinzendorf is in favour of infant baptism for the characteristic reason that it takes the place of circumcision. In the case of adult baptism, which he considers in connexion with the missionary task, he requires that it should be preceded by faith in the crucified Jesus.

His statements about the Church are very revealing and significant. He says that the bringing together of opinions and doctrines only leads to a 'religion' or 'religious community'. The significance of this was that it came at the end of a whole period of 'ecumenical' endeavour—that of the sixteenth and seventeenth centuries—which tried to establish the unity of the Church through unity of doctrine, and strove tirelessly to find common formulations of the faith. According to Zinzendorf the Church arises in quite a different way. It springs from the common relationship of hearts with Jesus. He sees three ascending aspects of the Church. First there is a 'spiritual' Church in which each experiences the same and which is by nature invisible. Then there is a 'living' Church in which the same is not only experienced but also personally confirmed, and this is partly visible and partly invisible. Above this is the 'corporal' Church, in which the same is experienced, believed, and made visible, and this is therefore by nature visible, even if small. In connexion with the last he no doubt has his own community in mind. The same classification applies to the organization and names of the church office-bearers. The 'servants of the Lord' in the religious fellowship are heralds, exhorters, and preachers. In the living Church, inasmuch as the

165

emphasis is upon establishing the content of belief, they are theologians and scholars. In the corporal Church on the other hand they are members who are appointed in virtue of their capabilities and spiritual gifts. He concludes with the assertion that the reformed Church is a religious community, while the invisible Church is that which all believers everywhere seek after. It is mixed because partly episcopal and partly presbyterian. The company of the Brethren in Georgia is cited as an example of the visible Church.[5]

It may be questioned whether Wesley really understood this way of presenting the problem or if he was able to estimate its importance. Apparently he did not reply to the points. It was however of the greatest significance for the history of the Church that Zinzendorf right from the start felt it necessary to propose a theological basis for their future meeting and their nascent association. While this was the case from Zinzendorf's side, it must have made a strong impression upon Wesley that so much intellectual strength was hidden in the simple community of the Brethren, which he had come to know mainly from its lay aspect.

On 14th May[6] he began to translate their hymns into English and in this way their influence upon his own faith was strengthened at a decisive moment.[7] It was on 27th October 1735, two weeks after the start of the voyage, that he had first come across the German 'Hymn-book', probably the first Moravian hymn-book of 1735.[8] It was through the singing-meetings that he had been drawn closer to the Moravians. Possibly they also had with them the classic hymn-book of Pietism, Freylinghausen's from Halle, first published in 1704. While the conversations with Spangenberg were presumably conducted in Latin,[9] he had by now become so proficient in German that he was able to attempt the translation. He had a German-English lexicon published in Leipzig in 1716,[1] and he appears also to have

---

[5] Zinzendorf's Latin is as follows: '*Religio sive civitas religiosa, ecclesia spiritualis, animalis, corporalis. Ministri Domini in re publica religiosa praecones sunt, in invisibili vel Apostoli, vel Evangelistae in mixta animali et rationali doctores, in corporali seu locali et visibili membra, pro viribus et charismasi collocanda. Ecclesia Reformata religio est; ad invisibilem in omni terrarum orbe properant animi, mixta est, quae vel Presbyterio vel Episcopatui, vel alii favet ritui, visibilis est, e.g. coetus in Georgia fratrum.*

[6] The date varies somewhat. According to *Journal*, I.211, Diary, it was 5th May in the Julian calendar, which would be the 16th in the Gregorian. In Töltschig's Diary it is 14th May according to the Gregorian reckoning: 'On the 14th (May) Mr Westli began to translate our hymns into English.'

[7] Cf. principally John L. Nuelsen, *John Wesley und das deutsche Kirchenlied*.

[8] *Journal*, I.114, Diary, 27th October 1735.

[9] Nuelsen (*John Wesley und das deutsche Kirchenlied*) thinks this is certain.

[1] Nuelsen, ibid. pp. 23 and 143, note 11.

planned one himself in virtue of his association with the Herrnhuters. The first four hymns which he translated and at the same time abbreviated were: 'O Jesu, Source of calm repose', from the hymn by Freylinghausen; 'My soul before Thee prostrate lies', by Christian Friedrich Richter; 'Jesu, to Thee my soul I bow', from the German of Zinzendorf; and 'To Thee with heart and mouth I sing', by Paul Gerhardt. By a happy touch he brought together in this way representatives of Lutheran Orthodoxy and the Pietism of both Halle and Herrnhut. If their contents are examined it will be seen that the first three, those of the two representatives of Halle and that of Zinzendorf, are expressly hymns about Jesus. What do they say about Him and in what way do they confess Him? Freylinghausen adores the miracle of the unity of the God-Man in the incarnation and in the work of salvation. In words reminiscent of Paul and John he gives concise expression to this great original Fact. The triad of light, love and life, the splendour of glory, and the fullness of time, reveal their power in the lines which Wesley chose. But Freylinghausen also expresses the longing of the believer to regain the true image of God in his soul. He prays for that heroic spirit which will not yield in the struggle with the world and the lusts of the flesh, but does its utmost to triumph, at the same time being prepared to sacrifice both life and possessions. John Wesley was here on familiar ground, and it is possible to locate each of these elements. The view of the incarnation, established in Christian tradition by Irenaeus, Athanasius, and Cyril, in which the christology is understood soteriologically, was the basic idea in Anglican theology. A yearning after the true image of God was the central idea in the thought of Scougal and Castaniza and the religious writings of Law. Romanic mysticism stressed the spiritual conflict against carnal lusts. Mystical tendencies are seen even more clearly in Richter's hymn. The emphasis is upon resignation and the purification of the love for God, which has to be freed from every self-centred motive. Everything depends upon grace, and there is a summons to the most severe struggle against 'false activity'. The emphasis upon love reaches its climax in Zinzendorf's bridal-song of the soul, in which the believer once again prays for purification from creaturely self-centredness, and seeks for that genuine fire to inflame his cold heart. He prays that he may have a part in the victorious power which streams from the blood of Jesus, by which sin shall be slain and the image of God made a living reality. The child has to find his way back to the Father's house. These were all themes to which Wesley was wholeheartedly devoted. Love as the basic motive was continually stressed; grace, as the activity of God to which man's effort was subordinated, governed the whole presentation. So the hymns indicated a step towards the fundamental insight of the Reformation that salvation is effected by grace alone. Characteristic- ally Wesley, by abbreviating Zinzendorf's hymn, omits its strangely powerful erotic touch and so takes from it—notwithstanding its im- provement [2]—something of its vitality. Paul Gerhardt took him into quite a different realm. In it the dominant note was from first to last a reverent gratitude to the Creator. Wesley translated only the first six verses, which one by one set out God's temporal gifts. In this case too there were points of contact for him, for in addition to the characteristic concepts of Jeremy Taylor there was his own feeling for God's creation and for material things, his delight in the beauty and fertility of the garden.

These hymns are all prayers and penetrate into that inmost place where God and man come face to face, and which provides the basis for a deep, abiding relationship. This same strongly personal aspect of prayer is also seen in the two hymns which are found, in addition to the ones already mentioned, in Wesley's first hymn-book, which appeared in Charlestown in 1736. The first, Ernst Lange's poem, 'O God, Thou bottomless abyss', is a hymn of adoration which extols the power and omnipotence of God in exalted and solemn words. It depicts His sovereign authority in heaven and His sway over all creatures. Another hymn about Jesus, Christian Friedrich Richter's 'Thou Lamb of God, Thou Prince of peace', takes the obedience and sacrifice of the Lamb as the pattern for the personal behaviour of the believer, and also expresses the desire that the transformation of the suffering lamb into the victorious lion might be accomplished in the Christian's own combat. Fellowship with Christ in this life and its eternal consummation in glory is the thread which runs through the whole poem and which colours each expression used.

John Wesley thus entered into the rich heritage of the hymns of Pietism, and his translations, both in their language and content, show a real understanding of the meaning of the originals. They helped him to penetrate still more deeply into the world of the Bible and so strengthened him in those principles of primitive Christianity on which he based his life. Later Wesley said that he had gained another

[2] Nuelsen (*John Wesley und das deutsche Kirchenlied*, p. 69) rightly draws attention to this. He sees it only as improvement.

valuable thing from his meeting with the Herrnhut Brethren, namely the use of the biblical lot in cases where he was faced with difficult decisions.[3] Yet as far as possible he tried to guard against using the text of the Bible mechanically like an oracle and always endeavoured to do justice to the context of the scripture references which he found by means of the lot.

Wesley's relationship with the Herrnhut Brethren was characterized by an open and lasting friendship, and yet it must have had its darker moments. Later he complained that the Brethren had mistrusted him. In particular they thought it likely that he had written letters to England against them; accordingly for a period of five months they broke off their association with him.[4] On many occasions also they did not reply to him, and when he was not immediately convinced by all they said, spoke no more with him about the point.[5] But all this was as nothing to the great amount he gained from them, and not a word about it appeared in his *Journal*.

At the same time the Salzburgers provided a corrective to this constant and close fellowship with the Herrnhut Brethren. Their settlement of New Ebenezer lay to the north of the Georgia colony, near to Purrysbourg. The distance from Savannah prevented frequent visits being made and a regular interchange was impossible. The commissioner, von Reck, who had brought them over from Europe in different batches, was also on this occasion a fellow-traveller in the second ship, the *London Merchant*. He had imbibed the Pietism of both Halle and Herrnhut, and vacillated between the two movements. Naturally he was reproached by both,[6] but in a real way this must have commended him to John Wesley as a mediator. During the first days Wesley had from him a detailed account of New Ebenezer and wrote a letter to the actual leader of the community, the minister Johann Martin Bolzius.[7] The two pastors—the other was Israel Christian Gronau—had come from the Orphan-house at Halle and had been active there as teachers before they answered the

---

[3] *Journal*, I.435, 3rd February 1738. The lot itself had been taken over by the Brethren Community from the old Bohemian United Brethren.

[4] Peter Böhler's Diary, London, 18th February 1738, until the end of May, handwritten, in the archives of the United Brethren at Herrnhut, R.13.A.No.4.

[5] Ibid., 15th March 1738.

[6] See below, pp. 171ff.

[7] *Journal*, I.182, Diary, Saturday 13th March 1736; cf. my study, *Die Anfänge der Kirchenbildung bei den Salzburgern in Georgia in 'Lutherische Kirche in Bewegung'*, *Festschrift des Martin Luther-Bundes for Friedrich Ulmer* (1937), pp. 21–40.

call to America. They had been ordained at the pietistic court of the
Count Christian Ernst of Stolberg in Wernigerode [8] by the chaplain
Samuel Lau, a man who had come to the justification of sinners
through grace after severe spiritual struggles, and who combined in
his preaching features of the Reformation and Pietism.[9] This is seen
in his ordination sermon, which applied the text from Isaiah 54[3-5]
entirely to the situation of the emigrant, and expressed the hope that
the great promises of divine aid might be richly fulfilled in them.
At the same time they should hold fast to them in every difficulty and
temptation. He exhorted them to fight boldly against internal and
external foes. Earlier the two men had been influenced by Spener's
ideas about 'the importance of the office of a shepherd of souls',
which the father of Lutheran Pietism had expressed in the preface to
his book *On Nature and Grace*. Shortly before their departure they
were brought up against these ideas again in Halle. In the first place
the ministers were faced with the demand for a personal, living
knowledge of Jesus Christ, but then their attention had been directed
to their congregation. They were to acquire a clear and true picture
of the state of their people, to take upon themselves their spiritual
and biblical suffering with compassionate love and yet not to offer
their words of comfort indiscriminately. Above all they were not to
console too hastily, lest they lull their people into a false security. If
it was Spener who urged the importance of the care of souls in the
true sense of the word upon the young ministers, it was Lau who
directed them to the fundamental ideas of Luther on the relationship
between promise and faith.[1] In their work among the members of
their congregation they themselves used the Bible and Luther's
Smaller Catechism, which became very dear to the simple miners.[2]
A typical example of the way in which they prepared themselves was

[8] The German sponsors of the Salzburgers, Professor Gotthilf August Francke
of Halle and Friedrich Michael Ziegenhagen, chaplain at the Court in Kensington,
stressed the importance of the ordination taking place in Germany, since in
London the Anglican bishop claimed the exclusive right to ordain. Similarly
Ziegenhagen, when he wanted an assistant for himself from the Orphan-house at
Halle, required that he be ordained. Ziegenhagen to G. A. Francke, 30th October
1733, archives of Francke's Institution at Halle, Missionary archive, Z.I.L.2.
[9] Concerning Samuel Lau, cf. L. Renner, *Lebensbilder aus der Pietistenzeit*,
pp. 331-2.
[1] For Luther cf. primarily the classical reference from *De captivitate Baby-
loniva*: 'For where there is the word of a promise-keeping God, there is needed
the faith of a man who accepts it' (W.A.6, 514, 13).
[2] Handwritten, Ebenezer Diary (1736) in the archives of Francke's Institution at
Halle, Missionary archive, 5.D.2 (formerly Z.IV.I.2.), p. 102, 2nd June 1736,
'Instruction for a convert from Catholicism to Lutheranism'.

their reading at the Whitsun of 1736 of a sermon by August Hermann Francke on Revelation 22 [17].[3]

Bolzius was undoubtedly the leading character of the two. His ability and prudence were constantly praised.[4] But Gronau worked admirably with him. The critical attitude which Halle and Wernigerode, as the homes of the classical Pietism of the type of August Hermann Francke, maintained against Count Zinzendorf and the Herrnhut Brethren was naturally shared by the Salzburger ministers. Above all von Reck, by his, to say the least, equivocal undertakings had contributed considerably towards further estrangement and constantly given cause for suspicion. Even during the first transportation Bolzius gained an unfavourable impression of him. At that time Friedrich Michael Ziegenhagen, the German chaplain at Kensington in London, still believed that he had more or less to take him under his care.[5] It was, however, during preparations for the second transportation in the autumn of 1734 that the decisive disagreement occurred, which from then on adversely affected the whole undertaking in Georgia.

Von Reck had returned to his home at Windhausen in Hanover. From there he set out to visit Gotthilf August Francke and also Samuel Urlsperger in Augsburg, the two spiritual fathers of the Salzburg emigrants. Urlsperger was minister of St Anne's and was the senior amongst the clergy of the town. Through his friendship with August Hermann Francke he had since his youth also been closely associated with the work of the Halle orphanage. At the conclusion of his student course he made an educational journey to England, where he found many friends and was also received as a member of the Society for Promoting Christian Knowledge. His position as the leading figure in the whole enterprise for the care of the Salzburgers was one into which he grew almost as a matter of course. On his journey south von Reck made a detour to Ebersdorf in Thuringia to Count Reuss. This household was the home of Zinzendorf's wife, Erdmuthe Dorothea. From there he was able to

[3] Handwritten, Ebenezer Diary, 1st January to the end of December 1736, ibid. in Halle Missionary archive, p. 68.
[4] Esp. Ziegenhagen to G. A. Francke, 28th January 1741 and 2nd December 1741, handwritten, in Halle, ibid. Z.I.L.5.
[5] Ziegenhagen to G. A. Francke, handwritten, 24th December 1733, ibid. in Halle, Z.I.L.2: 'Herr Commissioner von Reck is to be sure a young man, and, I presume, sanguine and therefore naturally still very fickle and somewhat indiscreet. However, it may be that Herr Boltzius looks at some things more strictly and sees them as worse than they really are, in that perhaps he arrived at a different and more favourable idea of the Commissioner, before he had seen and spoken with him. . . .'

make a personal visit to Herrnhut. Everything was made easy for
him, a carriage being put at his disposal, and he stayed with the
Moravian community from 17th to 21st October. He was greatly
pleased with what he saw and heard, and it was apparently then that
he conceived the plan for reconciling the contending parties of Halle
and Herrnhut, just as Zinzendorf himself while a student in Wittenberg had wanted to bring together the orthodox theologians of
Wittenberg and the Halle pietists. While still at Ebersdorf von Reck
wrote in this vein to Urlsperger,[6] who first sharply rebuked him for
the arbitrary way in which he had made such a considerable change
in his itinerary. Then followed 'complaints' about Zinzendorf and
his wilful, self-complacent innovations, how he knew better than
anyone else, the arrogance of his community, his peculiar teaching
about marriage, his abandonment of confession at the Communion,
and such like. Urlsperger said that he would be pleased if the
Brethren really were the leaven permeating the Church for its salvation, but as this was not so, and only ecclesiastical self-satisfaction,
Pharisaism and strife were produced, the congregations not yet
affected by the Herrnhut malady must be protected. He granted that
it was von Reck's lack of experience which prevented him from per-
ceiving things correctly. 'My dear Herr von Reck,' he wrote, 'you
have only recently been converted and you do not adequately grasp
the situation. Thirty years ago I also would have written as you have
done, but it really will not do. Count Zinzendorf must change completely, or I am bound by my conscience to do what I judge to be
right before God. My party is what is good, right and true. Most of
the people in Herrnhut do not understand what is now happening. I

---

[6] Von Reck to Urlsperger, Ebersdorf, 11th October 1734 (Extract), handwritten, in the archives of the United Brethren at Herrnhut, R.14.A.1.11b: 'I do
not know what I ought to say. Both parties labour earnestly in God's cause. Their
purpose is honest, they have wholly dedicated themselves to their Saviour, strive
solely after what is above, leave and sell everything to get the one pearl. They
have no wish to turn from the Evangelical Faith, and if they are put out they still
desire to confess it. They lie in tears and groan, they place their children before
God's face and beseech Him that He might prevent all separation or offence, be-
stow the spirit of love and good temper, forgive their sins and failings, and establish again a wholesome understanding amongst His children who have fallen into
error. I am not a little amazed and believe that if they were cut in pieces, killed
and burned, they would nevertheless live and die in love, such open humility,
lowliness and love is there found amongst them. Ought we to persecute such
folk? Ought we to put them out of our churches? Ought we to be ashamed of
such people, who bear the reproach of Christ in their own bodies? Ought we to try
and hinder them in their plan of going to the heathen in Georgia? Here is an
affair of conscience. God will forgive me if I have written anything against these
people. How much I have wished that your Excellency had only seen a few of
them and talked but once cordially and intimately with them.'

have nothing to do with the Herrnhut community.' He then went on to speak about the actual care of the Salzburg settlement in Georgia, a community scarcely yet established. Urlsperger continued: 'What do you think our worthy preachers in Georgia would think if people so contrary to them were placed at their side? Or our Salzburgers, if they should see such fraternities, hours of prayer and all the many other arrangements, which are more like the papal yoke than evangelical freedom? Our Georgian ministers, praise God, observe a true evangelical discipline. I beseech you to go piano and to remember how I called you at the first and how you were prevailed upon by God through His true servants: do not allow yourself to be still taken in.' At the end of the letter Urlsperger assumed again the paternal tone: 'I write this to you with affection as to my son.' He expected nothing from a consultation: 'And what shall I say about a conference? A guarantee of justice must be given beforehand.' His bad health prevents him from making the journey at the moment. Nevertheless in a postscript to the letter he left open the possibility but demanded a larger membership. In addition to Zinzendorf Spangenberg must be present, and one or two representatives from Halle and others both from Herrnhut and from the Church-pietists. He also mentioned the name of Herr Winkler, presumably the pietist Johann Joseph Winkler, minister of Magdeburg Cathedral. The determinative point for him, however, was the fate of the Salzburg community. 'If the Count has been given land, if folk from Herrnhut wish to go there, then I cannot prevent it. But I will have no part in it, for it is not necessary: and I must care for my people, and this includes preventing every kind of danger and scandal and disorder.' [7]

This was a clear and decisive refusal, nevertheless von Reck pursued his efforts at a reconciliation. He obtained from Zinzendorf a reluctant declaration of his readiness for a consultation in Augsburg. The Count to be sure declined to have Spangenberg taking part, since apparently he found him an encumbrance.[8] As was to be expected

---

[7] Urlsperger to von Reck, ibid.

[8] Zinzendorf to von Reck, Herrnhut, 11th November 1734, handwritten, in the archives of the United Brethren, R.14.A.2.19: 'The Lord dispose Herr Urlsperger's affairs according to His will. The Lord is in His house. I have always been willing to hold a conference. Friend Spangenberg is not essential for this, only my Herrnhut brethren and myself. We were under no obligation to give a report or account of our action to unfamiliar Lutheran ministers, even less to travel to them as far as Augsburg, for we have been attacked, defamed and condemned unheard by others unjustly and unfairly. But even this will not cost me or the Brethren anything, and where we are desired to go we will come, and the Saviour with us.'

as a matter of course, nothing came from the meeting. Von Reck also tried to make peace in Halle itself. He had scarcely arrived there when he wrote enthusiastically to Zinzendorf of how heartily they were devoted to him, the Count. The latter received the information with superior and indulgent scepticism, nevertheless he replied with great care and seriousness to each separate point which von Reck brought forward as from the Halle side.[9] At the same time he insisted very strongly that von Reck should not act in his name and that under no circumstances was he to take members of the Brethren fraternity to Georgia.[1] The professions of devotion by the young man towards himself and the Herrnhut community he completely ignored.

The most prominent feature in the further development of the Georgia affair was Urlsperger's own concern to guard the Salzburg community from Herrnhut infiltration. This fear overshadowed the whole situation. On 11th October 1734 Ziegenhagen wrote to Gotthilf August Francke that he had heard that Count Zinzendorf had inquired through an official of the Württemberg legation, von Pfeil, without mentioning his own name, of the trustees for the Georgia Colony, whether he could obtain land there. But at the same time he had laid down particular conditions to which the trustees were unable to agree. It could therefore be assumed that he had given up his plan. Ziegenhagen wrote: 'Meantime I have asked in advance, in case they [the trustees] should think fit to agree with him under certain conditions, that the land granted might be at a distance from that of the Salzburgers.' The fact that Spangenberg was to play a leading role in this was also already known.[2] A month later, on 15th November 1734, Ziegenhagen received a letter from von Reck which bore only the general mark 'on the borders of Bohemia and Moravia'.

[9] Von Reck to Zinzendorf, Halle, 26th October 1734, archives of the United Brethren at Herrnhut, R.14.A.3.8a = R.14.A.2.13. Zinzendorf to von Reck, Herrnhut, 30th October 1734, ibid. R.14.A.3.9.
[1] Zinzendorf to von Reck, Herrnhut, 30th October 1734, ibid.: 'I must moreover marvel how you, dear Herr von Reck, should come to take upon yourself a struggle on our behalf. We do not desire that *you* should lead our people to Georgia. . . . We disengage you from all connection and declare that we accordingly have not the smallest claim upon you. The Lord will lead us, and whoever seeks to prevent us will have to reckon with Him. . . .'
[2] Ziegenhagen to G. A. Francke, Kensington, 11th October 1734, handwritten, in the Missionary archives of Francke's Institution at Halle, Z.I.L.2. Gerhard Adolf Wauer's conjecture (*Die Anfänge der Brüderkirche in England*, p. 80) that Ziegenhagen's opposition to the Brethren was based on the fact that he, the agent of a visit by Spangenberg to Oglethorpe, was then pushed aside, is disproved by this letter.

Von Reck reports that he has met a hundred people who, for the sake of Jesus Christ, have had to suffer a great deal. These honest folk have decided to emigrate to Georgia. They will bear the expenses of their journey to London themselves and the rest will be found. Their aim in Georgia is 'to exalt Christ among the Indians', and for their bodily needs they wished 'to subsist on roots and vegetables among the Indians'.[3] The same information had been reported to Ziegenhagen on 3rd November by Francke with strong disapproval. He had, it is true, received the impression from personal conversation with von Reck that the affair had become much too big for him. Probably he would have preferred to be free from the commission. Soon, he says, he wants to bring the Salzburgers farther into Georgia, soon to Virginia or Carolina, soon, he does not know whether anything will come of the affair. Francke accordingly deplores that von Reck 'at his first awakening should have fallen into such hands'. Like Ziegenhagen he foresees that a great complication is developing. Zinzendorf will not fail 'to send on his type of teachers'. Francke has only the one desire 'that the people should not come there, because they will certainly move around and make a disturbance, and so it is only good if they do not come amongst the Salzburgers'.[4]

Ziegenhagen cannot find words strong enough to express his disapproval with all this. Von Reck knew perfectly well that the financial resources on the English side were limited. He has not said what sort of people his new friends are. He does not find out from England whether what he has proposed is possible, but himself decides the time and place of the arrival. '*Summa:* this project, come from whom it may, is so confused and immature, that its authors ought to be thoroughly ashamed of it. They must indeed have got it into their heads that people here are blind and that they would not see their cunning in concealing many essential points. Count Zinzendorf may now give up all thoughts of Georgia.'[5] In this way the differences were sharpened by a new note: on the side of Halle was order, work, responsibility, on the side of Herrnhut, lack of purpose, slothfulness, dallying. To this was added the fact that Ziegenhagen learned from Gotthilf August Francke that Zinzendorf had turned up in Stralsund in the guise of a private tutor, i.e. a candidate in theology. He was

[3] Ziegenhagen to Francke, 15th November 1734, ibid.
[4] Francke to Ziegenhagen, Halle, 3rd November 1734, ibid.
[5] Ziegenhagen to Francke, Kensington, 11th October 1734, ibid.

examined by the pastor there and so obtained recognition as a proper theologian. Ziegenhagen could only see this as an act of insinuating himself by false pretences. His opinion was expressed thus: 'For the communication of what happened with the Count Zinzendorf in Stralsund, much obliged. I supposed the intention was to dispose everything in apostolic fashion, but to run when one is not well, to preach when one has no call, and to force one's way in by pretence, does not at all seem to be what the apostles meant. And why Count Zinzendorf should believe that the Church of God is helped in this way, or that anyone should presume to be a teacher by his own personal whim and judgement, is a point of view about the nature of the Church and its improvement to express which I can find no words.'[6] Stralsund and Georgia seemed to him to proceed from one and the same spirit. The way of Herrnhut meant to him not only every kind of anarchy, but also usurpation by cunning and deceit. It was this which threatened the Salzburg community—and in a situation where it still could not be fortified in any way!

It was then a particular set of circumstances which brought Spangenberg at that time to London. He arrived shortly before Christmas in 1734 with fifteen people from Herrnhut and stayed with Ziegenhagen for six hours on 23rd December. Even if the court-chaplain also was not able to find the reason for his dismissal from Halle—it lay in Spangenberg's separatist tendencies—he nevertheless formed a favourable impression of him from further conversations. He wrote to Francke: 'It is a great sorrow to me that this young, lively, able, and so far as I can see honourable, man, because of so trifling a matter . . . is to be almost unusable all his life, when he could give to the Church of Christ very profitable service.' It pleased him that Spangenberg should feel no grudge against the Halle professors, and indeed spoke well of them. He only wished that he had the time to find a way again. He in no way concealed his own mistakes, and only found fault with the fact that he had been set against him (Spangenberg) on the question of authority and above all that there had been an appeal to the king.[7] But this purely personal impression was far

---

[6] Ziegenhagen to Francke, ibid.
[7] Ziegenhagen to Francke, 10th January 1735, ibid.; cf. also Spangenberg, op. cit. (see note 9, p. 151) pp. 16–17 and XI: 'After that I came to Halle in Saxony. A difference arose between the divinity professors on the one side and your humble servant on the other. Our weapons were not the same, but this is now in the past. One thing I regret, and that does not concern me but others, who must consequently suffer. The blame was laid upon the *Ordinarius Frater* for having been concerned with my affairs at Halle. Yet he was not only quite innocent of

too limited to have been able to resolve the opposition between the two worlds, an opposition which was fundamental and continually strengthened by the events referred to.

This much had already happened. Indeed the dispute over the Salzburg community was a decisive element in the story of mutual discord, and must have determined consciously and unconsciously the personal points of view and theological and ecclesiastical opinions of the pastors Bolzius and Gronau. Quite apart from their own wishes they could not dissociate themselves from what had happened previously. Bolzius was prejudiced by personal impressions and did not conceal the fact. On 17th May 1735 he wrote to Ziegenhagen in London: 'I soon informed him [sc. Spangenberg] that I had been more depressed than cheered by the arrival of himself and his people, because their character and peculiar ways, which I had observed myself in Herrnhut, were well known to me. . . . The heavenly Father keep the hand of His grace over His vineyard, that it may not be uprooted by wild boars and foxes, and according to His mercy bring back all those who are in error and those who have been led astray, whereas may He suppress and put an end to all factions and offences.' [8] When Spangenberg considered settling the Herrnhuters in the spot which the Salzburgers had left, he exclaimed: 'In this way confusion and trouble similar to that in Pennsylvania will arise in this country.' [9]

In spite of this the relationship between the two types of German Pietism, which met in this way in a corner of the New World, was at first surprisingly good. Spangenberg formed a very favourable impression of the Salzburgers, and recognized their industry and modest bearing. His first report ended with the words: 'They love us very much.' [1] Of course he thought otherwise about the views of

this but completely ignorant. For at the time he was himself undergoing personal persecution, was at the other end of southern Germany, and had no correspondence with me. So that he certainly experienced from afar how things went with me and was angry about it, but without knowing the nexus of the facts. The divinity professors were harshly judged by many people on my account, and they had certainly not been able to help themselves in any other way. The blame really lay there. Had I in the view of the divinity professors, whose accessory I had become, not been willing or able to work harmoniously I should not have become their helper. Yet after I had once allowed myself to be an assessor of their Faculty they could rightly demand that I ought to maintain a character in keeping with it.'

[8] Bolzius to Ziegenhagen, 17th May 1735, handwritten, in the Missionary archives of Francke's Institution, Halle, 5.A.3.
[9] Ebenezer Diary (1736), 25th February (*Diarium extraordinarium*), p. 36, handwritten, at Halle, ibid.
[1] Spangenberg's Diary, 2nd February 1736, handwritten, in Herrnhut archives, R.14.A.6.d.

the two pastors Bolzius and Gronau. From his separatist Herrnhut point of view he regarded their pastoral work as clumsy. He could indeed grant that they visited the members of their flock assiduously and especially that they took great pains over the instruction of the children, yet as a whole he had to find fault with them. 'They only lead their people as far as they themselves wish to go.' Accordingly they fail to understand the peculiar fellowship of the Brethren who have grown beyond average Christianity through their apostolic discipline and so have not attached themselves either to the Lutheran or Anglican Church. In such circumstances he was able to play off John Wesley against them, and Wesley could not have expected that the Brethren, the advanced Christians, would once again descend to the level of an unrefined, disorganized ecclesiastical troop undeserving of the name of a 'congregation'.[2]

Wesley came between two fires, and yet the meeting between him and the people of New Ebenezer in no way suffered from this fact. Gronau and von Reck paid him a brief visit on 16th March.[3] John Wesley, who had to go to Frederica during the very time when Bolzius came to Savannah, left a letter for him which the recipient found 'most excellent'. He obviously received the impression that Wesley's zeal for his duties was being highly spoken of. It was apparently an innovation in Savannah to hold daily morning and evening prayers and to have a sermon or instruction on Wednesday.[4] The relationship between them was in accordance with this first fleeting impression for the period of a year. All the time each listened to the other and shared in the work of the other. Thus on 16th March 1737 Bolzius wrote in his diary: 'Because of the insubordination of his auditors Mr Wesley is not a little troubled and cast down as to whether he should be at pains to correct them by a right solid and improving exposition of the divine Word.'[5] On 23rd May and 9th June 1737 Bolzius came again, and on the second occasion they talked about Count Zinzendorf. He was there again at the end of the month, on 28th and 29th June. He reports on this meeting in his diary: 'Mr Wesley is pleased that I should visit him when I come to Savannah. . . . He diligently sings German hymns from the Herrnhut hymn-book and praises the superiority of our Church over others with respect to this treasury of hymns.' Wesley suggested that most

[2] Spangenberg's Diary, 30th June to 28th October 1736, R.14.A.6.d.12.
[3] *Journal*, I.183, Diary, 16th March 1736.
[4] Ebenezer Diary, Missionary archives of Francke's Institution, Halle, 5.D.2.
[5] Handwritten, Ebenezer Diary (1737), 32 (16th March), Halle, 5.D.3.

178

of the hymns originated from Halle—a further indication that the Herrnhut Brethren had not prejudiced him against the Halle Orphanhouse. Bolzius had to deny the Halle origin of most of the verses, but he did not fail to indicate the particular value of the few examples which did in fact come from there. He referred in particular to two of Freylinghausen's hymns: 'I come, Lord Jesus, to thee' and 'O Jesu, Source of calm repose.' From the latter, which he knew particularly well from his own efforts at translating, Wesley concluded that the author must be 'endowed with much grace and strength', whereupon Bolzius told him a few things about Freylinghausen's life, particularly 'of his experience in the ways and conflicts of the Lord'. So the conversation turned to Spangenberg's dispute with the theological faculty in Halle, which had been brought about by his separatist tendencies. In particular, Bolzius gave Wesley the true facts about two things in Spangenberg's account of his life. In the first place he had not been called to the theological faculty as professor, as he himself had said, but only as an assistant. Then it was not true that he had been expelled at the royal command without a judicial examination, but only after repeated efforts on his behalf, particularly on the part of Freylinghausen, had come to nothing because of his refusal to take advice. In this way the conflict was explained to Wesley. He tried to defend Spangenberg, whom he regarded highly.[6] Nevertheless Bolzius gained the impression that Wesley was now beginning to have doubts about him.[7]

Three weeks later Bolzius was again there, and this time the two men got remarkably close to one another. Bolzius's account says: 'As I had occasion this time to stay longer in Savannah, I became really familiar with Mr Wesley, and we joined our hearts together in the Lord'.[8] Bolzius even asked to be admitted to the Anglican Sacrament. This Wesley refused, not indeed—as he later represented it[9]—on the grounds of exaggerated high-churchmanship, but because his instructions directed him thus. Bolzius suffered the slight in a way which made a very deep impression upon Wesley. It seemed to him at the time a model of Christian lowliness and meekness.[1] On his side Bolzius summed up Wesley at this time in these words: 'He does

[6] *Journal*, I.371, 27th July 1737: 'In the evening, I rejoiced to meet once more that good soldier of Jesus Christ, August Spangenberg.'
[7] Handwritten, Ebenezer Diary (1737), 28th–29th June, in Missionary archives of Francke's Institution, Halle, 5.D.3., p. 98.
[8] Ibid. 19th July, p. 112.
[9] *Journal*, III.434.
[1] Ibid. p. 370, 17th July 1737.

the work of the Lord, and since he is most affectionately disposed towards his Saviour and the souls of his congregation, the true and chief Shepherd will surely supply him with a greater measure of the *Spiritus Evangelici*. He performs the duties of Christianity very earnestly, and visits his people industriously and is well received by some.'[2] These words give clear expression of that ecumenical characteristic of Pietism, which laid chief emphasis on personal zeal in the service of God without at the same time abandoning objective criticism in the understanding of the Gospel. 'Try to have as close an acquaintance and friendship with Messrs Wesley and Ingham as possible.' So Ziegenhagen wrote in February, and this wish was fulfilled.[3] Only one thing divided them, and this was Wesley's Anglican conception of the ministry. He held that ordination and the laying-on of hands by the bishop were essential for the administration of valid sacraments. This alone guarantees the apostolic succession, the uninterrupted link of ministers from the early Church to the present day, and therefore also the purity of the ecclesiastical tradition. He could not find this in the Lutheran Church, nor therefore amongst the Salzburg ministers. On the other hand he agreed that it did apply to the Herrnhuters because they could produce an episcopal list in their Church which went back to the apostles. As Bolzius pointedly expressed it, he considered that the Moravians were 'the true Church'. The Salzburg ministers were obliged to deplore this, since it meant that the opposition between Halle and Herrnhut was strengthened by a fresh difference. But Bolzius did not make the mistake of reproaching Wesley for his open sympathy with the Brethren as he might easily have done. In a non-factious spirit he pointed out that Ingham was much more infatuated by them than Wesley. Bolzius went to the heart of the matter and lamented 'that this papistical leaven was to be found in this upright man', by which he meant the grounding of purity of doctrine in ecclesiastical legalism. Accordingly he did not hesitate to dispute with him about his principles. He emphasized in the first place that there was no actual word

---

[2] Ebenezer Diary (1737), loc. cit., p. 112 (19th July).
[3] Ziegenhagen to Bolzius and Gronau, Kensington, 22nd February 1737. Ebenezer Correspondence (1735–7), p. 296, Halle, ibid., 5.A.3; cf. also Bolzius and Gronau to Ziegenhagen, 29th July 1737, ibid., 5.A.3, p. 413: 'We have not only more frequent intercourse with Mr Wesley, preacher in Savannah, but we are united in warm brotherly love, since he does the work of God there which we carry on here. We do not heed the *Singularia* to which he is still attached.' Bolzius and Gronau to G. A. Francke, 29th July 1737, ibid., 5.A.3, p. 457: 'We live in friendship and good harmony with the preacher in Savannah, Mr Wesley; can also now fuse together in spirit.'

of the Lord in favour of ordination and succession, and then offered, as soon as Wesley should come to New Ebenezer, to demonstrate from the early Fathers the very opposite of episcopal authority.[4]

Wesley's long-projected visit to the Salzburgers took place at last on 1st August 1737. He was accompanied by Spangenberg, who had returned from Pennsylvania for a few months on a journey of visitation.[5] The day before the two men had discussed in detail the points of agreement and difference between Anglicans and Herrnhuters. The main debate between the two churches was on the nature of primitive Christianity and the early Church in so far as the confession of faith and the regulation of life were concerned. The points actually mentioned were conversion, faith, the Holy Spirit, the Church, together with the Mosaic precepts, fasting, and military service. In his conscientious rational way Wesley noted down exactly every answer, without himself making any comment. He had astutely asked thirty-one questions and thereby indicated, however cautiously, his own point of view. Obviously there was considerable agreement between the two men: the awareness of unanimity was stronger than that of difference.[6]

On the journey to New Ebenezer they passed the old settlement, which surpassed in its natural beauty all other spots in Georgia, but which had had to be abandoned because of the poverty of the soil. The new place made a most favourable impression on Wesley, so eloquently did the huts and fields testify to the industry of the inhabitants, who had done it all in the course of a year. Their lot had been extremely hard. Their pastors had repeatedly got the impression that the intention was to wear them out, perhaps even to break up the settlement and disperse the occupants as slaves for the Englishmen. In addition there was the conflict between the Germans and the British administration. In the year 1741 Bolzius wanted to have a lawyer to assist him, but the trustees would not have it. Even had they granted permission it would only have been for an Englishman and not a German, 'because as they had said before, it is not suitable to them that the Salzburgers should wish to remain Germans all the time rather than becoming Englishmen'.[7] The pastors had constantly to warn the members of their flock against 'shunning God in

[4] Bolzius and Gronau to Ziegenhagen, 20th July 1737, ibid., 5.A.3, p. 413.
[5] *Journal*, I.375ff, cf. also Reichel, *August Spangenberg*, p. 98.
[6] *Journal*, I.372–4.
[7] Ziegenhagen to G. A. Francke, Kensington, 2nd December 1741, Missionary archives of Francke's Institution, Halle, Z.I.L.5.

the school of the Cross' and looking for more congenial places.[8] But obviously they were successful too in their educational work. When Heinrich Melchior Mühlenberg, the patriarch of American Lutheranism, left the settlement in 1742 after a stay of several weeks, he commented: 'The worthy patrons and benefactors in Europe have not performed their good deeds in vain, for the situation appears in fact to correspond to the printed accounts in Germany and is in many respects better than has been represented. Physically it is a matter of wonder how the poor people by God's help have improved their conditions, and spiritually a blessed harvest is to be hoped for'.[9] Wesley was particularly impressed with the simple appearance of the two ministers' wives. Their dress was plain and their hospitality indicated that they would be the servants of all. A controversy arose between Spangenberg and the ministers in which Wesley was struck by the friendly and mild way they stated their objections against Herrnhut. The same points were discussed as on the previous day between Spangenberg and himself. Statements about the Count's exposition of scripture and method of prayer fortified Wesley in his conviction that he was likewise but a man.[1]

The association of the Methodists with the Salzburgers continued in Georgia. When he thought about returning to England, Wesley went to them again to say farewell[2] and to inquire as to their wishes. Twelve years later Bolzius wrote to Wesley and reminded him of their former association.[3] When George Whitefield came to know New Ebenezer later on he was so impressed that he collected money for the orphan-house there and the building of a church by his preaching in London and Bristol.[4]

Alongside these contacts with foreign associates, in which John Wesley was to a considerable extent a beginner and observer, were the problems and experiences of his own office. In these he had to take the initiative and act on his own. He wanted above all to be a missionary, for it was in this that lay the meaning and promise of his position. Yet this is what proved more and more impossible to attain, for he was thwarted both intentionally and unintentionally. Inten-

---

[8] Ebenezer Diary (1736) 14th May, Halle, ibid., 5.D.2, p. 173; 19th June, ibid. p. 205; ibid., 16th October.
[9] Heinrich Melchior Mühlenberg's Travel-Diary, London–Ebenezer (1742–3), Monday 11th October 1742, handwritten, in Missionary archives, Halle, Z.IV.D.2.
[1] *Journal*, I.374–6.
[2] Ibid. p. 396, 11th October 1737.   [3] Ibid. III.434–5, 25th July 1749.
[4] Ziegenhagen to G. A. Francke, Kensington, 26th December 1738 and 22nd January 1739, handwritten, in Halle Missionary archives, Z.I.L.5.

tionally—at least in part—by General Oglethorpe, whose chief purpose was to build up the colony by keeping the English inhabitants together, and unintentionally by the conditions themselves. It is quite touching to see how Wesley again and again tried to begin the mission to the heathen and yet failed to bring it about. He grasped at every possibility, however small and apparently hopeless. On 30th June 1736 he wanted to push forward farther into the Indian territory. His plan was connected with the Choctaw tribe, because they had the slightest contact with European civilization and therefore seemed to him the least corrupted. Oglethorpe advised against it, since Savannah could not be left without a minister. After consulting his companions and the Herrnhut Brethren Wesley reluctantly submitted.[5] Shortly afterwards two aged Indians, leading men, were with Oglethorpe, and Wesley sat with them at table. After the meal he got into conversation with one of them and asked him what he thought he was made for. The Indian replied: 'He that is above knows what He made us for. We know nothing. We are in darkness. But white men know much. And yet white men build great houses, as if they were to live for ever. But white men cannot live for ever. In a little time white men will be dust as well as I.' Wesley continued the conversation in the same simple way. 'If red men will learn the good book, they may know as much as white men. But neither we nor you can understand that book, unless we are taught by Him that is above; and He will not teach, unless you avoid what you already know is not good.' The Indian answered: 'I believe that. He will not teach us while our hearts are not white. And our men do what they know is not good: they kill their own children. And our women do what they know is not good: they kill the child before it is born. Therefore He that is above does not send us the good book.'[6] These words of Wesley reflect a feeling of solidarity with the heathen before God's Word similar to that expressed in his letter to John Burton in 1735. Three weeks later he had a fresh opportunity for conversation. From the Indians of the Chicasaw tribe, who for some reason or other had come to Savannah, five, together with their interpreters, sought out John Wesley and his companions. They were all warriors, and this was soon reflected in their conversation. Wesley questioned them about their faith and asked them first if they believed that an almighty One were over all

[5] *Journal*, I.238–9, 30th June 1736.
[6] Ibid. p. 239, 3rd July 1736.

things, to which he received the answer that they believed that there were four 'beloved things above', the clouds, the sun, the clear sky, and He who lives in the clear sky. Wesley then asked them more precisely whether they knew of only *one* such Lord, and was told that they accepted a sort of Trinity. To the question whether this three-fold Being created the sun and the other things the Indians did not know the answer. On the other hand they believed that all men had been fashioned out of the ground by His hand. They were not sure whether this Being loved them, but they affirmed that He had often preserved them when they were in danger of their lives. They be-lieved that He and the three other 'beloved things' could overcome their enemies, since they had often known times when mist, hail, and rain had decided the battle for them against the Choctaw Indians or the French. They knew that the four beloved things were always about them, making themselves perceptible by noises which they attributed to ghosts. When asked about the destination of the souls of the dead they replied that these must walk up and down at the place of burial for they had often heard cries there. When Wesley offered to give them fuller information about the 'beloved things' from the 'book of the white men' they declined, saying that as warriors they did not have time for it, but should peace come they would gladly be ready for instruction.[7] The beliefs of the Indians were obviously a queer mixture of heathen and Christian elements, originating from recollections of earlier missionary teaching. Much simpler and less artificial was a report which Ingham gave to the Herrnhuters about the Cherokese. In the main their beliefs bore the marks of a fertility religion. They drew a distinction between the good God 'South' and the evil God 'North'. The former sends them warmth, makes their crops grow, and takes up the good people after death to His kingdom, whereas the latter creates the cold and bad men go to Him.[8] John Wesley's impression of those with whom he had his talk was so favourable that he expected the Chicasaws would be the first among the Indians to become Christians.[9] Yet when almost a year later a Frenchman, after a month's imprisonment, gave him more precise information he radically modified his opinion. He expressed his horror at the effects of this high-sounding 'natural religion' and

[7] *Journal*, I.248–50, 20th July 1736.
[8] Töltschig's Diary (18th May 1736), in the archives of the United Brethren at Herrnhut, R.14.A.6.D.5.
[9] *Letters*, I.228–9, Savannah, 11th September 1736, to James Vernon.

found confirmation of the biblical word that the gods of the heathen are but devils.[1]

The continuous guerrilla warfare between the tribes was in itself an almost insurmountable obstacle to the missionary work.[2] When Wesley moreover saw how his immediate duties kept him to the English congregation and stood in the way of his plan, he invited his Oxford friends to help him in America. Some months before, Ingham had left him and lived in a house which Oglethorpe had built expressly for him near the Indian settlement of the Creek tribe, so that he might instruct the children there. He had already taught them Greek letters so that they could write out their language.[3] Charles had gone to England, Delamotte could only be used for teaching children. Wesley's intention was to make his companions assistants in Church work, and this activity among the English congregation was to prepare them for the difficult task of proclaiming the Gospel to the heathen. He thought that those who were trained in works of charity among their own countrymen and fellow-believers would then be able to take upon themselves the cross, and even martyrdom, should the occasion arise. Although the disciple of Jesus Christ expects persecution wherever he is, so far he and his three companions had only experienced it in Georgia in the form of words.[4] But his request produced no result and so he decided to send Ingham back to England to recruit some in person. Ingham travelled with Spangenberg and subsequently went over completely to the Herrnhuters.[5] Naturally his lack of success among his Oxford friends disappointed Wesley. When six months later he read the report of the first English missionary society, the Society for the Propagation of the Gospel in Foreign Parts, he found in it painful confirmation of the indifference shown by Christians in his native land. He felt the lack of the early

[1] *Journal*, I.367, 9th July 1737.
[2] Ibid. p. 298, 23rd November 1736.
[3] Correspondence and News of the Salzburgers in America: letter of Gronaus to G. A. Francke, Ebenezer, 13th October 1736, handwritten, in Missionary archives of Francke's Institution at Halle, 5.A.3, p. 189: 'The conversion of the heathen is very much the concern of Mr Oglethorpe. He has brought with him his own preacher, who is already learning the Indian language. At the place where the king lives Mr Oglethorpe has helped the Herrnhuters to build a school in which the aforesaid minister is to give instruction. When I was recently returning from Savannah and was prevented by the darkness from going farther I spent the night there. In the morning I saw some children coming into the hut which had been the first to be erected. They were carrying little books which I could see had some Greek letters written in them; I was told that the Indian language is to be learned in Greek characters.'
[4] *Letters*, I.211–12, Savannah, 16th February 1737, to John Hutchings.
[5] *Journal*, I.320–1, 24th February 1737.

Christian enthusiasm for missionary work, particularly of the blood of the martyrs, which in all ages had been the means of bringing the Church into being. Where today were men to be found who praise God in the midst of the flames and pray for their murderers? If they could be found, Satan, the grand ruler of the New World, would fall as lightning from heaven, and as the psalmist says, these lands would be full of the knowledge of the Lord as the waters cover the seas. Then the almighty power of God would cast down every high thing that exalts itself against the faith of Jesus Christ.[6] In such a way Wesley, from this remote spot, looked for an act of God which would be a typical example of God's conflict against the devil.

He was constantly preoccupied with the condition of the Indians. He observed with great concern their addiction to alcohol. Töltschig wrote to Herrnhut: 'These Indians live worse than cattle, drunk all day, so that they roll about on the ground.'[7] But Wesley reminded Oglethorpe that it was he who provided them with the opportunity in the first place.[8] These experiences may have contributed towards the bitter and on the whole unjust judgement he allowed himself to make at the end of his time in Georgia. He was then able to say that he had not heard of any Indians who had the least desire for Christian instruction. He denied that they had any sense at all of law and order, obedience or readiness to serve. He called them liars, thieves, and violent men.[9]

His missionary design extended beyond the Indians. On his first visit to Charlestown, the capital of the neighbouring province of South Carolina, he was asked by the local clergyman, Alexander Garden, to preach. Among the 300 members of the congregation Wesley noticed a few negro women, with one of whom he had a conversation. He learned that she came regularly to church. Her former mistress had often given her instruction in the principles of Christianity, but in spite of this Wesley discovered that she was appallingly ignorant. She had no real idea that a man was anything different from an animal. She knew nothing of the distinction between bodies and souls. All this led him to cry out to God, to ask when He would fulfil His promise (Malachi 3[20]) that the Sun of Righteousness would arise on these forlorn creatures. He was in this

[6] *Letters*, I.225, Savannah, 22nd July 1737, to Dr Humphreys.
[7] Töltschig to Friedrich Martin, Savannah, 5th January 1737, handwritten, in the archives of the United Brethren at Herrnhut, R.14.A.6.d.
[8] Töltschig's Diary, 30th June to 28th October 1736, ibid. R.14.A.6.d.
[9] *Journal*, I.396, Friday 7th October 1737, I.407 (general account of Georgia).

way brought to the question of the all-embracing nature of God's mercy. It also spurred him on to consider the possibility of action, and during a stop he later made in South Carolina this assumed definite shape. Wesley became acquainted with a young negro who had been sent as his guide and found that he had a great readiness to learn. This suggested to Wesley the idea of a systematic and organized mission to negroes, which he conceived on the following lines. A few earnest Christians from amongst the planters should be found who would select the most capable of their slaves and teach them, or allow them to be instructed in, the Christian faith. These should then be taken from one plantation to another, staying long enough at each until a few others were converted. Wesley discussed this with three or four landlords and obtained their consent. He himself gave to a negro girl a first brief lesson, which consisted of the following points. Starting with the transitory nature of life, it led on to the immortality of the soul, the meaning of the creation, and man's destiny for eternal fellowship with God as his supreme happiness. The attention of the girl, who was able next day to answer all his questions correctly, left a strong impression on Wesley.[1]

Finally he also directed his efforts to the Jews. He learned Spanish so that he might the better talk with them, and discovered from their first meetings that they were closer to an understanding of Jesus Christ than many who bore the Christian name. On another occasion he deplored the fact that he was not able to bear a strong enough witness to the truth in a debate about the Messiah he had with his Spanish teacher, Dr Moses Nunes.[2]

Yet all these were only brief interludes. His real work lay amongst the members of his English congregation. He visited them between twelve and three o'clock in the middle of the day because the heat then made work impossible for them.[3] He gave scarcely a thought to a midday break for himself. Individual pastoral work he took very seriously. He naturally regarded the visitation of the dying as

[1] Ibid. pp. 254–5, 31st July 1736; pp. 350–1, Saturday 23rd April 1737; pp. 352–3, 27th April 1737.
[2] Ibid. p. 237, 27th June 1736; p. 300, 3rd December 1736, Diary; pp. 345–6, 4th April 1737; p. 367, 7th July 1737. In I.345–6 Wesley uses one of his favourite expressions, 'the mind which was in Christ', of the Jews. The phrase looks back to Scougal, who stressed the image of God. The reference in Wesley runs: 'I began learning Spanish, in order to converse with my Jewish parishioners; some of whom seem nearer the mind that was in Christ than many of those who call Him Lord.'
[3] Ibid. pp. 213–14, 10th May 1736.

particularly important and repeatedly was deeply affected by what he regarded as an early-Christian readiness for suffering and departure from the world. Here was the same surrender to God's will which had so impressed him in the case of Spangenberg.[4] In a severe thunderstorm he had a repetition of the shattering experience which had come to him in the storm at sea at the end of the voyage. The prospect of death filled his heart with terror and not, as it ought to have done, with joy and longing for his eternal home. Sadly he asked himself: 'When shall I wish to be dissolved and to be with Christ?' to which he gave the reply: 'When I love Him with all my heart!'[5] So perfect love for God was once again defined as his real aim. As the number of the sick unexpectedly grew he made no progress with his regular visiting, and it was this which decided him to summon his young friends from Oxford. He addressed the letter principally to George Whitefield. He saw before himself an immense field of work and a tough battle-ground, but its varied character made it at the same time an example of a mission-field so full of promise that he could not adequately describe the urgency of the task. Every line of this letter gave expression to his conviction that the office of Christian minister and missionary, of service to Christians and to heathen, were fundamentally one.[6] Accordingly he wanted to extend the decision which a year before he had made for himself to include the whole of the Oxford circle, and events abroad once again confirmed his conviction that the matter of his own salvation was bound up with the spread of the Gospel and the lordship of Jesus Christ on earth.

Resolutely he applied himself to the indifference which all too frequently he encountered in the members of his congregation. One day somebody came to him and frankly declared his desire to discuss with him any subject except religion. Wesley replied with a suitable parable. His companion seemed to him like a man preparing to go to a foreign country where he would be dependent exclusively upon the language of the place. While still in his own land a teacher of languages is sent to him, but the man prefers to trifle with him rather than put himself to any trouble. In a similar way he, Wesley, has been sent to show his acquaintance the way to heaven: how then can he squander away his time in idle talk? He would rather not con-

---

[4] *Journal*, I.225–6, 6th June 1736; pp. 243ff, 8th–10th July 1736.

[5] Ibid. p. 246, 10th July 1736.

[6] *Letters*, I.204ff, Savannah, 10th September 1736, corresponds with the description of the situation in *Journal*, I.272ff, September 1736.

verse with him at all. Another man he asked why he had stopped commending true religion to those with whom he spoke, and received the answer that in doing so he had only put himself out and not made anyone better. Now he was only prepared to speak about religion with those folk who were disposed towards it. Wesley could not find words strong enough to condemn this defeatist attitude. Over against it he set the fact that in the early Church and at all times God's Word has been not only 'the savour of life' but also of death, as Paul said. Even if one has wounded somebody else, one's witness ought not to cease, but one must strive for God more humbly, more calmly, more cautiously, but strive one must without ceasing.[7] Here is the same religious radicalism as that which he had shown at Oxford in the correspondence with Richard Morgan.

It is understandable that with such principles he aroused considerable opposition. Reference has already been made to the fact that his ministry was not confined to Savannah. Every so often he had to go to Frederica, where his brother Charles urgently needed help. When Charles returned to England at the end of July 1736 to report to the trustees and in person to solicit help for the work in America, the congregation became the charge alternately of John and Ingham.[8] This created only greater difficulties. One of the leading men named Horton told John Wesley bluntly that he could not abide him. Everything he did was repugnant to him, his sermons were only allusions to particular people, and nobody wished to come to church to let themselves be censured before all the others without the possibility of replying. His behaviour had brought nothing but strife amongst the people. Horton declared that everybody was of the same mind as himself. Such being the case Wesley could preach for an hour, but nobody would any longer come to listen to him.[9]

Yet none of these things could damp his zeal. He went on with his strenuous work from five in the morning until ten at night and still found time to record every detail in his diary. He stayed now in Savannah, now in Frederica. He travelled through forest and swamp, water and cold,[1] sometimes on a pioneer expedition, sometimes on a pastoral journey. In this way he discovered the land route to Frederica. The comprehensive report on Georgia he made at the end of his stay in America shows his remarkable capacity for obser-

[7] *Journal*, I.231, 12th June 1736; I.235, 23rd June 1736.
[8] Ibid. pp. 217–18, 16th May 1736.
[9] Ibid. pp. 234–5, 22nd June 1736.
[1] Ibid. p. 304, 22nd December 1736.

vation. On the way to Frederica he sought out the Scots in Darien and found much to praise in them, particularly their industry, modesty, and friendliness. But he could not condemn strongly enough their presbyterian custom of extempore prayer, which seemed to him to show a pronounced lack of order and responsibility in their relationship with God.[2] Near Frederica was a settlement of Independents, members of a separatist congregation which originated in the great revolution under Cromwell. Naturally they were opposed to the Anglican Church. Their minister, Dison, who had pastoral care of the soldiers in the fort at Frederica, on one occasion made good use of John Wesley's absence from Savannah by going there and stirring up trouble amongst the congregation. In various ways he deviated from Church order and also sowed seeds of suspicion against Wesley as a man. Wesley stayed on at Frederica, as he was easily able to establish; when he returned Dison was still there and Wesley called him to account. He ended the entry in his *Journal* about this incident with the lament: 'O Discipline! where art thou to be found? Not in England, nor (as yet) in America.'[3]

On the other hand there were favourable impressions also. In the neighbouring colony of South Carolina he was struck by the receptive attitude of the people towards the Gospel. A man who heard Wesley preach on the text about victorious faith (1 John 5[4]) made the striking comment: 'A Christian man must have more courage than Alexander the Great.' After his first meeting with Garden, who was at the time the clergyman at Charlestown, a warm friendship developed between the two, based upon high regard for each other. It was this Garden who took him to the annual assembly of the clergy of the province, at which Wesley was present at a conversation lasting several hours on 'Christ, our Righteousness and our Example', and which he said was of a quality such as he had never known at any visitation in England.[4]

Upon the whole he was still happy twelve months after entering upon his position as minister of the Savannah congregation. He realized that he had to deal with folk who were essentially simple and he strove to feed them with the milk of the Gospel. He impressed upon them a few clear and straightforward principles of the Christian life, and suffered the reproach that they were perhaps too coarse.

---

[2] *Journal*, I.309–10, 2nd January 1737.
[3] Ibid. pp. 270–1, 6th September 1736.
[4] Ibid. pp. 347ff, 12th–19th April 1737.

His reply was that nice distinctions and uncertainties belong only to the intellectualistic and highly cultivated circles of England. He strove to be a pattern for the members of his flock. The only thing he recognized as essential was the doing of the will of God, and that will is sanctification, man's renewal in God's image in holiness and happiness.[5]

As pastor, John Wesley was at the same time the teacher. While at Oxford this had been indelibly impressed upon his character; hence in Georgia he gave his attention to the school. In actual fact Charles Delamotte taught the children, but Wesley examined them twice a week. At worship he made them repeat parts of the catechism.[6] That he might get to know the adults better he quite early on divided the congregations at Savannah and Frederica into smaller groups, which were to meet two or three times a week for mutual reproval, instruction, and exhortation. From these again he selected a small number which he and his friends could watch over individually and meet on Sunday afternoons in the parsonage.[7] This was completely in line with the Oxford practices and was an important step towards that which became characteristic of the Methodist order.[8] John Wesley could not think of the Church as 'the mass of the people under the Word' but only as a living fellowship of real members. It is uncertain whence this originated for him. One naturally thinks of Horneck's and Smithie's religious societies and of the Herrnhut systems of brotherhoods for mutual consultation and drawing of lots with the help of the Bible. When John Wesley shortly afterwards read the account of the life of the French mystic Gaston Jean-Baptiste de Renty he found confirmation of his own action in forming small groups of pious folk.[9] It was an age when Romanic mysticism, Pietism, and the religion of 'free spirits' (*Spiritualismus*) were in the air, and yet Wesley's model differed from all

[5] *Letters*, I.219ff, Savannah, 29th March 1737, to Mrs Chapman.
[6] *Journal*, I.322, 26th February, 1737.
[7] Ibid. pp. 197ff, April 1736; pp. 226–7, 10th June 1736.
[8] Curnock, *Journal*, I.198, note 1, referring to Wesley's *Ecclesiastical History*, IV.175 (which was not available to me).
[9] Cf. H. Bett, 'A French Marquis and the Class-Meeting', *Proc.W.H.S.*, XVIII.(1931–2).43–5, esp. p. 45. Against the immediate dependence on de Renty is the fact that Wesley apparently only began to read his biography carefully four to six weeks after he had subdivided the congregation in Savannah, that is on 20th May 1736 (*Journal*, I.219, Diary). The letter to Anne Granville, written on 3rd October 1731 (*Letters*, I.112), shows that he had some knowledge of de Renty's character even at that time. Curnock's statement in *Journal*, I.198, note 1, is in my opinion too one-sided: 'The plan was a Moravian draft upon the "Oxford Methodist" stock.'

other forms which were known at that time. His groups were not associations of independent people but subdivisions of the congregation. He did not create new organizations but deepened existing ones. He began with what was already in existence, and perhaps the only ones who can be compared with him were Spener and Martin Bucer in the Reformation era. Moreover he retained all the time the idea of the Church as an hierarchical institution: he chose people from above, and the dividing of the groups into two categories made it possible for the members to ascend as it were from below.

Outside his immediate Church work he undertook many additional duties. Assistance from England enabled him to build up a library for his congregation. As secretary to Oglethorpe he frequently had to write letters, deal with legal matters and problems of maintenance in connexion with the colonists, and pass on petitions and grievances. The question of commercial relations with the Indians was particularly difficult. It is interesting to observe how the Salzburgers tried to blacken the Herrnhuters in Wesley's eyes, on the grounds that they had violated the terms laid down by the English in this matter.[1] In fact, Wesley acted for everyone and had to be at everybody's beck and call.[2] He adapted himself to the tasks of administration and applied himself industriously to them. It was natural that he should in this way acquire a position of considerable influence in Savannah and that he should come to occupy a place in which he acted as a sort of counter-balance to Causton, the Chief Magistrate, as was to become evident later.

He felt himself called in the widest sense of the word to the proclamation of the gospel of salvation and the saving of souls. His position as a minister and his work among Jews and heathen he regarded as simply different aspects of one task. The famous claim which he made in 1739 to his Oxford friend James Hervey, 'I look upon the whole world as my parish',[3] was already being realised at this time. It was a natural consequence of this that he should give himself to any service in connexion with the Church which offered itself. One day in Frederica he met several Germans who could not understand a word of English. What did he do? Every day at noon he met them in his house, sang a German hymn with them, read to them a chapter from the New Testament and as best he could

[1] Ebenezer Diary (1737), 29th June, handwritten, in the Missionary archives of Francke's Institution at Halle, IV.3.
[2] Library: *Journal*, I.321, 26th February 1737; Oglethorpe: pp. 246ff, July 1736.
[3] *Letters*, I.286, 20th March 1736.

explained its meaning, said the Lord's Prayer, and ended the meeting with another hymn.[4] He did the same thing for the Germans in Hampstead and for the French and Italians in Highgate.[5]

In the Anglican congregation alone there were enough people to give him sufficient to do. This was especially the case with the women. While on the ship he had given them special pastoral attention, and seasickness in particular had disposed them to listen to readings from religious works! Indeed he was forced to confess that such a serious attitude was the normal accompaniment of their indisposition, and he also made the painful discovery that those whom he tried to reconcile with one another suddenly joined together against him. In particular a young woman, Mrs Hawkins, stood out. At one moment she seemed to be sensitive to the Word of God, and then the next just the opposite. Many of the passengers warned him of her insincerity, and he talked over with her all the points which had been raised against her. He came to the conclusion that she was completely innocent.[6] Spangenberg, with whom he discussed the matter when they landed, advised him in the words of Thomas à Kempis to avoid all good women and to commend them to God. In all probability he was led to say this as a result of his own bitter experiences. He was of the opinion that in view of the particular circumstances Wesley should speak only sparingly with her and ask God to do the rest.[7] But Wesley did not follow this advice; he had many talks with her and exchanged many letters. On no other member of his congregation did he expend so much effort, nor did he allow himself to be put out by any disillusionment. After every favourable expectation had gone and he had seen through her intrigue, he still believed that nothing would be impossible with her to God.[8] The young woman, who was married to a doctor and soon occupied with him a leading position in the settlement at Frederica, first conceived a strong dislike of Charles Wesley, presumably because quite early on he saw through her sham piety, while John Wesley was taken in by her. She succeeded in making Charles believe that she and her friend, Mrs Welch, had committed adultery with Oglethorpe. This confession, which was quite untrue, Charles fool-

[4] *Journal*, I.284–5, 18th October 1736.
[5] Ibid. pp. 396–7, 15th, 22nd October 1737.
[6] Ibid. pp. 135–6, 12th January 1736.
[7] Ibid. p. 155, 9th February 1736; on Spangenberg's experiences, cf. Reichel, *August Spangenberg*, pp. 27ff.
[8] *Letters*, I.200, Savannah, 20th April 1736, to Oglethorpe.

ishly did not keep to himself, and it came to Oglethorpe's ears. Naturally he was furious. He turned against Charles and made his pastoral work in Frederica impossible, which was precisely what Mrs Hawkins wanted. The excitement made Charles seriously ill, and John had to hasten from Savannah and, in addition to performing his brother's duties, to some extent straighten out the confused state of affairs. This succeeded for a time, but Mrs Hawkins did not let the matter rest. With several kindred spirits she had got hold of a letter from Charles to John which contained in Greek some unfavourable remarks about herself and her friends. When next time John was staying in Frederica she invited him to her house, and suddenly threatened him, all unsuspecting, with a pistol and a pair of scissors. A severe struggle ensued, and although several men came into the room, nobody at first interfered. John Wesley refrained from using force against her, but seized hold of her hands and succeeded in disarming her. She then bit him with her teeth so violently that he not only went home with the sleeve of his coat torn but was able to show the wound he had received to the Herrnhuters when he got back to Savannah.[9] That no one at first intervened between him and the enraged woman but merely watched what was going on says enough in itself. The aversion she had formed against him could scarcely have shown itself in anything more obvious and unprovoked than this wilful pleasure in hurting him. It was in Frederica that a conspiracy against him and his brother had actually been planned. Only a month after their arrival, in a letter written on 22nd March 1736, John stressed the differences in their respective situations. He encountered no sort of opposition in Savannah, everything seemed set for a fair course, and his work appeared to be full of promise. Yet he was sure that for him also this peace could not last and that the storm must break. But he saw immediately the good in the difficulties in which Charles was placed. When his people cast him out, the way to the heathen would be open to him and so God would lead him to the real objective.[1] Also for the time being Oglethorpe's attitude to John Wesley during these disputes became noticeably

[9] *Journal*, I.263–4, 22nd August 1736, and Töltschig's Diary (August 1736), handwritten, in the archives of the United Brethren at Herrnhut, R.14.A.6.D.5. 'On the 27th March Mr Westley returned from Fridrich [Frederica] and told us that a grand lady had wanted to shoot him, but that he had anticipated her by grasping hold of the pistol, and while he held her hands she had bitten large pieces of flesh in her rage. He showed us the places. The reason had been that he told her the truth too plainly.'

[1] *Letters*, I.198–9, 22nd March 1736, to Charles.

less cordial,[2] but he continued to hold the general in high regard. When the clouds were gathering against Oglethorpe in England and his direction of the colony became the object of envious and ground-less attacks, Wesley encouraged him to rely upon the justice of his cause. He stressed the fact that the social purpose which had led to the establishment of the colony was in such sharp contrast to the teaching of Machiavelli, whose works fell most justly under the con-demnation of God. He assured the general of his prayers and loyalty, and counted it a particularly favourable dispensation of God that he, Wesley, had been able to work under him. He almost regarded him in the manner of the prophet Deutero-Isaiah, who saw in the Persian king Cyrus a divinely sent instrument for the protection of God's true servant. At the same time he wished that God might ever renew him in His own image.[3] So closely did he feel himself bound to the general through God and before God that even temporary discord could not destroy their relationship. It was able to stand firm amidst all troubles because it was in the end grounded in this dimension.

Spangenberg, who came to know of the difficulties and disputes, saw their cause in the fact that Wesley was only willing to admit members of his congregation to the Lord's Supper after exact know-ledge and his judgement of their preparedness. With all the rigour of the older Separatists his judgement was: 'It is quite certain that Westli must either do what the English Church commands or he cannot be a minister of that Church. But he can forsooth become a free servant of Christ if they cast him out. It is easy to see how it is with all the sects and that it is impossible to remain in the Church apart from hypocrisy.' He reckons that should his own folk cast him out he should be taken in by the Herrnhut brethren. His words pointedly express their real relationship with Wesley: 'They can have nothing to do with the circumstances which prevail in his office, and yet at the same time they cannot be indifferent to the insult he has received.'[4]

A much more serious affair intruded itself into Wesley's private life and had repercussions upon his official position. On 13th March 1736 he met Sophia Christiana Hopkey at the house of her uncle, Thomas Causton, the director of supplies and chief magistrate of Savannah. She was then eighteen years of age, and was praised by

---

[2] *Journal*, I.286, 23rd October 1736.
[3] *Letters*, I.212–13, 24th February 1736.
[4] Spangenberg's handwritten Diary, 30th June to 28th October 1736, in the archives of the United Brethren at Herrnhut, R.14.A.6.d.12.d.

Wesley as a simple, modest girl, tender and ready to learn, whose good nature and adaptable disposition won for herself friends everywhere.[5] John Wesley, whose first contact with her was as pastor and teacher, soon took a great liking to her. He has described his relationship with her in attractive and completely candid terms. The fact that he records the sequence of events in detail and yet with reserve, at the same time concealing nothing against himself, is an outstanding testimony to a love of truth which gives his *Journal* a high degree of credibility.

The relationship began in his reading devotional works to 'Miss Sophy', as he soon came to call her, and this led to conversations about religion in general. He also read to her the hymns he had collected at the time for his first hymn-book, and even sections from his *Journal*.[6] They sang together and went walks. At first her friend, Miss Fosset, was also present, but after about five weeks Sophy usually came alone. In this way the summer passed, but even by 22nd March, nine days after their first meeting, it became clear to him that dangers threatened. He wrote to his brother Charles, taking the precaution to use Greek: 'I stand in jeopardy every hour. Two or three women are here, young, pretty, God-fearing. Pray for me, that I know none of them after the flesh.'[7] The meetings became more frequent and often took place daily. She also met John Wesley regularly when she went to visit a family of friends in Frederica. They were drawn closer to each other when he was once again there in October. His departure from Savannah foreshadowed this. He had gone to her uncle, Causton, to be able to take her his greetings and directions. The chief magistrate mentioned the subject of marriage, which he described as the real remedy for her fits of depression. It is significant that he said: 'I give her up to you. Do what you will with her. Take her into your own hands. Promise her what you will. I will make it good.'[8] It is likely that Oglethorpe and Causton already had plans for keeping Wesley permanently in Georgia by an appointment to a high ecclesiastical position: probably he was to

[5] *Journal*, I.291–2, 1st November 1736.
[6] Ibid. p. 259, 14th, 15th August 1736, **Diary.**
[7] *Letters*, I. 199: ' Κινδυνεύω πᾶσαν ὥραν· Δύω ἢ τρεῖς εἰσι γυναικες, νεώτεραι, ἀστεῖαι, φοβούμεναι τὸν θεόν. Προσεύχου, ἵνα μήτινα αὐτῶν γινώσκω κατὰ σάρκα.' ('I stand in jeopardy every hour. Two or three are women, younger, refined, God-fearing. Pray that I know none of them after the flesh.') By using the Koine form of γινώσκω, and the reminiscence of 2 Corinthians 5[16], Wesley shows how intimately he lived in the Greek New Testament.
[8] *Journal*, I.280–1, 12th October 1736.

become a sort of bishop of the new colony. It was supposed that it would be easier to make him abandon the mission to the heathen if in addition a suitable wife were available. In Frederica Wesley found that Sophy was merely a shadow of her former self. She was in a state of deep depression,[9] but he was affected most of all by her resolve to leave America and return to England. Not only was he afraid of losing her, but he saw in her decision a way of avoiding the cross, for he discovered in it the wish to escape from his earnest pastoral ministrations. Accordingly he considered it a God-given duty to oppose it. In his concern for her he perceived God's own concern, but it was only when he gave up introducing religious considerations into his argument and reminded her simply of their friendship that she began to change her mind.[1] But he as well as she was affected. At this particular time he was feeling disillusioned not only by the lack of response among the members of his congregation but also by General Oglethorpe himself. For this reason it was in Miss Sophy's power to console him. He told her that Oglethorpe's attitude took away his joy in pastoral work, therefore he could no longer devote himself to her personally. He declared that she was free to return to England, but she protested that she would not stir a foot and if need be she also would suffer Oglethorpe's displeasure. Then, accompanied by the boat's crew, the couple sailed for several days along the coast back to Savannah, sometimes putting ashore in the evening to sleep under a tent hastily erected from the sail because of the cold. Miss Sophy was extremely depressed. Wesley asked her if she were afraid of dying, to which she replied that she expected nothing but misery from the world. He regarded her with wondering eyes, and could only attribute her patience in suffering to her deep surrender to God's will. Her attitude during a conversation on holiness led him to the strong conviction that she herself would become a pattern of it, although as yet she showed considerable ignorance. On the question as to whether lying was permissible in order to do

---

[9] Ibid. pp. 283–4, 16th October 1736: 'Most of her good resolutions were vanished away; and, to complete her destruction, she was resolved to return to England. . . . I begged of her to pray earnestly to God to direct her to what was best. I then read to her some of the most affecting parts of the *Serious Call* and of Ephrem Syrus. I was at first a little surprised and discouraged; but I soon recollected my spirits, and remembered my calling and the word which cannot fail: "Greater is He that is in you than he that is in the world."

Non me, qui caetera, vincet
Impetus, ad rapido contrarius evehar orbi. (Ovid, *Met.*, II.73)
I began with earnest crying to God to maintain His own cause.'
[1] Ibid. p. 285, 19th October 1736.

good she was ready to follow Wesley's demand for unconditional truth, although her previous ideas and practice had been to the contrary. In this way he experienced at one and the same time the pleasure of a teacher in his pupil, the responsibility of a spiritual director for a trusting confidante, and the affection of a man for a maid. The result was that to an unusual degree he was devoid of his customary critical insight. During the night when, unlike the hardened crew, neither of them could sleep, he asked how far she was engaged to a certain young man of doubtful character. She replied that she had promised either to marry him or nobody at all, which led Wesley to say the decisive words, 'I should think myself happy if I was to spend my life with you', at which she burst into tears. She would not have her fiancé and she could not have anyone else. She gave him to understand that his proposal aroused the strongest response in her heart, but begged him to say no more about it. Wesley fell completely under her spell and declared that he had never known a character so patient, meek, or modest. More than anything she was upset at the prospect of having to live again in her uncle's house, whereupon Wesley suggested that she should make her home either with him at the parsonage or with the Herrnhuters. When they reached Savannah he came to an understanding with her uncle that she should stay in his house as before, but that every morning and evening she should come to the parsonage. At her uncle's she was to meet only those people she herself wished to see, nor was the matter of her suitor to be mentioned.[2]

As previously, the daily meetings provided opportunities for devotional reading and prayer. In addition Wesley gave the young lady lessons in French, and occasionally a woman friend shared in these. Soon he was forced to confess that he had taken on a task too great for his powers. It became ever more difficult for him to keep to his original and confessed intention of concentrating on the business in hand and the pastoral oversight. In order to fulfil his commission of going to the heathen he is firmly determined to forgo marriage. But he does not know how long he will hold out.[3] He becomes greatly alarmed. Several times only some interruption prevents him from taking Sophy's hand. Sometimes he experiences God's help directly, and it is at this point that he once again uses the biblical metaphor of the brand snatched out of the fire, which he had

[2] *Journal*, I.286ff, 23rd October to 1st November 1736.
[3] Ibid. p. 294, 1st November 1736.

applied to his childhood experience.[4] In this way six months went by. He asked his friends whether he should break off all association with her, but he concluded from their ambiguous attitudes that this was not required of him.[5] Nevertheless later on his protégé Delamotte presented him with an ultimatum. He found that he must part from Wesley when Wesley married Sophy. He could not then continue to live in the same house with him. When Wesley protested that he had no intention of marrying, Delamotte replied that he did not know his own heart. He ought to break completely with her, for he was losing ground every day, and Wesley had to admit that he was right. Resort was had to lots, and three answers were proposed: Marry; Think not of it this year; Think of it no more. After they had prayed for a true decision Delamotte drew the third answer, which forbade the association altogether. Since they also wanted to know if Wesley might converse any more with Sophy they once again resorted to the lot, and received the direction: 'Only in the presence of Delamotte.'[6]

Sophy became completely submissive to Wesley and agreed with every proposal that he made. Without his exerting any pressure she complied fully with his wishes.[7] Yet he was still perplexed, and so one day he went to the one of the Herrnhuters with whom he was most intimate, Johann Töltschig.[8] Töltschig asked him what was at stake in the matter, to which Wesley replied that by breaking off the relationship Sophy would relapse into a state of unbelief and worldliness, since there would be no one to keep these at bay, whereas if the acquaintance were to be continued marriage might be expected. To this Töltschig replied by asking what stood in the way of marriage? This advice brought no satisfaction to John Wesley, who once again repaired to his friends Ingham and Delamotte, who did not agree with Töltschig's counsel. Ingham quite justifiably warned him against overestimating her piety, which might be due either to her natural good temper or to her intention of marrying.[9] According to the account in his diary, which is written in cipher, the Herrnhuters again cast lots after much prayer, and the result was a declaration in favour of the marriage.[1]

[4] Ibid. p. 328, 7th March 1737.
[5] Ibid. p. 294, 1st November 1736.
[6] Ibid. pp. 324ff, 3rd, 4th March 1737.
[7] Ibid. pp. 313–14, 31st January 1737.
[8] Ibid. p. 315, 3rd February 1737.
[9] Ibid. p. 319, 3rd February 1737.
[1] Ibid. p. 316, 5th February 1737, Diary.

In response to Ingham's suggestion John Wesley left the town for a few days so as not to see Sophy each day and thus avoid being influenced. First he wrote her a letter in which he asked her to pray with him that God would show the right way.[2]

He betook himself to the neighbouring settlement of Irene, where he experienced an inner conflict more fierce than ever. He did not dare ask after God's will immediately on his arrival, since he did not feel prepared as yet.[3] Not until the following day does he speak of short fervent prayer, repeated for several hours, which made him feel freer and happier. Towards evening God hid His face from him for a period, that He might again send him His help. The next day he had to pay another quick visit to Savannah, in the town itself, and he felt an overwhelming desire to see Sophy. Quite suddenly a remarkable thing happened to him. He was summoned by One to cry to God for complete resignation to His will—on doing so John Wesley felt himself in a new world, born into a new life as from the dead. This is the only instance of which we know John Wesley to have actually had anything in the nature of a visionary experience. There came to him directly joy and happiness, coupled with the fear lest he might lose them once again.[4] He returned quite decided not to marry Sophy. Two reasons drove him to this conclusion. On the one hand he wanted under no circumstances to be untrue to his mission to the heathen; on the other he did not feel equal to the complicated temptations of the married state.[5] The next time he spoke to Sophy he declared to her that he would under no circumstances marry before he had gone to the heathen. From that time she became noticeably cooler, stopped visiting his home and having French lessons, although she invited him to her uncle's as often as he cared to come.[6] On another occasion with tears she called him her only real friend, who alone had remained true and devoted to her.[7]

Suddenly she became betrothed to a man who lived in her uncle's house.[8] John Wesley was taken completely by surprise, since only the day before she had assured him that she would take no such step without his concurrence.[9] He was now to experience the tension of

---

[2] *Journal*, I.316.
[3] Ibid., 6th February 1737: Being 'a man of so unclean lips'.
[4] Ibid. p. 317, 7th, 8th February 1737.
[5] Ibid. p. 318, 8th February 1737.
[6] Ibid., 14th February 1747.
[7] Ibid. p. 323, 24th February 1737.
[8] Ibid. p. 329, 9th March 1737.
[9] Ibid. p. 328, 8th March 1737.

the most conflicting sensations, pain over the deception, fears for Sophy's welfare in the hands of a man who was not above suspicion, and his own anguish at finally losing the girl.[1] In the difficulties which now beset him he missed above all the advice and authority of Oglethorpe. Shortly after Wesley's voyage in the boat with Sophy the general had sailed for England on 23rd November 1736. He had gone leaving Wesley and his friends with the bitter realization that they must put the mission to the heathen out of their minds.[2]

Three months after Sophy's engagement, Wesley asked his sister Keziah to join him in Georgia, but scarcely had he done this than he began to question his right to do so, since his position was so uncertain.[3] Although his personal relationship with Sophy was now at an end Wesley still felt that he had a pastoral responsibility towards her. On the basis of this—and this only—several conversations took place between them, mostly in the presence of her fiancé or husband. He warned her to consider carefully the step she was taking, stressed her responsibility before God, and reminded them both of the duty of a Christian approach to marriage. Sophy told him that she was marrying in order that she need no longer go on living in her uncle's house, a thing she found intolerable. Wesley replied that the desire to avoid the cross was not a true reason for marriage. Moreover she could never escape the cross. These conversations, from which John Wesley found good reasons to doubt her sincerity (among other things she had corresponded again with her former lover),[4] had two unfortunate consequences. In the first place her husband became suspicious of John Wesley and hostile to him.[5] Secondly, on the grounds of his knowledge of her conduct, chiefly in the neglect of her obligation to attend church services, but also of her insincerity,

[1] Ibid. p. 334, 9th March 1737. The marriage was performed in a neighbouring church against Wesley's advice in a hasty, informal way without publication of banns, only four days after the betrothal. John Wesley probably considered it illegal. In his *Journal* and all public statements he calls Miss Sophy Mrs Williamson, but in his private cryptographic Diary, Miss Sophy. In London he protested against the careless way in which the clergymen in the nearby congregation at Purrysburg had acted, and secured that in future no marriages should be performed without previous publication of banns. Was the reason for this hurried wedding the husband's fear that Miss Sophy might regret giving her consent, perhaps under Wesley's influence?

[2] Ibid. pp. 297–8, 23rd November 1736.

[3] Ibid. p. 263, 7th June 1737.

[4] Ibid. pp. 328–9, 8th March 1737; p. 360, 4th June 1737.

[5] Ibid. p. 338, 15th March 1737; p. 336 shows that John Wesley had a sharp tongue, which he used on one occasion. When Mr Williamson refused to allow any conversation between Miss Sophy and himself, Wesley replied: 'Tomorrow, Sir, you may be her director, but today she is to direct herself.'

John Wesley felt bound to exclude her from Communion.[6] He had received particularly strict directions about admission to Communion from the Society for the Propagation of the Gospel,[7] although personally he administered them generously.[8] In Sophy's case especially he proceeded with the greatest circumspection and conciliatoriness. He sought the advice of his friends and hers,[9] he asked her both directly and in writing to confess,[1] and made everything easy for her,[2] but Sophy had deliberately run the risk of it happening.[3]

On 7th August 1737 John Wesley repelled Sophy from Holy Communion. By 8th August her husband, Williamson, had obtained a warrant for his arrest. On the 9th, Wesley was brought before the magistrates. Williamson charged him first with defaming his wife and secondly with repelling her from Holy Communion. John Wesley refused to admit the first charge and denied the competence of the court to deal with the second, since it concerned only a point of ecclesiastical discipline. When he read the appointed Lesson from the 11th chapter of the Epistle to the Hebrews in the evening of 9th August he prayed for a similar measure of faith to enable him to prefer the reproach of Christ to the treasures of Egypt. The next day also he was helped by the Lesson for the day. In a letter Causton challenged him to state before all the inhabitants of the colony his reasons for repelling Sophy. Wesley refused because he was not prepared to expose a matter of ecclesiastical law to general judgement, and he was afraid that extreme measures might be taken against Causton, who was in many ways unpopular. As early as 11th June he had been compelled to inform the chief magistrate of a

[6] *Journal*, I.376, 7th August 1737. Since 19th March, that is almost four months previously, Wesley had considered keeping her away.

[7] Ibid. p. 335, note 1, Curnock.

[8] Examples of this, *Journal*, I.135–6, 12th January 1736, Mistress Hawkins; pp. 398–9, 4th November 1737, Mr Watson.

[9] *Journal*, I.356, 7th May 1737, from Delamotte; p. 361, 4th June 1737, the same; p. 365, 3rd July 1737, from Burnside, the husband of their friend, formerly Miss Bovey; ibid., from Causton.

[1] Ibid. p. 356, 16th May 1737; p. 364, 3rd July 1737, directly; *Letters*, 1224–5, Savannah, 5th July 1737, p. 226, Savannah, 11th August 1737, by letter. In the second letter he offered to receive her, after he had forbidden her: 'If you offer yourself at the Lord's Table on Sunday, I will advertise you (as I have done more than once) wherein you have done wrong. And when you have openly declared yourself to have truly repented, I will administer to you the mysteries of God.'

[2] *Letters*, I.226.

[3] *Journal*, I.376, 7th August 1737. Mrs Burnside said to Mrs Williamson: 'You was much to blame, after receiving the letter from Mr Wesley to offer yourself at the Table before you had cleared yourself to him. But you may easily put an end to this by going to Mr Wesley now, and clearing yourself of what you are charged with.'

number of complaints which the people had about his conduct of affairs. This had so aroused his anger that Wesley had seen himself in the place of the prophet Ezekiel who had to proclaim God's Word regardless of how it was received.[4] Accordingly Wesley now wanted his own case to be handled by the trustees of the colony. The Lesson for the day gave him strength. It was from the beginning of the 12th chapter of the Epistle to the Hebrews, where the call to the resolute follower of Jesus in the way of the Cross is combined with the reference to the great Conqueror.

The inevitable happened: Causton was enraged. In high dudgeon he came to Wesley's house and accused him of maltreating his niece and through her, himself. He warned Wesley that he had drawn his sword from its sheath and would not put it back until he was revenged. He repeated his demand that Wesley should vindicate himself before the whole congregation. He opened a regular campaign against Wesley. He drew up a report about Sophy for the trustees which was the direct opposite of Wesley's complaints against her. He worked on the jury, talked with them day and night, and kept a continually open table for them.[5] On 16th August Wesley read out after evening prayers a short account of the case which he himself had written.[6] Earlier, on 12th August and the days following, Causton had given as many people as possible a garbled version of Wesley's letters to Sophy, so that the impression grew that Wesley wanted to avenge himself for her refusal of his proposal of marriage.[7] On 22nd August the Court of Savannah met with Causton presiding. Because of their background twenty-three of the forty-four jurors of which it was composed were already committed to the desired result. John Wesley was indicted under a ten-point charge, nine of which were concerned with measures in which he had departed, or was alleged to have departed, from the regulations of the Anglican Church. Above all he had not declared, as he ought to have done, that he would exercise his ministry according to Anglican principles. The Sunday Service, which was meant to be a unity, he had divided into two parts. He held Morning Prayer early at five or six o'clock and sermon and Communion without Morning Prayer between nine and eleven o'clock. He wanted to enforce baptism by dipping, even when the child was frail. Two godparents were sufficient for him. He

[4] Ibid. p. 362, 11th June 1737.
[5] Ibid. p. 381, 15th August 1737.
[6] Ibid. p. 382, 16th August 1737.
[7] Ibid. p. 380, 12th August 1737.

had assumed the title 'Ordinary', which he had probably taken over from Count Zinzendorf. Further complaints were added from individual cases. Wesley maintained that a civil court had no competence to try these laboriously assembled charges. He recognized its right in only one point—the accusation that he had spoken with Williamson's wife against her husband's will. He declared his agreement that this question should be considered by the court immediately, but the court was not willing and Causton gave way. The trial was first adjourned until 2nd September and then moved elsewhere. Causton's questionable behaviour gradually recoiled upon himself and people became suspicious. A minority of the jury drew up a counter-declaration to the accusation, and this acquitted Wesley from each charge by giving different versions of the matter. Both accounts were forwarded to the trustees in England and in this way everything remained for the time being in a state of legal indecision.

At the same time other spiteful attacks continued to be made. A medical man, Dr Tailfer, made common cause with Sophy's husband. In England this person had seduced a young girl to whom he was related and enticed her, partly against her will, to Georgia, where he had brutally maltreated her with beatings, thus drawing a sharp reproof from Wesley. The two men drew up a tendentious report on the colony which they soon had printed. In this John Wesley was represented as Savannah's great tyrant, who enslaved people's minds in order to prepare for the subjection of their bodies by outward impositions. He was said to be a rigorous adherent of Roman Catholic principles and practices, even though he was expert at concealing them by his emphasis upon Anglicanism. He damned all Dissenters and cultivated the spirit of Pharisaism.[8]

At the same time another opponent appeared in the field. The dissenting minister Dison from Frederica seized the opportunity to usurp Wesley's rights in the pastoral office. He began by claiming that the Savannah magistrates had commissioned him to perform ecclesiastical duties there. At the same time he announced that in future he would hold a service to celebrate the Sacrament every Thursday. He conducted his first service on 8th September, and there were present Mrs Causton, Sophy and her husband, and eight or ten others. Wesley was very concerned at this high-handed action by the magistrates, but did no more than to bring the situation to their notice. At this same time Delamotte led him to consider whether

<hr/>

[8] *Journal*, VIII.304ff.

he ought not to return to England and immediately, to prevent false reports from spreading, since it became known that the Williamsons had decided to go to England and would leave on the next boat. At first Wesley decided against this, considering it better to wait rather than hasten to defend himself. When he preached on Sunday, 11th September, on the words of Jesus about the impossibility of avoiding offences (Matthew 18[7]) in his exposition of the text he justified his actions against the complaints which had been made. Characteristically he based his dividing of the Sunday Service on its correspondence with the practice of the early Church. He supported his case in admitting folk to Holy Communion from the strict regulations of the Anglican Church. Yet he was still preoccupied with the idea of returning to England. He brought it up again on 7th October when he was with his friends. On this occasion they all supported the proposal and even his own scruples began to weaken. The decisive factor in his own eyes was that now the mission to the heathen seemed to be impracticable. He did not consider that he was under an obligation to the congregation in Savannah; from the beginning he had looked upon his work there as a temporary means of going on to the missionary work. Moreover, he believed he would be able to serve them better by giving a true account in England of their material and spiritual condition than by remaining in a situation which was so unpromising. Yet in agreeing with his friends he reserved to himself the right of deciding when the time should be most appropriate. He had to wait six weeks longer. On 22nd November Causton invited him to a conference with himself, and at this Wesley learned that he had been branded by the court as a disturber of the public peace. He took this as the right moment to inform Causton on the next day that he wished to return immediately to England. It was not for an enemy of the public peace to remain where he caused only mischief. It went hard for him that he had to ask Causton for the money for the journey and that this request had to be repeated a week later. This was on 30th November. His opponents now realized that he was in earnest and on 2nd December they summoned him before the magistrates and informed him that he must not leave until he had been cleared of all charges. They stressed the fact that this had also been imposed upon him by the court, but Wesley denied that this had ever been decided. He had undertaken no such obligation at the time nor was he prepared to do so now. He had his business and the magistrates had theirs. In this way he was denying in a very sharp way his own subordination to the civil authority, and arguing for the separation of Church and State. In the afternoon the magistrates published an order to all security officers to prevent his leaving the colony and forbidding any person from helping him to do so. This was the signal for him. Since he now had to regard himself as a prisoner at large he set off quietly after evening prayers. The faithful Delamotte, who had been his companion almost without break since 14th October 1735 went with him as far as Charlestown. After many troubles, which included hunger, thirst, cold, and the taking of wrong directions, they reached the sea-port town, where he went on board the ship *Samuel* just before Christmas, on 22nd December 1737. This was to bring him to England. America now lay behind him, but not, he hoped, for ever.[9]

His disappearing was not really flight. He had informed the Savannah officials in no uncertain terms of his intention to leave, and he did not feel that he was bound by their inhibition. They too did not attempt anything that looked like pursuit, although he gave them opportunity of doing so by tarrying long in the country. Twenty days passed before he went aboard the ship. In Charlestown he conducted morning service and preached. Nevertheless the whole affair created a very bad impression. Bolzius and Gronau knew about the entire procedure of Sophy's exclusion from Communion, since Gronau was in the congregation in the summer when Wesley explained the issue to them. At the time Gronau wrote sadly to Ziegenhagen in London: 'It looks to me as if he is not long for this country. God will at last break in with His judgements.'[1] When he heard of Wesley's sudden departure he wrote in his diary on 15th December: 'At the same time received news that Mr Wesley had gone secretly at night to Charlestown by way of Purrysbourg, to go from there in all haste to London. I do not know at all what moved him to so quick a resolution, so hurtful both to his office and to God's honour. At least he was not intending to leave his congregation when I was recently with him in Savannah and talked much about the dispute between him and Causton, but he was to await the arrival of Mr Oglethorpe. He

---

[9] On this section, *Journal*, I.382–413.
[1] Gronau to Ziegenhagen, 19th August 1737, handwritten, in the Missionary archives of Francke's Institution at Halle, Correspondence and News from Ebenezer, 5.A.3, p. 349.

thought it scandalous that he had tolerated two men who had contracted debts and gone away without paying them.'[2]

What did the affair with Sophy mean for John Wesley? Through it all it can be seen that he was concerned about it at the deepest level and that he deliberately placed it under God. It penetrated the depths of his religious life. His visionary experience,[3] the only one which he is known to have had, shows how frightful the mental strain was. There is no doubt that he saw in her a suitable life-companion; he was attracted not only by her physical charm and the impression she made upon him as a man, but he also believed she would live as a true Christian.[4] It was for this reason that he attached such importance to their religious conversations. But increasingly he came to look at the relationship under negative religious categories: temptation,[5] spiritual conflict, sacrifice.[6] More and more she threatened to interfere with his mission, even with his relationship to God. He notes that God's will is one opposed to his own, he experiences conflicts in his prayers, but knows that God hears and answers him,[7] which is always an unusually significant thing for him. It is always a question of something to be renounced. He recognizes that this renunciation includes worldly and social comfort.[8] Behind all this of course there is the influence of the primitive Christian ideal of

[2] Ebenezer Diary (1737), ibid., 5.D.3, p. 142, Thursday 15th December 1737. Ziegenhagen had informed Gotthilf August Francke in Halle by 8th February 1738 of the return of 'the well-known minister Westley from Savannah' which took place on 3rd February. There are rumours about the real reason for his unexpected arrival concerning which Ziegenhagen wishes to be silent. Ziegenhagen to G. A. Francke, Kensington, 8th February 1738, Missionary archives of Francke's Institution, Halle, Z.I.L.5.

[3] Cf. above, p. 200.

[4] Cf. above, p. 197.

[5] *Journal*, I.294, 1st November 1737: 'This I began with a single eye. But it was not long before I found it a task too hard for me to preserve the same intention with which I began, in such intimacy of conversation as ours was.' Ibid. 318, 10–11th February 1737: 'I was not strong enough to bear the complicated temptations of a married state.' Ibid. p. 323, 26th February 1737: Wesley calls his being alone with her 'an hour of trial'; similarly, ibid. pp. 323–4, 27th February 1737, and pp. 328–9, 7th March 1737 ('shock of temptation'); cf. also p. 329: 'I lay struggling in the net, nay, scarcely struggling, as even fearing to be delivered.'

[6] Ibid. p. 325, 4th March 1737: 'A costly sacrifice.'

[7] Ibid. p. 327, 4th March 1737: 'From the directions I received from God this day touching an affair of the greatest importance, I could not but observe, as I had done many times before, the entire mistake of those who assert: "God will not answer your prayer, unless your heart be wholly resigned to His will." My heart was not wholly resigned to His will. Therefore, not daring to depend on my own judgement, I cried the more earnestly to Him to supply what was wanting in me. And I know, and am assured, He heard my voice, and did send forth His light and His truth.'

[8] Ibid. pp. 325–6, 4th March 1737.

poverty and the forgoing of a settled home.[9] Indeed, this renunciation extends into his most intimate relationship with God: after he has heard of Sophy's engagement he experiences a depression which can only be described as a spiritual trial.[1] Everything is shattered for him: never has he known so bitter a time. Even God departs from him, and yet—so unlike A. H. Francke—no doubts about the objective reality of God come to him. But the effects of the experience extend even to the way in which he recounts it in his *Journal*: the sentences are short and sharply compressed.

Thus Sophy had for John Wesley just the opposite meaning to that once possessed by Varanese[2] and Mrs Pendarves.[3] In both of these friends of his youth he had seen models for his own sanctification, and they had to say the least strongly determined the forms in which his religious life was expressed.[4] There had been temporarily introduced into his piety a fanatical trait which had frankly unhealthy results, but in the affair with Sophy everything was wholesome and natural. Whereas he allowed his personal religion to determine his relationship with Varanese and Mrs Pendarves, that with Sophy was affected in this way only indirectly, since it sprang out of the sphere of the natural which was covered for him by the first article of the creed. And yet his spiritual development received a stronger step forward from the affair with Sophy. God Himself drew near in a way such as he had never known before. He experienced the fact that God inclined His ear to him even when he himself was not wholly surrendered to the divine will. This was a starting-point for the understanding of prevenient grace, which is stronger than the human will; the moralistic-mystical effort after that complete preparation of the self for God is rejected.[5] The relationship with God is radically withdrawn from the sphere of the rational and moralistic, and becomes a reality painfully experienced. In this way it reached a new depth, the dimension of spiritual conflict.[6]

[9] Evidence of this is the way in which he thinks of his life in Georgia when reviewing it, as in *Journal*, I.418, 422.
[1] Ibid. pp. 334–5, 9th March 1737.
[2] See above, pp. 72ff.
[3] See above, pp. 112ff.
[4] James Harrison Rigg, *The Living Wesley*, p. 50.
[5] Cf. above, p. 207, note 7.
[6] It is significant that the meaning of the experience with Miss Sophy has been missed by all the biographers, even those careful interpreters, James Harrison Rigg, Augustin Leger, and Maximin Piette. Because of Wesley's living, divinely-related belief in the natural creation his renunciation was an important preparatory factor for his conversion.

The affair with Sophy was the factor which finally made John Wesley decide to leave the North American colony. What was the effect of these two years as a whole upon him? Was the result completely negative? His lack of success as a minister and the distress of his personal affairs both point in this direction. Wesley had gone to America with the highest hopes. One after another they were smashed. His main concern, the mission to the heathen, was forced by the pressure of events more and more into the background. It was the leading men of the colony who were responsible for this. The careful but pitiful attempts he made to keep it alive can only have revealed the actual situation the more clearly to him and made it more oppressive. The vast amount of work he did in his congregation, his involvement in the judicial and economic affairs of the settlers, left him scarcely any free time for himself, and this is precisely what he hoped to find in Georgia. In the event the contrary was true. The danger threatened of his getting lost in all these concerns which were really external to him, and the fact that he took them so seriously brought about the catastrophe.

At the time he was not in a position rightly to assess all the facts, but when he was staying in London at the beginning of February 1738 he wrote an account of what he had achieved and failed to do, which was marked by remarkable restraint and objectivity.[7] The outstanding characteristic of this retrospect was gratitude to God. Wesley saw God's hand in all that had happened just because it had turned out so differently from his expectations. Neither the decision to go to America nor his experiences there were anything like his original plans. They had gone contrary to his own wishes, and this led him to recognize as a deeper meaning in his life the fact that God had humbled him. God had proved him; God had shown him what was really in his heart and brought him to despair of himself. Above all God had cured him of all trust in man. God had shown that *He* knew how to direct affairs just when reason fails, either by the lot as used by the Herrnhuters or by other means of making known His will to man. Accordingly Wesley had now become obedient to God's commandments with a new devotion, and yet this went along with a blessed certainty that he was borne up by God Himself. And God had not only made him free from man but from natural forces also. He had taken away the fear of the sea which he had felt since his youth. All this had come about through his personal dealings with

[7] *Journal*, I.435, 3rd February 1738.

God. Moreover God had brought him into touch with new acquaintances whom he recognized as true servants of God. This was particularly the case with the Herrnhuters. God had also made accessible to him the writings of German, Spanish, and Italian holy men, and through them he had not only been able to see something of their piety but also to appreciate the reality of world-wide Christianity.

This is what he had gained personally. At the first, when he decided to go to America, he had spoken primarily about himself and his aims; he did the same at the end also. His relationship to God, or rather God's relationship to himself, was his first consideration, and this order of precedence was not at this stage any more an egotistic concern about his own salvation than it had been in the first instance. This way of putting it was merely an expression of the truth as he saw it. He could only speak about that which really applied to himself, so that this focusing of attention upon himself was an expression of modesty rather than egotism. All the time Wesley was declaring that for him 'Christianity' was not theory or a matter of abstract principles about religion, but personal encounter with God, the Lord of his life.

When in the second place he looked back and asked what others had gained from his sojourn abroad, he abandoned the note of definite assertion and said: 'I hope, too, some good may come to others hereby.' It is significant that now he spoke quite impersonally. He did not attach any particular significance to his own contribution or work; he merely kept to facts. 'All in Georgia have heard the word of God. Some have believed, and begun to run well. A few steps have been taken towards publishing the glad tidings both to the African and American heathen. Many children have learned "how they ought to serve God", and to be useful to their neighbour.' The men responsible for the care of the colony have the opportunity of knowing the true state of affairs and have been placed in the position of building better than before both peace and happiness for many generations.

This retrospect indicates that the significance of the stay in America was not exhausted in Wesley's experiences as a clergyman but lay more fundamentally in his own reaction to these experiences. Thus Georgia, which meant for him the almost complete disappearance of what was merely theoretical, brought him the task of authenticating to others what he had received and what was his own. In this undertaking he was frustrated: what was his own possession was not capable of being verified before others. Accordingly this interchange between what was his own and what he had received went on in increasing measure: what he received became stronger than that which was his own. Almost everything which came from his side was shattered, or at least was severely tested. This applied to his beliefs about the natural creation (Sophy) and to the individualistic way in which he conceived holiness. All that he received led in the last resort to the continued strengthening of his attachment to primitive Christianity. First and foremost this was due to his daily preoccupation with the New Testament, and then to his meeting with the Herrnhuters. His dealings with Spangenberg, the climax of his affair with Sophy, and his intense prayer-life, all helped to make conformity with primitive Christianity more and more a *personal* demand and a *personal* question. Confidence in his own designs increasingly dwindled alongside his confidence in men in general,[8] and he comes to suspect that the primitive Christian character cannot be attained without something more. The required presupposition is faith, and this indeed is the very heart of the matter. So there opens before him the beginnings of an understanding of the sequence: sin, conflict, justification, faith. For this reason a theological discussion at the assembly of the English clergy of South Carolina on 22nd April 1937 became so important for him, since it centred around the theme of Christ our Righteousness.[9] He caught a glimpse of what justification really meant, although the essential note and real systematic clarity were missing. It was still too much a matter of externals.

As a general conclusion it may be said that the reality of God became increasingly clear for Wesley through his ever-increasing penetration into the meaning of primitive Christianity, the frustrating of his hopes regarding himself and his work, and the experience of loneliness in his spiritual struggle.[1] The idea of God which he had from childhood, greatly modified and yet basically the same, disappeared in the sense that his belief in providence, though not destroyed, was radically recast. God had come near to him in His inconceivable greatness as One who opposed his own will and who

[8] *Journal*, I.435. This account shows how Wesley himself recognized this.
[9] Ibid. p. 350, 22nd April 1737, in Charlestown. J. H. Rigg, *The Churchmanship of John Wesley*, p. 32, rightly drew attention to the importance of this experience for Wesley.
[1] The fear of death has an important preparatory role in this connexion; cf. also Karl Holl, *Ges.Aufs.*, I, *Luther* (1932), p. 18.

demanded recognition. It was this humiliation which led him away from himself towards God.[2] As a result his religious point of view was decisively altered. His trust in the power of the law[3] as the way from man to God was shaken. His own resources and what he has received have proved inadequate to fulfil the task prescribed for him by God. He has failed to satisfy either of the two demands which at that time were the concrete expression of the law for him, namely, the claims of his work in Georgia (the mission to the heathen and the pastoral oversight of the congregation), and conformity to the primitive Christian character. It was at his conversion that he came to realize through awareness of sin the full depth and tension of the law. At this stage the spiritual conflict was experienced only indirectly through the law: he saw in Sophy one who endangered the fulfilment of his appointed task and his attachment to the ideals of primitive Christianity, particularly of poverty and the absence of a home. But the spiritual conflict had another meaning also. It was instrumental in enabling him to penetrate a dimension in the relationship with God which is right outside the province of 'law': one in which it is quite impossible to think of God as One who can be apprehended on the level of law or legal concept or action. This new idea of God is on the very edge of the *Deus absconditus* and an opportunity is given for the working of grace.

[2] *Journal*, I.325, 4th March 1737; p. 435, 3rd February 1738. In this connexion he attributes a meaning also to the use of the Herrnhut lot.
[3] Cf. above, p. 123.

SEVEN

The Conversion

THE VOYAGE back to England was quite different from the journey out to America. Wesley had no programme, no particular objective, not even the group of friends in Oxford. Disillusioned, defeated, if not despairing, an uncertain future lay before him. The enforced inactivity can only have driven him back the more upon his own troubles. In spite of this he immediately took up the work which provided the connecting link throughout his whole period in America and which once more brings out his real concern. Once again he became a missionary. He gave instruction in the Christian faith to a half-grown negro youth who was a fellow-traveller in the ship. Soon a second joined him. In this way Wesley was able to carry forward the task which he had begun earlier, for it was while he was in South Carolina that he realized the importance of proclaiming the Christian message to the negroes. Accordingly his efforts with the two young men on the boat revived a project which had been interrupted, and as before he also tried to approach his fellow-passengers as pastor and messenger of the Gospel. In this, however, he made the painful and surprising discovery that he had no real desire to do so. Several times he forced himself to act, and on these occasions he did experience a measure of relief, but on the whole he remained silent because he was worried by his own problems. He continued working and reading on his own account. In particular there was one book, the life of the French Count Gaston Jean-Baptiste de Renty (1611–49), which he finished reading at this time. This work, which first appeared in 1651, was written by the Count's Jesuit confessor, and was published in a second edition in 1701 by Pierre Poiret with the pretentious title, *Le Chrétien réel* (*The True Christian*). It is a significant and effective example of Romanic mysticism. In Germany its influence is seen most of all in Gottfried Arnold and Gerhard Tersteegen.[1] John Wesley had begun it on 20th May 1736[2] and it

---

[1] On this largely forgotten book, cf. my article '*John Wesley und die Lebensbeschreibung de Renty*', *Theologia Viatorum*, V.(1953). Gottfried Arnold, *Das Leben der Gläubigen oder Beschreibung solcher gottseliger Personen, welche in*

was his constant companion during the whole of his stay in America. Nor did it lose its hold upon him afterwards, and in his old age he still commended it as the ideal Christian life.[3]

Wherein lies the importance of the life of this Catholic believer? The Count was not outstanding because of any epoch-making works; his name occupies no special place either in the history of France or in the Church. His greatness lay in his personality. It is obvious that he combined qualities rarely found so completely and powerfully in one individual. He was of course utterly devoted to his Church and went to mass not merely with regularity but with ardent longing. The high esteem he showed for the priesthood exercised a powerful influence upon other people. He was extremely conscientious in the performance of those tasks prescribed for him by his confessor. But it was mystic solitude which he valued most of all; by sinking into the divine mysteries he was able to forgo the use of all external means of grace in the Church. Yet at the same time he cared for his family both as husband and father, and not only for it, but for all known to him who were in need.[4] He lived in the world and yet was not of the world. He was surrounded by many people and yet he was alone with his God. His source of strength was in mystical prayer with its three degrees of meditation, affection, and contemplation—reflection, sensation, and union. He mastered this to a very high degree. He thought of himself as an utter sinner, and was a perfect example of self-abasement. Humility was his guiding principle, and he carried it to such a degree of self-mortification that physical death became merely the organic counterpart of a process which had been

den letzen 200 Jahren sonderlich bekandt worden (Halle, 1701), gives on pp. 1–12 from the postscript to the biography of de Renty the 'Instruction how one is profitably to read from these accounts of holy men'. Johann Heinrich Reitz gives the life of de Renty in his Historie der Wiedergebohrnen, V.(1726).49–75; Gerhard Tersteegen in the selected Lebensbeschreibungen heileger Seelen, I.(1784).120–98. It was from de Renty that Tersteegen took over the symbolic practice of writing out a promise to the Saviour in his own blood (Geistliche und erbauliche Briefe, I.(1773), Introduction; cf. Albrecht Ritschl, Geschichte des Pietismus, p. 461).

[2] Journal, I.219, Diary, 20th May 1736; cf. also p. 435, 3rd February 1738 (Review of life in Georgia): 'Hereby my passage is opened to the writings of holy men in the German, Spanish and Italian tongues.' Of Wesley literature, cf. Luke Tyerman, The Oxford Methodists, p. 5. Henry Bett, The Spirit of Methodism, p. 62: 'Wesley had read most of these mystical writers while he was in Georgia.' It is noteworthy that this whole side is neglected by Maximin Piette, the catholic student of Wesley.

[3] Letters, VIII.171, near Bristol, 16th September 1789, to his nephew Samuel Wesley.

[4] Le Chrétien réel ou la Vie du Marquis de Renty (Cologne, 1701), pp. 159ff.

completed in thought long before.[5] Yet the more he gave himself in solitariness to this severe self-discipline the more he felt himself one with the true believers of all ages in a real and deep communion of the saints.[6] He was wealthy and yet longed to abandon everything, and like St Alexius to separate from his wife on their wedding-night in order to embrace the life of poverty of Jesus and the apostles. But it was this which God denied him and so provided that he learned to hold his possessions as if he had nothing.[7] God led him to similar experiences at the death of his wife, when he knew such a strange 'holy unconcern' at this most severe of human losses that it could only be seen as a demonstration of divine power.[8] On the other hand he was able to endure pains which would have been too much for any other person, for all the time his thoughts were centred upon the suffering Saviour and Redeemer.[9] God's honour, the salvation of his own soul, and the well-being of his neighbour were the focal points of his religion and his practice. On a certain day in his life he had written out a covenant with the Saviour Jesus Christ in his own blood.[1] Yet at the same time he devoted himself to the care of the sick and aged, he interested himself in the Catholic exiles from England, and was a benefactor of the Church in Canada.[2] He formed little groups of believers who helped to build each other up by spiritual discussions.[3] Everyone with whom he spoke looked upon him as a man in whom they could confide, and so he acted as a true spiritual father to many folk. His deepest attachment of all was to primitive Christianity, and his great desire was to make its spiritual power

[5] Ibid. pp. 81ff, 85, 91, 97, 148ff, 314, 325, 347, 359, 405, 409, 428ff, 460, etc. De Renty also used in this connexion the story of Isaac's offering, ibid. p. 353; cf. my article 'Kleine Nachlese zu Isaak's Opferung', Theol. Zeitschr. (Basel, 1952), pp. 469–70.
[6] Ibid. pp. 386ff.
[7] Ibid. pp. 60–1.
[8] Ibid. p. 365: 'L'ordre de mon Dieu est mon désir et lors qu'il m'est signifié, il me fait la grâce de m'y rendre.... J'apris sa mort entrant dans Paris: alors je me donnai plainement à Dieu de qui j'attendois la volonté pour la suivre.... L'an 1641, il lui mourut l'un de ses enfants, qu'il aimois beaucoup; quand on lui en aporta la nouvelle, il ne dit pas une parole et ne fit voir auqu'un mouvement si non de soumission aux ordres de Dieu, agréant dans une parfaite complaisance la disposition qu'il faisoit de cet enfant, et la perte qu'il lui envoioit.... Madame sa femme fut très grievement malade et pensa mourir.... Monsieur de Renty ... dit: Je ne peux pas nier que ma nature ne ressente une grande douleur de cette perte, mais mon esprit est remplis de tant de joie de me voir en état de donner et de sacrifier à Dieu une chose qui m'est si chere'.
[9] Ibid. pp. 123ff.
[1] Ibid. pp. 318–20 (Christmas 1643).
[2] Ibid. pp. 168ff, 186ff, 302–3.
[3] Ibid. p. 205.

evident in his own time.[4] In the light of all this it is not surprising that Peter Poiret should see his life as a proof of the claim that true mysticism is Christianity in its full power.[5] In spite of his great social activity he saw the heart of the Christian faith in personal communion with God. So deeply did he penetrate into the eternal mysteries by spiritual contemplation that he actually had a direct awareness of the presence of the Triune God.[6]

What was it that John Wesley found so attractive in the life of this modern saint? Fundamentally it was the way in which the thought of God dominated him which impressed Wesley so deeply. It was evident that de Renty was like Gregory Lopez, a man who lived continuously in the presence of God. In everything he was led by the wish to be wholly dedicated to God. He saw through all external things to an ultimate spiritual point, and there he perceived God. Wesley found in him a perfection which attains to holiness as a higher nature. To read de Renty's life is to gain the impression that he never needed to submit himself to law, although he does make incidental reference to his inner struggles. He was one in whom sanctification and joy in salvation had attained a deep unity. His perfection was rooted in love towards God. That all this appeared in the life of one person was bound to have a strong influence upon Wesley. Here was a vigorous and full vitality, an irrefutable proof of the reality of Christian values. It was a powerful answer to Wesley's own longings after the experience of salvation. De Renty was an individual witness, just as the Herrnhuters had been a corporate one, to the fact that primitive Christianity could be realized in the present. The Puritan characteristics of the observation, watching over, and education of the self were corroborated by the various spiritual experiences which came to de Renty. Wesley was able to find confirmation of what he himself was striving after, growth through self-discipline, through the mastering of his own thoughts and passions. He saw in de Renty the splendour of that final inner

---

[4] *Le Chrétien réal*, pp. 249, 379.

[5] Ibid. Preface, pp. 7b–8. '*En un mot, l'example vivant de Monsieur de Renty, ne doit-il pas convaincre tout le monde, que bien loin, que la vraie Mystique et la vraie Religion Chrétienne soit des choses mal accordantes ou incompatibles, cette mystique et le Christianisme en sa vigueur et en sa vive pratique ne sont qu'une seule et une même chose en sa substance et en sa nature?*' Similarly 3b–4.

[6] Ibid. pp. 335ff, esp. p. 338: '*Je porte pour l'ordinaire en moi, (dit-il en la déclaration qu'il donna de son état à son Directeur l'an 1645) une vérité expérimentale et une plénitude de la présence de la très-Sainte Trinité.*'

freedom from the world, the 'holy unconcern' about its so-called possessions and genuine values.[7]

Thus Wesley took over in the main those features which were biblical and in the Puritan tradition rather than those which were genuinely mystical. Neither the mystical prayer nor annihilation of self, which are the two central features of the biography, entered into Wesley's own life and thought.[8]

Wesley's judgement on the book as a whole was in the event very revealing and significant, and at the same time an eloquent testimony to his own critical ability at its best. He acknowledged without any qualifications the achievements of this unique life, and praised it in the highest terms, although in one respect he severely attacked the biography. By praising indiscriminately everything about de Renty, the greatest and the least, the unusual and the commonplace, it is possible to suspect this true example of a Christian life of superstition.[9] Wesley appears here as an advocate of what is natural and original over against an artificial arrangement of the material, the purpose of which is to edify the reader. His judgement in this instance is exactly in line with the objection he raised as a young man against Thomas à Kempis's summons to humility.[1]

Against the background of such a complete and accomplished Christian personality John Wesley could not help feeling that his own lack of integration was doubly painful. While still on the boat those tortuous thoughts set in which were the prelude to his conversion. As might be expected from one of his temperament, theoretical doubt and practical failure reacted upon each other. Once again it was the fear of death which aroused in him ultimate questions. The possibility of death indeed runs like a recurring theme through the whole period of his spiritual development. During his student days he was brought sharply up against the fact of death by the passing of friends and acquaintances: John Griffith, William Morgan, and a young girl whose name we do not know had died almost before his own eyes. On each occasion he was sharply con-

[7] *Letters*, VIII.253, London, 3rd January 1791, to Adam Clarke: 'But you startle me when you talk of grieving so much for the death of an infant. This was certainly a proof of inordinate affection; and if you love them thus all your children will die. How did Mr de Renty behave when he supposed his wife to be dying? This is a pattern for a Christian.'
[8] Further to this, cf. his radical rejection of the Mystics and their methods in *Letters*, I.207–10, Savannah, 23rd November 1735, to his brother Samuel.
[9] *Journal*, I.415, 6th January 1738.
[1] See above, pp. 83ff.

fronted by the question of 'conversion', that complete turning to God.
Each time also he appealed directly to the conscience of others in the
matter. In the letter written from Oxford in February 1733, when
his mother had recommended him to exercise restraint in thinking
about questions of belief, he insisted upon extreme plainness and
resolution in such matters.[2] He repeatedly stressed the shortness of
life as something which imperilled the process of sanctification.[3]
Then came the voyage to America, when the fearless attitude of the
Herrnhuters in the most severe storm both shamed and cheered him.
While in America death in his congregation moved him every time
it occurred, and the crises in the affair with Sophy aroused thoughts
of death. On the day of her marriage he made his will.[4] It seems
that during the first six months he wrote for his pastoral work a
poem about death and introduced it to his congregation.[5] Now once
again he was on the sea and he trembled before death. He recognized that in the two years since his outward voyage he had not
progressed. Indeed the fear he now felt was greater than on the
previous occasion. It not only took hold of him in moments of danger
but also oppressed him when the wind was light and the sea calm.[6]
But he found that he had been able to banish the fear of death by
crying to God in the storm,[7] so it was not the fear which was the
main trouble. More and more he reached the conclusion that it was
faith which he lacked. The fear of death was a sign of this, perhaps
the clearest, but by no means the only one. At such times he doubted
the truth of the Gospel, which admittedly he still understood essentially in a legalistic way as unconditional following of Christ, a preparedness for every renunciation. He found he could ask, 'Am I not
a fool if I prefer to sacrifice everything for a fable, as I have done
and still do?'[8] It became continually clearer to him, however, that
without faith he was not entitled to bear the Christian name at all.
Accordingly he prayed for a complete transformation, a spirit which
would glorify God alike in life and death.[9] He felt that his way of
life hitherto had been like a building without a foundation-stone,
and he applied to it the deprecatory judgement of Thomas à Kempis:

[2] *Letters*, I.134, 15th February 1733.
[3] Ibid. p. 120, 28th February 1732, to his mother.
[4] *Journal*, I.337, Diary, 12th March 1737.
[5] Ibid. p. 272, Diary, 9th September 1736.
[6] Ibid. p. 414, 28th December 1737.
[7] Ibid. p. 417, 13th January 1738.
[8] Ibid. p. 418, 24th January 1738.
[9] Ibid. p. 414, 28th December 1737.

'What I have hitherto done is nothing.'[1] In the light of the scrupulous watch he had kept over himself and the painstaking and rationalistic method of living to which he had subjected himself since his Oxford days, the meaning of this statement raises interesting questions. With this one sentence he crossed out all that he had so far undertaken and done, and he condemned as one of his greatest illusions the attempt to attain the goal of holiness in solitude. He is now quite enough by himself, but does this mean that he is any nearer the ideal of a true Christian? On the contrary when he measures himself by the standard of Jesus he feels he is so much more like Satan. Undoubtedly he is thinking of Jesus's solitary temptations. He, Wesley, would have sunk into the abyss had not God Himself rescued him, which He did through the works of the early church Father, Cyprian.[2] It is not known which these were, and it is possible to see in this reference an example of that attachment to the primitive Church to which John Wesley and the dominant tradition in his Church felt themselves bound. But it may be conjectured that Cyprian's attitude of glorying in the reality of the Church strongly neutralized his feeling of solitude.

Yet it may be asked whether he was not unjust to himself in this ruthless judgement on his past life. He had not cultivated solitude so much in Georgia as he had done at Oxford. Had he not been continually occupied in his work, in pastoral counselling, and in evangelistic activities on behalf of other people? Was it not from fellowship with the Herrnhuters that the strongest spiritual influences in his life and thought had come? Had he not also received a great deal from the more sober Salzburgers? On the other hand he had so steeped himself in the two mystics, Lopez and de Renty, that they seemed to him models of the Christian life. And it must be remembered that they were recluses, while similarly the picture of the intrepid religious man in August Hermann Francke's *Nicodemus* was drawn throughout on individualistic lines. It is an indication of Wesley's keen sense of self-observation that he clearly recognized how far in his strivings after holiness in the midst of the many claims of his spiritual and secular occupations he had been concerned with God as it were on his own. It was his inner struggles on the ship which first drove him really into the loneliness of hyper-

---

[1] Ibid. p. 416 (cf. Thomas à Kempis, *De Imitatione Christi*, I.19.1), repeats *Letters*, I.263, 30th October 1738, to his brother Samuel.
[2] Ibid. p. 416, 9th January 1738.

criticism and self-laceration. Soon he could no longer know whether he was being prompted by God's will or tempted by Satan.[3] So he cried: 'Lord, save, or I perish! Save me.'[4]

Of course there were also lights in the darkness. When still conscious of the fear of death he resolved to preach God's Word to all and to apply it to the condition of each individual, and he actually made a start, he immediately felt better. Straightway he clung anxiously to this 'success' as a sign of God's grace and launched a passionate attack against the idea that a man must remain in the depths if he would come to God.[5]

He continued to hover between unrest and quietness of mind, between uncertainty and the desire for assurance, between doubt and belief, between the sense of nearness to God and being abandoned by Him. He experienced the complete breakdown of his spiritual position, and this drove him to say: 'I went to America to convert the Indians; but oh, who shall convert me?'[6] Twice in close succession he put the same question to himself. On the second occasion it was intensified by a ruthless judgement on himself: 'It is now two years and almost four months since I left my native country, in order to teach the Georgian Indians the nature of Christianity. But what have I learned myself in the meantime? Why, what I the least of all suspected, that I, who went to America to convert others, was never myself converted to God.'[7]

This judgement was not simply a reaction against his lack of success. It was meant quite seriously and was intended to let all who doubted it know the truth. Of course he had at the same time all those qualities which others might regard as evidence of their Christian faith. He had been trained to think and had received a theological education; he was a fluent speaker on religious subjects. He had fulfilled such practical demands of Christianity as almsgiving and service of the brethren. He had given up all the things that could be sacrificed, friends, fame, comfort, home, had renounced all security and had risked his life—all for the sake of the Gospel.

But does all this make him acceptable to God? Is he justified in God's sight by all his knowledge, his sermons, his good deeds, and his suffering?[8] Is his position established by his constant use of all

[3] *Journal,* I.414, 28th December 1737.
[4] Ibid. p. 415, 8th January 1738.   [5] Ibid. pp. 417–18, 13th January 1738.
[6] Ibid. p. 418, 24th January 1738.   [7] Ibid. pp. 421–2.
[8] Ibid. p. 423: 'Does all I ever did or can know, say, give, do, or suffer, justify me in His sight?'

the means of grace?[9] Or by the fact that his conscience is clear and that he is aware of being outwardly upright? Or that he is rationally convinced of all dogmatic truths? Do any of these give him a right to the holy, heavenly, divine name of Christian? By no means.[1] If the witness of the Bible, 'God's oracles', is true, then all of these things without faith in Christ are merely dung and dross (Philippians 3[7-8]), fit only to be burned up in eternal fire, although all derive their value and right from faith.

At the ends of the earth he has learned that he has acted against God's honour. His whole heart is corrupt and abominable, and consequently his whole life must be so, since a corrupt tree cannot bring forth good fruit. Alienated from the life of God, he is a child of wrath, an heir of hell. His own words, his own sufferings, his own righteousness are so far from reconciling him to an offended God, that they need an atonement for themselves. He stands under the sentence of death. His only hope is that of being justified freely by God through the redemption that is in Jesus Christ. Then he will be found in Him, not having a righteousness of his own but that which comes from God (Philippians 3[9]).

The problem of justification, having been so clearly stated, could not again be avoided. It is particularly significant that John Wesley includes the things he has suffered amongst those which fall under condemnation: his one-time pride in the enmity of the world is shattered.

He then proceeds to consider the question of his own personal faith with the same analytical and self-accusing clarity. Should it be objected that he has faith, those who say this are miserable comforters. His faith is the faith of devils (James 2[19]), a sort of faith indeed, but the kind possessed by those who are strangers to the covenant of promise. At best his faith is like that of the apostles at the beginning when Jesus first manifested His glory at Cana in Galilee (John 2). But in no sense is this the faith which overcomes the world (1 John 5[4]). He lacks the faith which firmly trusts in God that his sins are forgiven through Christ's merits, and that he is once more reconciled to the favour of God. He lacks the faith which Paul commends to everyone, particularly in the Epistle to the Romans. He lacks the faith which enables its possessor to cry out: 'I live not;

[9] The fact that the means of grace are mentioned second and then not again shows that Wesley's main concern was not in them.
[1] *Journal*, I.423: 'Does all this give me a claim to the holy, heavenly, divine character of a Christian? By no means.'

but Christ liveth in me; and the life which I now live, I live by faith in the Son of God, who loved me, and gave Himself for me' (Galatians 2[20]). He lacks the faith which none can have without knowing he has it. Whoever has it is free from sin—the whole body of sin is destroyed in him. He is free from fear, because he has peace with God and rejoices in hope of the glory of God. He is free from doubt, since the love of God is shed abroad in his heart through the Holy Ghost (Romans 5[5]). The Spirit of God witnesses with his own spirit that he is a child of God (Romans 8[16]).

It is surprising that there is to be found here already a completely clear understanding of what is involved in justification.[2] No more severe judgement on himself could be made, and indeed John Wesley later modified it by a somewhat more favourable interpretation: 'I had even then the faith of a slave, although not the faith of a son.'[3] For this reason it is possible to describe the struggles which went before, with their negative result, as spiritual trials (*Anfechtungen*),[4] which stand in a polar relationship with faith in the sense that they are essentially bound up with it. The whole man is challenged and put on trial, and justification is given its full biblical import.

How can John Wesley's development up to this decisive point be described so that this advance became a possibility? Sufficient emphasis has been given to the negative presuppositions. At this point attention must once again be directed to that positive motive which in the last resort was decisive. This is that attachment to primitive Christianity, which John Wesley affirmed with ever-increasing emphasis determined his course. It became more and more clear to him that the essential feature of this was the faith which lays hold of justifying grace and allows itself to be transformed by the Spirit of God. The key to John Wesley's spiritual development is to be found in this living involvement in primitive Christianity. More and more he found that the practical confirmation of facts in the New Testament lay in the events in his own life. It is extraordinarily instructive

---

[2] This fundamental position has not been noticed hitherto in Wesley's scholarship. Without exception it is only the actual conversion which is drawn upon in the matter of justification. But only when the details are carefully analysed and interpreted at this point is justice done both to the conversion and its inner condition, and only in this way can the conversion be seen as anything other than something foreign to John Wesley's inner development.

[3] *Journal*, I.424, note 1.

[4] J. W. Bashford in 'John Wesley's Conversion', *The Methodist Review* (bimonthly) LXXXV.(1903).775ff, esp. 784, is the only one to have called attention to the significance of the spiritual trials or conflicts (*Anfechtungen*), but even he confines himself to those which followed immediately on the conversion-day.

and illuminating to follow through this coincidence of theological perception with reality as actually experienced. Each step forward became possible only when the conditions for it were present in real life. Thus it was only after the complete breakdown of his situation that John Wesley came to see the doctrine of justification as the central feature in primitive Christianity. On the other hand he is honest enough to distinguish between this perception and his own personal knowledge of it. The acquiring of this is not something to be achieved but is a gift, an experience of grace, which he has not yet attained.

Wesley was a true pastor. Even the radical self-examination he carried through on the voyage did not stop him carrying on with this essential activity. He could not confine his attention to himself. In spite of his disturbance of mind and his spiritual emptiness it is astonishing how strongly he felt the obligation to concern himself with other things. Immediately on landing he preached in Deal, just north of Dover, to a large company, and in an inn of all places. That very evening he did the same in Faversham, where he had only a few listeners. The mere fact that he compared the ignorance of his English hearers unfavourably with the wildest Indians he had met in America shows how deeply the mission to the heathen had become the principle which directed all his thinking. Next he visited the parents of Charles Delamotte at Blendon Hall near Bexley. He had expected a cold reception, for they had disapproved of their son going to America, but he found just the opposite. He was given so warm a welcome that he concluded that God Himself had prepared his way. On the evening of 3rd February he came to London and stayed with his friend John Hutton. There he met his brother Charles, and he soon went to visit his mother. He had a great many relations and friends in town; moreover Oglethorpe was also there. Several times Wesley reported to the trustees of the colony, and in accordance with his practice this would have been done most conscientiously. He was convinced of the rightness of his own position, and yet his heart was no longer in any of these proceedings. His *Journal* gives no indication of anything which betrays real concern.[5] It is most probable that his position was in fact very difficult, and that his behaviour was questioned.[6] But he had done with all this.

[5] *Journal*, I.437, 8th February 1738; p. 438, 15th February 1738; p. 440, 22nd February 1738.
[6] Ibid. p. 438, note 2, from Charles Wesley's *Journal*.

Since he had returned from a colony whose fate deeply concerned everyone in England he received more invitations to preach than he might otherwise have done. But his forceful manner and his religious radicalism often offended his hearers: on the other hand he was continually surprised how well he was received by his friends, and saw in this a sign that the time had not yet come when he should be hated by all men. He prayed to God that He might prepare him for that day,[7] and it was in this way that the martyr type of religion continued to exert an influence upon him, although it was not the desire for actual martyrdom which possessed him but rather the early Christian conviction of its necessity. He liked to choose texts for his sermons which gave expression to this, such as Luke 9^{23}: 'If any man will come after me, let him deny himself, and take up his cross daily, and follow me', or Galatians 6^{12}: 'As many as desire to make a fair show in the flesh, they constrain you to be circumcised; only lest they should suffer persecution for the cross of Christ.'[8] But the text which contained the master-idea was the one, so dear to Pietism, about the new creature (2 Corinthians 5^{17}).[9]

He gave his whole attention and interest to the proclamation of the Word of God and its effects. By a number of unpremeditated stages he came to occupy the position of a free evangelist, a process which was hastened by a meeting which proved decisive. In the house of a Dutch merchant named Weinantz, the trusted friend of Zinzendorf, Wesley met several of the Herrnhut brethren on 7th February. Of these the most important from his own point of view was Peter Böhler from Frankfort/Main.[1] Wesley found lodgings for them near his own, and so began those searching conversations which took place each day. Peter Böhler was accompanied by an aged merchant from Stralsund named Abraham Richter, in whose house Zinzendorf had in his early days acted as tutor. In addition Georg Schulius and Wenzel Neisser belonged to the group.

It was natural that Wesley should have become friendly with Böhler, since he was on his way to Georgia. The brief outline of his career is as follows.[2] Born in Frankfort/Main in 1712, he was still

---

[7] *Journal*, I.423ff, 1st February 1738. On his rejection: ibid. p. 438, 12th February 1738; p. 460, 7th May 1738, 9th May 1738; p. 462, 14th May 1738.
[8] Ibid. p. 440, 21st, 26th February 1738.
[9] Ibid. p. 436, 5th February 1738; p. 446, 19th March 1738.
[1] Ibid. pp. 436–7, 7th February 1738.
[2] Cf. J. P. Lockwood, *Memorials of the Life of Peter Böhler, passim.* This book is well done but should be supplemented from the German side by a treatment which makes the inner development its special concern. It would have to

only a young man. His father had decided that he should study medicine, but his own choice lay in a different direction. A great impression had been made upon him when he went with a pastor to visit a woman who was condemned to death, who faced her end trusting in the forgiveness of sins through the Saviour's blood. From 1731 he studied theology at Jena and joined the Herrnhut student fellowship which met there in the house of Professor Walch, although it was under the leadership of Spangenberg. Böhler lived with the pietist Pastor Brumhardt in Wenigenjena and he acted as a liaison with the pietest circles among the townsfolk.[3] But Brumhardt died, Sprangenberg went to Halle, and the student group threatened to collapse. Then Count Zinzendorf came to Jena in order to reorganize it, and Böhler, who was at this time fairly new to the group, experienced his real conversion through meeting with the Count. This meant that the course of his spiritual life was now determined, and he became fully identified with the Moravians. In 1734 he stayed at Herrnhut for the first time. Greatly moved by one of his sermons, Georg Schulius, his companion in England and America, was won for Jesus Christ. In the same year he matriculated at Leipzig, and was *magister legens* when Zinzendorf engaged him as tutor for his son Christian Renatus. The University released him only reluctantly. It was also Böhler who first procured a refuge for the Count in Frankfort in 1736 after he had been exiled from Saxony. From there the ancient fortress of Ronneburg could be visited, and there Böhler was ordained, although he had already served as deputy pastor in Berthelsdorf, near Herrnhut. In the succeeding period he became Zinzendorf's special commissioner for England and America, and in Pennsylvania he met Heinrich Melchior Mühlenberg.[4] He became a bishop and died on 27th April 1775 at Fulneck in England, following a paralysis which affected his mind.

draw upon unpublished material from the Herrnhut and Halle archives. My pupil Dietrich Schiewe will probably undertake this work. In addition to Lockwood, see Gerhard Adolf Wauer, *Die Anfänge der Brüderkirche in England*, Leipzig phil. dissertation (1900), *passim*, which is superior in its knowledge of the material, although at times one-sided in its judgements. Wauer made use of the archives of the English Brüdergemeine in Fetter Lane, London, which were destroyed in the Second World War. On basic principles, cf. above all, Arthur Wilford Nagler, *Pietism and Methodism. The Significance of German Pietism in the Origin and Early Development of Methodism*, esp. pp. 120ff, 133, 171ff; Thomas F. Lockyer, *Paul: Luther: Wesley*, and J. Ernest Rattenbury, *The Conversion of the Wesleys*.

[3] Cf. Gerhard Reichel, *August Gottlieb Spangenberg*, p. 20.
[4] Mühlenberg's Diary, 25th November 1742 to 17th March 1743, Thursday 30th December 1742, handwritten, in the Missionary archives of Francke's Institution, Halle, Z.IV.D.2, p. 14.

This simple and yet obviously very resolute and energetic man came closer to the two Wesley brothers than any of the Moravians. On 17th February they went with him by road to Oxford and on the way John told him a great deal about his relationships with the Brethren in Georgia. Surprisingly enough he said it was his intention to return there as a missionary, only he felt that the trustees were the real obstacle in the way. He had therefore decided to go to Herrnhut in July or August to see it for himself. Böhler himself, as he says in his account, was not convinced that as yet he really knew the Saviour but that he was willing to be taught. Böhler grew very fond of him and hoped that when he had seen Herrnhut he would be 'completely ours'.[5] From Oxford, where John Sarney, an old friend of their student days, entertained them, they went to the parsonage at Stanton Harcourt. John Gambold now lived there: he was a friend of John Wesley, a former member of Christ Church and of the Oxford circle, and after Wesley's departure its leader. Gambold was attracted by the mystics, and John Wesley had actually spoken about him on this account with Spangenberg in Georgia. Later he gave up his position as an Anglican priest and went over fully to the Herrnhut Brethren, becoming bishop in the English section of their church. Like Daniel Ernest Jablonski, the Polish-German bishop of the old *Unitas Fratrum*, he cherished the hope of union with the Anglican Church. Keziah, the youngest sister of the Wesleys, whom John had wanted to come out to Georgia, was actually staying in the parsonage as a guest. John, to his great satisfaction, believed that he could say that Gambold had freed himself from Johann Tauler and Jakob Böhme and was attached to St Paul's type of Christian faith.[6] In this he was deceived. Shortly afterwards Böhler and Gambold were together in Oxford, and from the very first Böhler came to the conclusion that 'he looked just like a mystic'. Since they shared a room and even the same bed they had a serious talk in the evening, and Gambold began by saying that Böhler probably had too favourable an opinion of him. He was by no means the sound and convinced Christian that he had been represented to be. On the contrary he had been a seeker for ten years. Three years previously Luther's writings had 'caused him to believe', and things 'had often gone well with him'. Then he had hit

[5] Peter Böhler's handwritten Diary, London, 18th February 1738 to the end of May, in the archives of the United Brethren at Herrnhut, R.13.A, No. 4. A part of this in English translation was published in the *Wesleyan Methodist Magazine* (1854), pp. 687ff.
[6] *Journal*, I.439–40, 18th February 1738.

upon the mystics, and now he was plagued with all sorts of doubts which were directly connected with the duties of his office. In particular he was troubled about the sacraments. He doubted whether baptism and the Lord's Supper 'still had their old power'. He had fasted and watched a great deal, but he knew that carnal desire was still strong in him. He gave every indication of being a hypersensitive spirit, given to mysticism and asceticism. Since he had been commended to Böhler as a true Herrnhuter, Böhler was very interested in him, but found himself unable to confirm the favourable judgement.[7]

John Wesley's time was divided between preaching and consultations. He also gathered together students in his room to sing with them and to read prayers from the Prayer Book. On one occasion Böhler was present, but he did not feel at home.[8] As in the days before he went to America Wesley again visited the prison and preached there, finding receptive hearers. Occasionally business with the trustees recalled him to London and every time he tried to commend the Gospel to his fellow-travellers on the road. Lack of success made him unhappy and he put it down to his using the wrong method. He blamed himself for having mixed up together light and serious topics in his conversation; he must reject absolutely the counsel of the mystics that those acquaintances who resist one's approach should be left to themselves. With inexorable self-criticism he acknowledged that the fault was his and he prayed that God would not lay the sin to his charge.[9] On another occasion he believed he could see the effect of his words upon a lady immediately from her face and the new way in which she spoke. Within a few moments she seemed to him to change completely, although he had been labouring with her to no purpose for an hour.[1] The zeal, which he had so conscientiously and decidedly made into a matter of law and which seemed absolutely essential to him for his evangelistic work, he expressed in four practical rules which he laid upon himself. He would speak with complete openness and unreserve to all with whom he should converse. He would strive after the utmost seriousness and would not allow himself the smallest carelessness in his conduct, not even a moment's

[7] Peter Böhler's Diary, 6th March 1738.
[8] Ibid.: 'March 7 at 7 in the evening several *studiosi* met at the elder Wesley's, with whom he sang and read the usual prayers from their prayer-book . . . but this gathering did not please me.'
[9] *Journal*, I.440–1, 27th February 1738.
[1] Ibid. p. 446, 17th March 1738.

laughter. He would speak no word which did not tend to the glory of God; in particular he would not talk of worldly things. Likewise he would not allow himself any pleasure which did not promote God's glory. Since he would be thankful to God at every moment he must reject everything for which he could not directly thank Him.[2]

It is tempting to regard all this as fanaticism. Does not this excessive self-examination and regulation of his concerns show a man completely devoid of humour, who, filled with a passion which is at the same time without feeling, strives regardlessly towards his goal and sacrifices everything for it? This view fails to recognize that the English character had been quietly moulded by a long thoroughgoing process of education by the Puritan religious writers. Wesley had grown up in this tradition and shows at this point that he was not thinking of anything like a new rule but was rather returning to his earlier principles. In doing this he was of course building upon his Puritan heritage and carrying it to its limits. Yet he never lost the sense of Christian freedom. As early as February 1735, while at the height of his Oxford career, he came out for it in a letter to his mother, in which he made the point that it is freedom from hard and fast rules which distinguishes the Christians from the Jews, who are bound to the law. It is true that he was inclined to admit such freedom only on extraordinary occasions, yet at the same time he considered that rules lose their justification through changed spiritual circumstances.[3] Although he may never again have put the point so clearly in writing, his practical activity shows that he kept to this line.

While still in London, where he was getting ready to visit his brother Samuel in Tiverton, news reached him that his brother Charles lay at death's door in Oxford. He hurried to him and found Peter Böhler at his bedside.[4] Charles was suffering from acute pleurisy, but soon recovered. Böhler had become the centre of a group of young men: it seemed that they were quickly attracted to him. He met with them each day either in groups or individually. According to his own account these meetings for fellowship were quite simple in character. They usually met at about three o'clock in the afternoon and began with prayer after the liturgical form of the Church of England, and then drank tea and 'spoke of divine things'. Böhler, like all Germans, found the strict liturgical practice of the

[2] *Journal*, I.441–2, 2nd March 1738.
[3] *Letters*, VIII.268–9, Oxon, 14th February 1734/5.
[4] *Journal*, I.442, 4th March 1738.

Anglicans strange. On 2nd March he wrote in his Journal: 'They always pray one after another from the printed book, and before they drink tea and afterwards they pray again. I always do so along with them and so far I have been able to endure it, though how much longer I know not.' Likewise he thought they put too much emphasis upon ordination. On 15th March he wrote, 'If at any time anyone from our Church should be sent here, it were good that he should be an ordained brother in view of the strange ideas of the people, for folk in the English Church are even more eccentrically churchy and liturgical than in the Lutheran.' On one occasion Böhler sang a Latin hymn which he had hastily composed because he had no other to hand and could not remember one, thereby emphasizing the importance the Herrnhut Church gave to the extempore hymn in contrast to the rigid written prayers of the Anglicans. The young people spoke to him wherever he was, especially when they met him in the library, where he worked for six hours every day. They were mainly undergraduates, although not exclusively so. In addition to the two Wesleys and John Gambold, there were two M.A.'s, Wolf and Hoare, two young clergymen, Wells and Charles Kinchin, both from the neighbourhood of Oxford, and the undergraduates Watson, Washington, Hutchins. Later the following are also mentioned: Bray, Edmund Clark, Otlee, Procker (probably Procter), Harphey, Sweetland, Shaw, Fish, Brown, Hatter and Greenwich.[5] In addition to the meetings for members of the university some took place at which ordinary men and women from the city were present. There might be forty, seventy, or even a hundred persons of both sexes. They were typical meetings of 'religious societies'. A student usually read some devotional passage, but naturally Böhler was also asked to speak, which he did partly in English and partly in Latin, which was translated by one of the students as he went along. He gave himself eagerly to learning English and strongly desired that people in Herrnhut itself might do this, for a great harvest was to be expected in the British Isles.[6] When he spoke about the Moravians in Germany he found ready listeners, so that he writes enthusiastically: 'When they hear of how in Germany there is grace in affliction they open their mouths in wonder and surprise . . . in their eyes I am like

[5] Böhler's Diary, 10th May 1738.
[6] Ibid., 12th March 1738: 'O how good it would be if there were a brother or sister in Herrnhut who understood English who could be sent to guide these poor folk. The poor people are awakened but do not know what they want. They toil at reading books and their prayer-book, but they know nothing of the Saviour.'

a miracle.' [7] In this way he grew closer to them; the outcome was that at their request he shared with them in the Sacrament of the Lord's Supper. The first time this happened was on 10th March at Charles Wesley's bedside, as he lay ill. Gambold had come to give the sick man the Sacrament and Charles wanted Böhler also to partake. Böhler was not very happy about this. He observes: 'I did not dare refuse, so I took it.' On 15th March another celebration took place and this time John administered the Sacrament to his brother. Böhler was very uncertain as to whether he ought to take part, and carefully weighed up the pros and cons. In favour of participating was the fact that he had created a precedent on the previous occasion, and this still bound him. Moreover, he was afraid that by refusing he would adversely affect the celebration, and that meant giving offence. On the other side it could be urged that it was 'a regular Church sacrament' after the Anglican usage, with its proper liturgy. Moreover, he was apprehensive lest the young Englishmen in their naïve self-confidence were doing something 'not understanding what they did'. It therefore appeared that the reasons for and against his taking part were of equal weight. He did not know what to do. Accordingly he first withdrew and went out of the city to be alone and to follow the Herrnhut custom of seeking information by means of the lot. First he put the question whether he might go to Communion with them and received the answer, 'Yes'. He then inquired whether he should first speak with them and the answer was in the negative. He had still a third question and this put the point definitely and unambiguously as to whether in fact he *ought* to participate. This he postponed until he was back in the house. When he arrived the service was almost ended, so a delicate situation was avoided. [8]

This vacillation indicates clearly the scrupulous attitude of the Moravians to a different type of churchmanship. Böhler obviously was not convinced that the Anglican communion-rite was a true expression of the early Christian sacrament. On the other hand brotherly love would not allow him to hurt his friends. In the same way that Zinzendorf in his meeting with Wesley deemed it necessary at the outset to make a thoroughgoing and comprehensive statement of his theological and ecclesiastical principles, so Böhler did not want fellowship at the sacrifice of truth. The fact that he was not able to solve the problem but merely to avoid it was indeed a failure

[7] Böhler's Diary, 3rd March 1738.
[8] Ibid., 10th and 15th March 1738.

on his part, yet it is to his credit that he took it so seriously and probed the matter so deeply.

Böhler had come to England as a Herrnhuter. With an inflexibility equal to that with which the Anglicans held to their ecclesiastical forms he believed that he was not only entitled but in duty bound to enjoin upon them his own. So he strove energetically to organize closely-knit fellowships, the 'bands', as they were called in Herrnhut,[9] where they had been started on 9th July 1727. A week before this the Herrnhuters had joined with the State Church of Saxony in celebrating the feast of the Visitation of Mary and her going to Elizabeth, the mother of John the Baptist, and the whole occasion had been elaborate and marked with deep feeling. Pastor Schwedler of Niederwiesa, near Görlitz, the friend of Zinzendorf, had preached to thousands, according to the count's report. The local pastor, Johann Andreas Rothe, preached in the open air to those who were unable to get into the Berthelsdorf church. The count himself held two meetings in the hall at Herrnhut, the one immediately following the other. The day made an unforgettable impression on all who took part. Zinzendorf expressed it in the following way: 'The visit of Mary to Elizabeth, which is remembered to this day by Christianity, and the divine emotion which these two women with their hidden children experienced, you may have in the visitation of the children of God, for whom the Saviour is always present as the third Man who is brought forth in the *Bands* or *Societies*.'[1] The 'bands' were based upon the closest personal unity of their members, a unity derived from an awareness of the life of God hidden in them. Since this was expressed in mutual conversation a band consisted originally of only two or three persons. The result was that the Moravians naturally divided themselves into very small groups of this kind. Each was under the direction of a 'band-keeper', who was usually chosen by lot, sometimes by acclamation, or, as when numbers later grew, by vote. As considerable scope was given to individual authority and freedom many bands originated from the personal initiative of one of the brethren or sisters. The band-keepers also held other offices in the Church and sometimes had to be away on journeys: accordingly assistants are found in association with them as substitutes from 1733. These had also to act if the leaders, perhaps for

[9] On these, cf. Gottfried Schmidt, *Die Banden oder Gesellschaften im alten Herrnhut Zeitschr. f. Brüdergesch.*, III.(1909).145–207.
[1] August Gottlieb Spangenberg, *Leben des Grafen Zinzendorf* (1772), pp. 432–3.

231

spiritual reasons, felt incapable of doing so for the time being. The band-keepers did not function entirely on their own, but were under the direction of the Count, whom the lot had expressly chosen as leader of the men's bands on 5th March 1731. The band-keepers saw him individually or in groups, and if he was away written reports on all their concerns had to be sent to him. Thus in the Herrnhut Diary there appears the entry for 3rd March 1733: 'Her Ladyship the Countess, the secretary Tobias Leupold and all the band-keepers wrote down the state of every soul, as they were from week to week, for His Lordship the Count.'[2] He seems to have given up the position in about 1734, owing to the number of other tasks. As a result the band-conference became an institution on its own, and this increased its importance.

This was the practice which guided Peter Böhler at Oxford. In the deliberations of the band-conference people shared their experiences, and so there developed a distinctive and highly-organized type of pastoral care. People were described as 'foundering', 'improving', 'nice', 'serious', 'anxious', 'ready', 'awake', 'watchful', 'confused', 'fervent', 'sensual', 'strong', or 'dejected', and new characterizations were continually being found. The bands met once a week, usually between six and seven in the evening. Since they were formed without any kind of restraint the whole congregation was not subdivided all at once into bands, but they developed gradually over a number of years. It was the married men who made the beginning on 9th July 1727. They were followed seven months later, on 9th February 1728, by the married women, and a few days later, on 14th February 1728, by the single women. The single men were the last to follow. The bands grew rapidly in number; in 1732 there were seventy-seven; in 1733, eighty-five; in 1734, one hundred. In addition to these voluntary fellowships there were the regular organizations, the 'classes', called 'choirs' after 1736. These were arranged on the basis of sex and age, so that there were classes for single and married men and women, widowers and widows, young men, young women, and children. A strict form of mutual examination was practised in the bands. In the words of Christian David the aim was 'to spie out the hidden territory', the secret sins and secret resistance to God, and 'to cleanse the old leaven'.[3] As everything was so personal and

---

[2] Handwritten; in the archives of the United Brethren at Herrnhut.
[3] Christian David, in *Beschreibung und zuverlässige Nachricht von Herrnhut in der Ober-Lausitz* (1735), p. 44.

intimate the bands were of a charismatic rather than an institutional character. They formed themselves and then broke up; people joined and then left to go into another, or a band could cease to meet for a period.

Peter Böhler wanted to form close fellowships like these in Oxford, and at the beginning at least he was successful. He frequently notes in his Journal that he 'held band' or that he 'appointed the band brethren'.[4] His aim was to reproduce in Oxford a copy of the Herrnhut congregation, but in this he failed. He told John Wesley about his disappointment.[5] The settled group which he had in mind actually came into being in the Fetter Lane society. Yet Böhler's achievement in Oxford was considerable, even if his extravagant accounts cannot be taken at their face value. He used every opportunity to witness to his Saviour. When he was being conducted by a university don through the famous Bodleian Library in Oxford they stood for a time before a book. At once Böhler began to recount the history of the Moravian Brethren. He had very soon discovered that the library possessed a copy of the Brethren's History by Johann Amos Comenius in the Amsterdam edition of 1660 and that this was superior to the new edition by Buddeus. In particular he informed Zinzendorf of the rich sources which would help him particularly in the writing of his Church history.[6] After relating the story of the Moravians in the past he came finally, in his own words, 'to our Lamb'. For two hours his companion listened to him, and assured him that although he had not understood everything because he did not have the experience of salvation, he would not forget what he had heard. This was the first time that Böhler had used Latin for proclaiming the Gospel.[7]

This was an example of his method in dealing with a scholar, yet

[4] Böhler's Diary, 6th March 1738: 'In the evening Mr Wels came and held band with me, but did not finish because four *studiosi* came.' 8th March: 'In the afternoon I went for a short walk with Washington, Watson and Hutchins, and spoke with them about their basic foundation, which is still weak, saying that it would be a good thing if they would band themselves more closely together; they were willing to do this and wanted to meet again early tomorrow morning to talk further about it.' 5th May: 'I have determined now before I leave to bring it about that the Englishmen should agree to begin bands amongst themselves. The Saviour be merciful to these poor folk of His, so that my hopes shall come to pass.'
[5] Ibid., 20th March 1738: 'I talked with the elder Wesley alone (after the conversation with the Band-brethren) about conditions in Oxford because it was not permitted me to make any further arrangement.'
[6] Böhler to Zinzendorf, Oxford, 9th March 1738, handwritten, in the archives of the United Brethren at Herrnhut, R.13.A, No. 4 (in Diary).
[7] Böhler's Diary, 28th February or 1st March 1738.

he applied himself with equal directness and enthusiasm to humbler folk. In the room of the undergraduate Hutchins he met the young man's washerwoman. Others said that she was tormented by exaggerated scruples, their judgement being similar to that which Luther's fellow-monks in Erfurt once brought against the future reformer. Böhler on the other hand was convinced through conversation with the woman that she was on the right road, for she felt she was a great sinner. She maintained she was too stupid for the Kingdom of God and thought that for such people as herself there was no Saviour. But this was just the right frame of mind to receive the message of Jesus Christ. He spoke to her about the Saviour. He succeeded in making Him absolutely central, real, and living, and if he did not see any obvious result from his words he nevertheless gained the impression that 'they were not without blessing'. Immediately after she had left the room he discussed her case with the students there, whom he called 'Latin brethren', and he emphasized the gracious disposition of the Saviour whose help exceeds our asking and understanding.[8]

Naturally he had also to meet opposition. It is reported that some of the undergraduates laughed at him and John Wesley when they went through the college quadrangles. When Wesley showed concern at this treatment of his guest Böhler is said to have replied: 'It does not even stick to our clothes.'[9] But it was a more serious matter that such 'religious societies' as were already in being and organized under stewards, made a sharp differentiation between themselves and the Herrnhuters, and refused membership to anyone 'who is attached to the doctrine of the German sects'.[1]

Böhler looked for great things from England, and from Oxford in particular. On his way there he had been greatly concerned. He had asked himself 'what he was to do there of all places'. But whether it was the conversations with the Wesley brothers or whether he received a special inner experience, when he was in the university city itself he felt ready to wage a successful battle. He wrote to Herrnhut: 'But now my heart has been opened within me and through grace I have courage to go to these people in the name of the great Reconciler and to tell them what they know not.' He went on: 'Carry the summons into ear and heart, and when I point to Thyself, shine forth!

[8] Böhler's Diary, 8th March 1738.
[9] Journal, I.440, note 1.
[1] Böhler to Zinzendorf, Southampton, 19th May 1738, handwritten, in the archives of the United Brethren at Herrnhut, R.14.A.9.B.

I desire that the whole church might say this with me, so will the
Saviour do something, that we may be able to rejoice and thank
Him.' [2] When he learned that Charles Delamotte's brother, who was a
student in Cambridge, was doing a successful work there in connexion
with the religious societies, he concurred with the opinion of his
brother who was in America. 'He believes that an awakening will
come in that university through these men. He is in great earnest.'[3]
So Böhler recognized that in his work amongst the students, in which
he gave himself to each individual, he was also engaged in a great,
even ecumenical undertaking. When he had to go he left a succession
of grateful young men, who brought joy to him through their affectionate letters. They had discussed the possibility of inviting him
back to Oxford and at their own personal cost enable him to stay for
a while at least.[4]

What was the particular contribution which Böhler brought to
them? The outstanding characteristic of the frequent conversations
was his forthright rejection of all 'philosophy'. This implied the
emphatic repudiation of natural theology, which was particularly
highly esteemed and pursued both in the tradition of English thinking
running from the Middle Ages and in the contemporary Enlightenment. Like Zinzendorf[5] Böhler rejected every idea of God which
was derived, however indirectly, from any general principle of human
reason. He would allow only the Jesus Christ of the Bible. This was
the primary thing, yet he seems in addition to have included under
'philosophy' ethics, and—again following Zinzendorf[6]—all ethics not
derived directly from the Saviour or which did not make His love the

[2] Ibid., 28th February/1st March 1738.
[3] Ibid., 8th March 1738.
[4] Ibid., 1st May 1738. Ziegenhagen, who was orientated towards Halle, of
course regarded Böhler's success and the close attachment to him of Wesley and
Ingham with regret. At the same time he declared that Ingham's preaching was
causing a sensation. Böhler had professed that he wanted to visit Zeigenhagen,
but had not done anything about it. Ziegenhagen to G. A. Francke, Kensington,
15th March 1738, handwritten, in the Missionary archives of Francke's Institution, Halle, Z.I.L.5.
[5] On Zinzendorf's antipathy to natural theology, cf. esp. Bernhard Becker,
*Zinzendorf und sein Christentum im Verhältnis zum kirchlichen und religiösen
Leben seiner Zeit*, pp. 31ff; Otto Uttendörfer, *Zinzendorfs religiöse Grundgedanken*, pp. 22ff; Wilhelm Bettermann, *Theologie und Sprache bei Zinzendorf*, pp.
176ff; Samuel Eberhard, *Kreuzes-Theologie. Das reformatorische Anliegen in
Zinzendorfs Verkündingung*, pp. 20ff, 114ff.
[6] On this, cf. esp. Otto Uttendörfer, *Zinzendorfs christliches Lebensideal*, pp.
70ff, 86ff, 273ff. Uttendörfer works out the basically elastic character of the
Christian ethic determined completely by love and rooted in the attitude of full
faith in the Saviour. This makes it entirely opposed to all types of abstract
philosophical moral theory.

starting-point. In conversation the young clergyman Wells remarked to Böhler that the majority of scholars in England, in particular the theologians, laid greater stress on the fact that a man should live worthily than anything else. It was not necessary for him to believe anything particular, for the Saviour did not speak about belief but expressly laid down rules of conduct, as the Sermon on the Mount proves. Böhler's comment was that this would place Jesus merely on a level with the prophets.[7] Moreover he felt that the constant pre-occupation of Englishmen with Thomas à Kempis was, to say the least, dangerous, if not altogether misleading.[8]

Accordingly it is understandable why Peter Böhler's first word to John Wesley was a challenge to give up his philosophy and why this should have seemed so strange to the Englishman.[9] In the talks which followed they discussed sin, the new birth and faith, and Böhler stressed faith in the strongest possible way. From the first it was incomprehensible to him how quickly the young Englishmen were done with it. They always assumed from the start that they had it, and their only concern was to prove it by works. They falsely imagined it to be a form of imagination or self-persuasion. Against this view Böhler strove to make clear to them that its essential nature consisted in coming to know Jesus. This was on the one hand much more simple than their scheme required, but on the other hand it was much more difficult, because it offended the susceptibilities of the natural man.[1] On 5th March, in conversation with him, John Wesley became convinced that he lacked the faith which alone leads to eternal salvation. Immediately the thought flashed through his mind that he should give up preaching. How could he preach to others if he had not faith himself? Here was a further instance where the question of his own salvation and that of others, the concern for his own soul and those of his fellows, were indissolubly bound up with each other. Here once again was that sense of intimate solidarity between the bearer and the recipient of the word of salvation. But

---

[7] Böhler's Diary, 8th March 1738.

[8] Ibid., 18th February and 3rd April 1738.

[9] *Journal*, I.440, 18th February 1738: 'All this time I conversed much with Peter Böhler; but I understood him not, and least of all when he said, *Mi frater, mi frater, excoquenda est ista tua philosophia.*' So far as I know this word of Böhler has not been explained in the Wesley literature. James Harrison Rigg (*The Living Wesley*, pp. 95-6) thinks it refers to Wesley's considerable capacity for formal logical argument. Christoffel Nicolaas Impeta (*De leer van de heiliging en volmaking bij Wesley en Fletcher*, pp. 97-8) follows him in this—although in another connexion (in a general judgement upon Wesley's character).

[1] Böhler's Diary, 18th February 1738.

Böhler would not have it, and he answered him in the well-known words: 'Preach faith till you have it; and then, because you have it, you will preach faith.'[2] In this pregnant statement lies the deep truth that the task of the preacher is not to bring before his hearers himself or his own spiritual attainment but the authoritative Word, the greater reality of God. Böhler was asserting the objective reality of the Word over against that tendency towards Donatism which besets Pietism, whereby the efficacy of salvation is made to rest upon the subjective condition of the minister. Wesley took his advice and the next day attempted to put this precept into practice, although he was still very conscious of resistance deep within him. It was a prisoner under sentence of death to whom he spoke. Until then Wesley had always avoided this undertaking, because he did not believe in the possibility of a death-bed repentance. Although Böhler had repeatedly asked him to go to the prisoner Wesley had not been able to bring himself to do so. Now, after the challenge to preach faith even without possessing faith, he obeyed, so powerful had the objective authority become for him.[3]

The next conversation did not take place until seventeen days later, Böhler in the meantime having had to go to London. Both the Wesleys were present. According to Böhler's account[4] they began by asking what was the right way to fight sin. It is probable that the two brothers put forward views which were moralistic, for they 'brought up various objections ... especially from Thomas à Kempis'. This implied that they wanted to urge a Christian ethic against sin which was strongly ascetic. Böhler refused to give way. He said that everything depended upon their coming to know the Saviour, and only in this way could they help people. When they asked him further to explain this he expounded 'to them in a very deep discourse' the difference between 'living externally to the Saviour' and 'living in the Saviour'. This presumably dealt in the first place with the difference between having Christ as an ideal and having Christ as a Saviour, and then the pietist idea of Christ within us, since Böhler attached the greatest importance to the new birth, which was the main tenet of Pietism. Time and again he dealt with this in his meetings, and it is significant that it was still the theme of his last gatherings.[5] His intention was to help the Wesley brothers to

[2] *Journal*, I.442, 5th March 1738.
[3] Ibid., 6th March 1738.
[4] Böhler's Diary, 3rd April 1738.
[5] Ibid., 5th March, 25th April, 10th, 12th, 13th May 1738.

come to an assurance that Jesus Christ by His power was working within them and near to them at all times. This is what he meant by having faith, and his conversation must have gone along these lines. He also took great care to express himself correctly, and it all came as a surprise to the two brothers. Charles was of the opinion that if it were true there was nobody in Oxford who really knew Christ, while John went even farther by saying that he had never seen one Englishman like this or one who had experienced this. Böhler was proclaiming a completely new gospel, one which he had never heard in the whole of his life. Böhler felt that his efforts to make clear the meaning of the Gospel had not been wholly success-ful,[6] but Wesley interpreted what he heard in terms with which he was familiar, namely that holiness and happiness were the true fruits of living faith. It must be left an open question whether Wesley really understood Böhler's meaning by this reminiscence of Henry Scougal's phrase. This was always the circle of ideas which was the most congenial to him, since it was to hand in his own reading. When next morning according to his usual practice he opened his Greek New Testament his hope was that God through His Word would confirm or refute Böhler's teaching.[7]

The third conversation of which we have information took the results of the other two a stage farther.[8] It seems as if the various meetings followed one another without being definitely planned, and yet in a natural sequence. In this third discussion, which took place in London, the nature of faith was so carefully explained that Wesley makes use of the language of the Lutheran Reformation as it was known to him from the Homilies of the Church of England. These state that faith is a firm trust a man has in God that his sins are for-given through the merits of Christ and that he stands in the favour of God. Wesley found that the New Testament confirmed this. Like-wise he was able to establish from the Bible that happiness and holi-ness are the fruits of such faith. Happiness is confirmed by Romans 8^{16} and 1 John 5^{10}, and holiness by 1 John 3^9 and 1 John 5^1. In this way he connected the new birth and the overcoming of sin with justi-fication, and so returned to the favourite theme in his conception of religion. This combination of the main ideas of the Reformation and of Pietism, which he achieved in this way, is a foretaste of his actual

[6] 'I could not get any farther with him even before this.'
[7] *Journal*, I.447, 23rd March 1738.
[8] Ibid. pp. 454–5, 22nd, 23rd April 1738.

conversion. Yet one point remained which caused him concern. Böhler's contention that saving faith was a gift to be received suddenly and once for all astonished him, but this doubt was once again dispelled by the New Testament. In particular he examined the Acts of the Apostles, the classic record of the early Christian mission, and discovered to his surprise that Böhler's idea was confirmed. Everywhere he found sudden conversions; that of Paul, which lasted three days, was actually remarkable for the length of time it took before it was completed. Only one way still remained of avoiding Böhler's conclusion. It was conceivable that God might have brought people to Himself by sudden conversions in the beginnings of the Church, but who would say that He still does this at the present day? Are not the times changed? It is surprising to find Wesley putting forward this objection, for did he not take early Christianity as his standard almost as a matter of course? Was not the attempt to return to the early Christian way of life the real driving-force in his personal behaviour and ecclesiastical activity? The question must therefore be asked whether his objection, as an evasion he himself could not take seriously, was used as a last show of resistance before he yielded? Or was he refusing, in full consciousness of theological responsibility, to use the New Testament as a merely external standard? Was he opposing a mechanical idea of the Canon? Is this for once an example of the influence on his theological thinking of the historical sense of the Enlightenment? Be that as it may, it is an indication of the energy of his thinking and of extreme concern for the clarification of the truth, that he did not simply fall back upon some spiritual authority. Neither Böhler, whom he held in such high regard, nor the New Testament by itself, that is, neither the man nor the book as such, exercised a wholly decisive influence upon him. Step by step assent was wrung from him, but it was done only with difficulty.

The next day approached. It was Sunday. Early in the morning Böhler heard Wesley preach at St Ann's. By this time he had learned sufficient English for him to follow all that was said: accordingly he was able to form a judgement on the sermon. He was dissatisfied with it. 'It was not what I wished.' The discussion in Wesley's room in the evening followed on from this, but Böhler chose a different method. Since Wesley still objected to the sudden beginning of faith, he refuted him by living witnesses which he had brought with him. He let the three 'relate the way they had been led'. In the manner of the Herrnhut 'life-experiences' one after the other spoke simply and forcibly of how they had come to have faith. One in particular, named Wolf, who had been recently converted and whose impressions were still fresh in his mind, 'spoke very cordially, force-fully and instructively about his experience of grace', as Böhler says in words characteristic of Pietism.[9] Wesley summarized their account by saying that God gave to them 'in a moment such a faith in the blood of His Son as translated them out of darkness into light, out of sin and fear into holiness and happiness. Here ended my dis-puting. I could now only cry out, "Lord, help Thou my unbelief".'[1] It might well have been the original of the Methodist 'love-feast', that service of Christian witness.

Böhler describes the course of events in even greater detail. At first 'Westley and the others who were with him' were 'as though struck dumb at these narratives'. Nevertheless he still held out. He said that four examples—obviously including Böhler's own account with the others—were not sufficient to convince him as yet. Straightway Böhler offered to bring eight more in London. After a short time Wesley stood up and proposed that they should sing Christian Friedrich Richter's hymn, *My soul before Thee prostrate lies*. It was one of the hymns he had translated in Georgia. During the singing he repeatedly wiped his eyes. Then he took Böhler into his bedroom with him alone and said he was now convinced of what he had said about faith and that he would not raise any further points. He saw indeed that he did not possess this faith, which he had to recognize as the genuine kind. 'But how could he now help himself and how should he attain to such faith?' He said that he was a man who had not sinned so grossly as other people. Böhler answered, just like Zinzendorf and Luther, that he had sinned enough in not believing in the Saviour. He ought not now to go away from the door of the Saviour until He had helped him. Wesley then asked Böhler to pray with him. 'So I called upon the blood-covered name of the Saviour for mercy on this sinner',

---

[9] Wolf was apparently an Englishman whom Böhler had only recently won over (cf. also *Journal*, I.481, 29th May 1738). The other two were 'Müller Abra-ham' and 'the Captain'. 'Müller' is probably a slip of the pen for 'Richter'. Abraham Richter could be the Stalsund merchant with whom Zinzendorf ap-peared in 1734 allegedly as private tutor and then examined as to the othodoxy of his belief by the pastors of the town. Later he became the father-in-law of Baron Johann Christian Adolf von Hermsdorf, who was with the Herrnhuters in Georgia and looked after Wesley during his stay in Herrnhut. 'Captain' cannot be further explained.

[1] *Journal*, I.455, 23rd April 1738.

wrote Böhler in typical Herrnhut language. Wesley assured him that if he gained a true and complete relationship with the Saviour he would then preach only about faith.[2]

In this way Böhler brought Wesley to that state in which he wished him to be, and at the same time Wesley was prepared for it by many circumstances. At the psychological moment Böhler provided personal witness of the living faith which lays hold of justification. He helped Wesley in an important way to rid himself of placing too great an emphasis upon a Christian ethic, and so from a certain restrictive factor which had been present in his striving after holiness. He made him realize that a simple personal relationship to Jesus the Saviour is the heart of the relationship with God, and he pointed him to Luther's deep insight that lack of faith is the most serious sin. His insistence upon a sudden awakening restored the 'historical' character of faith, such as the New Testament expresses in its emphasis upon the 'moment'. As a consequence it became evident that faith indicates a completely new creation by God, and not merely a restoration of the divine image, as the more mystical and naturalistic theology of Scougal and Taylor claimed. It became clear that it was not sufficient for salvation that something should be destroyed or removed; rather it was a question of a complete new beginning. But this only God could accomplish. Wesley was now aware of the fact that faith, which trusts God for everything and the self for nothing, was the one fundamental truth of Christianity. This knowledge had now been removed from the realm of the theoretical into that of personal reality. He had come through spiritual struggles, which unlike those in Georgia, sprung not from failures connected with his work or his personal difficulties, but directly and solely from the question of God and salvation. This makes it intelligible why this young associate could mean so much to him. The degree of concentration, indeed monotony, with which Böhler stressed faith is shown by a letter which he sent to Wesley shortly after leaving England.[3] In this he concentrated in the typical manner of Herrnhut upon the one fact of the love of Jesus Christ as it was expressed in the Cross. Over against this he sets the one sin of unbelief and so reaches the conclusion, briefly expressed and challenging in the

---

[2] Böhler's Diary 4th May 1738.
[3] *In Agris Southamptonianis, Die 8vo Maii, 1738* (*Journal*, I.461). How closely Böhler followed Zinzendorf is shown by Otto Uttendörfer, *Zinzendorfs religiöse Grundgedanken*, pp. 34, 75ff; cf. also (with a certain reserve) Gösta Hök, *Zinzendorfs Begriff der Religion*, pp. 13ff, 36ff.

sharpest way, that unbelief actually shows itself as absence of love. It was made in consequence a completely personal concern and was branded with an extraordinarily grievous stigma. Böhler warned Wesley three times in the course of this brief letter against going astray from Jesus in this way, and warned him further against postponing the act of faith. But not only did he bring together the love of the crucified Jesus Christ and faith in this negative way, but he also called attention to their positive connexion. When you believe on Him, he asserted, you also experience His life within you, in your flesh. Böhler might have used at this point an expression much loved by the Pietists, the promise of 2 Peter 1^4 about partaking in the divine nature.

Two emphases can be seen in this unusually important and significant letter: that of Luther, in which faith lays hold of the promise to forgive sins, and that of Pietism, in which faith conveys the power of God into the heart of the believer. The greetings which Böhler sends on to his friends, particularly Wesley's brother Charles and his brother-in-law Westley Hall, consist in the first place in the summons to admonish one another to believe. To be sure he also speaks about walking properly in the sight of God, fighting with the devil and the world, crucifying sin and treading it under their feet, but all this is associated with the great theme that it is the second Adam who gives them power to act in this way, for His life far exceeds the death of the first Adam, just as His grace surpasses the corruption and damnation of the first Adam. The whole emphasis is upon this life and this grace; man's own activity is put entirely into the shadow.

The decisive occasion when Böhler overcame Wesley's opposition by producing living witnesses led Wesley to raise the old question whether it would not be better for him to leave off preaching. Böhler had not agreed, and said to him: 'Do not hide in the earth the talent God hath given you.' [4] Wesley acted in accordance with this advice and one evening preached, as Böhler heard, to more than 4,000 people on 1 Corinthians 1^{23}: 'We preach Christ crucified, unto the Jews a stumbling-block, and unto the Greeks foolishness.' This caused a very great stir. Such preaching had not been heard before. He began by saying that he considered himself unworthy to preach Christ crucified. This encouraged many of his hearers, who felt that he was fully identified with them. Apparently a number of them came to Böhler and told him about it, for he writes: 'The three English

[4] *Journal*, I.455, 24th April 1738.

brethren who are going to Herrnhut today visited Mr Bray,[5] where a few had gathered and told how they had seen the Saviour and what they had come to know of the Saviour. They were all greatly moved, and many confessed that they did not yet have the Saviour. When they heard Westley say just the same thing from the pulpit many recognized that they were great sinners and wept copiously in their desire for the real thing.' It was this consciousness of personal unworthiness which Böhler had wanted to arouse in Wesley and all his English friends. Now he could write of Wesley: 'He is a poor sinner, who has a broken heart and who hungers after a better righteousness than that which he has had up till now, namely after the righteousness which is in the blood of Jesus Christ.' He now considered it his duty to rescue him from despair of himself; accordingly he told Wesley that he should 'not put' the grace of the Saviour 'so far' from himself, but believe that it was near him. The Saviour's heart was open to him. Wesley asked him whether in conversation with others he should speak about his own spiritual state or keep silent. The day before he had found some difference of opinion among his serious clergymen friends when he had informed them about what was now troubling him, and what he had come to understand about the nature of Christianity, and what he still lacked in his own experience. Böhler gave him no directions on this point, but advised him to do 'what the Saviour would teach him', a reference to the use of the lot.

If Böhler was successful in bringing about a remarkable movement among the undergraduates, young university teachers and clergymen in Oxford, he also found the ground ready prepared in London. No doubt it would be a mistake to take as literally true the lyrical words in his Journal. He says: 'What shall I write? The miracles in London are too many for all to be told. It is too sublime a matter to describe what the Saviour does to souls. We are continually astonished when we call it to mind.' He is not referring to the number of people affected. The meaning lies deeper. In these rapturous words Böhler is showing his feeling for the New Testament truth that the faith of each individual person is a miracle—a miracle wrought by God. Thus he happens to mention that two Presbyterians who were affected by his sermon came to him, desiring to speak with him about the righteousness of Jesus Christ and faith. In words which are true

[5] Who the three English Brethren were who proposed to visit Herrnhut unfortunately cannot be known. John Bray, a brazier, was Böhler's representative in England, and after his departure, his successor (*Journal*, I.460, note 1).

to the language of Herrnhut he could rejoice that 'noble sinners are brought down thus'.[6] He also went to the Quakers and surprisingly was able to come to an understanding with them on the subject of the new birth.[7] Offers came to him from all sides to speak in meetings of the Religious Societies. He was particularly happy when he had overcome the language difficulties and was able to testify as easily as in German about Jesus, 'who through His blood is the only Saviour'. He believed also that he could immediately see its effect. 'It was seen in these souls that the Gospel did to them what it is accustomed to do when the Saviour opens heart and mouth to speak.' All this filled him with humility, gratitude, and new love for Jesus, and he confessed: 'I can do no other than bow myself low because of this, and ever anew dedicate myself and all that is mine to the Lamb, because my Lamb is willing to use me because of the prayers of my beloved people for me, and will sustain such a poor, very poor shepherd as I with the power of His blood. Since this abides I am His with all my heart. I love Him in a right childlike way and I should dearly like henceforth to abide in Him each hour as one stem, and remain so at one with Him that I shall ever be green and fruitful in His service.'[8] Böhler did not hesitate to testify also before General Oglethorpe himself of the grace of Jesus Christ through His blood and of the forgiveness of sins. He formed the impression that 'his feelings are touched. He sees clearly that he has it not, for he cast down his eyes and became red in a way which is quite different from his wont', which was also an admission that the general had some perception of what the heart of Christianity was. When Böhler accompanied John Wesley on 7th May as far as Kensington on his way back to Oxford he impressed on him again that faith should be the object of his striving as a Christian. It is significant that Wesley replied 'that now he found everywhere in the Bible the grace of the Saviour and saw how great He was and what He does to poor sinners'. Böhler comments in his Journal: 'I am truly hopeful that he will become completely the Saviour's and ours.'[9]

Böhler's main concern in London, as it had been in Oxford, was to organize 'bands' after the Herrnhut pattern. Even John Wesley decided to join one, although this is not surprising, since all that had

---

[6] Böhler's Diary, 6th May 1738, where see all the preceding paragraph. On this central thought in Zinzendorf, cf. esp. Samuel Eberhard, *Kreuzes-Theologie. Das reformatorische Anliegen in Zinzendorfs Verkundigung*, pp. 12, 155ff.
[7] Ibid., 25th April 1738.   [8] Ibid., 30th April 1738.
[9] Ibid., 7th May 1738.

happened to him in the past was wholly in this direction. The group of students at Oxford and the organization of the two congregations in Savannah and Frederica were significant steps towards it. So on 1st May the little group of Böhler's English friends met and drew up its rules in eleven points. Later it met in Fetter Lane. In the constitution they refer to James 5¹⁶, 'Confess your faults one to another, and pray one for another, that ye may be healed', and thus they brought into being a modern evangelical form of the monastic confession of the Eastern Church. In comparison with the Herrnhut pattern the bands were fairly large, for they were to comprise at least five and at most ten persons. As at Herrnhut the intention was to meet once a week. Complete candour towards each other was required, both in speaking about personal religious experiences and difficulties, and in complaints about other members. When new members wished to join they were formed into one or two separate bands under the leadership of an experienced member, and after two months were admitted into the large group known as the 'Society'. Discipline was to be exercised so that anyone who failed to conform to the decision of the 'Society', after being admonished three times, was no longer to be reckoned as a member. Every fourth Saturday was to be observed as a day of general intercession, and on every second Sunday a 'love-feast' or service of testimony was to be held, to last from seven until ten. In spite of Böhler's powerful influence, which can be seen in these arrangements, the new society does not seem to have been organized after the pattern of Herrnhut in the strict sense, but was rather a compound of elements taken from the Religious Societies within the Church of England, and the Herrnhut model, and Wesley's own ideas and experiences.[1]

Thus Peter Böhler's influence upon the early beginnings of Methodism was twofold: it was evident in the theology and the organization. Both preaching and doctrine on the one hand, and the care of souls and ecclesiastical discipline on the other, show the marks of his influence. From this it is easy to understand why Wesley held such a high opinion of the part played by Böhler, and his judgement reflects his feeling for primitive Christianity: 'Oh what a work hath God begun, since his coming into England! Such an one shall never come to an end till heaven and earth pass away.'[2] Even if this

[1] Curnock (*Jounrnal*, I.458, note 2) seems to me to claim too easily that it was a Church of England religious society.
[2] *Journal*, I.459–60, 4th May 1738.

comment was added later[3] he had at the time a real awareness of the profound significance of this simple man. The Herrnhuters in Georgia had given him a demonstration of primitive Christianity as a present reality, but now it was a question of personal call and theological perception, even if this was expressed in simple formulae. The rejection of ethics as the way to God, the assertion that there are 'noble sinners', the understanding of faith as personal trust in Jesus, the forgiveness of sins and a sharing in the living power of Jesus, the realization of the meaning of the new birth—all this was of decisive importance to Wesley. The association with Peter Böhler anticipated his meeting with Zinzendorf himself and went a long way to compensate for it. It meant that the impulse which Spangenberg had aroused in him was carried a stage farther. Böhler confirmed him in the belief that faith, and indeed faith in the forgiveness of sins by the blood of Christ, was the very heart of primitive Christianity. At the same time he demonstrated to him that this faith as a living reality determines the spiritual condition of people in the present.

On 4th (15th) May Böhler left London to go to the Herrnhut Brethren in Georgia. Before he went a discussion between Oglethorpe, John Wesley, and himself took place about the possibility, should the need arise, of his carrying on the duties, as Wesley's successor, of the ministry in the English Church in Savannah. This was to happen only if no Englishmen were there.[4]

This very definite influence and spiritual strengthening were not the only consequences which came to Wesley through his association with this man. He was also led to detach himself expressly and decisively from one who up until then had been an authority which he held in highest esteem, and whom he had allowed to exercise a determinative influence upon his mode of life. This was the religious writer William Law. The correspondence between them, which all took place within a few days, does not present a pleasing picture. Wesley wrote passionately, harshly, almost offensively; Law replied calmly and not without dignity, but also with superior irony. It was an encounter between a young man and an old man. Whatever the actual facts of the case Wesley represented them as if Law had only told him of the law when he ought to have acquainted him with the truth about justifying faith. As a result he doubted whether Law himself had been 'born of God', to use the language of Pietism. In

[3] So Curnock, ibid. p. 460, note 1.
[4] Böhler's Diary 1st May 1738.

all probability he himself did not have true faith in Jesus. So Wesley accused him of having laid another foundation than that which God had laid, Jesus Christ. What he, Wesley, had received from Law's instruction was not more than the shadowy, empty, and purely rational knowledge that there is a God. This is the faith of a devil, of a Judas. But not only Böhler's words contradict Law, but also his, Wesley's, experience. He has been preaching in accordance with Law's directions and his hearers have been convinced of the greatness and dignity of the law and have recognized that it is holy, just, and good, or as he himself puts it, 'great, wonderful, and holy'. But both they and he have perforce been more and more convinced that a man cannot live by it, for it leads inevitably into ever deeper captivity to sin, since the 'law in our members' continually wars against it. Even the means of grace, which like his Anglican listeners he understood as enabling a person to obtain God's grace, have proved themselves in the end powerless. Only living, justifying faith in the blood of Jesus can help. A man must abandon his own righteousness and lay aside all his own works and fly naked to Him. Law had told him none of these things and it had been necessary for Böhler to come before he knew of them. Only through him had be been saved from despair. Further, Law, in a conversation which Böhler [5] had had with him shortly before, had been silent and embarrassed about the subject of faith in Christ, and had spoken about mystical matters. Why, asks Wesley, had he never heard from Law the Name of Jesus? At the end he refers to Law's personal disposition. His exceedingly morose, rough, and repelling nature could not be the fruit of a living faith in Christ. Could the reason be that he lacked that which was most important? [6]

In his reply Law in the first place agreed with the claim Wesley had made when he had solemnly opened his letter of censure by referring to a command of God which he had to obey. Wesley had gone on to describe himself as one under sentence of death, meaning the death which the law brings upon him. Law ignored this second disparaging description of himself by Wesley and merely referred ironically to the first as a high-falutin sense of prophetic mission. He

[5] The letter speaks anonymously of a 'man of God' who had recently had an interview with Law. This refers to Böhler (cf. Law's last letter to Wesley, May [no day given] 1738 [*Letters*, I.242]). The remarkable thing is that Böhler, who usually notes down even the least significant experience, makes no mention of this important conversation. Presumably he did not regard it as part of the heroic epic of Herrnhut in England.
[6] *Letters*, I.239–40, London, 14th May 1738.

was prepared to humble himself before this call of God and, aware of his own guilt, to keep silence, because as a monster of iniquity he had corrupted all those who had conversed with him. The only thing which remained for him was to implore God's grace. This was really all he had to say in reply, at least if he were to accept Wesley's assumptions.

But should there be another, more modest and generally more ordinary possibility of speaking about the situation, then he had the following to say. In the first place he must remind Wesley that he, Wesley, had published a new translation of Thomas à Kempis. As he now claimed that for two years his preaching had been based upon his, Law's, writings, he would suggest that the blame for the erroneous doctrine should be shared between him and Thomas. Should not Thomas also give an account before God for this corruption? At all events he, Law, was conscious that he was in full agreement with Thomas and therefore he had at all times strongly recommended him. Or will Wesley perhaps maintain that by his translation he has been the first to rid him of a meaning which, though false, had been universally accepted? Quite seriously, however, he, Law, must say on his own behalf that in every conversation he had with Wesley he spoke about the very doctrine of faith of which he is said to have been completely silent. To prove this he would remind Wesley that the second time he visited him he put into his hands the book, the *German Theology*. If that book does not lead him to Jesus Christ then he, Law, must certainly admit that he understands almost nothing about Christianity. If Wesley maintains that a man ought to strip and loose himself from all that is his own to a degree greater than this little book directs, certainly he could not have had such teaching from himself. For such he disclaimed all responsibility. Moreover, Law recalls that in his recent book there are two sayings of Jesus which run through and govern everything that he wrote: 'Without me ye can do nothing' (John 15[5]) and 'If any man will come after me or be my disciple, let him take up his cross and follow me' (Matthew 16[24]). If Wesley was for separating in his teaching the Cross and discipleship from faith he should not count Law on his side. Thomas à Kempis more than any other Christian writer leads to living faith in Jesus Christ. Let Wesley take heed lest the new way of expressing things which he has taken over does not obscure his awareness of the value of the earlier one. He, Law, remembers very well the conversation with Böhler to which

Wesley refers, but it was different from what he had maintained. He, Law, had not been asked about faith in Christ nor did he begin to speak about 'mystical matters'. Should he be deceived in this point, however, he must ask on the other hand whether that would really have been a receding from the subject under discussion? He feels that faith in Jesus Christ is the sum and substance of what is meant by 'mystical religion'. Finally with reference to his uncivil behaviour, he allows the reproach to stand in its full force and he is grateful for the reference to it.[7] In spite of the sarcasm this was essentially a friendly letter, the main point being the claim that the German mystics had both the same doctrine of justification as the Lutheran Reformation and of the new birth as German Pietism. They lead to real living faith.

This idea was not entirely mistaken. Law was acute enough to notice the similarity between the emphasis upon the new birth and inward power in both spiritual mysticism and Pietism. Similarly he had remarked the connexion between renunciation in mysticism and the stress upon the sole sovereignty of grace in the reformers, such as led Luther in his early days to praise the *Theologia Germanica.*[8] Would all this pacify Wesley?

Wesley pushed on one side all secondary points, some of which were quite important, and merely repeated with the sharpest precision the main question: had Law either in person or through other books ever directed him to seek first living faith in the blood of Jesus Christ? He then examined the facts to which Law appealed as proof that he had done so. These were the *Theologia Germanica,* Law's own most recent book on the Sacrament of the Altar, and the two sayings of Jesus which he had described as maxims that governed what he had written. In the *Theologia Germanica* Wesley was indeed able to find something about Christ as pattern, but nothing about Christ our atonement. The book about the Sacrament he put on one side because it was not relevant to the matter. In the two Scripture maxims he misses a third which would have completed them: 'He is our propitiation, through faith in His blood' (Romans 3^{25}). He then condensed his disappointment into definite accusa-

---

[7] 19th May 1738, *Journal,* VIII.320–3.
[8] *WA,* I.153 (Foreword to Luther's edition of 1516), pp. 378–9 (Foreword to his edition of 1518). Walther Köhler, *Luther und die Kirchengeschichte,* pp. 236ff; Hermann Mandel, Introduction to his edition of *German Theology* (1908), pp. 1ff; Erich Seeberg, *Luthers Theologie, Motive und Ideen,* I, *Die Göttesanschauung* (1929), esp. p. 116.

tions. The right to do this he deduced from the fact that Law claimed to have discerned in their conversations his, Wesley's, real condition. He brought before him five points which showed Law's neglect. First, he did not openly tell him, Wesley, that he did not have faith in Christ's blood. Secondly, he never advised him to seek or pray for this faith. Thirdly, his advices were only suitable for such as had this faith already. Fourthly, the counsels he gave were such that the more he followed them the farther they led him away from true faith. Finally, he recommended books which were in no way likely to call forth this faith. And to attribute part of his guilt to Thomas à Kempis was inadmissible, since if he, Wesley, had misunderstood Thomas it was Law's duty to explain him correctly.

Wesley's second letter was extremely severe, yet Law once again sent him a detailed reply, even if the tone was somewhat less friendly.[9] In the first place he quietly corrects one important detail in Wesley's letter. Wesley had said that Böhler's account of his conversation with Law, which included Law's silence on the question of faith, had been confirmed by two witnesses. Law points out that these two were not in a position to establish anything since the conversation was conducted in Latin, which neither of them understood. He then turned to Thomas à Kempis. He had not wished in any way to impugn Wesley's translation; on the contrary he was convinced of its worth. It is precisely for this reason that he is puzzled that Wesley shows he has so failed to penetrate the author's mind. An attentive reading would have led him to all the truths he found missing.

Similarly he is astonished that Wesley found nothing about Christ the Mediator in the *Theologia Germanica*, and declares that he only came across Christ the Pattern. Law directed him to this book, which to be sure is not suitable for beginners in the faith, just because he considered that Wesley, as an ordained clergyman who had studied theology, would benefit from it. Moreover he got the impression that Wesley had a particular aptitude for meditation and a disposition to probe to the root of things.[1] In his judgement the *Theologia Germanica* contains the whole system of Christian faith and practice and is excellently suited to keep believers from all mis-

---

[9] *Letters*, I.242–4, May 1738.
[1] Ibid. pp. 242–3: 'I put that author into your hands, not because he is fit for the first learners of the rudiments of Christianity who are to be prepared for baptism, but because you were a clergyman that had made profession of divinity, had read as you said with much approbation and benefit the two practical discourses and many other good books, and because you seemed to me to be of a very inquisitive nature and much inclined to meditation.'

takes in faith and works.[2] Again, when Wesley says he feels his two governing maxims are incomplete he, Law, in one sense agrees with him. Obviously the whole content of Scripture cannot be reduced to two sayings of Jesus. On the other hand he is bound to claim that the whole meaning of the atonement is in fact contained in them. When Wesley doubts this, is he not merely striving about words? As to his own book on the Sacrament of the Altar the reason he referred to this was to indicate his faith in Christ as the Atonement, which faith Wesley found lacking. Then Wesley says he deliberately passed over a number of points in Law's letter because they were not relevant to the matter at issue. But none of these had been raised in the first place by him, Law, but were brought up in Wesley's first letter. Perhaps they were relevant only to that, which Wesley maintained he had written under divine guidance, but not to Law's merely human reply? In the first letter Wesley had found fault with him because he did not teach that faith in Christ which strips men naked of their own works and their own righteousness, yet he must repeat that all mystical books are full of just this.[3] He could fill a whole volume with what he, Law, had said on this subject, but at this point Wesley raised a second question. He demanded that Law should advise him how to seek a living faith in the blood of Christ, but the real subject of the first letter was the fact that a 'man of God' had revealed to Wesley the miserable condition of Law's soul. If Wesley honestly examines himself he will have to admit the truth of this. If he reflects once again it will at least seem curious that a 'man of God', to whom he, Law, was a stranger, should put a friendly conversation to such use. In this conversation it was the man of God who had said practically everything, while he himself had only listened and allowed himself to be instructed. But now the man of God has gained the impression that his companion is in a pitiable spiritual condition. He says nothing about this to him, but betakes himself to another man of God and imparts this insight to him. He charges his former companion with defamatory things which in no way correspond to

[2] Ibid. p. 243 : 'In this view nothing could be more reasonable than that book, which most deeply, excellently, and fully contains the whole system of Christian faith and practice, and is an excellent guide against all mistakes both in faith and works. What that book has not taught you I am content that you should not have learnt from me.'

[3] Ibid.: 'In your first letter I was blamed for not calling you to such a faith in Christ as strips us naked of our own works, our own righteousness; for not teaching you this doctrine—"Believe in the Lord Jesus Christ with all thy heart, and nothing shall be impossible to thee." This is the faith in Christ which all Mystical spiritual books are full of.'

the truth. The other man of God confirms this grave sentence as if it had come straight from the mouth of God, since he is quite sure that his authority for it possesses the Spirit of God. In obedience to God's call he lets the one who is concerned know of his sentence. All this is extremely odd!

In conclusion Law asked point blank: 'Who made me your teacher? or can make me answerable for any defects in your knowledge? You sought my acquaintance, you came to me as you pleased, and on what occasion you pleased. . . . If it was my business to put this question to you . . . may you not much more reasonably accuse them who are authoritatively charged with you? Did the Church in which you were educated put this question to you? did the Bishop that ordained you . . . do this for you? did the Bishop that sent you into Georgia require this of you?'

So ended the exchange of letters. Wesley's case appears to be the weaker and the less pleasant side of his character is shown. But what was the real situation? Law had unequivocally declared himself for the mystics, especially the German mystics. He was to become the chief representative of the Jakob Böhme type of piety in England.[4] To break with him necessarily meant for Wesley the renunciation of the mystics. In Georgia especially he had been influenced by two examples of Romanic mysticism, the biographies of Lopez and de Renty, and he had gained essentially favourable impressions of these. Moreover, on Law's recommendations he had steeped himself in the *Theologia Germanica*, Tauler, and Molinos. All the time he had taken this so seriously that he reduced their main ideas to a sort of system and asked his older brother Samuel for his opinion about it.[5] In doing this he had not confined himself to their books only but also drew on letters and conversations with actual representatives of this kind of piety, which meant that a particularly favoured place was given to John Gambold and Spangenberg. He perceived that two things were central: the high value given to love, and the depreciation of definite means towards salvation. Prayer, the reading of religious books, the use of the sacraments, fasting, and all the usual exercises of the religious life count for nothing. Perfect love, centred

---

[4] Cf. Wilhelm Struck, *Der Einfluss Jakob Böhmes auf die englische Literatur des 17 Jahrhunderts;* Nils Thune, *The Behmenists and the Philadephians;* Konrad Minkner, *Die Stufenfolge des mystischen Erlebnisses bei William Law*; August Lang, *Puritanismus und Pietismus, Studien zu ihrer Entwicklung von Martin Butzer bis zum Methodismus*, pp. 281ff.

[5] *Letters*, I.207–10, Savannah, 23rd November 1736.

wholly in God, and which no longer asks any reward for its good deeds, must clothe him around. Time and again, beginning from his mother's faith, this had been stressed as the goal of his religious life. On the other hand the contempt for the means of grace could only have seemed strange to him, for it went contrary to the strict self-discipline which he practised and enjoined upon his friends—while still in Georgia he had sent letters of spiritual counsel along these lines to England. Just as he strongly resisted the idea that by 'Christianity' he understood an austere, sullen disposition which was incapable of flexibility and joy, so he upheld with equal vigour that God's clear commandments in Scripture are fixed.[6] But it was just at this point that he no longer found in the mystics what he had so admired in de Renty and Lopez, namely that complete subjection of one's own will to God's. On the contrary he perceived a malicious light-heartedness which wantonly allowed this or that to be done or left undone. He might not himself have seen anything like such gross misdemeanours as sexual libertarianism, yet what he noticed was an unlimited individualism which permitted each person to attain salvation in his own way. He found that clearly-stated standards were set aside, he found an attitude of complete passivity, he found that sight was being emphasized to the exclusion of faith, and a self-sufficient attitude which neglected that sense of responsibility for others that had driven him to seek to do good ever since his time at Oxford. If it was no longer necessary to be an example to one's fellow-men or to attend to their needs, if it was enough to feel compassion without doing anything practical, if speaking about salvation was forbidden, if nothing other than a great silence remained, in which the mystic was plunged solitarily in God, then he was unable to detect in such a faith the presence of the Spirit of God. He had already reached this position by the end of November 1736, when he had described the writings of the mystics as the rock on which faith most easily suffered shipwreck. When he examined his spiritual state on the voyage home from Georgia and found that the greatest form of self-deception was reliance upon solitude as the way to God, he reiterated this categorical No to the mystics. He made the point against them that under the cloak of love they avoid every concrete, practical act of obedience and leave a person fluctuating in a state of uncertainty between a sense of obligation and freedom. It was of course their promise of final

---

[6] On this, cf. esp. the letter to William Wogan on the question of trifling conversation (*Letters*, I.217–18, Savannah, 28th March 1737).

union with God and of being inwardly bound to Him which he found so attractive. Yet what presented itself to him in no way corresponded to the religion which Jesus Christ and the apostles lived. It was for these reasons that all other enemies of Christianity seemed harmless to him beside the mystics. He saw in them the most dangerous adversaries, people who succeeded in seducing precisely the best and most serious Christians.[7]

In both of these statements Wesley rejected mysticism because of his concern for holiness and for social responsibility, and contrary to it he argued for a genuine Christian ethic. This was also the reason why he had not been able to break entirely with Law, for his writings contained so many ethical exhortations, which counterbalanced his predilection for the mystics. But now, since he had become acquainted with Böhler, he saw this type of religion in a new light. Böhler made him see that its error lay in trying to attain to salvation through a high Christian ethic. He taught him that there were 'noble sinners' and also faith in the living power of the blood of Christ. Accordingly it was first through him that Wesley came to understand mysticism as the highest and most dangerous form of legalism. He saw more clearly than Law, who concealed both from himself and from Wesley the real problem in mysticism. When Wesley again took up the *Theologia Germanica* three and a half years later he was conscious of the difference between it and the plain language of the Bible, and he thanked God that he had learned to prefer the clarity of the prophets and apostles.[8]

Nevertheless, Böhler would not have been able to influence him so strongly had not the actual circumstances of his life first prepared the way. The fact that he had been so frustrated in Georgia meant that he had taken a decisive step away from the design which had filled him with the desire of becoming like Jesus and of adopting the early Christian way of life. The aim was not abandoned, but the prospect of attaining it directly had become problematic. Everything about him had been shaken, and much was destroyed. This meant that because of what he had come through and undergone, he was in the right situation for the antitheses between law and grace, and sin and forgiveness, to become something real in his actual experience. This was the reason why he was prepared to entrust himself so completely to Böhler, who was able to formulate what he really felt and

[7] *Journal*, I.420, 24th January 1738.
[8] Ibid. II.515, 18th November 1741.

which was struggling after expression. Under his guidance Wesley learned to understand faith as the central motivating force in Christianity, and to bring it entirely into relation with God's promise. The truths which Böhler taught him to express in Zinzendorf's terms he then found confirmed in everything which actually happened to him.

On 26th March he preached at Whitam,[9] near Oxford, on the new creature. The next day, in company with his friend Kinchin, he visited a man under sentence of death in the Oxford prison. They found him deeply troubled and concerned about his sins, but after they had proclaimed to him forgiveness and prayed with him, he stood up after remaining for a while on his knees and said: 'I am now ready to die. I know Christ has taken away my sins; and there is no more condemnation for me.' With 'composed cheerfulness' he went to the place of execution and in his last moments was filled with the assurance that he was accepted with those beloved of God. On 2nd April, which was Easter, Wesley preached in the chapel of his own college, Lincoln, in Oxford on John 5[25]: 'The hour cometh, and now is, when the dead shall hear the voice of the Son of God, and they that hear shall live.' Twice during the afternoon he again spoke from this text. The few words which he uses to refer to these occasions in his *Journal* really say everything: 'I see the promise; but it is far off.' In the hope that it would be fulfilled in him he thought it better to go into retirement, and he spent two and a half weeks with his friend Kinchin in the country. The deep stirring within, which had now seized him, showed itself outwardly in the fact that he now sometimes gave up strictly liturgical set prayer, a practice he had greatly abominated in Georgia as a sign of irregularity in the relationship with God.[1] What this meant can be judged when seen in relation to the principal features and character of the Anglican Church, which regards prayer as the true expression of its spirituality, or when the fact is recalled that prayer was given special emphasis in both the religious literature and the mysticism of the eighteenth century. But even more revealing in this connexion was John Wesley's own practice of prayer. In Georgia he translated the hymns of German Pietism, and the Herrnhuters expressly explained to him through Spangenberg that they must be thought of as prayers.[2] He fre-

---

[9] The suggestion that this was High Wycombe (*Proc.W.H.S.*, V. [1906].94), must, as Curnock suggests (*Journal*, I.447, note 2), be rejected.
[1] This section, *Journal*, I.447–53, 26th March to 18th April 1738; for the opposite attitude in Georgia, cf. ibid. p. 309, 2nd January 1737.
[2] Ibid. p. 374, 31st July 1737: 'Our hymns are forms of prayer.'

quently prayed with Delamotte, particularly in times of stress;[3] and in the spiritual conflicts which the unhappy affair with Sophy Williamson-Hopkey brought about, prayer and singing were continual sources of strength to him. He constantly cried, 'Lord, help Thou my unbelief!' and his *Journal* contains ejaculations to God.

Having disagreed with Böhler about the possibility of instantaneous conversion, and then being convinced by the Bible and the living examples of its truth, he immediately testified passionately to others of his newly-won knowledge. The first to whom he spoke were Delamotte's parents in Blendon, his brother Charles, and a young man named Thomas Broughton. Mrs Delamotte left the room, put out by his words; Broughton objected that he could not conceive how a man who had done and suffered so many things as John could not be said to have faith. Charles was indignant at the obstinate way in which John persisted in his point of view. John on his part only considered that their opposition confirmed the truth of his position. He thanked God that it had pleased Him to kindle this fire.[4] He now seized every opportunity of declaring this faith in the forgiving grace of God through the blood of Christ. Many refused the message, others did not even trouble to do this, but merely remained indifferent, whilst a few received it.[5] So the parable of Jesus about the four different kinds of soil was repeated in Wesley's experience. He strove hard to win over his brother, and was disappointed that even upon his sickbed he continued to hold out against the 'new Faith'.[6] When he was again staying at Blendon with Delamotte's parents a week after his previous visit, he found to his surprise that they were ready to accept his message.[7] In the meantime even Charles had been won over to the Herrnhut gospel, and Peter Böhler wrote in his Journal: 'The younger Wesley now also believes that he is a poor sinner and that he lacks the Saviour. He seeks grace in the blood-stained wounds of the Redeemer.'[8] This came as great a surprise to John as had the case of Delamotte's parents, and when Charles began to recover from his illness immediately after this, John exclaimed in the language of the Bible: 'Who is so great a God as our God?' He

---

[3] E.g. *Journal*, I.271, 6th September 1736.
[4] Ibid. pp. 455–6, 25th April 1738. Thomas Broughton is probably to be identified with a subsequent secretary of the Society for Promoting Christian Knowledge. As such he corresponded between 1743 and 1776 with the governors of the Halle Orphan-house; cf. Missionary archives of Francke's Institution, Halle, Z.I.L.9.
[5] Ibid. p. 457, 26th April 1738.   [6] Ibid. p. 458, 1st May 1738.
[7] Ibid. p. 460, 5th, 6th May 1738.   [8] Böhler's Diary 12th May 1738.

felt that he was in the presence of a miracle of healing as in the early days of Christianity.[9] On the other hand he was finding that his preaching on free grace and faith in the blood of Christ was not received in a number of churches,[1] but this only confirmed for him the truth of what a friend, probably John Gambold, wrote about this time to Charles Wesley, that it had become quite clear to him that the message of justifying faith was highly presumptuous to religious men in particular. Everything else is tolerated more easily, even unchristian statements like those of the deism of the day, or the fanatic utterances of religious enthusiasm, such as were met with in this place and that, or the demand for the most rigorous mortification which leading writers put forward—probably a reference to Law. What is found intolerable is the rejection of self-glorification and the acceptance of the fact that man is a sinner. Should anyone reveal how deeply the religious man is entangled in his own pharisaical self-righteousness and then indicate the deliverance he needs, that person will find that his hearers turn indignantly away from his message. Even a Montanist or Novationist, who from the height of his moral purity looks down contemptuously upon poor sinners is not considered to be acting so subversively as one who takes seriously the fact that the Saviour was the friend of publicans and sinners. It is the religious people who believe that through their long exercise of piety they have accumulated a treasure for time and eternity. They think they can rely on this. The doctrine of faith on the contrary takes this from them and acts just like a robber. That they should now once again be ranked with the poorest, most miserable and needy folk in God's sight, the very people from whom they had lifted themselves by severe and self-renouncing moral effort, is contrary to all their ideas. It shocks their reason more than any intellectual pretension like the doctrine of transubstantiation as an explanation of the holy sacrament.[2]

Böhler's idea of 'noble sinners' can be detected in every line of this passage. For the last time before the great transforming experience itself Wesley was brought up against the doctrine which for

---

[9] *Journal*, I.464, 19th May 1738. The language he used shows this: 'His bodily strength returned also *from that hour*' (Italics mine).

[1] Ibid. p. 460, 7th, 9th May 1738; I.462, 14th May 1738; I.464, 21st May 1738. The one-sidedness of Peter Böhler's account of the situation becomes clear at this point. He tells of his overwhelming success in dithyrambic style, whereas Wesley reports both the favourable and unfavourable reception given to his preaching and conversation; cf. Böhler's Diary.

[2] Ibid. pp. 462–3.

months had so disturbed him. Theory and practice, doctrine and experience, preaching and witness, were keeping closely in step, just as always they had gone together during his own life.

Three days of deep dejection now followed. Two weeks earlier it had been just the same: he had found it impossible to read or meditate. Praying and singing were out of the question, and he was not able to give himself effectively to any activity. What was happening in his heart is seen from a letter which he wrote to a friend on the decisive day itself, 24th May.[3] In it his mode of thinking is theocentric to a degree unattained previously. The situation itself indicates this, for although he is writing to a friend, to whose words he refers, he constantly loses sight of this fact. In reality he is standing before God, God alone, and the result is that imperceptibly he falls into a manner of speaking which is really only suited to prayer. The problem of his own personal salvation deepens for him into insight into the nature and activity of God. God, incomprehensible in His creative love, will actually use him as His instrument! Though

[3] *Letters*, I.244–5. It has been suggested that the 'friend' may have been Gambold, Kinchin, Kinchin's sister Molly, or Clayton (cf. Telford, in ibid. p. 244). In my opinion only Gambold is a possibility. It must have been someone who like Wesley was strongly influenced by the Herrnhut gospel, yet who had assimilated it with similar independence. Only Gambold answers to this. In addition it must have been somebody who was particularly close to Wesley. In trouble of this kind Wesley would only have opened his heart to a trusted friend. Concerning his relationship with John Gambold, Wesley wrote on 5th November 1763 (*Journal*, V.40): 'I spent some time with my old friend John Gambold. Who but Count Zinzendorf could have separated such friends as we were? Shall we never unite again?' Similarly, he said on 16th December 1763 (ibid. p. 43): 'I spent an agreeable hour, and not unprofitably, in conversation with my old friend, John Gambold. Oh how gladly could I join heart and hand again! But, alas! thy heart is not as my heart!' In his Diary for 6th March 1738, Peter Böhler wrote of Gambold: 'In the house I met a pastor from the country named Gämbul, who had been described to me as a true Herrnhuter who had truly mortified himself. He looked like a Mysticus. . . . Gämbul was to share a bed with me, and when we were together in our room he began to confess that he was not really as I had said. For ten years he had sought something better, but he had not rest of spirit; he was also without rest because of his office of a clergyman, for he doubted whether baptism and the Lord's Supper still had their old power. I explained this matter to him as well as I could and invited him to disclose to me his actual condition: He did not know whether he could do this, or whether it was God's will, but in the morning he would do so. I remained quiet and still: he bid me take evening prayers, which I did in Latin, and before he got into bed he himself began to confess his sins and told how he had been trying to live as a Christian, having been awakened to faith by reading Luther's writings three years before, which had often done him good; but then he had come across mystical works, and had fasted and watched much, yet carnal desires were still active in him and he could not be rid of them. I spoke only a few words to him and made him come to bed, although he remained awake for a long time, groaning much. On 7th March he went back to his own village again, and I accompanied him for a good half-hour, speaking with him once more and holding a lengthy band with him. He took affectionate farewell of me, which was also pleasing to me.'

contrary to human understanding, He sends the dead to awaken the dead. 'Yea,' Wesley exclaims, 'Thou sendest whom Thou wilt send, and showest mercy by whom Thou wilt show mercy. Amen! Be it, then, according to Thy will! If Thou speak the word, Judas shall cast out devils.'

He then turns to his friend. 'I feel what you say (though not enough), for I am under the same condemnation. I see that the whole law of God is holy, just and good. I know every thought, every temper of my soul ought to bear God's image and superscription. But how am I fallen from the glory of God! I feel that "I am sold under sin". I know that I, too, deserve nothing but wrath, being full of all abominations, and having no good thing in me to atone for them or to remove the wrath of God. All my works, my righteousness, my prayers need an atonement for themselves. So that my mouth is stopped. I have nothing to plead. God is holy; I am unholy. God is a consuming fire; I am altogether a sinner, meet to be consumed.'

'Yet,' he continues his soliloquy, 'I hear a voice (and is it not the voice of God?) saying, "Believe, and thou shalt be saved. He that believeth is passed from death unto life. God so loved the world that He gave His only-begotten Son, that whosoever believeth in Him should not perish, but have everlasting life." '

Again he looks to himself and his friend. 'Oh let no one deceive us by vain words, as if we had already attained this faith! By its fruits we shall know. Do we already feel "peace with God" and "joy in the Holy Ghost"? Does "His Spirit bear witness with our spirit that we are the children of God"? Alas! with mine He does not. Nor, I fear, with yours. O Thou Saviour of men, save us from trusting in anything but Thee! Draw us after Thee! Let us be emptied of ourselves, and then fill us with all peace and joy in believing; and let nothing separate us from Thy love, in time or in eternity!'

This letter is a most significant document, both with reference to its subject-matter and the style in which it is written. He says what he has to say in the shortest possible sentences, all charged with meaning. Without any sense of having been chosen artificially his words re-echo the language of the Bible. He begins with God and ends with God. The whole emphasis is upon God's working. He is consuming fire and sacrificial love. God is holy, man is sinful. God brings life out of death and turns judgement into grace; in place of despair He gives joy. Everything in man is wicked, his action and that upon which he bases his righteousness, and even his prayers, that is, the very acts which are directed immediately to God. The background of the idea of God is the predestination which throws into relief His incomprehensible grace in all its greatness and shining clarity. God condemns justly—and yet by His unbounded love He forgives. Sin is violation of God's honour and loss of His image; faith is not a human capacity, but response to God's call, obedience to His command.

In all this there is a very striking similarity between John Wesley and Martin Luther.[4] Wesley goes beyond Peter Böhler, which means beyond Zinzendorf also. For them God, the Father, recedes completely behind the historical, incarnate, crucified Saviour. It is true that Zinzendorf did pursue speculative ideas about God and that he referred to them in his first letter to Wesley, but he did this only to give force to the basic dogma that the Redeemer is also the Creator, that Jesus Christ is God Himself. Perhaps he only made use of them so that subsequently he could reject them with greater force. His real protest was, like the Alexandrian theologians of the early Church, against the Two-Natures doctrine as a rationalistic speculation. Like them he recognized only *one* Nature, the Divine, which entered into union with the flesh.[5] Wesley on the other hand knew that he was in the immediate presence of God Himself. Without showing a similar tendency towards speculation the idea of God was itself for him much

[4] Cf. Karl Holl, *Ges. Aufsätze*, I: *Luther*, pp. 37ff; Fritz Blanke, *Der verborgene Gott bei Luther*; Erich Seeberg, *Luthers Theologie, Motive und Ideen*, I, *Der Gottesanschauung*, 107ff, 131ff, 155ff, with its wilful transposition of Luther's existential categories into the philosophic; Paul Althaus, *Gottes Gottheit als Sinn der Rechtfertigungslehre Luthers, Lutherjahrbuch*, XIII.(1931).1–28=*Theologische Aufsätze*, II.(1931).1–30, *Gottes Gottheit bei Luther, Lutherjahrbuch*, XVII.(1935).1–16.

[5] On this, cf. Luther's '*Grosses Bekenntnis vom Abendmahl*' (1528), *WA*, pp. 16, 320, 324, 332, 334, and especially clearly on p. 333: 'Man is more closely joined to God than is our skin with our flesh and closer than body and soul. While the man is alive and healthy skin and flesh, body and soul, make up one thing and person, which cannot be divided . . . where one is there must the other be also. Similarly thou canst not separate the divinity from the humanity and put it away apart from the humanity, for then thou wouldst divide the person from the humanity and make it a shell. . . .' Concerning the problems raised, cf., above all, Werner Elert, *Der christliche Glaube*, pp. 396ff. For the young Luther, cf. Erich Vogelsang, *Die Anfänge von Luthers Christologie nach der ersten Psalmenvorlesung*, pp. 171ff. He interprets the Two-Natures doctrine completely in terms of justification and accordingly is not able to do full justice to Luther's use of this formula. Quite different is the interpretation of Erich Seeberg, *Luthers Theologie*, II: *Christus. Wirklichkeit und Urbild*, pp. 26ff, 241ff. From the standpoint of his strongly philosophical, ethical-idealistic interpretation he seeks to prove that Luther's interest was in the separation of the Natures. The sharp differences between the commentators lead to the conclusion that there are problems which have not been sufficiently elucidated, even if the dogmatic position of the different interpreters contributes materially to their conclusions.

more an expression of the actual reality of God. It may well be all of a piece with his doctrine of perfection or perfect love, which derived its standard from God Himself. Moreover, the Puritan custom of self-observation may have been a contributory factor, since it constantly raised the question of God's judgement, and made the individual aware of the need to walk all the time in God's presence, regarding conscience as God's witness in man. Then there were the Romantic mystics, whose constant aim was to surrender themselves completely to God's will and to inquire only after it. Finally, it was precisely this characteristic about the Herrnhuters which made the greatest impression upon Wesley, as seen principally in Spangenberg's account of his life and in the daily use of the lot. For these reasons he could not abandon the idea of God by allowing the first article of the creed to be merged entirely in the second.

When this point is taken into consideration this letter will have to be regarded as a legacy from Böhler's teaching, and yet independently thought out. Previous to this his influence on Wesley had been great and perhaps overwhelming. To be sure Wesley had tested his statements and claims by the Bible and demanded that they should be confirmed by living contemporary witnesses; nevertheless he had to a large extent taken over Böhler's actual expressions. It was because he had been so shocked by them that he held on to them so tenaciously. Even before his meeting with Böhler he was convinced of the basic truth of the principle of justification and the distinction between law and grace, sin and forgiveness, as the review he made of his life in America indicates. Böhler taught him afresh to stress faith in the redeeming blood of Christ in place of a Christian ethic, and made him conscious of the fact that this faith is inseparably bound up with God's promise. In this way the lines which Wesley had only faintly sketched were made definite, notwithstanding the fact that the idea of God Himself was pushed into the background. The letter to the friend shows Wesley's independent understanding of the teaching he derived from Böhler.

Finally, the letter is significant because of its complete devotion to truth. As was the case in the review of his life, Wesley in this instance also shows that he had a complete grasp of the essential elements of the doctrine of justification. He has clearly seen it both as a judgement made by God and as something which happens to man: yet he knows that he himself does not possess this faith. It is not his personal spiritual possession. Just because of his own bitter experiences he tries to avoid every temptation to deceive himself at this point. It is possible to see here traces of Puritanism, for which self-delusion, especially religious self-delusion, was a constant theme.[6] But the thing that stands out most clearly is Wesley's principal characteristic, an inexorable regard for truth. This was true of him during the whole of his life: it was also the characteristic which led him on occasions to make such harsh judgements or to break with other folk.

The letter shows the direction his spiritual pilgrimage was taking; he was further helped by certain things which happened to him at this critical time.[7] At five o'clock on the morning of the day of his conversion, immediately after getting up, he opened the Bible at a text which was a favourite with the Pietists: 'There are given unto us exceeding great and precious promises, even that ye should be partakers of the divine nature' (2 Peter 1[4]).[8] He gave a shortened translation of the Greek text, which brings out the promise for which, in his heart of hearts, he was longing. As he was leaving the house, he opened his Bible again and lighted this time on the words: 'Thou art not far from the Kingdom of God' (Mark 12[34]). In the afternoon he went to the service in St Paul's. The words of the anthem, which Wesley wrote out in full in his *Journal*, were from Psalm 130: 'Out of the deep have I called unto Thee, O Lord.' It may well have been sung to the setting of W. Croft which was published in 1742, and which by constant repetition emphasized the words: 'Trust in the Lord.'

He was now on the verge of the conversion, which was so soon too follow. In the evening Wesley betook himself unwillingly to a small group which had assembled in Aldersgate Street. It was probably a

---

[6] Cf. William Perkins, *The Foundation of Christian Religion*, pp. 3–8; Daniel Dyke, *The Mystery of Self-Deceiving*, published by his brother Jeremy Dyke in 1615 and often praised (especially by Philipp Jakob Spener, *Consilia theologica latina* I.[1700].158, III[1709].351); Richard Sibbs, *Bowels Opened* (1641); Richard Baxter, *Mischiefs of Self-Ignorance and Benefits of Self-Acquaintance* (1662); John Bunyan, *The Pilgrim's Progress* in *Grace Abounding and The Pilgrim's Progress*, ed. John Brown, Cambridge English Classics (1907), pp. 244ff, 263.

[7] On this, cf. R. Kissack, 'Wesley's Conversion. Text, Psalm and Homily', *Proc.W.H.S.*, XXII.(1939–40).1–6.

[8] *Journal*, 1.472; cf. e.g. A. H. Francke, *Nicodemus*, pp. 149–50: 'The divided character is not acceptable to GOD. And although God suffers this in men with patience nobody ought to abuse the patience of God to cover his sloth, indolence or little faith, but rather make use of it the more to arouse himself to press on to a true joy in believing, which God without partiality will gladly give to such a man. For why should He have given so great and precious promises to men if it were not the wish and longing of His heart that men who hear or read the same should become partakers of the divine nature, which has certainly no part with the fear of man?'

meeting of a Religious Society, possibly even a Herrnhut 'band', which met there. Someone was reading Luther's Preface to the Epistle to the Romans, the document in which German Pietism found the reformer giving classical expression to its great concern for living faith.[9] The reader came to the point where it says: 'Faith is a divine work in us, which changes us and makes us newly born of God, and kills the old Adam, makes us completely different men in heart, disposition, mind and every power, and brings the Holy Spirit with it. O faith is a lively, creative, active, powerful thing, so that it is impossible that it should not continually do good works. It does not even ask if good works are to be done, but before anyone asks it has done them, and is always acting.'[1] John Wesley felt his heart warmed in an unusual way. He was gripped by a new power. He felt that now he really did trust in Christ, and looked for his salvation from Him alone. 'An assurance was given me that He had taken away *my* sins, even *mine*, and saved *me* from the law of sin and death.'[2] He put the time at which this happened as about 8.45 p.m., and this precise fixing of the moment may at first sight look like Pietist pedantry. Perhaps Wesley was still under the influence of those examples given by the Herrnhuters and the New Testament in which the awakening of faith is experienced in a moment. But the exact determining of the time has also another deeper significance. Its intention was to guard the experience from the dissolving effects of time and from the suspicion that it was an illusion.[3]

This was Wesley's conversion-experience. Theory had become actual fact, expectation had become fulfilment, desire had become possession. The final, decisive step had been taken. Step by step Wesley had come to the climax. In the first instance he had believed that the message of justification by grace alone through faith in the forgiving power of Christ's blood was foreign to the truth. Then he had followed Böhler's counsel and preached faith without possessing it himself. He had done this from a sense of being responsible to something outside himself, in the last resort out of responsibility to God. Then the idea of the sudden beginning of faith had aroused his opposition, but in the end he had been compelled to accept it. By the time he had returned from Georgia he had already seen his spiritual

---

[9] Spener, *Pia Desideria* (1675), ed. Aland (1940), p. 34, 1; *Erste geistliche Schriften* (1699), p. 3; *Der hochwichtige Articul von der Wiedergeburt* (1715), p. 153. For Zinzendorf, cf. Otto Uttendörfer, *Zinzendorf und die Mystik*, p. 143.
[1] *WA*, German Bible, pp. 7, 9–10.
[2] *Journal*, I.475–6.   [3] Cf. John 1[39].

situation in terms of the contrast between law and grace. But it was the letter which he wrote to a friend on the day of his conversion which first made it clear that this doctrine had been fully brought into line with the conception of God which governed his whole outlook. In this the last link was added to the chain: the attainment of actual assurance arose from insight into the truth, and this occurred in the overwhelming and solitary meeting between God and himself, between the Thou and I.

Nevertheless it was not only his relationship with God which was affected by the conversion; John Wesley was not left standing alone before the Eternal. His first impulse after the encounter with God was to think of his fellows. As he says, he prayed with all his might for those who had in a more especial manner despitefully used him and persecuted him, and at this point also a great change can be seen. He may have been thinking of the bantering which the Oxford circle of students had endured. Only a few weeks earlier they had been repeated in a different form, when he and Böhler were walking through the familiar quadrangles there. Perhaps too his experiences in Georgia were in his mind. Or again it could have been the recent opposition which he had encountered through his preaching. Yet until this moment he had in fact cherished these things, because he regarded them as signs of the world's hatred, which necessarily went along with being a Christian. He had looked upon them merely as things which contributed to his own welfare, whereas now he began to think of the other people concerned and recognized that he had a responsibility before God for the scoffers. It is true that on 5th December 1726, in correspondence with his brother Samuel about a sermon, he had recognized that the New Testament ethic transcended the Old Testament ethic in that it made love of wicked men obligatory. Yet quite apart from the fact that the question under discussion at that time was in the main theoretical, he had immediately gone on to say that the Christian undoubtedly ought to love good men more than others.[4] But now not only had it become an actual commission but also a spontaneous act. The definite social disposition, which went as far as love of enemies, proves how little there was in his conversion of even a sublimated using of God for his own ends. Finally Wesley went on to tell all who were present of what had happened in his heart.

How serious his spiritual conflicts were is indicated by the fact that

[4] *Letters*, I.32.

they now returned. He describes the situation in the following words: 'But it was not long before the enemy suggested, "This cannot be faith, for where is thy joy?" Then was I taught that peace with God and victory over sin are essential to faith in the Captain of our salvation; but that, as to the transports of joy that usually attend the beginning of it, especially in those who have mourned deeply, God sometimes giveth, sometimes withholdeth them, according to the counsels of His own will.' Once again it is the thought of God which determines everything else. The type of expression which is basic is 'God doeth, God willeth'. The whole feeling-aspect of the conversion, everything which can be summed up as the 'experience' of it, is given a subordinate part. All the stress is laid on the actual content, peace with God and victory over sin. In this way his spiritual conflicts were in principle overcome and their strength broken just because the claims they made were contested.

When they did return they were always directed at the same point, the absence of joy. This shows how earnestly Wesley desired this, although it had become clear to him that it was not essential. He longed that his newly-found faith should be fully felt by him, not to base assurance upon this, but in order to bring his new conviction completely into line with reality. In that age of sentiment reality was for him in the main psychical reality. He overcame the spiritual difficulties in different ways. First he was helped by prayer, which was often nothing more than the crying-out of a tormented man. Then he was struck by texts from the Bible which he came across in the course of his own reading or in the Psalms from the Anglican liturgy, or through opening the Bible at random, similar to the Herrnhut use of the lot. On one occasion the Herrnhuter Töltschig, who by then had come back from Georgia, told him not to fight his temptations but to flee from them the moment they arose and take shelter in the wounds of Jesus.[5] On another occasion it was as if another voice spoke through his own to the tempter, and set his own

[5] *Journal*, I.476ff, 24th–27th May 1738. The significance of prayer in the spiritual conflicts is shown in ibid. p. 479, 27th May 1738: 'Believing one reason of my want of joy was want of time for prayer, I resolved to do no business till I went to church in the morning, but to continue pouring out my heart before Him. And this day my spirit was enlarged; so that though I was now also assaulted by many temptations, I was more than conqueror, gaining more power thereby to trust and to rejoice in God my Saviour.' Rudolf Hermann (*Das Verhältnis von Rechtfertigung und Gebet nach Luthers Auslegung von Röm.3 in der Römervorlesung* [1926] = *Zeitschr.f.syst.Theol.*,3.[1925–6].603ff) has worked out the fundamental structural connexion between justification and prayer in Luther with distinction. At this point Wesley is very close to the reformer.

incontestable peace with God against the enemy's question as to why there was not a more sensible change. When the tempter went on, Wesley found his answer in the New Testament, which he opened at 2 Corinthians 7^5: 'Without were fightings, within were fears.' In this way he was conscious of being in the same situation as Paul, and following his example said to himself that even if there were fears within his heart he must nevertheless go on and tread them under his feet.[6]

The first practical outworking of his conversion had been a heightened sense of responsibility for his fellow-men, and this continued to develop. A week later it happened that he spoke sharply instead of with charity about someone who was not sound in the faith. Immediately he was conscious that God was hiding His face. He himself was troubled, and this state lasted for a day. The next morning he was consoled by the words from the Epistle to the Hebrews ($10^{19, \ 22-4}$): 'Having therefore boldness to enter into the holiest by the blood of Jesus, let us now draw near with a true heart in full assurance of faith. Let us hold fast the profession of our faith without wavering (for He is faithful that promised); and let us consider one another to provoke unto love and to good works.' These words spoke to him of the promise of grace.[7] One other event that day shows how little he thought of putting himself on a pedestal as one who was confident of victory because of what he had attained. He was walking in the country with a young friend of Böhler, named Wolf. In the course of their conversation Wesley became strongly convinced of the man's superior faith. On the one hand he was encouraged by the fact that God's grace was so effective in the man, but he was at the same time troubled about his own condition. He doubted whether they both had *one* faith. Without giving way to fruitless or morbid preoccupation with this problem, he reasoned in the following way: 'Though his faith be strong and mine weak, yet that God hath given some degree of faith even to me, I know by its fruits. For I have constant peace; not one uneasy thought. And I have freedom from sin; not one unholy desire.'[8] Here he acknowledges as the fruit of his conversion the things he had always stressed, and which he was to bring out with even greater emphasis in the years to follow. Not only had it brought him personal assurance of faith, but dominion over sin.[9]

[6] *Journal*, I.478, 25th May 1738.   [7] Ibid. pp. 481–2, 31st May–1st June 1738.
[8] Ibid., 29th May 1738.
[9] He expressed this most clearly and distinctly in a letter written on 30th October 1738 to his brother Samuel, in which he definitely describes the content

By this he did not mean sinlessness, although this is one root from which his later 'perfectionism' sprang. It is rather a conviction derived from primitive Christianity that a new life begins when a person is fully united with Jesus Christ. 'If any man be in Christ, he is a new creature: old things are passed away; behold, all things are become new' (2 Corinthians 5¹⁷). The Epistle to the Romans, in which in chapters 7 and 8 descriptions of the pre-Christian and the

of his conversion-experience (*Letters*, I.262–3.): 'With regard to my own character, and my doctrine likewise, I shall answer you very plainly. By a Christian I mean one who so believes in Christ as that sin hath no more dominion over him; and in this obvious sense of the word I was not a Christian till May the 24th last past. For till then sin had the dominion over me, although I fought with it continually; but surely then, from that time to this it hath not, such is the free grace of God in Christ. What sins they were which till then reigned over me, and from which by the grace of God I am now free, I am ready to declare on the house-top, if it may be for the glory of God.' Wesley has here abandoned the deeper conception of sin expressed in the letter written on the day of his conversion. Sin is for him no longer the radical negative condition of the whole human existence standing in opposition to God, but individual sins separately considered. This follows the thought of Puritanism and Pietism, and differentiates Wesley from the reformers' conception of sin. It is however characteristic that it is difficult to place him finally in either camp; his distinctive peculiarity lay rather in his fluctuation between the two.

Somewhat different, richer and therefore less sharply defined, is the entry in the *Journal* for 14th October 1738 (II.89–91), which does not expressly refer to the conversion of 24th May 1738. The subject is the new creation. To have faith is to be a new man. The newness manifests itself in the first place in a changed judgement about himself and the goal of salvation. Concerning self it leads to a radical judgement that everything about the individual on his own is earthly, sensual and devilish. Wesley describes the goal of salvation in terms of living wholly in God and for God and bearing again the lost divine image. Next the believer's designs are new, so that he now aims at regaining the divine image and the life of God in the soul. His desires which unconsciously or half-consciously accompany his designs have also been changed. They are no longer centred upon earthly treasures but heavenly. Again his way of living is also new; it shows greater wisdom and a stronger sense of responsibility. His whole activity is new because it is directed to God's glory. When Wesley tests his own condition, which he does in accordance with 2 Corinthians 13⁵—a text beloved of the Puritans for self-examination—he has to confess that all the foregoing points have actually been fulfilled. He does recognize himself as a new creature. On the other hand the seven fruits of the Spirit of Galatians 5²² have only partially been realized in him.

When these statements are examined it can be seen that the main emphasis is upon actual things rather than a spiritual relationship. The standpoints of both the Reformation and Pietism appear alongside each other. The basic underlying theme seems Pietist, yet the emphasis which leads to the critical judgement, and the governing attitude which implies the *accusatio sui*, belong to the complex of the reformers' doctrine of justification. To be sure this structure is not consistently carried through. Combined with the Reformation point of view are Augustinian-mystical ideas about satisfaction in God, or the life of God in the soul as Scougal used it, so that the overall impression is of a syncretism. The stress on the 'new creation' does not contradict the equal emphasis on 'dominion over sin'.

Christoffel Nicolaas Impeta (*De Leer der Heiliging en Volmaking bij Wesley en Fletcher* [Dissertation Amsterdam]) was not able to recognize this distinction but confines himself to the subject of 'sanctification'. He characterizes the difference

Christian man are placed immediately alongside each other,[1] was one of the strongest pieces of evidence for this. Wesley's point of view here corresponded exactly with the basic outlook of German Pietism.[2]

Even before his conversion Wesley had been a keen evangelist, preaching everywhere the Gospel-message, particularly repentance, in churches and chapels and inns, even on the highway. His reception had been very varied. In March he made a journey with his friend Kinchin through a part of England, and in Newcastle they were looked upon with astonishment as men who had risen from the dead. Often they were ridiculed and laughed at, and sometimes they found grateful hearers. At other times Wesley reproached himself because he had not taken a sufficiently decisive line or had refrained from exhorting because of indolence. Thus he looked upon a shower of hail in Birmingham as God's punishment for such negligence.[3]

He experienced similar opposition when he came to tell of his conversion. In particular this happened in John Hutton's house, where he lived in London. When John Wesley maintained on 28th May that previous to 24th May he was not a Christian, but that now he had become one, people thought he was mentally deranged. The Reverend Mr Hutton, like a true Anglican, warned him not to disparage the effect of the two sacraments which he had of course received. Mrs Hutton told him that if he had not been a Christian before he was a great hypocrite, since he had made everybody believe he was one. She wrote, reprovingly and anxiously, to his eldest brother Samuel, the schoolmaster, whom she obviously credited with

between the periods before and after the conversion as the advance from 'external' to 'internal' sanctification and the substitution of justification on the basis of works by justification through faith. Faith is in this way understood as a disposition, that is as a 'work' in the deeper theological sense.

In the subsequent years Wesley's judgement of himself varies repeatedly. He denied once again that he had reached the stage of a 'new creation' and he could refuse to himself the name of a Christian (*Journal*, II.115–16, 16th December 1738; II.125–6, 4th January 1739).

Julia Wedgwood (*John Wesley and the Evangelical Reaction of the Eighteenth Century*, pp. 140ff.) gave a 'liberal' interpretation of the conversion experience, imparting to it an ecclesiastical significance. She regards the experience of 24th May 1738 as fundamentally the release of Wesley from the Anglican sacramental conception and so from Anglicanism in general, since conversion takes the place of baptism. James Harrison Rigg (*The Churchmanship of John Wesley*, pp. 40ff; *The Living Wesley*, pp. 118ff) followed her with reservations. The primary sources give no support to this view. Wesley's highchurchmanship was something he took over and not a theological position worked out by himself. It weakened imperceptibility before the conversion, but this was only completed after his separation from the Anglican Church.

[1] Cf. esp. Werner Georg Kümmel, *Römer 7 und die Bekehrung des Paulus*.
[2] Cf. above p. 142, note 6.
[3] *Journal*, I.444–5, 14th–16th March 1738.

considerable skill as a teacher.[4] Already on a previous occasion John had displeased Samuel with his religious radicalism when he urged his brother to avoid using with his pupils ancient works like Virgil's *Aeneid* and Terence's *Eunuchus* because they fed the lusts of the flesh. John considered that the lessons which his brother had to give were in the same category as his own mission to the heathen[5] and therefore they ought not to be abused by reading bad material. Mrs Hutton implored the older man to put his younger brother right. The conversation in their house had become so animated because their two children, a son and a daughter, revered John Wesley almost as if he were a saint. He was now branded as a heretic, an enthusiast, and a seducer. After a fruitless discussion he went away. Although he had succeeded in controlling his anger he found that his state of mind was not as quiet or as charitable as he would have wished. The only conclusion he could come to about the others was that they 'were seeking death in the error of their life'.[6] When on another occasion he was attacked in a similar way by one of his old friends he was able to obtain the self-control he needed through prayer.[7]

In addition to prayer he drew strength to an even greater degree from the Bible. It was principally the New Testament which helped him. On 28th May, four days after his conversion, and in the morning of the day on which in the evening there was an altercation at the Hutton's, he preached on 1 John 5[4]: 'This is the victory that overcometh the world, even our faith', and in the afternoon on the God who justifies the ungodly. Through these classic texts he passed on to others the central message of Luther, Zinzendorf, and Böhler. The result was, as so often before, that he was not to preach in either church, Bloomsbury or Long Acre, again. Had he been able to carry on his evangelical work in the main along traditional lines perhaps he might have become accustomed to this experience. To be sure he was no longer surprised, yet each time he was repulsed he felt it afresh, because he thought of every sermon as a new encounter with the Gospel. Probably the disappointments of the morning and afternoon contributed towards the unpleasant experience in the evening at the Hutton's house.[8] The following Sunday affected him quite differently. It seemed to him like a veritable feast-day! From

[4] Ibid. p. 479, note 2, 28th May 1738.
[5] *Letters*, I.192, 15th October 1735, to Samuel.
[6] *Journal*, I.479–80, 28th May 1738.
[7] Ibid. p. 482, 3rd June 1738.
[8] Ibid. p. 480, 28th May 1738.

morning until past midday all his thoughts and actions were filled with God alone. He read the Bible, prayed, sang, and preached, or, as he himself put it, he praised God and called sinners to repentance. Involuntarily he recalled the example of his ideal, Count de Renty, for whom life in the constant presence of God ceased to be a state that had to be induced or striven after, because it had become his natural state. The Bible itself became for Wesley that day an experience of a special kind. Every time he opened the New Testament he hit upon a great promise, and this led him to a deep insight into the character of the Book as a whole. He expressed this very happily in the words: 'I saw more than ever that the gospel is in truth but one great promise, from the beginning of it to the end.[9]

Yet although the conversion came as the climax of a long process it did not solve every problem: indeed the new religious attitude brought fresh difficulties for Wesley. Just when he imagined that he had settled the question of his lack of joy in salvation, he received a letter from Oxford which threw him once again into perplexity. Presumably it was from a member of the group which Böhler had got together, who wrote to the effect that doubts were incompatible with even the smallest degree of faith. Whoever feels doubts or fears is not merely weak in faith, but has no faith at all. Wesley let Paul answer for him. He found the actual refutation in Chapter 3 of 1 Corinthians, where the apostle addresses those of his spiritual children who had to be fed with milk rather than strong food as true members of the Body of Christ. It is to none other than these that he says: 'Ye are God's building, ye are the temple of God.' But the objections and doubts had aroused afresh in Wesley the feeling that he was not yet restored, or, as he himself expressed it, that his wound was not yet fully healed. This led him to pray that God would save him and all who were weak in the faith from doubtful disputations.[1]

It was this which prompted him to carry out at this time the project which he had long had in mind of visiting Herrnhut. He says expressly that his own spiritual need, coupled with this intention, was the reason for his decision. 'My weak mind could not bear to be thus sawn asunder.'[2] He hoped that meeting with the Brethren, the living

---

[9] *Journal*, I.482, 4th June, 1738.
[1] Ibid., 6th June 1738.
[2] Ibid. pp. 482–3, 7th June 1738: 'I determined, if God should permit, to retire for a short time into Germany. I had fully proposed, before I left Georgia, so to do, if it should please God to bring me back to Europe. And I now clearly saw the time was come. My weak mind could not bear to be thus sawn asunder.'

witnesses of the full power of faith, would be the means of so building him up that he 'might go on from faith to faith and from strength
to strength', as he says in words which are reminiscent of August
Hermann Francke.[3] But in addition to the admiration he had felt for
the Brethren on the sea voyage, in Georgia and England, and the
gratitude he felt towards Spangenberg, Töltschig, and Böhler, there
was a fresh reason. He was looking for help, although no longer
from instruction, but by experiencing the fellowship which the strong
gave to the weak. Here was a further feature of primitive Christianity
coming to expression. Now he was no longer regarding the Brethren
from the outside as an example of New Testament fellowship, but
he was actually going into their midst, that is, into the reality of the
early Church, where, in giving and taking and mutual sympathy and
suffering, the unity of the members in the one body was looked upon
as the basic principle of life.[4] First he went to Salisbury to take
farewell of his mother. She had long since ceased to play so important
a role in his spiritual life as during his first days at Oxford. He had
not written to her about the events in Georgia or of his experience
with Sophy Hopkey in particular, but—if at all—only told her about
them when he returned.[5] He no longer submitted theological questions to her. She only heard about his conversion from the Hutton
family in an account which was distorted and tendentious, and it was
for this reason that John read his own version of it to her. This
pleased her, and she thanked God for her son's experience of salvation, yet it is remarkable that she did not recognize this document a
year later when it was sent to her by 'a relation', accompanied by an
unfavourable judgement about it.[6] Furthermore, she agreed without
reservation with this adverse opinion. Therefore the contents and
the circumstances did not suggest to her that it was about John, and
he himself was extremely surprised about this.[7] This experience is

[3] *Nicodemus*, p. 158: '*Selig ist der / welcher also in allen Streit und Kampff /
auch wenn der Feind sich rühmet / dass er ihn überwunden hab / aushält /
und fort Kämpffet* (Jos. 4[10]) *der wird aus Glauben / in Glauben / aus Krafft in
Krafft gehen / und endlich mit Christo alles ererben.*' English in Wesley's
Abridged Edition, p. 27: 'Blessed is he that thus standeth his Ground in all Com-
bats and Assaults; he shall go from Faith to Faith, from Strength to Strength,
and finally overcome and inherit all things with Christ.'
[4] 1 Corinthians 12.
[5] It is extraordinary that there are no letters from Wesley to her during his time
in America. There are two possible explanations—either the correspondence has
been lost or there was none.
[6] The 'relation' was most probably his brother Samuel; cf. Curnock, in *Journal*,
II.219, note 2.
[7] *Journal*, I.483, 7th June 1738, and ibid. II.219-20, 13th June 1739.

sufficient to show how far she was now removed from him and his problems.

From Salisbury he went to Stanton Harcourt to see John Gambold and preached there on faith in Christ. In the afternoon of the same Sunday—it was 11th June—he preached his great sermon on Salvation by Faith [8] in St Mary's Church, Oxford. The text was Ephesians 2[8]: 'By grace are ye saved through faith.' In his calm, precise manner Wesley set out his subject in strictly logical order, and described first faith, then salvation. Finally he answered the objections which are raised against salvation through faith. This style of preaching, which consists mainly of argument and very rarely exhorts, and which addresses itself to the reason rather than to the will or even feeling, is most strongly reminiscent of the rational empiricism and psychological emphasis in the religious literature of the Puritans, and the same feature is evident in their sermons.[9] John Wesley openly acknowledged this when he reprinted a series of them in his *Christian Library*.[1] A necessary consequence was that faith received a greater emphasis than salvation, but the strong stress on subjective factors continued in the treatment of salvation. It was principally set forth as a living and present experience, and less as the act of God. In this way the theocentric line, which ran through the letter written on the day of his conversion, was abandoned. On the other hand faith was endowed to a great degree with objective qualities. It was defined in good Herrnhut fashion as complete trust in the blood of Christ. Salvation included remission of all past sins, deliverance from fear, and also deliverance from the strength of sin, the result of Christ's living power in us. It was justification [2] and regeneration in one, but regeneration took precedence. In the concluding section Wesley spoke of the effect of the doctrine of justification in the history of the Church and called it, with the Homilies of the Church of England, the strong rock and foundation of the Christian religion, which

---

[8] *Standard Sermons*, I.25–52; *Works*, V.7–16.

[9] Cf. for this, mainly William Haller, *The Rise of Puritanism*, and my essay, *Eigenart und Bedeutung puritanischer Eschatologie*, Theologia Viatorum, IV. (1952), esp. pp. 214ff.

[1] Cf. above, p. 42, note 3.

[2] From the point of view of the English tradition it was significant that justification and salvation were placed alongside each other, since the most frequently read Puritan writer before John Bunyan, Lewis Bayly, wrote in his *Practice of Piety*: 'From the doctrine of justification by faith only a carnall Christian gathereth, That good works are not necessary (p. 130). . . . But hee should know, though good workes are not necessary to justification: yet are necessary to salvation' (p. 131).

brought about the fall of the papacy in the land. But in addition he ascribed a decisive role to Martin Luther as its herald. The enemy of God, he continued, knew very well that the doctrine of justifying faith guarantees protection like a strong shield against his assaults. Now, for reasons of self-preservation, he has to attack it with all his might. When Wesley compared its apparent insignificance with a child overpowering a giant it is probable that he had the story of David and Goliath in mind. Because Satan rightly estimated the power of the message of justification he summoned all his cunning, strength, and lies against Luther in order to frustrate his work. In this way Wesley gave the reformer an important role in the drama of salvation and almost made him into the mythological figure of the devil's adversary. It is a curious fact of history that this reformation-pietist message of justification and living faith was proclaimed in the same Church in which a hundred years later John Henry Newman through his sermons ushered in the Anglo-Catholic movement.[3]

On 14th June 1738 Wesley set out from Gravesend for Rotterdam with four Englishmen and three Germans.[4] The names of some of his companions can be given with certainty, but the others are a matter of conjecture. Johann Töltschig, who had formed a close friendship with Benjamin Ingham while they were in Georgia, was undoubtedly one of the Germans. The English party included Ingham, Richard Viney, who was Böhler's interpreter in London, and John Holmes. The last two were tailors, who were making the journey partly for business reasons. The fourth Englishman was probably John Brown, a young draper, who belonged to the Moravians and later served among them in Ireland as a lay-preacher. He was the only one who went with John Wesley as far as Herrnhut.[5]

Their journey showed the influence of Herrnhut at every point. Where possible they put up at settlements of the Brethren and visited friends of the Church. In Rotterdam, their first stop, Wesley made the acquaintance of a man who became a lasting friend, the physician Dr Johan te Koker, who followed the development of the Methodist

[3] On John Henry Newman, cf. P. Thureau-Dangin, *La Renaissance catholique en Angleterre au 19me siècle;* R. W. Church, *The Oxford Movement, 1833–45;* Yngve Brilioth, *The Anglican Revival;* W. Ward, *The Life of Newman;* Bertrand Newman, *Cardinal Newman, a Biography and Literary Study.*

[4] Ziegenhagen wrote to G. A. Francke, Kensington, 13th June 1738: 'Ingham has gone to Zinzendorf at Frankfurt with several Herrnhuters. Time will reveal whether Wesley will soon follow.' Missionary archives of Francke's Institution, Halle, Z.I.L.5. The chaplain had thus no exact information.

[5] *Journal,* II.14, 15th July 1738, see note 2 (Curnock); II.57, 18th August 1738.

movement with warm sympathy and also translated into Dutch several of Wesley's tracts.[6] In Ysselstein, which was reached from Rotterdam via Gouda, they were on the outskirts of the Moravian settlement which was beginning at Herrendyk. The Community House was just being built, and on his return journey Wesley found it completed. In the meantime several families and the single members of the fellowship, German and English, were living in three or four houses. They were all under the direction of Baron von Watteville, Zinzendorf's Swiss friend, who later became his son-in-law. Wesley shared one of their 'Community Days'.[7] These monthly occasions meant a great deal to the life of the Moravians and were among their great events. People came from far and wide, and it was inconceivable for any to be absent except through necessity. The celebration lasted the whole day and consisted of three great gatherings. The first was from 8 to 11 o'clock, the second from 2 to 6 o'clock, with an interval of half an hour round about 4 o'clock. The other lasted the whole evening. The forenoon was spent principally after the custom of Herrnhut in singing, and it was in this way that the hymns of the old Moravian Church of the United Brethren, most of which were about the Church, came to occupy such a prominent place. In singing them the people were happy to recall that they had given spiritual strength to their fathers during the Roman Catholic persecutions at the time of the Counter-Reformation. The spirit of former times came to life. Then a passage from one of the prophets or a psalm was read, interspersed with chorales, which so far as possible were suited to the subject of the Bible-reading. Then followed the reading of letters to the community. These frequently came from a distance and consisted of simple words of greeting; sometimes they were requests for admission into the community. But in almost every case the writer of the letter told of his own spiritual condition, and in this way the fellowship was deepened into a truly personal communion. In the afternoon they looked at the wider world by reading letters and journals from settlements abroad or from the mission-

---

[6] John Wesley had some correspondence with him (*Letters*, I.262, 14th October 1738; p. 268, 22nd November 1738). He wrote to John Wesley about the translation of *A Plain Account and The Character of a Methodist* (10th October 1749, *Journal*, III.445–6).

[7] John Wesley calls it an 'Intercession Day' (*Journal*, II.5). On these 'Community Days', see principally Ludwig Carl Freiherr von Schrautenbach, *Der Graf von Zinzendorf und die Brüdergemeine seiner Zeit* (1851), pp. 261ff, and Otto Uttendörfer, *Zinzendorfs Gedanken über den Gottesdienst*, pp. 37ff. Nehemiah Curnock's note 2 in *Journal*, II.5, shows that he had no clear idea about these days and their significance.

field, providing in this way an overall picture of the growth of their Church. This session too was interspersed with prayers and hymns, as in the morning related to the people or subject under consideration. On the other hand the evening meeting was again of an intimate character, to which only members of the community and specially invited friends were admitted. In this the day reached its climax. It consisted of an address of instruction and the reception of new members, ending with prayer, for which all knelt. The very simplicity of the basic outline made all that went on most effective. A balance was maintained between the personal and the objective, between local affairs and wider interests, between diversity and unity. This prevented those present from becoming too weary and gave each member some sense of responsibility for the work of the whole community. Since great and small without distinction had the opportunity of speaking, the feeling was engendered in each individual that he was of equal importance to the community, while ambition and disputes about precedence were kept in check. In general the 'Community Days' were means of giving the Moravians a distinct historical and ecclesiastical consciousness. They made them aware that they were part of the movement of the Church in history and that their activity was to be understood as a fulfilment of that process. God was exercising His sovereign authority in spreading His Name abroad, and in awareness of this the little local congregation as a true Church of God was joined with the many units of that Church then existing in the world, through praise, thanksgiving, prayer, and intercession with the Church of former days. This attitude was a further feature they had in common with the early Church.[8] Afterwards it is true it only occupied a position on the circumference of the work of the Brethren, and this was a weakness. But Zinzendorf clearly recognized and gave expression to both aspects. In 1756 he finely described the character of a Community Day as a 'gathering at which people hear and observe how much our concerns mean to the Saviour, how it is with our brethren in the world, and how He carries out the things about which we speak with Him in a fairer and happier way than we could ever have deserved'.[9] On the other hand he feared lest the Brethren, in the way typical of the vanity of the sects, should regard themselves too highly. 'We

[8] For the fundamental idea of the Church, cf. the epoch-making guide to the clarification of early Christianity by Rudolph Sohm, *Kirchenrecht*, I.16ff.

[9] Jüngerhaus Diary for 30th September 1756, handwritten, in Herrnhut community archives, cited by Uttendörfer (see p. 274, note 7), op. cit. p. 38.

must . . . pray God that, as far as possible, we do not even know who we are, since it belongs to the Saviour and not ourselves if men are to be struck by the purpose which He has for us.'[1]

Wesley was deeply impressed by the genuine primitive Christian eschatological character of the Community Day. He found that it was in line with his own way of ecumenical thinking, which had led him to take active interest in the persecution of Polish Protestants in the blood-bath at Thorn,[2] and also with his expectation of the decisive intervention of God, which lay behind his zeal for missionary work.[3] With real joy and a sense of personal interest he listened to the reports and saw in them evidence of a great work which God was beginning all over the world, and which proved the full power of His Kingdom in contemporary events. This impression was strengthened because he took part in the afternoon and evening meetings only. At the request of the other Englishmen he held a special Communion Service for them in the morning.[4]

As always Wesley paid detailed attention to what he saw on the way. When he left Rotterdam he admired the road leading to Gouda, with walnut-trees planted on both sides. The ancient church there, with its coloured windows, reminded him of the English Gothic cathedrals. On the other hand he was not pleased with the unsatisfactory and desultory service in the inn, which he thought would not be possible in England. He went from Ysselstein to Amsterdam by boat and was delighted with the beautiful gardens they passed and by the sight of the tree-lined canals in Amsterdam. He praised the cleanliness of its streets and the attractive exteriors of the houses. All the greater was the contrast he found later in Cologne, which seemed to him the ugliest and dirtiest city he had even seen.[5] In Amsterdam he stayed with a Mennonite minister named Decknatel, who had translated part of the Herrnhut Hymn-book into Dutch. However, in the meeting of the Society the exposition was given in High German. From Amsterdam they went to Rheinberg via Jutphaas, Buren, Nijmwegen, and close by Cleve. On the way it troubled him that the Reformed inhabitants of the Lower Rhine, whom he mistakenly took to be 'good Lutherans', profaned the Sunday evening by dancing and

---

[1] Jüngerhaus Diary, 19th December 1751, Uttendörfer, ibid. p. 39.
[2] *Letters*, I.20, Oxon, 29th July 1725, to his mother; p. 26, Oxon, Christ Church, 22nd November 1725, to his mother.
[3] Ibid. I.222, Savannah, 16th June 1737, to James Hutton; p. 225, Savannah, 22nd July 1737, to Dr Humphreys.
[4] *Journal*, II.5, 17th June 1738.
[5] Ibid. p. 7, 26th June 1738; *Letters*, I.249, Colen, 28th June 1738, to his mother.

fiddling. By the roadside crosses he was able to tell when they passed from the Protestant into the Catholic district. Cologne was reached by way of Uerdingen and Neuss. He visited the cathedral, which at that time was still unfinished in two separate parts. The lack of proportion and symmetry offended his taste as much as did the windows covered with dust and cobwebs or the dirty plaster. In the Roman Catholic devotion as he saw it he missed the sense of corporateness, which is all the more understandable after the strong impression of it he had received from the Moravians: each individual prayed for himself before an altar without any connexion with others. When he was watching a procession, a passer-by in the street was slow in removing his hat, whereupon a zealous Catholic shouted: 'Knock down the Lutheran dog!' On the other hand he comments favourably on how much better the Catholics observed the outward forms of religion; on the boat they said their morning prayers with bared heads, and never took the Name of God in vain or laughed when religious questions were discussed.

The beautiful country of the central Rhine, which they were able to enjoy to the full since the boat was drawn upstream by horses, pleased Wesley exceedingly with its steeply uprising hills, covered to the top with vineyards, and its churches and castles. On 2nd July they reached Mayence and the next day stood before the gates of Frankfort, where they had to wait a long time because they had no passes. After waiting an hour Wesley sent a messenger to Peter Böhler's father, the brewer Johann Konrad Böhler, who gave the required security and in a most friendly way provided them with lodgings. By the next morning they were on their way to Marienborn Castle, where Count Zinzendorf had been staying since shortly after his banishment from Saxony (1736).[6] The Brethren who accompanied him from Herrnhut had found as their first refuge in the Wetterau a half-ruined castle, which was in the territory of Count Isenburg. Later they succeeded in renting from Count Isenburg-Meerholz another, called Marienborn, which was large enough to accommodate eighty-eight people. From this an unusually elaborate establishment, the Herrnhaag, near Büdingen, originated, and until 1750 this was the second headquarters of the Moravian Brethren. Then it had to be given up and disbanded because of differences with the ruling authorities in Büdingen. A series of high buildings in the

[6] *Journal*, II.8–10.

eighteenth-century style with curved roofs similar to those of Francke's Orphan-House at Halle was erected there very rapidly.

But all this was still at a very early stage when Wesley arrived. The Count had been staying in Marienborn only a few months, and since his banishment had visited the Baltic and Berlin. He had found a very friendly reception everywhere and through the good offices of his stepfather, the Prussian General Gneomar von Natzmer, had even been allowed to go to Herrnhut for a short while. The year previously he had been ordained in Berlin by Daniel Ernst Jablonski, Bishop of the United Brethren. He stood on the threshold of a great work. 'No event contributed as much to the expansion of the community as the expulsion from Saxony.' [7] It is therefore quite understandable why he did not give Wesley as much attention as he deserved and might have expected after their previous correspondence. The meeting between the two men was to all appearances disappointing, although the cautious comments of Wesley, in spite of all his admiration, admit of no certain conclusion. What impressed him from the first at Marienborn was the close bond of brotherhood, which, since the folk lived together, extended to the externals of life also. Perhaps half-consciously the memory of Oxford and his beloved Lincoln College was awakened in him as he exclaimed at Marienborn: 'Oh how pleasant a thing it is for brethren to dwell together in unity!' (Psalm 133[1]). Perhaps also pictures of the Herrnhut settlement in Savannah and of Ebenezer, the Salzburgers' town, were in his mind. At first he exchanged only a few words with the Count and then lay down. He stayed near by at Eckershausen with one of the brethren, but spent the day at Marienborn, talking with those who could speak either Latin or English, not being sufficiently fluent in German. He stayed for fourteen days, ten days longer than he had intended. The fact speaks for itself.[8]

His first brief reception by the Count was so surprising an experience for him that words failed him to describe it properly. He saw himself in the presence of a person who was quite outside the usual run of men. But he was even more surprised by the unbounded respect paid to him by his own people. When he compared the Count's behaviour with that of Jesus as He took the children into His arms and blessed them, and when he expressed the opinion that the Brethren followed him in the same way as the Count

---

[7] Heinz Renkewitz, *Zinzendorf*, p. 74.
[8] *Journal*, II.10–11, 14.

followed his Master, there lay in such remarks both high praise and gentle reproof. He found a combination of natural nobility, easy condescension and genuine love in the Count, but perhaps a nobility and condescension fitting only to the Son of God and not to a man. At the same time he noticed that the Count tied his people to his own person. But the main thing about the community was its early-Christian love, love for the Saviour and one another, and this led him to repeat Julian's admiring words about the Christians: 'See how they love one another.' [9] But it was equally important for him that, as in England, he found people amongst them full of the power of faith, who through the love of God had overcome inward and outward sin, and by the witness of the Holy Spirit had become free from doubt and fear.[1] He wrote the following words to his brother Charles: 'The spirit of the Brethren is beyond our highest expectations. Young and old, they breathe nothing but faith and love at all times and in all places.' He goes on to say that he does not concern himself any longer with 'points that touch not the essence of Christianity', for he has learned once for all the truth that 'every one that believeth hath peace with God and is freed from sin, and is in Christ a new creature'. So he warns his brother and the friends who had remained in England against receiving grace in vain and summons them to become living witnesses of the great and precious promises which are made unto everyone through the blood of Jesus. It is easy to understand why Charles wrote on this letter the words: 'Panegyric on Germans.'[2] John wrote in similar terms about the merits of the Brethren to his brother Samuel.[3] God has given him at last his heart's desire. He is with a Church whose conversation is in heaven, in whom is the mind that was in Christ, and who walk as He walked. All the members have *one* Lord, *one* faith, all partake of *one* Spirit, the spirit of meekness and love. It grieves him all the more when discontented, passionate, resentful, earthly-minded Christians bring the name of Jesus into disrepute among the heathen: the mission to the heathen is still the real standard by which he judges all things! He makes use of the opportunity to write a few home-truths to Samuel, and especially to Samuel's wife Ursula, and de-

[9] *Letters*, I.250, Utphe, 6th July 1738, to his mother; *Letters*, I.251, Utphe, 7th July 1738, to his brother Samuel. On Utphe, near Marienborn, cf. Theophil Mann in *Proc.W.H.S.*, XXI.(1937/8).211.
[1] *Journal*, II.13, 6th July 1738.
[2] *Letters*, I.250-1, Utphe, 7th July 1738, to his brother Charles. Charles Wesley described this letter as 'Panegyric on Germans'.
[3] Ibid. pp. 251-2, Utphe, 7th July 1738, to his brother Samuel.

plores the fact that Christians judge one another, ridicule and speak evil of each other, instead of bearing one another's burdens. With this model of primitive Christian fellowship before them he urges his sister-in-law to show that universal love which intercedes for others.

Such was the impression the Brethren made upon him. It was much greater than that of the Count himself. One day he took Wesley with him to the Count of Solms at Utphe. The Englishman was struck with the modest German style in which the whole of this nobleman's family lived, both in food, drink, and dress.[4] On the other hand Zinzendorf was important for Wesley as a theological instructor. At a Conference for Strangers a visitor from Frankfort proposed the question as to whether a man could be justified and not know it. Zinzendorf affirmed that this was so. It could happen that the actual facts of a case might only become clear to a person long afterwards. In this way he held resolutely to the objective character of justification, which was for him in the first place—as it was for Luther—God's judgement before it became a human experience.[5] In reply to the separate points raised Zinzendorf gave a detailed exposition of the doctrine as a whole, which Wesley summarized under eight headings as follows:

(1) Justification is the forgiveness of sins.
(2) The moment a man flies to Christ he is justified;
(3) And has peace with God; but not always joy.
(4) Nor perhaps may he know he is justified, till long after;
(5) For the assurance of it is distinct from justification itself.
(6) But others may know he is justified by his power over sin, by his seriousness, his love of the brethren, and his 'hunger and thirst after righteousness', which alone prove the spiritual life to be begun.
(7) To be justified is the same thing as to be born of God.
(8) When a man is awakened, he is begotten of God, and his fear and sorrow, and sense of the wrath of God, are the pangs of the new birth.

It must have seemed to John Wesley as if his own experience was being put into words and explained. His deep concern is shown not so much by his clear, almost prosaic sentences as by his precise report of what was said. It is probable of course that it was coloured by his

[4] *Journal*, II.12, 6th July 1738.
[5] Cf. esp. Karl Holl, *Ges. Aufs.*, I, *Luther*, pp. 111ff (*Die Rechtfertigungslehre in Luthers Vorlesung über den Römerbrief*), and Althaus (see p. 260, note 4) op. cit.

own point of view: he heard what he wanted to hear. Later he added to point seven the comment, 'Not so'. The basic assertions correspond with what he already knew. Justification brings dominion over sin, and a new life begins with rebirth. It must remain a matter of uncertainty whether, in view of other statements he made, Zinzendorf actually said this. To be sure these statements are not all of a piece, but generally he would have kept more strongly to Luther's affirmation that the believer is at the same time a righteous man and a sinner. He is righteous according to the judgement of God, and a sinner according to his actual condition.[6] Wesley compared Zinzendorf's teaching with what he had heard from Böhler and found a difference in the emphasis given to living faith with its psychically perceptible fruits, particularly joy. According to Böhler it was impossible to be justified without knowing it. Wesley therefore understood him to mean that justification and the assurance of salvation were parts of the same experience, whereas for Zinzendorf they were distinct from each other.

Once again Wesley shared in a 'Community Day' at which many strangers were also present. Benjamin Ingham did not go on with the group, and soon afterwards became a member of the community. Wesley set out for Herrnhut with John Brown and a man from Dresden named Hauptmann. They went via Gelnhausen, Anfenau, Fulda, Bronzell, and Rückers, and through the Rhön to Marksuhl and Eisenach. Wesley was exceptionally taken with the magnificent expanse of broad country. From Eisenach onwards he observed how the terrain became more level and open. Nobody called his attention to the places associated with Luther, not even to the Wartburg. He found Gotha neat and pleasant, but he notes nothing of the rich and important history of Erfurt, the Electoral town of Mainz, with its centres of Catholic life and examples of ecclesiastical architecture, its university, and its memories of Luther. Here too he was entertained by a Herrnhut brother to whom he had been directed in Marienborn. At Weimar he once again encountered the difficulties which usually arose when he wanted to be admitted to a town. In the end the group of travellers were brought before the Duke and had to satisfy him as to why they had undertaken the long journey to Herrnhut. When Wesley replied shortly and tersely, 'To see the place where the

[6] Cf. on this, Rudolph Hermann, *Luthers These Gerecht und Sünder zugleich* (1930). For Zinzendorf, esp. *Evangelische Gedanken*, published by Otto Uttendörfer (1948), pp. 32–3.

Christians live', the prince 'looked hard' and let them go. They came next to the university town of Jena. Wesley was immediately struck by the fact that although the students, unlike their English counterparts, lived amongst the townspeople and not in a separate building, there was one great difference between them and the inhabitants. The students always wore swords. This only served to increase Wesley's feeling that the Herrnhut student group amongst whom he spent the time during his short stay were a true picture of brotherliness in their behaviour, and his wish for them was that this spirit of brotherhood might abound more and more among them. From Jena they began to see the milestones and direction pillars, and he strongly recommended that this excellent arrangement by the Elector of Saxony should be copied elsewhere. The group went down the river Saale to Weissenfels and then to Merseburg on their way to Leipzig.

From Merseburg Wesley wished to take in Halle. August Hermann Francke had already created something of a stir in England, where he had gained many friends.[7] John Wesley had for a long time held the founder of the orphanage and his work in high regard, and news about the Danish-Halle mission had been given a prominent place in his parents' home. He read Francke's account of the orphanage on the voyage to Georgia, and from then on *Nicodemus* was among his favourite books. The descriptions of the Salzburg ministers from their own observation and personal experience had coloured for him the world of Halle and given him some sort of picture of it. Now he came himself to the famous spot. Once again he had first to get by the German police, who caused him fresh annoyance every time. For two hours the 'tall men' of the King of Prussia sent him from one city-gate to the other, but he was not allowed to enter anywhere. At last he got in by sending a message to Gotthilf August Francke, who was not himself there, but another leading person from the Orphanage came to the help of the visitors and secured their admittance into the city. Wesley was amazed when he saw the great buildings. He thought that the whole lay-out, which included an apothecary's shop and printing-office as well as the school and educational buildings, was very conveniently arranged, in spite of being on so large a scale. He considered the school-children's rooms were models of cleanliness. The fact that 650 children were housed there and 3,000 given instruction seemed to him astonishing and an unprecedented

[7] Cf. my article, '*Das hallische Waisenhaus und England im 18 Jahrhundert*', *Theol. Zeitschr.* (Basel, 1951), pp. 38ff.

sign of God's rule in history.[8] He regarded it as a proof of the words of Jesus that 'all things are possible to him that believeth'.

They did not stay long in Leipzig with the Herrnhut students, who then accompanied them for an hour on their journey. On 30th July, a Sunday, they arrived early at Meissen, where Wesley was impressed in particular by two things, the china and the cathedral. The fine shapes and colours which at the time were being produced by the works in the castle under the direction of the rococo sculptor Johann Joachim Kändler seemed to him to rival those from the Indies and China. At the service in the cathedral he was surprised by the elaborate dress of the congregation and by the rich robes of the minister, whose gown or vestment had a huge cross on the front and back. To Wesley's amazement the men kept their hats on during the prayers and sermon, and he was equally scandalized by the fact that the whole congregation stayed for the Holy Communion, but only a few actually communicated.

Once again at Dresden it took them two hours to get into the city, and here at last Wesley's patience gave way. He unbosoms himself in his *Journal* and comments severely on the senseless, inhuman treatment of strangers, which violates every law of hospitality. He cannot understand why the ordinary common feeling which he took for granted existed in Germany as in his own country does not make an end of it. In the town he saw the building left unfinished by Augustus the Strong and the new Church of St Mary by Georg Bähr, which seemed to him like a theatre. The sight of the baroque splendour all over the city produced in him thoughts typical of a prophet of woe, and he exclaimed: 'Where will all these things appear when the earth and the works thereof shall be burned up?'

Leaving Dresden he finally reached Herrnhut in two days via Neustadt in Saxony. Its fine situation in the Lusatian highlands, embedded in woods and surrounded by fields and gardens, was very much to his taste. He was pleased with the plain style of the houses, which were nevertheless carefully looked after, and with their unpretentious uniformity which avoided grandeur or splendour. In particular he noticed this characteristic in the Count's house. He was full of anticipation as he went into the room which had been prepared for him in the lodging. Now he would see whether the reports of his friends had been exaggerated or whether they had been no more than

[8] He implies that he is giving the numbers from memory only (*Journal*, II.17).

the sober truth. His stay lasted two weeks, from 1st to 14th August 1738.[9]

He met one of his old acquaintances from Georgia, Baron Johann Christian Adolf von Hermsdorf, who had accompanied the Herrn-huters there in 1735. Hermsdorf made it his business to see that Wesley saw as much as possible of Herrnhut.[1] The days were given

[9] *Journal*, II.19–56. In the Herrnhut archives the only reference to Wesley's visit is the non-committal note (*Gemein-Diarium*, 1738, R.6.A.b.13): 'Aug. the 12th (new style) the English clergyman Westley arrived here and with him a wig-maker from England. They stayed here a time.' The previously related journey—ibid. pp. 14–19.

[1] On Johann Christian Adolf von Hermsdorf, born 4th February 1709, in Dahme in Saxony (now Brandenburg), died 18th November 1767, at Herrnhut, the best source is the handwritten account of his life in the archives of the United Brethren at Herrnhut, R.22.No.49, 23. All his life Hermsdorf was closely connec-ted with the Brethren. At nine years of age he went to the nobles' school at the Halle Orphan-House, but had to leave three years later because of bad health. He stayed with his mother, who was a widow living in Dresden. It was there that he became acquainted with Count von Zinzendorf, who took him as his page. As such he took part in the wedding between the Count and Erdmuth Dorothea von Reuss in Ebersdorf in 1732. Next he entered the Herrnhut establishment for young noblemen, and accompanied the Count on important journeys, in 1723 to Bohemia and in 1726 to Moravia, where Zinzendorf in vain asked the Bishop of Olmütz, Cardinal Schrattenbach, to discontinue the counter-reformation measures against the Moravian Brethren. In 1727 he went with the Count to German Pietist courts, such as Saalfeld, Bayreuth and others. In 1725 he went with Friedrich von Watteville to Paris and received the blessing of Cardinal Noailles. For a brief period he belonged to the cadet corps in Dresden and was to have received a position in Poland, which at that time was united with the electorate of Saxony, but he went back to Count Zinzendorf. On 15th November 1734 he married Carolina Regina, the only daughter of the Stralsund merchant, Abraham Ehren-fried Richter, who had taken Zinzendorf into his house in 1734 ostensibly as tutor, in order to supply him with theological recognition. From 1735 to 1737 Hermsdorf was in Georgia, where he became ill and often cried out ardently on his sick-bed: 'The Brethren, the Brethren!' In 1737 he returned to Herrnhut and was later in Marienborn, Barby, and again Herrnhut. Not until 1741 was he accepted into the Herrnhut Community. Just as he apparently had not been able easily to adapt himself during his youth to the order of the Brethren, so the more strongly he held to it in his riper years, and 'often stuck to the liturgy for hours at a stretch'. According to Zinzendorf's ideal and method this meant the daily inti-mate association with Jesus in prayer, conversation and intercourse, which the Count called 'the liturgical existence' (cf. Otto Uttendörfer, *Zinzendorfs religiöse Grundgedanken*, pp. 114ff; *Zinzendorfs christliches Lebensideal*, pp. 184ff). He stressed that this should proceed quite naturally and not have anything rigid or cramped about it. Hermsdorf's biography also makes the expression 'liturgical dying' understandable: it means an easy, happy, confident departure (on 'litur-gical dying', cf. Wilhelm Bettermann, *Theologie und Sprache bei Zinzendorf*, pp. 135ff). Zinzendorf repeatedly became irritated with Hermsdorf. He regretted his diffidence at committing himself. Cf. Hermsdorf to Zinzendorf, 12th January 1732, in the Herrnhut archives, R.20.B. No.6.b.B; Zinzendorf to Hermsdorf, n.d., ibid. R.6.A.No.29. Especially significant for their relationship is Zinzendorf's letter to him written on 19th August 1735, in which he gives him directions about his going to Georgia (ibid. R.14.A.6.c.4): 'My dear Hermsdorf, whom I have most affectionately loved these many years! I have nothing to say about his reso-lution to go to Georgia. It is his affair, and I only desire that he should rid his

up to services and conversations. Wesley got a true picture of the rich liturgical life of the Brethren. On one occasion a love-feast of the married men took place, which was a contemporary repetition of the early Christian Agape meal. He was present at many musical services and took part in a Bible Conference, led by Polykarp Müller, a former headmaster of a school in Zittau, and at this a portion of Scripture was read in the original. He gives an accurate description in his *Journal* of the order of the liturgy in the nearby church at Berthelsdorf, which was conducted by Johann Andreas Rothe, and he does not forget to mention even the two large candles burning on the altar nor the style of gown worn by the minister. He relates with equal exactness how a child was buried in Herrnhut, and in so doing describes the arrangement and division of the burial-ground. Finally, he gives an account of the unmarried men's prayer-procession, which they carried out on Sundays after the evening service. They went around the town with musical instruments and sang hymns of praise to God. Finally they formed a circle on a little hill and joined together in prayer. Wesley was also present at meetings of private bands, and so carried out his intention of letting himself be helped by those who were strong in faith, which was the real purpose of such gatherings.[2] He was even more deeply affected by the conversations he had, and this was particularly true of the sermons he heard from Christian David.

mind of all chimeras which arouse in him doubt and fear. Do not let Satan blind you! He can do nothing but alarm you. . . . Now I must let him have a few grateful memories, and request my dear Hermsdorf that he would allow them to take root. I presume that he is a tender object of grace and that the Saviour desires to make him His servant. For this reason He has specially led him, and whenever he has let himself be led good has resulted. But I add this. If he is to become something through Him he must no longer *will to be*. If he is to become my Resident in Georgia he must first be the servant of all, as I am, and not in an affected way or in merely external eye-service, but truly from the heart. When there is not much to do but prepare and cultivate the land he must quietly let the years pass, and not try to regulate, command or contrive, and at least allow himself to see and discuss with those people whose business and practice makes them understand better than he. . . . His position as Resident must be won by his *merita*; until then he must remain among the Brethren at my expense. . . .' Curnock's remark, in Journal, II.20, note 1, that he accompanied the Salzburgers to Georgia is an error. One so committed and devoted to Herrnhut and its ways would have reacted violently against the transport of the Halle brethren.

[2] On this, cf. esp. Christian David, *Beschreibung und zuverlässige Nachricht von Heerrnhut* (1735), pp. 33–4, and August Gottlieb Spangenberg, op. cit. (see p. 151, note 9), p. 50, para. 55: 'It is not in conformity with our principles that sins must be confessed in the small groups which twelve years ago came to be known as bands . . . rather they are intended for friends and neighbours to grow and increase amongst themselves in love and trust by spiritual conversation.'

He had intimate talks with eleven members of the community,[3] namely, Christian David, Michael Linner, David Nitschmann, Albin Theodor Feder, Augustin Neisser, Wenzel Neisser, Hans Neisser, Zacharias Neisser, David Schneider, Christoph Demuth, and Arvid Gradin. As the majority of these were laymen, the conversations probably took place in German; only in the case of the Swedish theologian Gradin does Latin seem to have been used to help Wesley.[4] He recorded all the talks with very great care, so that they can easily be reconstructed. They all took a very similar form, and were auto-biographical testimonies in which the main point was the way in which faith arose. In each case the experience of salvation was central. Michael Linner said that his spiritual history began sixteen years before,[5] and it was due to the fact that he took the New Testament quite seriously. He found that it required perfection, but he acknowledged with grief that he was far from it. He asked the best authorities he knew how to resolve this difficulty, but their answer that perfection was only attainable by the first Christians gave him no satisfaction. He held to the Bible, but heard from its pages only condemnation, which drove him into a state of despair. Suddenly there came to him the message of John 3[16]: 'God so loved the world, that He gave His only-begotten Son, to the end that all who believe in Him should not perish, but have everlasting life.' He asked: 'All? Then I am one. Then He is given for me.' But he had not yet obtained the full assurance of faith, and had to wait more than two years for it. Then fear and doubt disappeared. From his experience, and Wesley followed him in this point, he concluded that God deals differently with different people. Usually He grants assurance immediately after forgiveness of sins itself, sometimes, however, He allows a certain time to elapse in between. Linner's point of view in this instance agreed exactly with Zinzendorf's in Marienborn, and must have served to confirm it for Wesley. The statement of the student Albin Theodor Feder was along the same lines.[6]

David Nitschmann's struggle for faith took a more complicated course and was consequently more significant.[7] He too was brought into a state of despair through the law of God with its sentence of

---

[3] So far as I can see these reports have not yet been taken into account with reference to the history of the Moravian Brethren. They would supplement the brief accounts of Joseph Theodor Müller in *Zeitschr.f.Brüdergesch.*, VI.190ff, and *Geschichte der Böhmischen Brüder*, III.327ff, 368ff.

[4] *Journal*, II.49 ends the conversation with Gradin with a detailed account of the assurance of faith in Latin.   [5] Ibid. pp. 36–7.

[6] Ibid. p. 40.   [7] Ibid. pp. 37–40.

judgement. But this was not all. He argued that this was all very well if God existed, but what if there were no God? How could he know there was? In this way he was seized by the sickness of the age, the atheism which first overtook August Hermann Francke in 1687, the year of his conversion.[8] Then he heard the Berthelsdorf minister Johann Andreas Rothe say in a sermon that when you cannot believe you should merely suppose the assertions of the Bible were true. This idea of an hypothetical, heuristic faith helped Nitschmann further. Then another kind of doubt came upon him. He believed in God but not in Christ. But St Paul's classic word about reconciliation came to his aid: 'God was in Christ, reconciling the world to Himself' (2 Corinthians 5[19]). From this he concluded that God and Christ were one and the same. Straightway the beginning of St John's gospel came into his mind: 'The Word was with God, and the Word was God. And the Word was made flesh, and dwelt among us.' This filled him with great joy, but it did not continue for long. He was then suddenly thrown into disquiet by the fact that though he believed Christ was the Saviour of the world he had not laid hold of Him as his own Saviour. He was tortured in mind for a long period, and the relief which he experienced from time to time could not deceive him about his spiritual emptiness. In Arndt's *True Christianity* he read the momentous sentence: 'If all the sins of men upon earth were joined in one man, the blood of Christ was sufficient to cleanse that man from all sin.' Yet the comfort this brought also lasted only a short time: sadness and unbelief held him prisoner. He would have become impatient, but then he thought on the fact that the Saviour knew best, and that He would not allow the trouble to last so long if He did not see that it was good for him. At this point the decisive, lasting change came. He gave himself into the Saviour's hands, and he knew that he was gathered into the number of the reconciled children of God.

Augustin Neisser described in the clearest way Luther's doctrine of justification in its pure form.[9] He said that from childhood he had lived a 'good life', but that it was just this which had stood in the way of his coming to Christ, since he had trusted in his own good works and in the Church's means of grace. When he recognized the deep sinfulness of his heart and lost all trust in himself and fled naked to his

---

[8] Francke, *Anfang und Fortgang meiner Bekehrung* (1692), in Leopold Cordier, *Der junge August Hermann Francke*, pp. 31ff.
[9] *Journal*, II.40–1.

Saviour, his soul found rest in the assurance that his sins were forgiven. Yet he was not able to tell the day or the hour when he first received full assurance. He had not possessed it from the beginning, nor had it been given him in a moment, but rather it grew up in him by degrees. But from the time when it had fully come he had not lost it again.

Wenzel Neisser described his earlier condition as one which combined two positions.[1] As a good Lutheran he knew that he could only be saved by the death of Jesus Christ, yet alongside this he fell back upon his own righteousness as a second prop. Through the great number of sects he was tempted to abandon any form of Christian belief for atheism. Then one day it pleased God to grant him the assurance that Jesus Christ was also his personal Saviour, and since then he had not doubted any more.

Hans Neisser, Augustin's brother, gave an account of himself which was almost the same.[2] He also had built upon Christ and his own righteousness at the same time, but he deceived himself about himself because he hid his own part from himself and imagined that he was trusting only in Christ. When on one occasion he was walking in the wood near Herrnhut and thinking about himself, he saw through his self-delusion and recognized the depth of the misery of his sins. Despair laid hold of him, but suddenly he saw a vision of the Lamb of God taking away his sins. Since then he possessed the peace of the assurance of salvation without fear or doubt.

Zacharias Neisser had experienced a double awakening.[3] The first occurred while he was still in Moravia through the preaching of a distinguished representative of the later Pietism of the Halle type, Pastor Johann Adam Steinmetz in Teschen.[4] While receiving the Lord's Supper the assurance was given him that Jesus Christ died for him, but he retained it for only eighteen months. Later he came to Herrnhut and was greatly shocked by a sermon of Count Zinzendorf on the nature of sanctification. As he had never experienced what the Count described, he was terrified and asked his cousin Wenzel Neisser about it. On the latter's advice he buried himself in chapters 3, 4 and 5 of the Epistle to the Romans and read them with new eyes. They made him aware of the fact that God justifies the ungodly. During the singing of the Lutheran Confessional hymn in the church

---

[1] *Journal*, II.41–2.   2 Ibid. pp. 42–3.   [3] Ibid. pp. 43–4.
[4] On him, who finally as follower of Joachim Just Breithaupt became 'abbot' of the educational establishment in Klosterbergen, near Magdeburg, cf. L. Renner, *Lebensbilder aus der Pietistenzeit*, pp. 31–140.

of them.[7] The book had so impressed him that he asked the book-seller whether what it said were really true or whether it were not a picture of an ideal Christian community, something in the nature of a Utopian fiction in the style of Thomas More. When he was assured of the truth of the account his supreme desire was to see for himself how things were. As his pupil's father wished his son to get to know the world, Gradin combined educational travel with his own design and went with the young man to Central and Western Europe for two years. They spent a year at various places in Germany, and then went on to Holland and Paris. They spent the second year there and on the return journey Gradin left his pupil at Leipzig with his elder brother, who was travelling from Italy on his way back to Sweden. Gradin himself went to Herrnhut. He even declined the attractive offer of a theological professorship at Uppsala. He had now been staying for three months in the place he had so much wished to see, and his comment on it was: 'Here I was in another world.' He found everyone there building on the same foundation, and his only wish was to become inwardly and outwardly cleansed from all sin by the blood of Christ. Although he did not agree with the Brethren in all points of doctrine, he waived these aside and singly pursued reconciliation through Christ. On 22nd May he had been able to think of nothing but the words, 'He that believeth hath everlasting life' (John 3^{36}). For five days this truth had been realized in him through an abiding joy and a deep inward peace, yet he was afraid of deceiving himself. On 28th May he was strongly impressed with the words of Jesus, 'If ye, being evil, know how to give good gifts to your children, how much more shall your heavenly Father give the Holy Ghost to them that ask him?' (Luke 11^{13}). This drove him to pray with strong desire for the witness of the Holy Spirit. The next day he received this, and he then had the full assurance of faith. His storm-tossed heart had found rest in the blood of Christ, the troubled sea was calmed, peace and serenity prevailed. An unshakable confidence in God and assurance of grace had taken possession of his heart.

Wesley must have felt that in this account there was much which was directly akin to his own case. Even the dates of Gradin's experience in Herrnhut recalled his own conversion in London. Yet it was not precisely the same. While both men had been deeply impressed by their first contact with the Brethren, Wesley through people and

---

[7] *Journal*, II.47–8. Gradin as the pupil of Zinzendorf has recently been treated by Gösta Hök, *Zinzendorfs Begriff der Religion*, pp. 147ff.

at Berthelsdorf, and in particular at the second verse, 'We b(
also in Jesus Christ', he saw Jesus Christ clearly as the Saviour.
then he had had continual fellowship with Him, characterize
thankfulness, quiet joy, and love.

David Schneider had also been inwardly gripped through S
metz, whose preaching had aroused in him the conviction of
His great temptation was drunkenness, but it was the means o
recognizing increasingly the meaning of sin both inwardly and i
outward form. Gradually he received the assurance that it was
given him, although he was unable to name any definite mor
when this happened. While still in Moravia he held meetings
his brethren, and this caused him to be brought before the Catl
authorities and eventually put into prison. Finally he was condem
to the galleys with David Nitschmann, but escaped with him
went to Sorau in Silesia, where he taught the children in the Orph
house. Many of the brethren followed him there. One day t
went to Herrnhut, having being urged to do so by Christian Da
At first Schneider was very unhappy there, because he found
proper work. Accordingly the relationship between him and the ot
brethren was not good, and he cut himself off from them. Sin, m
likely his taste for drink, got hold of him. Then the Brethren, w
meanwhile had turned from him, as a result of the lot decided
admit him to the Lord's Supper. In this way peace entered his he
and he received the assurance that he was fully reconciled with G
through the blood of Jesus Christ.

Christoph Demuth related what had happened to him in t
counter-reformation movement against the Moravians.[6] He h
been deceived into subscribing to a statement in which he abjur(
the evangelical faith. Owing to untoward circumstances his fir
attempt at flight miscarried, but the second was successful. Durir
the long journey from Moravia to Herrnhut God gave him the assu
ance that his sins were forgiven.

Arvid Gradin, a learned theologian, who had a religious upbring
ing as a child in Dalecarlia, had subsequently entered the world (
politics and society as domestic tutor of a Swedish Secretary of Stat(
and was won over to the Brethren through reading a printed accoun

[5] *Journal*, II.44–5; cf. also '*Erzählungen der mährischen Exulanten in Herrnhu
von ihrer Herkunft*' related by Joseph Theodor Müller, *Zeitschr.f.Brüdergesch*
VI.(1912).186–95; also briefly mentioned by the same in *Gesch. der Böhm
Brüder*, III.(1931).327ff.
[6] *Journal*, II.46–7.

Gradin by a book, yet Gradin, unlike Wesley, did not come to it through an experience of the law. Hence the message of justifying faith did not presume this, nor did it require a decisive breach with the past. On the other hand high society and its particular codes of behaviour had never been any temptation to Wesley. As might be expected, Gradin afterwards became the leading figure amongst the Swedish Herrnhuters.

But by far the most important of all the personal biographies was that of Christian David.[8] This carpenter, who came to Herrnhut as leader of the religious refugees, had cut down the first trees in the wood and in this way laid the foundation of the settlement. He was accordingly better qualified than anybody to give an account of the growth of the community from its first association with the Moravians. His own life previous to that time had been remarkable and significant. Born in Senftleben in Moravia on 31st December 1690, he was brought up a Catholic but from an early age had begun to reflect independently on religious questions. He was upset when somebody declared that the pope was Antichrist, and when afterwards he read polemical Lutheran books he was persuaded of the falsity of the Catholic position, but not that the Lutherans were right. He could not understand what they meant by justification by faith, by faith alone, by faith without works. Also, as one brought up in the atmosphere of a fanatical devotion to the Virgin, he did not like the continual mention of the name of Jesus Christ. He asked, how can Jesus be the Son of God? This went to such lengths that he even experienced an aversion to the name of Jesus. During his wanderings as a travelling workman he fell into the company of some Jews, and their objections against the New Testament plunged him into fresh doubts. He read the Old Testament for himself to see whether the promises contained in it were fulfilled. He was forced to admit that they were, and so the difficulty he had felt about salvation through Jesus Christ was removed. In this way controversy with the Jews led him to recognize the truth of the Lutheran Christo-centric position, but then a new problem arose. Are the promises of the New Testa-

[8] *Journal*, II.26ff; cf. also Theodor Bechler, *Christian David*, and v. Koenneritz-Appel, *Christian David, ein munterer Zeuge*. A scholarly biography of this man, based upon the handwritten material in the archives of the United Brethren at Herrnhut, is urgently needed. David's own account of his life, which he gave to Wesley, in relation to David has been treated for the first time in Otto Uttendörfer, *Zinzendorf und die Mystik*, pp. 161–2, but in accordance with the subject of the book only with reference to the meaning of mysticism in the life of David and the early community of the Brethren.

ment fulfilled? This too he had to recognize, and this proved to him the divine origin of Scripture. Yet his soul was still not at peace, which was bound to be the case, because he had not yet openly renounced the Roman Catholic faith. This he did in Berlin, where he went over to the Lutherans. He now endeavoured to lead a strict life, to struggle vigorously against sin, yet he had to come to the distressing conclusion that his efforts were without success. One day he decided to become a soldier, hoping to get more time for prayer and reading. He had with him a New Testament and a hymn-book, but one day both books were stolen from him, which almost broke his heart. All that he had hoped for from his life as a soldier was bound up with them, and after six months he returned to his trade. He came to Görlitz and for almost six months was kept in bed there by illness. He was visited each day by Zinzendorf's friend, Pastor Johann Christoph Schwedler, from nearby Niederwiesa, a theologian and an original type of man, who is said to have preached sometimes on a Sunday for ten hours![9] Through him David came to have faith. Like Wesley on 24th May 1738 there was given him the certain conviction that God had forgiven him directly his own sins. Nevertheless he was still in the grip of the Pietist misconception that he ought to be completely finished with sin in the sense that he should feel nothing more of it. He forgot that it was only its dominion which was to be broken, and not that temptations were abolished. Similarly he was not clear that justification could be separated from the full assurance of faith. These were the two questions which had given Wesley so much trouble. Later, evidently under Zinzendorf's guidance, the true position was made clear to David, who tried to give it scriptural basis from the Last Discourse in St John's Gospel. Shortly before His departure Jesus had said to the disciples, 'Ye are clean', but they were not assured of it until many days later, when they received the Holy Spirit. As soon as he had recovered from his illness, Christian David set out for his home in Moravia in order to preach Christ there in accordance with his new-found understanding. He returned thence to Görlitz, where he stayed for five years. On two occasions he went to Moravia, and each time he won over more people who believed as a result of his preaching, and desired to follow him when he was in a position to offer them a home. One day,

---

[9] Cf. the eloquent and perceptive characterization of him by Zinzendorf, Περὶ Ἑαυτοῦ d.i. Naturelle Reflexiones über allerhand Materien (1746) Anhang Reael Beylagen, pp. 12-13.

through the pastor Johann Andreas Rothe, who himself had been called to the church at Berthelsdorf from Görlitz, he was brought to the notice of Count Zinzendorf and received an invitation to settle on the Count's estate near Berthelsdorf with as many of his friends as he could bring with him. He returned to Moravia with this good news, but at first he could only persuade ten of his fellow-countrymen to come, followed by ten more the next year. From these small, unobtrusive beginnings Herrnhut came into being. Christian David then told Wesley, who was eager to hear every scrap of information, about the first doctrinal controversies at Herrnhut which broke out over the question of predestination, through the Calvinist steward Johann Georg Heitz from Zürich. The belief that they were amongst the reprobate had thrown many of the settlers into a state of dejection, and they attributed the distresses and lack of success which had come to them to God's hatred of them. They feared that their whole enterprise would fail. It is possible that this narrative was partly responsible for Wesley's decided antagonism to the idea of predestination.

The young Count Zinzendorf then sent David to Johann Adam Steinmetz at Teschen, and David was persuaded by him that Jesus Christ had died for all men. Further he told Wesley about the trials which the Moravian Brethren endured in the Austrian Counter-Reformation. When the possibility of a peaceful life opened out before him through Zinzendorf and the secret emigration to Herrnhut began, an official declaration about their faith was presented by those who escaped to the Emperor on 12th August 1729. Wesley was told about this also by David and included it in his *Journal*, together with the statement about their history made on 24th January 1732.[1]

David then showed Wesley the different stages through which the Brethren had passed in their understanding of the meaning of faith. After a time a great remissness of behaviour had crept in, because only faith was stressed, and holiness and good works were forgotten. This was an abuse of the message 'Christ for us', which was then combated by stressing more than ever before the 'Christ in us', in the manner of mystical spirituality and Pietism. Everyone was asked: 'Is Christ formed in you? Have you a new heart? Is the whole body of sin destroyed in you? Are you fully assured, beyond all doubt

[1] *Journal*, II.32ff; on this, cf. Joseph Theodor Müller, *Geschichte der Böhmischen Brüder*, III.(1931).372–3. Of the German originals so far as I know only the first has been printed in Christian David, *Beschreibung und zuverlässige Nachricht von Herrnhut* (1735), 98ff.

and fear, that you are a child of God? In what manner, and at what moment, did you receive that full assurance?' Only those who could give satisfactory replies were recognized as true believers and were admitted to the Lord's Supper.

This was the predominant belief when David went to Greenland in 1733, where from correspondence with Hans Egede, a Danish pastor, he was further taught that in justification, while Christ-in-us and Christ-for-us belong together, yet Christ-for-us ought to be chiefly stressed, since everything depends upon it. In this way David came to see that the spiritualistic-pietistic emphasis upon feeling was fundamentally only another form of justification of self through works. He saw clearly that justification as an act of God is quite different from a person's experience. Now for the first time he received full assurance of salvation, and henceforth in all his trials he relied upon the fact that Jesus had done everything for him. All the points on which hitherto he had placed so much importance, action and feeling, long repentance and due preparation for believing, bitter sorrow for sin, and deep contrition of heart, he now laid on one side as not essential to justification. He actually went so far as to maintain that a sinner in the midst of his sin could probably receive the free grace of God, provided it were rightly preached, before one who insists on preparation.

David's point in this instance was of very great significance, both formally and in actuality. He had attained to insights which in some ways went farther than Luther's understanding of repentance in the 95 Theses, where the stress, thought of in the context of the medieval sacrament of penance, was entirely on repentance and self-accusation,[2] whereas in David's case it was completely on free grace.

When David returned from Greenland to Herrnhut he found it difficult to reconcile the Brethren to these newly discovered truths, but he was successful in the end. Since then, he assured Wesley, 'Christ given for us' has been consistently and vigorously proclaimed at Herrnhut in the strong conviction that as a result Christ will surely be formed within us. This preaching had always been accompanied with power and divine blessing. It had made the Brethren willing to submit themselves in all things with gladness to God's appointments.

It is scarcely too much to say that in the course of a few days these personal stories took John Wesley completely by storm. They served to clarify and intensify the formal aspects of justification and faith,

[2] *WA*, I.233–4.

the dogmatic structure of both receiving equal emphasis alongside their individual, personal character and practical effectiveness. They presented a complete account of the different interpretations which had been given to these doctrines in the history of Christian thought, and this in no theoretical way, for every sentence had been verified by painful or joyful experience. Each of the many witnesses provided an answer to some aspect of the problems which had concerned Wesley for over six months. It is quite understandable why he should feel the full force of this united testimony to justification. Since he saw them all passing before him in rapid succession as in a kaleidoscope, he must have been more impressed by their unity than by their diversity. Christian David's story both heightened and deepened the personal aspect because he represented the question of justification as the chief factor in the spiritual history of Herrnhut. For this reason Wesley owed more to him than to anyone else, with the sole exception of Peter Böhler. The four sermons which he heard David preach only strengthened his obligation.[3] On each occasion the subject was one which John Wesley would have wished him to take.[4] The account Wesley gives of them is so full that a clear and detailed impression emerges. The texts themselves are significant: Matthew 5^3, Romans 7^{21}–8^1, John 15^3, 2 Corinthians 5^{18-20}. They penetrate into the very heart of the Christian message. In the first three sermons Christian David spoke about those who are weak in faith, of those who know about forgiveness but do not yet have the Holy Spirit constantly dwelling in their hearts, for whom accordingly regeneration has not yet been brought to completion. He stressed the fact that they have long been God's children and heirs of the promise, that therefore grace precedes the human experience of it not only objectively, but also in time. Even a weak faith, threatened and deeply shaken by temptations and doubts, is still faith, as can be seen in the case of the disciples between Good Friday and Pentecost.[5]

The fourth sermon on the ground of faith, based on 2 Corinthians 5^{18-20}, made a deep impression on Wesley, like all the critical events in his life. Christian David applied himself to the question whether a man could or should prepare himself, for example by remorse, for justification. He rejected absolutely all human preparation, since repentance is the work of God Himself. There is no connexion between God and the ungodly. It must be completely miraculous: God Himself bridges the gulf. Sin is the only thing which absolutely

[3] *Journal*, II.25ff. [4] Ibid. p. 25. [5] Ibid. p. 26.

divides man from God. Sin is also the only thing which unites man to God. The daring with which these two statements are set alongside each other is reminiscent of Luther.[6] The only thing for a man to do with his sin is to hasten in all his ungodliness to God Himself, who justifies us through Christ.[7] This sermon is wholly Lutheran in character. All activity in justification lies with God;[8] God's sovereignty is unconditionally maintained.[9] A deep understanding of sin, which is diagnosed in all its seriousness as an assault upon God, makes justification appear in the light of an unheard-of miracle, whereas from justification also a new-creating power proceeds.

Thus the association with this man meant for Wesley a second important point of contact with the central ideas of Luther. The various strands which had come together in the conversion-experience were now separately laid out. The questions were put with extreme clarity and answered with similar decisiveness. Every obscure point was removed and every evasion exposed. Christian David had set free the hidden impulse which had brought Wesley to the point of conversion.

As an Anglican churchman, a practical Englishman, and one fanatically devoted to a methodical way of life, Wesley did not miss the opportunity of describing the ecclesiastical discipline at Herrnhut, and of submitting it to a detailed examination.[1] The basis of this he saw to be the officers of the Church, the dividing of the people, and the conferences. He was struck by the thorough way in which the officers were arranged. Supreme over the whole community was an Eldest: likewise there was one over each of the divisions, which were known as 'classes'. The community had four teachers, a number of deacons, eleven overseers or censors, eleven monitors, eleven almoners, and seven attenders on the sick. It was divided into five male and five female classes, three in each case consisting of the children, who were placed in them according to their ages. This arrangement showed a remarkable understanding of the minds of children, and an awareness of their capacity for learning and ability to adapt themselves, as well as of the different lengths of time they took to master spiritual truths. This was the way in which Herrnhut played its particular part in the new contribution which Pietism was making to the critical examination and treatment of human nature.

---

[6] *WA*, III.429, 432, 437, IV.34, from the lectures on the Psalms and the Epistle to the Romans, ed. Ficker, II.1, *magnificare peccatum*.
[7] *Journal*, II.27.   [8] *WA*, VI.520, *De captivitate Babylonica*.
[9] Cf. Paul Althaus, op. cit. (see p. 260, note 4).   [1] *Journal*, II.49ff.

The other four classes were for the single men, the single women, the married men, and the married women. Then there were about ninety bands, which met at least twice, and most of them three times, a week. The conferences of the officers each met once a week, and in addition an open meeting for strangers was held each week, in which anyone could take part and bring forward questions. In the schools they taught reading, writing, arithmetic, Latin, Greek, Hebrew, French, English, history, and geography. In this strong emphasis on technical studies and the great variety of subjects, which anticipated modern types of schools, Herrnhut made its own contribution to the reorganization which Pietism was effecting in school affairs, and which the Halle Orphan-house had already achieved on so large a scale.[2] As a teacher Wesley was also particularly interested in the day's programme in the Orphan-house. This lasted from five in the morning until eight in the evening for the smaller children, and until ten for the bigger ones. He was especially impressed with the fact that the children went for a walk in the open air three times a day: between eleven and twelve in the morning, after dinner until one, and from seven to eight in the evening. In the school which he later organized at Kingswood he drew on the experience of the Herrnhut Brethren.

He then turned to the arrangement of worship, the series of services. Every morning at eight there was a singing-meeting and exposition of Scripture, and again at eight in the evening. In the morning this included a short prayer, but in the evening every one prayed on his own. He could not refrain from finding fault with this individual silent prayer, which lasted for a quarter of an hour. The evening singing-meeting closed with the kiss of peace. On Sunday morning they met at six o'clock for service, and at nine they took part in public worship at Berthelsdorf. At one the Eldest gave separate exhortations to all the members of the community, which was divided into fourteen classes for this purpose, four being added to the existing ten. Each class was occupied in this way for about a quarter of an hour. At four, evening service at Berthelsdorf began, at eight the usual evening service at Herrnhut, followed by the aforementioned procession of the young men. The Lord's Supper was administered on the first Saturday in the month, and in connexion with this the Eldest spent from ten in the morning until two in the afternoon speaking with each communicant personally about his spiritual state. Dinner

[2] Cf. Gustav Kramer, *August Hermann Francke, Ein Lebensbild*, II.411ff.

was at two, after which the members of the community washed each other's feet, and this was followed by singing and praying. About ten in the evening they received the Sacrament without any particular ceremony, and remained together in silence until midnight. The second Saturday in the month was a solemn prayer-day for the children, the third was the Community Day; on the fourth the great monthly conferences of all the officers of the community were held.

The overwhelming impression produced by this general survey is of the number of observances which were prescribed. The question which naturally arises is how these people found time for their daily work and family life or for recreation in the home or in the country? The whole of life, particularly in its private aspects, was occupied with God and the promotion of the fellowship which the Brethren had in Jesus Christ. All other concerns receded until they completely disappeared. Here was the logical realization of Zinzendorf's theological principle that it is the Saviour who is also the Creator.

John Wesley was immersed in the atmosphere of this little world for two weeks. All that happened was confined within this very narrow area, and he was surrounded with it everywhere. The impression he gained, to an extent even greater than in all the other places where he had seen the Herrnhut type of life, was that he was amongst the early Christians. This comes out in a striking way in the two letters he wrote to England while he was there.[3] For a long time his language had included many biblical expressions, and time and again in letters and entries in his *Journal* he directly transcribed sentences or phrases from the Greek New Testament. But on this occasion the whole thing was modelled on the style of St Paul's letters, both in construction and in the arrangement of the material. Probably this was done quite unconsciously. Both letters were written on the same day. In the first, which he wrote to his brother Charles, he began by thanking God for having brought him to Herrnhut. There followed greetings and exhortations to the friends in Oxford and London—the groups brought into being by Peter Böhler—and he urges them to pursue the Gospel with all seriousness. He ended by commending them to God and with a request for their prayers. In the second letter, written to his friend James Hutton, the first part was devoted to the condition of the Christian lives of the brethren. Wesley expressed the hope that they stand steadfast in grace and carry on zealously

---

[3] *Letters*, I.252–3, Herrnhut, 4th August 1738, to Charles; pp. 253–4, on the same day, to James Hutton.

with their declaration of God's goodness and their witness to their Lord. He reminded them of the greatness and glory of the promises which attach to martyrdom. In the second part he described the Herrnhut community in glowing and thankful language. The closing section was made up of exhortations to humility, seriousness, and watchfulness—he had written in precisely the same terms to Charles —and ended with a benediction and a request for their prayers.

This was the only occasion on which he employed this stereotyped style. He gave his brother to understand that he would give him a full account on his return, but he opened his heart to Hutton. Herrnhut was for him a cloud of witnesses to the great truths of God. Now he knows, nay, sees daily with his own eyes and really understands, that God waxeth not old, that His arm is not shortened. It is as true of Christianity as of its Author, that it is the same yesterday, today, and for ever; the same gifts are still given to men, the same holiness and happiness, the same freedom from sin, the same peace and joy in the Holy Ghost. All the brethren testify with one accord that there is only one way of attaining to a fellowship in these great and precious promises, namely faith in Jesus Christ. Jesus Christ has loved all men and given Himself for them; He has borne their sins in His own body to the tree. Whosoever seeks this finds, if only he seeks humbly, earnestly, and perseveringly. He must absolutely renounce his own righteousness and his own works, and come to Jesus Christ poor and miserable and naked.

The concluding sentences immediately call to mind some expressions of Zinzendorf.[4] In the course of his visit Wesley strikingly comprehended the heart of the evangelical doctrine as it was proclaimed in Herrnhut. Although he was open to every impression he certainly did not stop at externals, and he saw the underlying unity in everything—an indication of the convincing form the Brethren had been able to give to the fact of reconciliation and the doctrine of justification. One other fact was also significant. Count Zinzendorf had been away from the organization he had created for more than two years, but apparently this had not produced any serious consequences; on the contrary it showed that the community as a whole was built upon sound foundations. If need be it could get on without the personal presence of its leader, and the dispassionate and critical Wesley derived his impressions not from him but from the

---

[4] Cf. esp. his hymn, *'Christi Blut und Gerechtigkeit'* ('Jesu, Thy blood and righteousness').

community. This was in line with tendencies which had shown themselves previously in his life. It had always been groups from which he had gained benefits; individual people influenced him usually only as representatives of such groups. His parents' home, his boarding-school at Charterhouse in London, the life of an English university, centred in a particular college, had all contributed to his training, but above all there had been the circle of Oxford Methodists, the Herrnhuters and the Salzburgers in Georgia, Peter Böhler's student fellowship in Oxford, and the Religious Societies in London, remodelled by Böhler into 'bands' in the manner of Herrnhut.

Yet had he really succumbed to the Herrnhuters and was he really one of them? When he left on 14th August he confessed that he would gladly spend his life there, but that God had directed him to another part of His vineyard. This wish was not merely occasioned by his sense of personal gratitude and indebtedness, for he immediately coupled with it the larger hope that the Christianity which he had found there might cover the whole earth with the vastness and irresistible force of the waves of the sea. He viewed Herrnhut in the light of a world-wide mission.[5]

But it was precisely because he had apprehended the root of the situation that he was aware that he was not committed to every feature. Hence he was able to raise queries. At the very beginning of the letter to Charles there is a surprising wish, and this impression is strengthened when it is compared with the earlier enthusiastic account of Marienborn. On that occasion John Wesley had nothing but praise for the Brethren, but now he hoped that God would enable him thoroughly to prove all things and to call no man master. In faith, practice, and discipline, he desires to hold fast only that which is good.[6] In addition to this general principle he could also bring forward certain individual points. In particular, as an Anglican trained in the liturgical tradition, he was concerned about prayer. With Herrnhut in mind he warned James Hutton and his group against neglecting vocal prayer under the pretext of mental prayer, a practice he had already criticized in the case of the mystics.[7] Soon

[5] *Journal*, II.28: 'I would gladly have spent my life here; but my Master calling me to labour in another part of His vineyard, on Monday the 14th I was constrained to take my leave of this happy place. Oh when shall THIS Christianity cover the earth, as the "waters cover the sea"?'

[6] *Letters*, I.252: 'Oh that after I have proved all things, I may be enabled thoroughly δοκιμάζειν τά διαφέροντα, and calling no man master, in faith, practice, and discipline, to hold fast that which is good!'

[7] Ibid. p. 254.

after his return he wrote in London a letter to the Brethren in Marienborn and Herrnhut which he never actually sent.[8] In this he first expressed his joy over their faith, their love for the Redeemer, their meekness, temperance, chastity, and love for one another. Once again he made use of Pauline expressions. He mentioned with approval their deadness to the world and amongst their practical arrangements he particularly praised the conferences and bands, the methods of instructing children, and the care in pastoral oversight in general. But then with complete frankness he proposed a whole succession of questions and doubts which were in his mind, and they show with remarkable clarity the limits of Herrnhut's influence upon him, and demonstrate not merely his acuteness and integrity, but also his Anglican sense of churchmanship, his Puritan strictness, his unconditional regard for truth, and his comprehensive understanding of the Christian ethos. He reproaches the Brethren for completely neglecting joint fasting. He believes he detected a certain levity in their behaviour, a lack of seriousness. In a similar vein was the question as to whether they really made the most of their time or whether they were not guilty of the very thing which he had tried so earnestly to avoid since the days of his youth in Oxford—trifling conversation. It appeared to him that they were not always careful enough about the truth,[9] but in many cases used cunning, guile, and dissimulation. Is not the spirit of secrecy the spirit of their community? Are they not aware of a close and impenetrable temper? Do they not mix human prudence with divine wisdom? Wesley was not able to discover altogether amongst them that childlike openness and genuine frankness of the apostles. A final set of questions centred around their opinions of themselves, and it was introduced by the sentence which might be said to have become notorious, 'Is not the Count all in all? Are not the rest mere shadows, calling him Rabbi, almost implicitly both believing and obeying him? Do they not magnify their own Church too much and do they not believe that any who are not of it are not in gospel liberty?' This led on to the question which was really the most serious reproach of all, because it went to the heart of the matter: 'Do not the Brethren set limits to their love? Do they love their enemies, do they love wicked men as themselves?' Doubtless this list, haphazardly drawn up, contained some things which

[8] Ibid. pp. 257–8, London, September 1738. John Wesley published the letter in September 1741 after his breach with the Herrnhuters (*Journal*, II.496–7).
[9] On this, cf. the pertinent judgement by Gerhard Adolf Wauer, *Die Anfänge der Brüderkirche in England*, p. 95.

were unjust. All through his life Wesley was regarded as a man without a sense of reserve, and he was well aware of this. Yet he did perceive the dangers which resulted from such a close fellowship and from the cloister-like character of their whole enterprise. He may well have seen them all the more clearly because of the fact that to such a high degree he too was devoted to, and had been influenced by, a similar ideal. Behind this criticism of Herrnhut, and in sharp contrast to such an attitude, lies the great word he wrote to James Hervey on 20th March of the following year: 'I look upon all the world as my parish.' [1]

When Wesley left Herrnhut he was accompanied for about an hour on the way by several of the Brethren. The return journey, made mostly on foot, was entirely under the aegis of the Moravians. They came first to Neukirch in Upper Lusatia, and from there to Hauswalde the travellers were accompanied by a friend of the Brethren, Theodor Gottlob Manitius, the pastor of Hauswalde, who told them of the implacable hostility of both Lutherans and Catholics against the Herrnhuters. He himself had been forced to defend himself before the Consistory at Dresden on account of a little Christian society, because it was suspected of being tainted with the sect-spirit of Herrnhut. This time Wesley met Gotthilf August Francke in Halle; in spite of being generally regarded as haughty, he received Wesley in a very friendly manner. In Jena John Wesley visited the Pietist schools, which went back to Stolte, Buddeus, and Spangenberg. He noticed with approval that their teaching laid special emphasis upon the Bible and Luther's *Smaller Catechism*. Shortly after they had left Weimar they were met by Benjamin Ingham, who was then on his way to Herrnhut. This time they stayed only two days in Marienborn, since the Count was away. In Mayence a dispensation by Pope Clement XII that had only recently been posted up evoked Wesley's astonishment and reproof, and he transcribed it in his *Journal* as an indication of Roman Catholic superstition. He had no appreciation at all for the cathedral, which he described as a huge heap of irregular building, full of altars overloaded with silver and gold. In Herrendyk he stayed for only one night in the newly built Moravian house. In Rotterdam he was again the guest of Dr te Koker, and this time he visited the Synagogue. He was shocked

[1] *Letters*, I.286, 20th March 1739, to James Hervey: 'I look upon all the world as my parish; thus far I mean, that in whatever part of it I am I judge it meet, right, and my bounden duty to declare, unto all that are willing to hear, the glad tidings of salvation.'

by the Jewish service, which seemed to him a mockery of God, and which he thought was responsible for the spread of atheism amongst thinking Jews. Just before going on board the ship for England he tried to comfort an English woman school teacher who was in spiritual trouble. He preached on the boat, and so followed his inevitable custom of using every opportunity for evangelism and pastoral work. By 16th September he was once again in London.[2]

What had Wesley's conversion meant in his life up to this moment? He himself stressed its importance by prefacing the account of it in his *Journal* with an autobiographical review.[3] Although the facts mentioned in this are well known it is well to repeat them here because of the selection he gives and the light that is thrown upon them. He says that during the first ten years of his life he had not yet 'sinned away' the 'washing of the Holy Ghost' which he received in baptism, for the careful teaching of his parents' home led him to believe that he would be saved by outwardly obeying God's commandments. But he understood nothing about inward obedience or holiness. During the next six years, spent in London at Charterhouse, sin really began in his life, although not in a gross form. In the eyes of the world he was still a respectable young man. He based the hope of salvation upon three things: his moral superiority to others, his continuing inclination for religion, and his reading of the Bible, going to Church, and saying his prayers. This was not materially changed at the university, and although he kept up the outward forms of piety, he went on in his sins, in spite of knowing them to be such. Yet especially before and after Holy Communion, which he received three times a year, he struggled against them. If he were to say by what he hoped to be saved at this time, it could only be by those transient 'fits' which many divines had taught him to call 'repentance'.

When he was twenty-two he was ordained. At this time he was directed to Thomas à Kempis's *Imitation of Christ*, and this opened up a new world to him. It taught him that religion was seated in the heart and that God's law extended not only to our words and actions but to all our thoughts. In many things he found the book too strict, yet he derived 'sensible comfort' from it. A meeting at this time with

[2] *Journal*, II.56–63, 12th August to 16th September 1738. A slight discrepancy lies in the fact that according to *Journal*, II.28, Wesley left Herrnhut on 14th August, while *Journal*, II.56, says that he had already left it.
[3] In my opinion this is sufficient to contradict the opinions of Leger and Piette that Wesley's real 'conversion' took place in 1725 and not 1738.

a likeminded religious friend completely changed his way of life. He submitted his time to regular discipline, so that one or two hours each day were set apart for private devotion; he went each week to Communion, and he watched against all sin in word or deed. He now began his striving after inward holiness and to pray for it. It seemed to him that in this way he was a good Christian.

When he moved to Lincoln College as a Fellow, he regulated his life still more strictly and increased his efforts at self-discipline. Above all he came increasingly to see the importance of time. Law's book on *Christian Perfection* and his *Serious Call* convinced him more than ever of the greatness of the Divine Law. In 1730 he began visiting the prisons, the sick, and the poor in the town, and brought them what help he could, giving up for this purpose personal luxuries and even necessities. Following early Christian practice he began to fast on Wednesday and Friday, taking no food at all until three o'clock on these days. Whilst he let no opportunity of doing good pass by, he knew very well that the important thing was not the outward work but inward holiness. His aim was directed wholly at the image of God.

It was at this point that he became familiar with the world of the mystics, and this had the effect of strengthening the emphasis upon inward holiness. The end was now union with God, and the chief means towards it, inward 'mental' prayer,[4] yet these injunctions only served to confirm him, albeit in a refined form, in the sense of his own righteousness.

Then he left England and on the ship met the Herrnhuters, for whose way of faith he was still too learned and too wise. His life in Savannah seemed to him like an incessant battle with the law and against sin, in the terms of the seventh chapter of the Epistle to the Romans. Sometimes he conquered, but mostly he was overcome. Yet anticipations of the consolation of the Gospel already came to him. After his return home God sent Peter Böhler to him at the right moment, and he helped him by the evidence of faith and of the two fruits which he showed ought to attend it, namely dominion over sin and constant peace derived from a sense of forgiveness. This was all very strange to Wesley. Scripture and experience—strange, present experience—were to confirm the truth of Böhler's doctrine! When

---

[4] This shows something of the significance which Romanic mysticism had in the England of the eighteenth century.

this had actually come about, he renounced dependence upon his own righteousness and sought for the righteousness of faith which is a gift from God.

This review shows how he brought his whole situation under the Pauline antithesis of the righteousness established by self and that which is of faith, the antithesis between law and grace. He sees the whole of his spiritual development in terms of the leading ideas of the Epistle to the Romans, and this was the result of Böhler's teaching on justification and reconciliation, although not only of this. It was his experience in Georgia which prepared him for it. No doubt his view of the past was one-sided; he deliberately sought for examples of the basic antithesis and ascribed to mysticism in particular greater significance than it in fact had possessed for him. He failed to give due weight to that non-antithetical tendency which worked counter to the stress on law, such as Jeremy Taylor and Henry Scougal had formulated in their synthesis of the doctrines of creation and salvation, as well as to that natural walking in the presence of God such as he had learned about from Lopez and de Renty. He did not do justice to that particular form which the law had assumed for him in his efforts to return to primitive Christianity, nor to the educational and theological heritage of the whole Puritan tradition.

Yet more important than these quite understandable omissions was the fact that he had gained a basic principle of judgement and a comprehensive category of interpretation. It was Böhler who gave him the decisive and final impulse and David who confirmed the insight for him. Yet neither had actually laid the original foundation. This came from his reading of the New Testament each day in the original, a practice which he had pursued for many years and by which he was in the habit of testing every theological doctrine. From the pages of the New Testament it became clear to him that justifying faith was the inward focal point. It was quite in character that this objective perception should become a matter of personal assurance for him through the reading of Luther's *Preface to the Epistle to the Romans*.

Yet Luther's effect upon him at this point was brought about by personal encounter rather than literary influence. This is the significance of the fact that Wesley heard his words rather than read them, and thus in a sense which was characteristic of the reformer himself something objective was uttered. Luther had laid very great emphasis upon the truth that the word of Scripture becomes fully active and living in preaching, through actual dialogue, and by being heard.[5]

But can it really be said that Wesley really understood Luther's deep concern?[6] The answer can only be given approximately, since Wesley does not expound any of his convictions in a strictly formal theological way. He is satisfied with plain, straightforward statements. He felt no need of a detailed exposition of an idea, such for instance as might relate it to the ultimate purpose of God or bring it within the scope of a constructive system. He never worked out the implication of his concepts for systematic discussion. He kept to the existential assertion and confession, and anything in the nature of a system, related to the spiritual and historical situation or comparable in method or content with the intellectual culture of the scholasticism of the Middle Ages, is entirely lacking. It is only possible to pick out and compare motifs. There is no doubt that the force of the law and its unconditional demands laid hold of Wesley in a way similar to Luther. He thought of God as the Lord to whom man was in all things responsible, and because of the seriousness with which he took this obligation he could not get away from the fact of sin. The purpose of his detailed self-examination was that he might free himself from every sinful impulse, and this was the expression of a tendency, which was never far removed from Pietism, of regarding sin in an atomistic way. But immediately prior to his conversion it came upon him that the nature of man as a whole, which included of course his own, was sin. If God was to be thought of as consuming fire, then he himself was the object which must be consumed. This was not only to affirm the reality of the primary sin, what Luther called *Hauptsünde*,[7] but implied at the same time insight into its personal character. Sin's ultimate seriousness arose not in connexion with law, but from God and man coming face to face. It was enmity against God, an insult to His honour. For this reason, shortly before his conversion Wesley came to realize that spiritual trial or temptation, God's assault on man, was a new dimension in the relationship

---

[5] Cf. Heinrich Bornkamm, *Das Wort Gottes bei Luther*, pp. 31–2.

[6] On this cf. my detailed treatment, 'Die Bedeutung Luthers für John Wesleys Bekehrung', *Lutherjahrbuch*, XX.(1938).143ff, the conclusions of which are here briefly summarized.

[7] *Schmalkaldische Artikel*, III, Edition of the *Deutschen evangelischen Kirchenausschuss* (1930 and 1952), 433, 16.

with God. The decisive factor in such a situation was that God hid His face from him. Like Luther he did not know whether it was God or Satan at work in him.

In this perception of the nature of law, sin, and spiritual conflict the essential factors in the matter of justification are already present. But how did Wesley understand the actual event? He does not often refer to the primacy of God, the fact that in the first place it is always a question of God's judgement, yet each time he does allude to it his reason for doing so is important—once in his review of his life in Georgia and then in the letter to a friend written on the day of his conversion. Since, however, it was not the actual relationship but rather personal assurance which was brought into being by his conversion, it became justification as an experience of man which he placed increasingly in the central position. It was Peter Böhler who influenced him in this direction by his over-emphasis upon one aspect of faith, and as a result the question of the meaning of faith for Wesley grew out of the question of justification. An even deeper significance lay in the fact that Wesley's conversion-experience followed on Luther's great words on the power of faith. Yet both men are close to Luther inasmuch as they both relate faith to promise; indeed on one occasion Wesley was able to describe the whole of the New Testament from beginning to end as one great promise.

This particular emphasis upon faith was bound to lead to greater importance being placed upon its psychical features. A desire for inward peace and joy in the fact of salvation continually break forth, and Böhler, and still more Wesley, saw in these the new creation. It was at this point that they deviated from Luther in the direction of Pietism. Regeneration as complete transformation, the power of Christ living within us, the new man as a demonstrable effect, and therefore also the visible congregation of the regenerate, all constituted for Wesley objects to be desired, and the longer he lived the more impossible it appeared to give them up. It was for this reason that he was so attracted to the Herrnhut community. To be sure Christian David once again emphasized very strongly the objective aspect, the Christ-for-us. But it was not possible that this should become Wesley's final point of view. For he was concerned with actual dominion over sin and not with a continuing sinfulness which points ever anew to the grace of God.

This leads to a final difference. One of John Wesley's favourite expressions was the equation: holiness is happiness. This association of the impulse towards holiness with joy in salvation, which is a characteristic of Methodism as a whole, is to be found very early in Wesley, and is the demonstrable constant in all his theological statements. It is rooted in a long English tradition.[8] The noteworthy fact is that it was maintained by Wesley both before and after his conversion,[9] although only subsequent to the conversion is it referred to the Holy Spirit. It is the Spirit who brings both into being. Behind this lies a profound awareness of the final unity of the divine action: in salvation God realizes the happiness of man; in redemption is fulfilled that after which man, in accordance with the constitution of his created nature, strives. Yet Wesley overlooked the fact that this fulfilment is reached only by a denial of the natural desire for happiness. Although he places the idea of the Cross very strongly in the actual experience of the Christian, he lacks that 'theology of the Cross' which was common to both Luther and Zinzendorf.[1] He was not sufficiently aware of the fact that God acts according to the law of opposites, and through His strange work realizes His own, His true work. It was for this reason also that the truth of Luther's principle of the Christian as 'both righteous and a sinner at the same time' remained hidden from him.[2] His fundamental concept, that creation and redemption, happiness and salvation, the fulfilment of man's life and God's will, always go together, looks back rather to Augustine.

[8] Cf. e.g. Arthur Dent, *The Plain Man's Path Way to Heaven* (1625), pp. 85, 115ff; Richard Sibbs, *The Christian's Portion* (1637), pp. 12–13, *The Saint's Happinesse* (1638), pp. 29ff, *Mary's Choice* (1638), p. 38; Thomas Hooker, *The Soul's Benefit from Union with Christ* (1638), pp. 60–1; Robert Harris, *God's Goodness and Mercy* (1622), p. 20; Henry Mason, *The Tribunall of the Conscience* (1626), p. 56; Robert Bolton, *The Saint's Self-Enriching Examination* (1634), pp. 19–20, 104, 284; Jeremy Dyke, *The Righteous Man's Honour* (1639), pp. 6, 10–11, 26, 30, 59; Richard Alleine, *Remains of Joseph Alleine* (1674), A.3.b.A.5.a; William Beveridge, *Private Thoughts upon Religion* (1709), pp. 19–20, *An Account of the Life and Death of Mrs Elisabeth Bury* (1721), A.4.b.2; Henry Scougal, *The Life of God in the Soul of Man* (1733), pp. 16ff, 30ff, 40ff, 50, 56, 74, 90, 96ff; William Law, *Christian Perfection*, p. 11, *A Serious Call to a Devout and Holy Life*, p. 116.

[9] *Letters*, I.89, 17th June 1731, to Anne Granville; pp. 92–3, 19th July 1731, to Mrs Pendarves; p. 114, 17th November 1731, to Samuel; p. 128, 19th October 1732, to Richard Morgan; pp. 217ff, 29th March 1737, to Mrs Chapman; *Journal*, I.447, 23rd March 1738; p. 454, 22nd April 1738. After the conversion: *Letters*, I.254, 4th August 1738, to James Hutton; *Journal*, II.89–90, 14th October 1738.

[1] In addition to the literature cited in note 4, p. 260, cf. Walther v. Loewenich, *Luthers Theologia Crucis*, and Samuel Eberhard, *Kreuzes-Theologie. Das reformatorische Anliegen in Zinzendorfs Verkündigung.*

[2] Cf. Rudolf Hermann, *Luthers These Gerecht und Sünder zugleich* (1930).

Yet none of this had at this stage been realized. The tensions showed themselves only from afar. They were overwhelmingly outweighed by the enrichment and deepening which came from the encounter with German Pietism in the different forms of Halle and Herrnhut. The English heritage and the German contribution formed in John Wesley a true and authentic alliance.

Select Bibliography of Principal Works referred to in the Notes

Annesley, S. *The Morning Exercise of Cripple Gate*, 1662 (1671).

Arch. f. Reformationsgesch.

Arminian Magazine.

Bayly, L. *Practice of Piety* (1634).

Bechler, T. *Christian David* (1925).

Becker, B. *Zinzendorf und sein Christentum im Verhältnis zum kirchlichen und religiösen Leben seiner Zeit* (1900).

Bertram, Ernst. *Nietzsche. Versuch einer Mythologie* (1918).

Bett, H. *The Spirit of Methodism* (1937).

Bettermann, W. *Theologie und Sprache bei Zinzendorf* (1935).

Blanke, F. *Der verborgene Gott bei Luther* (1926).

Bornkamm, H. *Luther und das Alte Testament* (1948).

——, *Luther und Böhme* (1925).

——, *Das Wort Gottes bei Luther* (1933).

Brilioth, Y. *The Anglican Revival* (1925).

Bunyan, J. *Grace Abounding to the Chief of Sinners* (ed. John Brown, Cambridge, 1907).

Butler, D. *Henry Scougal and the Oxford Methodists* (Edinburgh and London, 1899).

Calamy, E. *An Account of the Ministers, Lecturers, Masters and Fellowes of Colleges and Schoolmasters who were ejected or silenced after the Restoration in 1660* (London, 1703).

Church, L. F. *Oglethorpe* (1932).

Church, R. W. *The Oxford Movement, 1833–45* (1922).

Clarke, A. *Memoirs of the Wesley Family* (1823).

Clarke, E. *Susanna Wesley* (London, 1886).

Collier, F. *John Wesley among the Scientists* (New York).

Corbet, J. *An Enquiry into the Oath required of Nonconformists by an Act made at Oxford* (1682).

Cordier, L. *Der junge August Hermann Francke* (1927).

Danielowski, E. *Die Journale der frühen Quäker* (1921).

Dent, E. *Händel in England* (1936).

Diestel, L. *Geschichte des Alten Testaments in der christlichen Kirche* (1869).

Eberhard, S. *Kreuzes-Theologie. Das reformatorische Anliegen in Zinzendorfs Verkündigung* (1937).

Elert, W. *Der christliche Glaube* (1940).

Exner, H. *Der Einfluss des Erasmus auf die englische Bildungsidee* (1939).

Fitzmaurice-Kelley, J. *The Relations between Spanish and English Literature* (Liverpool, 1910).

Fox, G. *Journal* (1694; ed. John L. Nickalls, Cambridge, 1952).

Foxe, J. *Acts and Monuments of the Christian Church* (1563).

Francke, A. H. *Kurtzer und einfältiger Unterricht* (1702 and 1748; new edn. by Otto Frick, 1889).

——, *Nicodemus* (1707).

Freund, M. *Die grosse Revolution in England* (1951).

Fries, A. L. *The Moravians in Georgia* (Raleigh, N.C., 1905).

Funk, T. *Die Anfänge der Laienmitarbeit im Methodismus* (1941).

Gairdner, J. *The English Church in the Sixteenth Century from the Accession of Henry VIII to the Death of Mary* (1902).

——, *Lollardy and the Reformation* (1908 and 1950).

Galvez, J. M. *Guevara in England* (Berlin, 1916).

Green, V. H. H. *The Young Mr Wesley* (London, 1961).

Gundolf, F. *Cäsar. Die Geschichte seines Ruhms* (1924).

Hagedorn, M. *Reformation und spanische Andachtsliteratur* (1934).

Haller, J. *Papsttum und Kirchenreform* (1903).

Haller, W. *The Rise of Puritanism* (New York, 1947).

Harrison, E. M. *Son to Susanna* (1937).

Heber, J. *The Whole Works of Jeremy Taylor* (London, 1847–54).

Herder, J. G. v. *Sämtliche Werke.*

Hök, G. *Zinzendorfs Begriff der Religion* (1948).

Holl, K. *Ges. Aufs. z. Kirchengesch.* I: *Luther* (1932), II: *Der Osten* (1928).

Impeta, C. N. *De Leer der Heiliging en Volmaking bij Wesley en Fletcher* (Leiden, 1913).

Jackson, T. *The Life of the Rev. Charles Wesley M.A.* (London, 1841).

Jacobs, H. E. *A Study in Comparative Symbolics* (1908).

Kapp, R. *Heilige und Heiligenlegenden in England* (1934).

Kirk, J. *The Mother of the Wesleys* (London, n.d.).

Kittel, H. *Oliver Cromwell. Seine Religion und seine Sendung* (1928).

Knappen, M. M. *Tudor Puritanism* (Chicago, 1939).

—— (ed.). *Two Elizabethan Diaries* (Chicago, 1933).

Koenneritz-Appel. *Christian David, ein munterer Zeuge* (1952).

Köhler, W. *Luther und die Kirchengeschichte* (1900).

Kramer, G. *August Hermann Francke, Ein Lebensbild* (1882).

Kümmel, W. G. *Römer 7 und die Bekehrung des Paulus* (1930).

Lang, A. *Puritanismus und Pietismus. Studien zu ihrer Entwicklung von Martin Butzer bis zum Methodismus* (1941).

Lau, F. *'Aeusserlich Ordnung' und 'weltlich Ding' in Luthers Theologie* (1933).

Law, W. *Works* (New Forest, 1893).

Leger, A. *La Jeunesse de Wesley* (1910).

Lerch, D. *Heil und Heiligung bie John Wesley* (1940).

Leube, H. *Kalvinismus und Luthertum im Zeitalter der Orthodoxie* (1928).

——, *Reformation und Humanismus in England* (1930).

——, *Die englischen Kulturideologie* (1941).

Liljegren, S. B. *The Fall of the Monasteries and the Social Changes leading up to the Great Revolution* (Lund Universitets Arsskrift, 1924).

Lindström, H. *Wesley and Sanctification* (1946).

Lockwood, J. P. *Memorials of the Life of Peter Böhler* (1868).

Lockyer, T. F. *Paul: Luther: Wesley* (1922).

Loewenich, W. v. *Luthers Theologia Crucis* (1929).

Luther, M. *Werke* (W.A. 1883).

Mason, H. *Tribunal of the Conscience* (1626).

Meissner, P. *England im Zeitalter von Humanismus, Renaissance und Reformation* (1952).

Meyer, A. O. *England und die katholische Kirche unter Elisabeth und den Stuarts* (1911).

Meyer, J. *Historischer Kommentar zu Luthers Kleinem Katechismus* (1929).

Mozley, J. F. *William Tyndale* (1937).

Müller, J. T. *Geschichte der böhmischen Brüder* (1922).

Nagler, A. W. *Pietism and Methodism. The Significance of German Pietism in the Origin and Early Development of Methodism* (Nashville, Tennessee, 1918).

Newman, B. *Cardinal Newman, a Biography and literary Study* (1925).

Nuelsen, J. L. *Kurzgefasste Geschichte des Methodismus* (1929).

——, *John Wesley und das deutsche Kirchenlied* (1938).

Nuttall, G. F. *The Holy Spirit in Puritan Faith and Experience* (Oxford, 1946).

Pauck, W. *Das Reich Gottes auf Erden. Utopie und Wirklichkeit* (1928).

Pearson, A. F. Scott. *Thomas Cartwright and Elizabethan Puritanism* (London, 1925).

——, *Church and State* (Cambridge, 1928).

Philipps, J. D. *Salem in the Seventeenth Century* (Boston, 1933).

Piette, M. *John Wesley in the Evolution of Protestantism* (1937).

Pollard, A. F. *Thomas Cranmer and the English Reformation* (1904).

Powell, C. L. *English Domestic Relations 1487–1653* (New York, 1917).

Proceedings of the Wesley Historical Society.

Rattenbury, J. E. *The Conversion of the Wesleys* (1938).

Reichel, G. *August Gottlieb Spangenberg, Bischof der Brüderkirche* (1906).

Renkewitz, H. *Zinzendorf* (1939).

Renner, L. *Lebensbilder aus der Pietistenzeit* (1886).

Rigg, J. H. *The Churchmanship of John Wesley* (1886).

——, *The Living Wesley* (1891).

Ritschl, A. *Geschichte des Pietismus* (1880).

Rupp, E. G. *Studies in the Making of the Protestant Tradition in the English Reformation* (1948).

Schempp, J. *Seelsorge und Seelenführung bei John Wesley* (1949).

Schleiermacher, F. D. E. *Ueber die Religion* (ed. R. Otto) (1926).

Schöffler, H. *Protestantismus und Literatur. Neue Wege zur englischen Literatur des 18. Jahrhunderts* (1922).

——, *Die Anfänge des Puritanismus* (1932).

Schüking, L. L. *Die Familie im Puritanismus* (1929).

Scougal, H. *The Life of God in the Soul of Man* (1733).

Scupoli, L. *Il Combattimento spirituale.*

Seeberg, E. *Zur Frage der Mystik* (1921).

——, *Gottfried Arnold* (1923).

——, *Luthers Theologie, I* (1929).

Simon, J. S. *John Wesley and the Religious Societies* (1921).

Sippell, T. *Werdendes Quäkertum* (1937).

Smithen, F. J. *Continental Protestantism and the English Reformation* (1927).

Sohm, R. *Kirchenrecht* (1892).

Southey, R. *The Life of John Wesley* (1820).

Steinlein, H. *Luthers Doktorat* (1912).

Stevenson, G. J. *Memorials of the Wesley Family* (London and New York, 1876).

Strobel, P. A. *The Saltzburghers and their Descendants* (Baltimore, 1855).

Struck, W. *Der Einfluss Jakob Böhmes auf die englische Literatur des 17 Jahrhunderts* (1936).

Südliche Romania (1950).

Sweet, W. W. *Religion in Colonial America* (New York, 1949).

Telford, J. *The Life of John Wesley* (1953).

Theologia Viatorum (*Jahrbuch der Kirchlichen Hochschule Berlin-Zehlendorf*).

The Whole Duty of Man, necessary for all Families (1659).

Thomas, H. *The English Translations of Guevara's Works* (Madrid, 1930).

Thorndyke, H. *Works* (1670).

Thune, N. *The Behemists and the Philadelphians* (Uppsala, 1948).

Thureau-Daugin, P. *La Renaissance catholique en Angleterre au 19me siècle* (1899–1906).

Törnvall, G. *Geistliches und weltliches Regiment bei Luther* (1947).

Townsend, Workman and Eayrs. *A New History of Methodism* (London, 1909).

Tyerman, L. *The Life and Times of Samuel Wesley* (London, 1866).

——, *The Oxford Methodists* (New York, 1873).

——, *The Life of the Rev. George Whitefield* (London, 1890).

——, *The Life and Times of John Wesley* (London, 1890).

Uttendörfer, O *Zinzendorfs Gedanken über den Gottesdienst* (1931).

——, *Zinzendorfs religiöse Grundgedanken* (1935).

——, *Zinzendorfs christliches Lebensideal* (1940).

——, *Zinzendorf und die Mystik* (1950).

Vogelsang, E. *Die Anfänge von Luthers Christologie nach der ersten Psalmenvorlesung* (1929).

Völker, W. *Das Vollkommenheitsideal des Origines* (1931).

——, *Der wahre Gnostiker nach Clemens Alexandrinus* (1952).

Waldberg, M. Frh. v. *Studien zur Geschichte des modernen Romans* (1912).

Ward, W. *The Life of Newman* (1912).

Wauer, G. A. *Die Anfänge der Brüderkirche in England* (1900).

Wedgwood, J. *John Wesley and the Evangelical Reaction of the Eighteenth Century* (1870).

Weingarten, H. *Die Revolutionskirchen Englands* (1868).

Wernle, P. *Der Schweizerische Protestantismus im 18 Jahrhundert* (1923).

Wesley, J. *Works* (3rd Edition, 1829–31).

——, *Journal* (Standard Edition, ed. Curnock, 1938).

——, *Letters* (Standard Edition, ed. Telford).

——, *A Christian Library*.

Wesley, S. *Dissertationes in librum Jobi* (1736).

Whiting, C. E. *Studies in English Puritanism from the Restoration to the Revolution, 1660–88* (London, 1931).

Wieser, M. *Peter Poiret* (1932).

Woodward, J. *An Account of the Rise and Progress of the Religious Societies in the City of London and of their Endeavours for Reformation of Manners* (1698).

Zeitschrift f. *Brüdergesch.*

Zeitschrift f. *Kirchengesch.*

Index of Principal Subjects and Names

Date Due